HUDSON'S
HISTORIC HOUSE & GARDEN
— DIRECTORY —
GREAT BRITAIN AND IRELAND

GW00362892

STANFORD HALL, LEICESTERSHIRE (PHOTO: ARTHUR PICKETT)

Published by

NORMAN HUDSON & COMPANY

High Wardington House, Upper Wardington, Banbury, Oxfordshire. OX17 1SP

0295 750750

Planning and Project Co-ordinator: Jan Bowman
Colour Origination by Riverline Reprographics Ltd, Oxford
Printed in Great Britain by BPC   Waterlow Ltd

Cover Picture: Althorp House, Northamptonshire (Photo: Arthur Pickett)   © Norman Hudson & Company 1994

Crathes Castle, Aberdeenshire

T he likelihood of witnessing Aurora Borealis, the Northern Lights, as seen in the picture opposite, above Crathes Castle in Aberdeenshire, is a matter of chance and good fortune. The oportunity of seeing or in some way using the houses included in the following pages need not be left to chance.

No feature of Britain contributes more to the country's beauty and character than its profusion of historic houses. Bigger and more opulent palaces may be found in other countries, but none can rival in number and splendour Britain's stately homes with their parks and gardens. Their outstanding range of contents not only includes works of art but also objects intrinsically bound to national, local or family history.

These houses have grown in importance as an economic as well as a cultural asset. Opening to interested visitors is still their main activity, but a whole range of others have become an important part of the historic house owner's response to new markets.

This Directory provides information not only about houses to visit, but also venues for conferences and functions, film locations, accommodation and the wide range of other uses for which houses are now made available.

Norman Hudson

Norman Hudson

Leith Hall, Aberdeenshire

HOW TO USE THIS DIRECTORY

The directory is divided into three sections, each coded with a separate colour band at the margin.

1. Houses open to the public and those offering facilities for conferences, functions and special events. (Some offer accommodation).

2. Houses occupied as family homes but where accommodation is offered on the basis of previous booking.

3. Hotels in Historic Houses.

Section 1 is listed by country: England (counties in alphabetical order), Scotland, Wales and Ireland.
Section 2 is divided into Great Britain and Ireland. Listings are alphabetical in each.
Section 3 is alphabetical.

1. A *Special Events Diary* lists some of the events taking place at various houses during 1994.

2. An *Accommodation Index* lists those houses in section 1 providing overnight accommodation. All houses in sections 2 and 3 provide accommodation.

3. The *Alphabetical indexes* list all houses and hotels included with illustrated entries.

Prices, times and events mentioned are those for 1994
(unless otherwise stated)

THE PAST:
SOMETHING TO LOOK FORWARD TO.

LINDISFARNE PRIORY,
NORTHUMBERLAND

DOVER CASTLE, KENT

OSBORNE HOUSE, ISLE OF WIGHT

THE PAST IS ALL AROUND us waiting to be discovered. Throughout the countryside England's history is landmarked by standing stones, ruined abbeys, powerful castles and great houses.

The properties and gardens for which we care each has its own unique atmosphere and most are open daily for you to visit. You'll find some of our properties listed in this book; you can also pick up our leaflets at a Tourist Information Centre or just follow the signs. Why not plan a few days out and look forward to the past?

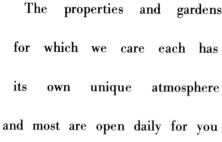

AUDLEY END, ESSEX

RIEVAULX ABBEY,
NORTH YORKSHIRE

English ⊞ Heritage

FIND YOURSELF A PLACE IN HISTORY

"Batoni's "Col Wm. Gordon of Fyvie Castle, Scotland

Heritage Events

The event management company specialising in the research, management and promotion of the arts and stately home events.

Event Research & Management

We assist businesses in the research, conception or selection of events to meet their marketing and corporate communication objectives. Our dedicated and highly professional team then manage all the elements.

Event Promotion

We promote events including the Stately Homes Music Festival to corporate and consumer markets, taking care of such matters as the packaging of sponsorship and corporate entertaining benefits, logo and print design, PR and advertising.

Business Entertaining

With a clear understanding of the corporate communication objectives and an eye for detail, we create a congenial environment in which to entertain. We take care of all the arrangements including catering, choice of venue and entertainment, seating plans, accommodation, transfers, gifts and other special requirements.

Historic House Marketing

We advise, encourage and where necessary, assist historic houses with strategies aimed at attracting a greater market share of corporate business.

For further details contact Philippa Bovey, or Douglas Reed on
071-636 4121

Heritage Events Limited 91 New Cavendish Street
London WIM 8HL

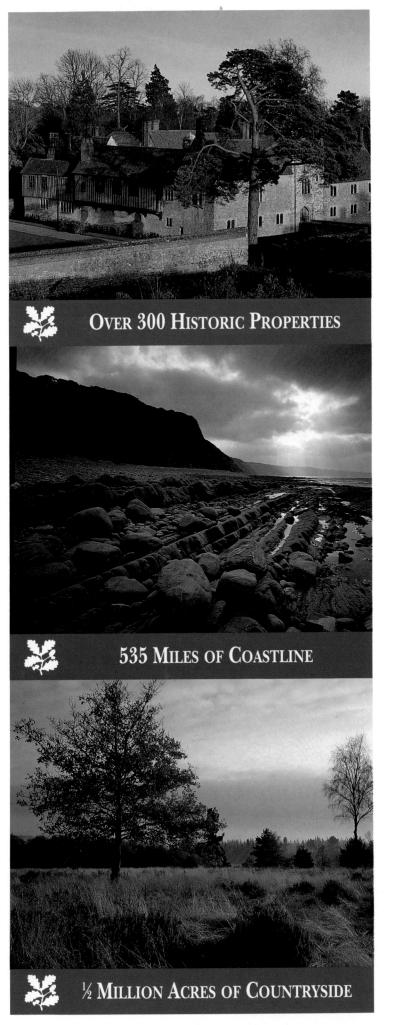

OVER 300 HISTORIC PROPERTIES

535 MILES OF COASTLINE

½ MILLION ACRES OF COUNTRYSIDE

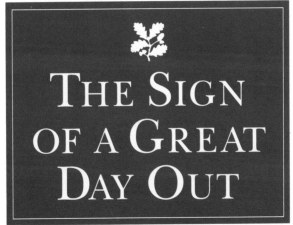

Whether you're an art-lover, nature lover or just an out-and-out explorer, the National Trust has something for you.

Magnificent houses and castles restored, with their priceless treasures, for all to enjoy.

Ancient woodlands and centuries-old gardens preserved for today's visitors.

THE SIGN OF A GREAT DAY OUT

And mile upon endless mile of unspoilt beaches and winding rustic lanes that lead to all sorts of wonderful and unexpected places.

Places you can find only with the National Trust as your guide.

Please 'phone the Travel Trade Office on 071-227 4810 for further information.

The National Trust

1 ROYAL CRESCENT
Bath, Avon

NUMBER 1 was the first house to be built in the Royal Crescent, John Wood the Younger's fine example of Palladian architecture. The Crescent was begun in 1767 and completed by 1774.

The House was given to the Bath Preservation Trust in 1968 and both the exterior and interior have been accurately restored. Visitors can see a grand town house of the late 18th Century with authentic furniture, paintings and carpets.

On the ground floor are the Study and Dining Room and on the first floor a Lady's Bedroom and Drawing Room. A series of maps of Bath are on the second floor landing. In the Basement is a Kitchen and a Museum Shop.

CONTACT

The Administrator
1 Royal Crescent
Bath
Avon
BA1 2LR

Tel: (0225) 428126

LOCATION

Exit 18 from the M4, then the A46 to Bath. 2¹/₂ hours.

Rail: Bath Spa Railway Station (1hr, 20 mins from London).

Taxi: Streamline

ADVICE TO COURIERS & DRIVERS

Please make sure you are familiar with restrictions in The Royal Crescent and parking regulations in the centre of Bath.

FACILITIES FOR THE DISABLED

The house is not suitable for the disabled.

CATERING

There is no restaurant or tea room, but there are many facilities in Bath.

GUIDED TOURS

There are guides in every room. Tours in French and Italian are available on request. Average time taken is 45 minutes.

GIFT SHOP

The Gift Shop is open at the same time as the house, and sells such items as classical creamware and books.

GUIDE BOOKS

A guide book with colour photographs is available, French, German, Spanish, Italian, Japanese, Chinese, Danish and Dutch translations are available on request.

SCHOOL VISITS/CHILDREN

School visits are welcome. The cost per child is £2.00 and guides can be provided.

OPENING TIMES

Summer
1 March - 30 October

Tues	
Wed	
Thur	10.30am - 5pm
Fri	
Sat	
Sun	

Closed Good Friday and Mondays except for Bank Hols and Bath Festival Mondays.

Winter

1 Nov-11 Dec.
Mon   Closed

Tues	
Wed	
Thur	10.30am - 4pm
Fri	
Sat	
Sun	

January & February Closed

Last admissions 30 minutes before closing. Special tours by arrangement with the administrator.

ADMISSION

All Year

Adult	£3.00
Child*	£2.50
Student	£2.50
Senior Citizen	£2.50

GROUPS	
Adult	£2.50
School*	£2.00
Student	£2.50

*Aged 5-16

Barstaple House (Trinity Almshouses), Old Market St., Bristol.
(0272) 265777 ½ mile from City Centre.

Beckford's Tower, Bath.
(0225) 312917 2 miles from Bath Spa Station via Lansdown Road..

GATCOMBE COURT

OPEN

Open by written appointment.
Please apply to
Mr Charles
Clarke
Gatcombe Court
Flax Bourton
Bristol BS19 1PX
Fax: 0275 394274

CLAVERTON MANOR

OPEN

26th March to
6th November
Grounds 1-6pm
Museum 2-5pm
(except
Mondays)
Bank Hol
Weekends, Suns
& Mons.
11am-5pm

GATCOMBE COURT, BRISTOL, TEL: 0275 393141
(Mrs and Mrs Charles Clarke)

A Somerset Manor House, dating from early 13th century, which has evolved over the centuries since, it is on the site of a large Roman Village, traces of which are apparent. There is a garden terraced by old stone walls, with many climbing roses, yew hedges and a herb garden.

Location: 5 miles west of Bristol, north of the A370, between the villages of Long Ashton and Flax Bourton.
Admission: By arrangement.

THE AMERICAN MUSEUM, BATH TEL: 0225 460503
(The Trustees of The American Museum in Britain)

Situated overlooking the valley of the River Avon and housed in a Georgian mansion, the Museum has 18 period furnished rooms from the 17th to 19th centuries. Special sections devoted to the American Indian, the Pennsylvania Germans, the Shakers etc. New Gallery with seasonal exhibitions. Many exhibits in beautiful gardens. A replica of George Washington's garden at Mount Vernon. American arboretum.

Location: Off the A36 (not suitable for coaches) other route via Bathwick Hill, Bath.
Admission: Adults £5.00, OAP £4.50, Children £2.50

Blaise Castle House Museum, Henbury.
(0272) 506789

Clevedon Court, Clevedon.
(0275) 872257 1½ miles East of Clevedon on the Bristol Road B3130.

Dyrham Park
(027237) 2501 12 miles east of Bristol approach from A46, 2 miles south of Tormarton interchange with M4, 8 miles north of Bath.

Horton Court, Horton.
3 miles north east of Chipping Sodbury, ¼ mile north of Horton, 1 mile west of Bath/Stroud Road (A46).

The Manor House, Walton-in-Gordano.
(0275) 872067 West of Bristol via B3124 from Clevedon to Portshead..

Sherborne Garden (Pear Tree House), Litton.
(0761) 241220 Litton, 8 miles north of Wells on B3114 off A39.

Vine House, Henbury, Bristol.
(0272) 503573 4 miles north west of Bristol centre, next to "Salutation" Bus Stop.

LUTON HOO
Luton, Bedfordshire

LUTON HOO is famous for housing the world famous Wernher Collection, formed primarily by Sir Julius Wernher, who purchased the mansion in 1900, and altered the House with opulent Edwardian interiors, by the designers of the Ritz Hotel in London.

There is also a large collection of Russian Fabergé jewellery and jewelled objects in addition to mementoes of the Russian Imperial family. This is the only collection of work by Carl Fabergé on public view in the country.

Recent additions to the collection included memorabilia of the Tsarevitch, which are displayed in the beautifully restored Chapel, which is now consecrated as a Russian Orthodox Church to the memory of Tsar Nicholas II, and the Imperial Family.

Visitors can view the full splendour of the 18th Century Capability Brown landscape from the terraces, together with the formal gardens by Romayne Walker from earlier this century. In addition the most peaceful area is the Rock Garden, a quiet retreat, always with some colour and a variety of most interesting plants.

CONTACT

The Administrator
Luton Hoo
Luton
Bedfordshire
LU1 3TQ

Tel: (0582) 22955
Fax: (0582) 34437

LOCATION

M1, Exit 10.
London 30 miles
Birmingham 85 miles.

Rail: Kings X Thames link to Luton/ Harpenden.

Bus: Green Line 747 Jet Link.
London Country 321 from Watford.
United Counties X1, X2 or X3 from Bedford.

Air: Luton Airport 1 mile.

SUITABILITY FOR OTHER EVENTS

Fashion shows, archery, clay pigeon shooting, garden parties, shows, rallies, filming, product launches and still photography. Meetings, conferences, luncheons and dinners.

ADVICE TO COURIERS & DRIVERS

No dogs or photography. There is a picnic area.

FACILITIES FOR THE DISABLED

Parking and cloakroom facilities provided.

PARKING FOR COACHES & CARS

There is unlimited parking for coaches and cars.

CATERING

The restaurant seats up to 90 people, plus an additional 45 in the annexe. The latter is normally used for groups booking in advance. Menu suggestions are available on request. Catering facilities are offered for special functions and conferences.

GUIDE BOOKS

New colour guide book.

GUIDED TOURS

Only available for pre-booked groups. Average time 2 hours. fee payable. Special viewing can be arranged for morning or evening visits with or without supper. Details on request.

GIFT SHOP

Open at the same time as the House

CONFERENCE/FUNCTIONS

All modern conference facilities and services can be provided. Banqueting facilities include the Pillared Hall, Dining Room, Ballroom, Drawing Room and Small Conference Room, and can be booked all year round.

OPENING TIMES

Summer
29 March - 16 October

Closed Mondays but open Bank Hol Mons
10.30am - 5.45pm

Tuesdays, Wednesdays and Thursdays.
Open for Coaches and Groups only by prior arrangement for both morning and afternoon visits.

Fridays, Saturdays and Sundays
Gardens open 12 noon
Restaurant opens 12 noon
House 1.30pm-5.45pm

Winter
17 October - 28 March
Closed.

Conference/Function Facilities available all year.

ADMISSION

Summer
HOUSE & GARDEN
Adult	£5.00
Child*	£2.00
OAP/Student	£4.50

GROUPS**
Adult	£4500
Child*	£1.50
OAP	£4.00

**Minimum 25 persons, pre-paid within 14 days.

GARDEN ONLY
Adult	£2.50
Child*	£1.00
OAP/Student	£2.25

*Must be of school age

Winter
Closed

CONFERENCE AND FUNCTION FACILITIES

ROOM	DIMENSIONS	CAPACITY	LAYOUT	POWER POINTS	SUITABLE FOR A/V
Ballroom	24'x69'	200	Theatre	3	✓
Dining Room	38'x24'	50	Any Function	3	✓
Pillared Hall	57'x37'		Any Function	3	✓
Conference Hall	25'x25'	35	Any Function	3	✓
Sitting Room		50	Any Function	3	✓

MENTMORE TOWERS
Nr Leighton Buzzard, Bedfordshire

MENTMORE TOWERS is an example of the Victorian 'Jacobethan' revival at its best. Built in 1855 for Baron Meyer Amschel de Rothschild, this grand romantic house is a reminder of the enormous wealth and power of the Rothschilds in the 19th Century.

The architect was Sir Joseph Paxton, designer of the Crystal Palace, whose early experience designing greenhouses is reflected in the liberal use of glass to open up Mentmore's glittering interior. The main rooms of the House are grouped around the vast Entrance Hall dominated by the magnificent white marble Grand Staircase.

The use of marble in the reception rooms contrasts with the ornate gilded style of the living rooms. De Rothschild plundered Europe for his great house, the gilded boiseries in the Dining Room were from the early 18th Century Hotel de Villars in Paris and the striking black and white marble fireplace in the Hall is reputed to have been designed by Rubens for his home in Antwerp.

The House is now the administrative Headquarters of Maharishi University of Natural Law.

CONTACT

Events Manager
Mentmore Towers
Mentmore
Nr Leighton Buzzard
Bedfordshire
LU7 0QH

Tel: (0296) 662183/
661881
Fax: (0296) 662049

LOCATION

M1 Junction 9
Join A5, past Whipsnade Zoo, then turn left, following signs for Ivinghoe, Cheddington and Mentmore.
London: 1hr (40 miles)

Rail: Cheddington Station 2 miles, Leighton Buzzard 4 miles

Taxi: Valcars (0296) 661666

SUITABILITY FOR OTHER EVENTS

Corporate hospitality, archery, shows, filming, sales exhibitions, fairs, concerts, conferences, product launches.

EXTRA FACILITIES

Parkland. Tables for 100 and chairs for 200 people. Lectures can be given on the property, contents, gardens and history. The Lecture Room has a max. capacity of 250 people. Cost of hire of the room and lecture negotiable. Projector and screen can be provided.

VIDEO FACILITIES

We can now offer 3 machine high-band editing, including time-coded computer list editing. Cameras (Sony DXC3000PK), a prompter, and portable and studio high-band recorders are also available for hire.

Standard conversion and VHS duplication from low-band, high-band and one inch are also available at very competitive rates.

ADVICE TO COURIERS & DRIVERS

Do not enter grounds through front gates. Use trade entrance by Church or South Entrance. No dogs except guide dogs. No smoking. No unaccompanied children.

FACILITIES FOR THE DISABLED

Disabled and elderly visitors may alight at the entrance to the property. Vehicles can then be parked in the allocated area. There are no toilet facilities for the disabled.

PARKING FOR COACHES & CARS

Capacity of the car park - 100 cars and 10 coaches, near to the House.

GUIDED TOURS

Up to 40 people per tour. Average time taken is 45 minutes.

GIFT SHOP

Postcards are available.

SCHOOL VISITS/CHILDREN

Groups of children are welcome. A guide can be provided on request.

OPENING TIMES

Summer
April-October

Mon	Bank Hol Mons 1.45pm-4pm Last tour 3.15
Tues Wed Thur Fri Sat	Groups by appointment only.
Sun	1.45pm-4pm Last tour 3.15

Winter
November-March

Closed

ADMISSION

Summer

Adult	£2.00
Child*	£1.00
OAP	£1.00
Student	£2.00

GROUPS**	
Adult	£1.75
Child*	£0.90
OAP	£0.90
Student	£1.75

* Aged under 14
** Min. 20 People

CONFERENCE AND FUNCTION FACILITIES

ROOM	DIMENSIONS	CAPACITY	LAYOUT	POWER POINTS	SUITABLE FOR A/V
Grand Hall	34'x43'	35-250	Various	8	✓
Dining Room	36'x27'	35-125	Various	6	✓
Gold Room	22'x30'	26-110	Various	18	✓
Conservatory	21'x55'	35-150	Various	6	✓

WOBURN ABBEY
Woburn, Bedfordshire

THE ABBEY, home of the Dukes of Bedford for over 350 years, was built on the site of a Cistercian Monastery, founded in 1145. During the 17th Century, it was restored, with further re-designing and rebuilding by Henry Flitcroft and later Henry Holland in the 18th Century. Today the house is more or less as Flitcroft and Holland left it, with the exception of the East Wing which was demolished in 1950 along with the huge Indoor Riding School and the Real Tennis building.

The interior is richly decorated and furnished and has one of the most important private art collections in the world, with English and French furniture; paintings by many of the world's famous artists, including 21 views of Venice by Antonio Canale in the Canaletto Room; English, Continental and Oriental porcelain and silver by some of the famous Huguenot silversmiths.

Within the 3,000 acre Deer Park landscaped by Humphrey Repton there are nine species of deer, including the Milu, better known as Pere David, which was saved from extinction by the 11th Duke of Bedford.

Nearby is the 350 acre drive-through Safari Park.

CONTACT

Peter A Gregory
Woburn Abbey
Woburn
Bedfordshire
MK43 0TP

Tel: (0525) 290666
Fax: (0525) 290271

LOCATION

From London, either M1 exit 12/13 or A5, turn off at Hockliffe (1¼ hrs).

Rail: Euston-Leighton-Buzzard, Bletchley or Milton Keynes.

Air: Luton Airport 14 mls
Heathrow Airport 39 mls

Taxi: Farmer, Milton Keynes (0908) 583484

SUITABILITY FOR OTHER EVENTS

Fashion shows, product launches, wedding receptions and filming. Company 'days out' can also be arranged.

EXTRA FACILITIES

Use of parkland and garden. Lectures on the property, its contents, gardens and history can be arranged.

ADVICE TO COURIERS & DRIVERS

No unaccompanied children. No photography in House. Dogs in park on leashes. Guide dogs only in House. Special 'out of hours' tours can be pre-booked during either summer or winter - special rates apply.

FACILITIES FOR THE DISABLED

Wheelchairs can be accommodated in the Abbey by prior arrangement There are toilet facilities for the disabled.

PARKING FOR COACHES & CARS

There is a very large hardstanding and grass area for coaches and cars.

CATERING

Day to day catering in the Flying Duchess Pavilion Coffee Shop, whenever the Abbey is open to the public. Conferences, banqueting, luncheons, dinners etc may be arranged in the Sculpture Gallery, Lantern and Long Harness Rooms.

GUIDED TOURS

Parties are taken round in groups of 15. Tours can be conducted in French, German and Dutch. There is an additional charge of £7.50 per guide.

GIFT SHOP

There are two gift shops, one in the Abbey, the other in the grounds. Both offer a wide variety of attractive and useful gifts.

GUIDE BOOKS

Colour, 48 page guide book, £2.00.

SCHOOL VISITS/CHILDREN

Groups are welcome. Special schools programme is available on request. Cost per child £2.50 (group rate). A guide (extra charge) can be made available if required. Particular interests for children include: Study Trail and Woburn Safari Park

OPENING TIMES

Summer
27 March - 30 October

Mon	
Tues	
Wed	11am-5pm
Thur	
Fri	
Sat	
Sun	

NB: Bank Hols Abbey closes 5.30pm

Winter
31 October-Mid-March
Open weekdays by appointment only.

Open Saturdays, Sundays and Bank Hols from the first Saturday after Christmas.
11am-4pm

ADMISSION

All year

HOUSE (including Private Apartments)
Adult	£6.50
Child*	£3.00
OAP	£5.50

GROUPS***
Adult	£5.50
Child**	£2.50
OAP	£4.50

* from 12 to 16 years
**from 7 to 16
***15 or more

Reduced Rates apply if Private Apartments not available.

CONFERENCE AND FUNCTION FACILITIES

ROOM	DIMENSIONS	CAPACITY	LAYOUT	POWER POINTS	SUITABLE FOR A/V
Sculpture Gallery	130'x25'	400	Reception	✓	✓
		300	Theatre		
		250	Dinner/Dance		
Lantern Room	24'x21'	100	Reception	✓	✓
		80	Theatre/Dinner		
		20	Boardroom		

Luton Hoo: The Chapel

✿ **Bushmead Priory,**
(023062) 614 4 miles west of A1 at St Neots.

Chicksands Priory, Shefford.
(02302) 4195 In RAF Chicksands. 1¼ miles from Shefford. Entrances on A507 and A600.

Cecil Higgins Art Gallery & Museum, Castle Close, Bedford.
(0234) 211222 In centre of Bedford, just off The Embankment.

WREST PARK HOUSE & GARDENS

OPEN

1 April - 30 Sept.

Wednesdays & Bank Holidays only

10am-6pm

WREST PARK HOUSE AND GARDENS, SILSOE TEL: 0525 60152
(English Heritage)

Here is a history of English gardening in the grand manner from 1700-1850, which would not, of course, be complete without some designs by 'Capability' Brown. Every whim of fashion is represented, whether it be for a Chinese bridge, artificial lake, classical temple or rustic ruin. The present house was built aabout 1839 by the Earl de Grey whose family had lorded over the Manor of Wrest for 600 years. The State Rooms and gardens are open to the public.

Location: ¾ mile eaast of Silsoe off A6, 10 miles south of Bedford. Bus; United Counties X1, X2, X5 Station; Flitwick.
Admission: Adults £1.80, Concessions £1.35, child 90p

Wrest Park

DORNEY COURT
Windsor, Berkshire

"One of the finest Tudor Manor Houses in England." Dorney Court is an enchanting, many gabled pink brick and timbered manor house with more than just a taste of history.

The Grade 1 listed Dorney Court offers a most welcome, refreshing and fascinating experience. Built about 1440 and lived in by the present family for over 400 years.

The rooms are full of the atmosphere of history: early fifteenth and sixteenth century oak, beautiful seventeenth century lacquer furniture, eighteenth and nineteenth century tables, 400 years of family portraits, stained glass and needlework. Here

Charles II once came to seek the charms of Barbara Palmer, Countess of Castlemaine, the most intelligent, beautiful and influential of ladies. St James' Church, next door, is a lovely cool, cheerful and very English village church.

"The approach to the house is through ancient Buckinghamshire woodland which transports the visitor into a dreamland. Suddenly the early Tudor house, a ravishing half timbered vision in gabled pinkish brick, comes into view, prettily grouped with a church. This is Dorney Court, a surprisingly little known manor house ... happily genuine...an idyllic image." *Daily Telegraph*

CONTACT

Peregrine and Jill Palmer
Dorney Court
Windsor
Berkshire
SL4 6QP

Tel: (0628) 604638
Fax: As Telephone

LOCATION

25 miles west of London via M4, 40 mins. depending on traffic.

Stations:
Windsor 5 miles,
Burnham 2 miles.

London Airport
(Heathrow) 20 minutes

CORPORATE HOSPITALITY

Dorney Court is a privately owned and lived in family house and because it is in no way a 'tourist attraction' hotel or commercial banqueting hall, is the perfect place for an 'upmarket' group visit or for exclusive private functions for companies and tourist groups from overseas.

Dorney offers exclusivity and privacy combined with a superbly convenient rural location, only 25mls west of London.

The house is ideal for private dinners etc., often matched into conferences held elsewhere, and makes a complete change from the work environment.

Catering can either be done by the best of outside caterers or by ourselves. We farm the surrounding land as we have

for centuries, producing some of the best of England's lamb, growing strawberries, raspberries and other delicious fruit and vegetables. As far as possible we use fresh home produced food such as lamb and asparagus in spring but if not appropriate then the best available fresh ingredients such as summer salmon, grouse or partridge in autumn with venison or beef in winter.

On a cold and dark winter's night, the Great Hall flickers in candlelight and the large wood fires glow with warmth. In summer you can stroll the lawns with a cooling cocktail. The cocktail might be the famous Palmer cocktail, winner of the Grand Prix in Paris in 1934, the secret recipe given to the family by an Hungarian barman in Budapest, the only recognisable ingredient being the topping up champagne, cooling and refreshing.

SUITABILITY FOR OTHER EVENTS

Activity and family fun days, product launches, spouses programmes and garden parties, overseas tourist groups, filming, photography. No private family parties, weddings or dancing.

GENERAL ADVICE

No facilities for disabled, unaccompanied children, dogs or photography in the house.

SCHOOL VISITS

£1.75 per child plus £15 per guide required. No charge for accompanying adults

PYO FRUIT

June-August everyday. 10% discount Mons-Weds 10.30am - 5.00pm.

GIFT SHOP

Open for visitors to the House. Guide Book £2.00.

GUIDED TOURS

Are available for private visits: one and a half hours.

OPENING TIMES

Summer
Easter-September
Mon   June-Sept
       2pm-5.30pm
       Bank Hol Mons
       2pm-5.30pm
Tues   June-Sept
       2pm-5.30pm
Wed ⎫
Thur ⎬ By appointment
Fri ⎪ only.
Sat ⎭
Sun   May - end Sept
       2pm-5.30pm
NB Open at other times for booked groups by appointment. Open all Easter weekend: 2-5.30
Last admission 5pm

Winter
October-Easter
Pre-booked tours only, at any time.

ADMISSION

HOUSE & GARDEN
Adult   £3.50
Child**   £1.75
OAP   £3.15
Groups*
  Adult   £3.00
  Child   £1.75

PRIVATE VISITS   £5.50

10% discount NT, NADFAS and OAP's
* Minimum 10 people
**Age 10-16 years

CONFERENCE AND FUNCTION FACILITIES

ROOM	DIMENSIONS	CAPACITY	LAYOUT	POWER POINTS	SUITABLE FOR A/V
Great Hall	33'x24'	65	Various	3	✓
Dining Room	20'x20'	18	Various	3	✓

STRATFIELD SAYE HOUSE
Reading, Berkshire

AFTER Waterloo the first Duke of Wellington, or the Great Duke as he was universally known was regarded as the saviour of his country and of Europe. A grateful nation voted a large sum of money to buy him a house and an estate worthy of a national hero, and in 1817, after carefully considering many other far grander houses, he chose Stratfield Saye.

The south stable block houses the Wellington Exhibition which portrays the Great Duke's life both as a soldier and a politician. A major feature of this exhibition is the 18 ton Funeral Hearse which was constructed, from the metal of French cannons captured at Waterloo, for the Great Duke's funeral in 1852.

GARDENS

The gardens have been completely restored since 1975 after being virtually abandoned for several decades.

They include a rose garden and the American garden, so named because of the vogue for American shrubs in the early 19th Century, created in the first Duke's time, and a walled garden dating from the 18th Century.

In the Ice House paddock stands a spreading Turkey Oak planted in 1843. The tree and a headstone mark the place where Copenhagen, the Great Duke's favourite charger was buried with full military honours in 1836 at the age of 28.

CONTACT

P Aubrey-Fletcher
Wellington Office
Stratfield Saye
Reading
Berkshire
RG7 2BT

Tel: (0256) 882882

LOCATION

Equidistant from Reading (Junct 11 M4) and Basingstoke (Junct 6, M3), on A33: 1 hour from Hyde Park Corner.

Rail: Reading/Basingstoke Station.

Taxi: Concorde Cars (0734) 595959

SUITABILITY FOR OTHER EVENTS

The House and grounds are available for events and corporate hospitality functions. Functions in the House can range from dinner for 20 to cocktail parties for 200 whilst, in the grounds, garden parties of any size are a possibility. Game Fairs, Country Fairs and Craft Fairs with numbers ranging from 20,000 to 200,000 visitors have all been held here.

Filming within the House and Grounds will be considered on request.

ADVICE TO COURIERS & DRIVERS

If possible, please book in advance; if not, telephone with arrival times and numbers.

FACILITIES FOR THE DISABLED

Disabled and elderly visitors may alight at the entrance before parking in the allocated area. There are toilet facilities for the disabled.

PARKING FOR COACHES & CARS

Free parking for up to 250 cars and 20 coaches 500 yards from the house.

CATERING

There is a restaurant (capacity 80 people). Parties can booked in advance for tea and other meals, special rates given to groups. Menus available on request. Prices from £1.50-£10.00. Special functions can be catered for.

GUIDED TOURS

There are no guided tours, but there are stewards in all rooms. Tours can be arranged for groups on payment of an extra charge.

GIFT SHOP

Open at the same time as the house and contains many items which can only be purchased at Stratfield Saye.

GUIDE BOOKS

Colour Guide book, French and Spanish translations available.

SCHOOL VISITS/CHILDREN

Groups are welcome at £2.25 per child. A spotter pack can be provided at an additional cost of 20p. Areas of interest include: state coach, 18 ton funeral hearse, wildfowl sanctuary, ice house, Copenhagen's grave.

OPENING TIMES

Summer
1st May - Last Sunday in September

Mon	
Tues	11.30am-4pm
Wed	
Thur	
Friday	Closed
Sat	11.30am-4pm
Sun	

Winter
October - April

Closed

ADMISSION

Summer

Adult	£4.50
Child*	£2.25
GROUP**	
Adult	£4.00
Child*	£2.25
OAP	£3.00

*Aged 5-15
**Min payment £70

❧ **Basildon Park,** Lower Basildon, Reading.
   (0734) 843040 7 miles north west of Reading between Pangbourne and Streatley on A329. Leave M4 at Junction 12.

Frogmore Gardens, Windsor
   Entrance to garden through Long Walk Gate.

Frogmore House, Windsor.
   (0753) 868286.

THE SAVILL GARDEN

OPEN
DAILY
10am-6pm
(7pm weekends)
or sunset when earlier.

Closed:
25th/26th
December

THE SAVILL GARDEN, WINDSOR TEL: 0753 860222
(Crown Property)

World renowned woodland garden of 35 acres, providing a wealth of beauty and interest at all seasons. Spring is heralded by hosts of daffodills, masses of rhododendrons, azaleas, camellias, magnolias and much more. Roses, herbaceous borders and countless alpines are the great features of summer, and the leaf colours and fruits of autumn rival the other seasons with a great display

Location: Wick Lane, Englefield Green. Clearly signposted from Ascot, Bagshot, Egham and Windsor. Nearest station: Egham.

Admission: Adults £3.20, OAP £2.70, Parties of 20+ £2.70. Accom. children under 16 free .

The Old Rectory, Burghfield.
   5½ miles south west of Reading between M4 junctions 11 and 12.

Valley Gardens, Windsor Great Park, Windsor
   (0753) 860222 Approach from Wick Road off A30 - 1 mile walk.

Welford Park, near Newbury.
   (048838) 203 6 miles north west of Newbury, 1 mile north of Wickham off B4000.

Windsor Castle. Windsor.
   (0753) 868286 3 miles off Junction 6 of M4.

HIGHCLERE CASTLE, HAMPSHIRE

DORNEY COURT

CHICHELEY HALL
Newport Pagnell, Buckinghamshire

CHICHELEY HALL is the home of the Honourable Nicholas Beatty, grandson of Admiral the Earl Beatty Commander of the Battle Cruiser Squadron at the Battle of Jutland in 1916.

The house, one of the finest and least altered 18th Century houses in the country was built between 1719-23. Here is some of the finest Georgian craftsmanship in brick, stone, plaster, wood carving and joinery.

It was designed by Francis Smith of Warwick, a well known Midland architect and master builder with many outstanding features, including the doors and windows which were inspired by four of the leading architects of Baroque Rome.

The interior contains some beautifully panelled rooms, and a grand Palladian Hall, designed by Henry Flitcroft with its ceiling painted by William Kent. Among the paintings are a magnificent collection of sea pictures.

There is a museum with photographs and memorabilia of the Admiral.

CONTACT

Mr J N Robertson
Administrator
Chicheley Hall
Newport Pagnell
Buckinghamshire
MK16 9JJ

Tel: (0234) 391252
Fax: (0234) 391388

LOCATION

From London: M1 Junct 14 (3/4 hour). Milton Keynes, 10 miles.

Rail: Milton Keynes 10 miles.

Air: Luton Airport 25 miles.

Taxi: Saxon Cars, Newport Pagnell 615340.

SUITABILITY FOR OTHER EVENTS

Suitable for filming, fashion shoots etc. Weddings in marquees.

EXTRA FACILITIES

Grounds available for clay pigeon shooting etc.

ACCOMMODATION

Chicheley Hall offers 4 four-poster suites, 1 double/twin with bathroom and 8 singles with 5 bathrooms. Groups can be accommodated with prior booking.

ADVICE TO COURIERS & DRIVERS

No dogs. No photographs inside Hall.

FACILITIES FOR THE DISABLED

Disabled and elderly visitors may alight at the entrance to the House. Ramp available for wheelchairs. Ground floor access only.

PARKING FOR COACHES & CARS

There is parking for up to 60 cars, 50 yds from House and for 2 coaches, 80 yds from House.

CATERING

There is a tea room (capacity 60 people). Pre-booked menus available for lunch and supper.

GUIDED TOURS

All tours are guided. They are available for groups of up to 60 people (which will be divided into smaller groups). There is no additional cost for this. The owner will occasionally meet groups visiting the house. Average time taken to see the house, $1^1/4$ hours.

GIFT SHOP

The Shop is open the same times as the House.

GUIDE BOOKS

Guide book with colour photographs price £1.25.

SCHOOL VISITS/CHILDREN

Groups are welcome, cost £1.00 per child. A guide is provided and there is a schoolroom for their use.

OPENING TIMES

Summer
Easter-31 May & August.

Mon	Closed except Bank Hols 2.30pm-5pm
Tues Wed Thur Fri Sat	Closed
Sun	2.30pm-5pm

NB parties welcomed at any time.

Winter
October-Easter

Closed

ADMISSION

Summer
| Adult | £3.00 |
| Child* | £1.00 |

GROUP**	
Adult	£2.40
Child*	£1.00

* Aged 0-16
**Min payment £50.00

CONFERENCE AND FUNCTION FACILITIES

ROOM	DIMENSIONS	CAPACITY	LAYOUT	POWER POINTS	SUITABLE FOR A/V
Hall	30'x21'	100	Theatre	1	
		100	Buffet		
		40	Lunch/Dinner		
Conference Room	18'x18'	16	Boardroom	4	✓
		12	U-Shape		
Dining Room	18'x18'	24	Lunch/Dinner	2	

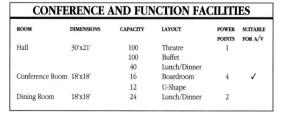

STOWE
Buckingham

STOWE owes its pre-eminence to the vision and wealth of two owners. From 1715 to 1749 Viscount Cobham, one of Marlborough's Generals, continuously improved his estate, calling in the leading designers of the day to lay out the gardens, and commissioning several leading architects - Vanbrugh, Gibbs, Kent and Leoni - to decorate them with garden temples. From 1750 to 1779 Earl Temple, his nephew and successor continued to expand and embellish both Gardens and House.

The House has now become a major public school.

Around the mansion is one of Britain's most magnificent landscape gardens. now in the ownership of the National Trust. Covering 250 acres and containing no fewer than 6 lakes and 32 garden temples, it is of the greatest historic importance. During the 1730's William Kent laid out in the Elysian Fields at Stowe, one of the first 'natural' landscapes and initiated the style known as 'the English Garden'. Capability Brown worked there for 10 years, not as a consultant but as head gardener, and in 1744 was married in the little church hidden in the trees.

CONTACT

The Commercial Manager
Stowe School
Buckingham
MK18 5EH

Tel: (0280)6 813650
(House only)
(0280) 822850 (Gardens)

LOCATION

From London, M1 to Milton Keynes, 1$^{1}/_{2}$ hrs or Banbury 1$^{1}/_{4}$ hrs.

Bus: from Buckingham
4 miles

Rail: Milton Keynes
15 miles

Air: Heathrow Airport
50 miles

SUITABILITY FOR OTHER EVENTS

Venue for International Conferences, prestige exhibitions and private functions of all kinds.

EXTRA FACILITIES

Indoor swimming pool, sports hall, tennis court, squash courts, parkland, cricket pitches and golf course.

ACCOMMODATION

Single, twin and dormitory accommodation available..

FACILITIES FOR THE DISABLED

Disabled and elderly visitors may alight at the entrance to the property. Vehicles can then be parked in the allocated areas. There are toilet facilities for the disabled in the gardens. 'Batricars' are available.

PARKING FOR COACHES & CARS

There is extensive parking for cars and coaches.

CATERING

The National Trust Restaurant/Tea Room can cater for up to 100 people. Parties should book in advance.

GUIDED TOURS

At an additional cost, parties can be given a guided tour in groups of 30. Average time taken for a tour of the house and grounds 2$^{1}/_{2}$ hours. House only - 30 minutes.

GIFT SHOP

During term time, open Monday - Friday 9am-12noon 12.50pm-5pm ; Saturday 1pm-5pm;. During school holidays, open Monday - Friday 9am-5pm; Saturday and Sunday 11am-5pm. Items include: postcards, books, gifts, souvenirs and prints.

GUIDE BOOKS

Guide book, £1.20 and £6.00. There is also a guide to the gardens £1.30.

Summer

HOUSE
2-5pm
26-29 March
5 April -17April
5 July - 25 August
30 August-2 September

GARDENS
10am-Dusk
26 March-17 April Daily
18 April-1 July
Mon, Wed. Fri & Sun.
3 July-4 Sept. Daily
5 Sept-21 Oct.
Mon. Wed. Fri & Sun.

Winter

GARDENS
Daily (10am-Dusk)
22 - 30 October
17 - 23 December
27 - 31 December

NB: It may be necessary to close the house at times when it is being used for private functions. Please telephone first to check.

ADMISSION

Summer

HOUSE ONLY
Adult	£2.00
Child	£1.00
OAP	£2.00
Students	£2.00

10% discount for parties of more than 30

GARDENS ONLY
Adult	£3.60
Child	£1.80
OAP	£3.60

Winter

House closed (Sundays by appointment only). Gardens as above

CONFERENCE AND FUNCTION FACILITIES

ROOM	DIMENSIONS	CAPACITY	LAYOUT	POWER POINTS	SUITABLE FOR A/V
Roxburgh Hall		600	Theatre	✓	✓
Audio Visual Room		50	Theatre	✓	✓
Music Room		120	Various	✓	✓
Marble Hall		150	Various	✓	✓
State Dining Room		180	Various	✓	✓
Garter Room		200	Various	✓	✓
Memorial Theatre		120	Theatre	✓	✓

WADDESDON MANOR
The Rothschild Collection
Waddesdon, near Aylesbury

Bookings
Waddesdon Manor
near Aylesbury
Buckinghamshire
HP18 OJH

Tel: 0296 651282
Recorded message: 0296 651211
Fax: 0296 651293

LOCATION

Waddesdon Manor lies at the west end of Waddesdon village, 6 miles north west of Aylesbury on the Bicester road (A41).

From London 1 hour 20 minutes, M40 Junct. 7.

Rail: nearest station Aylesbury BR.

Buses: 1,15, 16 from Aylesbury Bus Station.

WADDESDON MANOR was built in the late 19th century by Baron Ferdinand de Rothschild with the French architect Destailleur. The Manor is open once again following an extensive restoration programme which has included work on the fabric of the house, the collection, the gardens and several of the outbuildings.

The Renaissance style chateau was conceived as a showcase for the Baron's collection of French decorative arts of the 18th century. The collection which he and subsequent members of the family established at Waddesdon is exceptional in its quality and breadth including French Royal furniture, Savonnerie carpets and Sévre porcelain.

Among the great paintings are important portraits by Gainsborough and Reynolds and works by Dutch and Flemish masters of the 17th century.

The Wine Cellars are open to the public for the first time. They contain several thousands of bottles of Rothschild wine including rare vintages of Chateau Lafite and Mouton dating back to the last century.

GARDENS

The Garden and Park were laid out by Baron Ferdinand and Lainé, the French landscape designer. The Partérre on the South Terrace has now been returned to its high victorian glory.

SUITABILITY FOR OTHER EVENTS

Special visits of the collection may be arranged. In addition, facilities are available for lunches, receptions, wine-tastings and dinners as well as lectures and small business meetings. Film location use may also be possible.

EXTRA FACILITIES

Large park, Aviary, formal gardens. Parking, childrens play area. Special party rooms in the House and Stables.

ADVICE TO COURIERS & DRIVERS

Private cars/coaches are to enter through the main gates and proceed past the kiosk where a member of staff will meet the visitors.

FACILITIES FOR THE DISABLED

Wheelchairs and Ramp Access.

PARKING FOR COACHES & CARS

Capacity for 250 cars in the new car park near the ticketing office, walking distance from the House. Capacity for 10 coaches.

CATERING

Tea Room seating up to 120 people. Groups are encouraged to book in advance for afternoon tea and lunch. Catering for special events can be discussed with the Head of Banqueting.

GUIDED TOURS

Entry to the House is strictly by timed ticket every 15 minutes. Tours of the House last approx. an hour and a half and the maximum size of each party if 35 at any one time.

GIFT SHOP

Gift Shop and Wine Shop open 31st March-23rd Dec, Wed -Sun 11am to 6pm. A large range of high quality gifts and a unique selection of Rothschild wines from a Grand Cru to the most reasonable of vintages.

GUIDE BOOKS

Garden leaflet, Aviary leaflet £1.00. Garden Guide £4.95. House Guide approx. £3.00

SCHOOL VISITS/CHILDREN

Children are now admitted to the House.

31st March-16 October

HOUSE, BACHELORS' WING & WINE CELLARS
Wednesday. 1pm-6pm (July & August only)

Thurs to Sat. 1pm-6pm

Sundays. & Bank Holidays 11am-6pm

Last ticket 5.00pm

GARDENS, AVIARY, TEA ROOM, WINE & GIFT SHOP

Wed to Sun 11am-6pm
Last ticket 5.00pm

Shop & Tea Room close at 5.00pm during House Closed Season

ADMISSION

NT Members Free of Charge

Grounds, Aviary & Parking £3.00
House etc. Gardens, Aviary inclusive £7.00
Additional charge on Sunday & Bank Holidays £1.00

Children 5-17 yers
Grounds, Aviary & Parking £1.50
House etc. Gardens, Aviary inclusive £5.50
Additional charge on Sunday & Bank Holidays £1.00

✼ **Ascott,** Wing, Leighton Buzzard
(0296) 688242 ¹/₂ miles east of Wing, 2 miles south west of Leighton Buzzard on the south side of A418.

Chiltern Open Air Museum, Newlands Park, Gorelands, Chalfont St Giles.
(0494) 871117 4¹/₂ miles from Amersham, 8 miles from Watford.

✼ **Claydon House,** Middle Claydon, Buckingham
(0296) 730349/730693 13 miles north west of Aylesbury. Signposted A413, A421 and A41.

✼ **Cliveden,** Taplow, Maidenhead.
(0628) 605069 2 miles north of Taplow on Hedsor Road. Main entrance opposite Feathers Inn.

Cowper & Newton Museum, Market Place, Olney.
(0234) 711516 North of Newport Pagnell via A509.

✼ **Hughenden Manor,** High Wycombe.
(0494) 532580 1¹/₂ miles north of High Wycombe.

CHICHELEY HALL

THE MANOR HOUSE CHENIES

OPEN
April-Oct.
inclusive

Wednesdays,
Thursdays and
Bank Holiday
Mondays.

2.00pm-5.00pm

THE MANOR HOUSE, CHENIES TEL: 0494 762888
(Mr and Mrs MacLeod Matthews)

Early Tudor House in picturesque village, original house of the Russell family. Contemporary furniture, tapestries. "Secret" passages, hiding places. Lovely gardens with famous tulip display in spring and brilliant plantings throughout the year.. Physic garden, 2 mazes. Still a family home. Delicious teas. Corporate days with clays, archery etc., in beautiful location. Free parking.

Location: In Chenies village off A404 between Rickmansworth and Amersham. London 25 miles. M25 junction 18, 2¹/₂ miles.
Admission: Adults: House and gardens £3.50, gardens only £1.75. Child half price.

Milton's Cottage, Chalfont St Giles.
(0494) 872313 ¹/₂ mile west of A413 on road to Seer Green and Beaconsfield.

Nether Winchenden House, Aylesbury.
(0353) 290101 1 mile north of A418 Aylesbury/Thame road.

✼ **Princes Risborough Manor House,** Princes Risborough.
(08444) 3168 Opposite church off Market Square in town centre.

The Thatched Cottage, Duck Lane, Ludgershall, Aylesbury.
(0844) 237415

✼ **West Wycombe Park,** West Wycombe.
(0494) 524411 2¹/₂ miles west of High Wycombe.

Winslow Hall, Winslow
(0296) 712323 At entrance to Winslow on A413 (Aylesbury Road).

🏛 **Wotton House,** Wotton Underwood, Aylesbury.
(0844) 238368 2 miles south of A41 between Aylesbury and Bicester.

CLAYDON HOUSE

ELTON HALL
Elton, Peterborough

ELTON HALL, the home of the Proby family for over 300 years, stands in the midst of unspoilt landscaped parkland on a site where there has been a house since the Norman Conquest. Sir Peter Proby, Lord Mayor of London and Comptroller of the Royal Household, was granted land and property at Elton by Queen Elizabeth I. His grandson, Sir Thomas Proby, completed the main House in 1666. In the 18th Century John Proby was created the first Earl of Carysfort. He and his successors enlarged it to the 18th Century character that it has today.

Elton is a fascinating mixture of styles. Every room contains treasures - magnificent furniture from many countries and fine paintings from early 15th Century Old Masters to the remarkable Pre-Raphaelite work of Alma Tadema and Millais. Great British artists are well represented by Gainsborough, Constable and Reynolds. The Library is one of the finest in private hands containing some 12,000 books. The collection includes the unique Henry VIII's Prayer Book in which can be seen the writing of the Tudor King and two of his wives.

GARDENS

The formal gardens have been carefully restored in recent years. The Victorian Rose Garden contains some 1,000 roses including many old fashioned varieties whose fragrance in the summer months is quite memorable.

New herbaceous borders provide great interest to gardeners and non-gardeners alike. An arboretum has recently been planted. Picnics may also be taken in this pleasant area.

CONTACT

The House Manager
Estate Office
Elton Hall
Elton
Peterborough
PE8 6SH

Tel: (0832) 280468
Fax: (0832) 280584

LOCATION

From London, A1(M), A605 to Elton. 86 mls. From Leicester, A47, B671, A605 to Elton.

Bus: Peterborough-Kettering bus passes the Hall.

Rail: P'borough 8mls.

Air: Private Airport 3mls.

Taxi: Norwood, Oundle 273585.

OPENING TIMES

Summer

Easter, May & August Bank Holidays, Sun & Mon   2-5pm

July
Wed & Sun
            2-5pm

August
Wed, Thurs & Sun
            2-5pm

Winter
Private parties by appointment

ADMISSION

Summer

HOUSE & GARDEN
Adult	£3.80
Child*	£1.90
OAP	£3.80
Student	£1.90

GARDEN ONLY
Adult	£1.90
Child*	£0.95
OAP	£1.90
Student	£0.95

GROUPS**
Adult	£3.80
Child*	£1.90
Free ticket to all party organisers

* Aged 5-15
** Over 20 people. Over 50 people gain additional 10% discount.

Winter

Private Parties by appointment only

SUITABILITY FOR OTHER EVENTS

Corporate Entertaining, product launches, promotions, photographic and film location work

EXTRA FACILITIES

Parkland available for rallies etc. Clay Pigeon shoots can be arranged. Special lecture-tours of Hall. Please apply for details.

ADVICE TO COURIERS & DRIVERS

Elton Hall is not suitable for disabled visitors because of the steps. It is, however, of great interest to art lovers. No dogs in Hall or formal gardens. No photography in Hall. Ploughmans suppers and buffet suppers are available for parties being taken on a guided tour. Parking for 200 cars and 10 coaches, 50 yards from the house.

FACILITIES FOR THE DISABLED

Disabled and elderly visitors may alight close to the entrance. Vehicles can then be parked in the allocated areas. There are no toilet facilities for the disabled and steps at the entrance and in the Hall.

CATERING

The elegant State Dining Room is available for Banquets, Receptions etc. Up to 70 can be seated or 100 for buffet-type functions. Menus and prices on application. The Billiard Room seats 50 people. Prices on application. Meals can be booked in advance and menus are available on request.

GUIDED TOURS

Parties of up to 100 people can be split into groups of 20, except on Bank Holidays. Average time taken for a tour 3/4 hour.

SCHOOL VISITS/CHILDREN

Elton Hall is suitable mainly for 5th and 6th forms. There is a special question sheet with a competition for younger children. Grassed picnic area available. Guided tours available; please apply to House Manager for costs.

CONFERENCE AND FUNCTION FACILITIES

ROOM	DIMENSIONS	CAPACITY	LAYOUT	POWER POINTS	SUITABLE FOR A/V
Billiard Room	38'x28'	60	Buffet Lunch/Dinner	✓	✓
State Dining Room	38'6"x23'6"	100	Banquets/Receptions Product Launches	✓	✓
Old Laundry	21'x20'	40	Product Launches Receptions	✓	✓
Conference Room	21'x20'	20	Conferences	✓	✓

Anglesey Abbey and Garden, Lode, Cambridge.
(0223) 811200 6 miles north east of Cambridge on B1102.

Oliver Cromwell's House, 29 St Mary's Street, Ely.
(0353) 662062

Denny Abbey
(0223) 860489 6 miles north of Cambridge on A10.

Docwra's Manor, Shepreth
(0763) 261473/261557/260235 Opposite War Memorial in centre of village.

Kimbolton Castle, Kimbolton.
(0480) 860505 8 miles north west of St Neots on A45.

Longthorpe Tower
(0733) 268482   2 miles west of Peterborough on A47.

Peckover House and Garden, Wisbech.
(0945) 583463 In centre of Wisbech on north bank of River Nene.

Prior Crauden's Chapel, The College, Ely.
(0353) 662837 In the precincts of Ely Cathedral.

Wimpole Hall, near Cambridge
(0223) 207257 8 miles south west of Cambridge.

Wimpole Home Farm, near Cambridge
(0223) 207257 8 miles south west of Cambridge.

ELTON HALL

WIMPOLE HALL

ADLINGTON HALL
Macclesfield, Cheshire

ADLINGTON HALL, the home of the Leghs of Adlington from 1315 to the present day, was built on the site of a Hunting Lodge which stood in the Forest of Macclesfield in 1040. Two oaks, part of the original building, remain with their roots in the ground and support the east end of the Great Hall, which was built between 1480 and 1505.

The Hall is a Manor House, quadrangular in shape, and was once surrounded by a moat. Two sides of the Courtyard and the east wing were built in the typical 'Black and White' Cheshire style in 1581. The south front and west wing (containing the Drawing Room and Dining Room) were added between 1749 and 1757 and are built of red brick with a handsome stone portico with four Ionic columns on octagonal pedestals.

Between the trees in the Great Hall stands an Organ built by 'Father' Bernard Smith (c.1670-80). Handel subsequently played on this instrument, and now fully restored, it is the largest 17th Century organ in the country.

GARDENS

The Wilderness was landscaped in the style of Capability Brown in the mid 18th century and incorporates both earlier 17th century plantings and sympathetic Victorian additions. The formal french style has given way to an apparently wild, but very carefully cultivated informality. Dotted about the circuitous paths are a number of decorative buildings.

CONTACT

The Guide
Adlington Hall
Macclesfield
Cheshire
SK10 4LF

Tel: (0625) 829206
The Hunting Lodge
Tel: (0625) 827595

LOCATION

5 miles north of Macclesfield (A523), 13 miles south of Manchester. London 178 miles.

Railway stations: Macclesfield and Wilmslow 5 miles.

Manchester airport 8 miles.

OPENING TIMES

Summer
Good Friday-30 Sept.

Sundays and Bank Holidays 2pm-5.30pm.

Parties by appointment any day or early evening.

Winter

By appointment only.

The Hunting Lodge is open all year round.

ADMISSION

Summer

HALL & GARDENS
Adult £2.70
Child £1.25

GROUPS
Per Person £2.50
Minimum 25 people

GARDENS ONLY
Per Person £1.00

Winter

GROUPS
Per Person £2.50
Minimum 25 people

SUITABILITY FOR OTHER EVENTS

Suitable for corporate activity events, clay pigeon shooting, product launches, business meetings, conferences, concerts, fashion shows, garden parties, shows, rallies and filming.

CONFERENCE/FUNCTION FACILITIES

The Great Hall and Dining Room available for use when the Hall is not open to the public.

ADVICE TO COURIERS & DRIVERS

Special requests are considered.

FACILITIES FOR THE DISABLED

Disabled and elderly visitors may alight at the entrance to the Hall. No toilets for the disabled.

PARKING FOR COACHES & CARS

Capacity of the car park - 100 cars and 4 coaches, 100 yards from the Hall.

CATERING

Teas and light refreshments in the Hall. Banqueting facilities in the Hunting Lodge.

GUIDED TOURS

Tours are available.

SCHOOL VISITS/CHILDREN

School parties are welcome. Cost per child £1.25. A guide can be provided for the tour.

CONFERENCE AND FUNCTION FACILITIES

ROOM	DIMENSIONS	CAPACITY	LAYOUT	POWER POINTS	SUITABLE FOR A/V
Great Hall	37'x26'x38'	125	Theatre	5	✓
		60	Schoolroom		
		60/80	Buffet		
		80/100	Dinner/Dance		
Dining Room	35'x23'x18'	50	Theatre	3	✓
		25	U-Shape		
Hunting Lodge	60'x30'x28'	150	Theatre	15	✓
	40'x30'x20'	70/80	U-Shape		
		130	Dinner/Dance		
		150	Lunch/Dinner		

ARLEY HALL AND GARDENS
Northwich, Cheshire

ARLEY HALL, the home of the Hon Michael and Mrs Flower, was built about 1840 by the owner's great great grandfather, Rowland Egerton-Warburton, to the design of the Nantwich architect, George Latham. An important example of the Victorian Jacobean style, it has fine plaster work and wood panelling as well as interesting furniture, pictures and other contents. Adjoining Arley Hall is a large private Chapel designed by Anthony Salvin .

An impressive range of activities can be held both in the Hall and in the grounds, from Corporate Conferences of any size to Cocktail Parties and Ambassadorial Receptions. Arley Hall offers all its visitors an elegant setting combined with the professional approach to top class management. Catering to the highest standards.

GARDENS

Overlooking beautiful parkland, and providing great variety of style and design, the Gardens extending over 12 acres rank among the finest in the country. Winner of the Christie's HHA 'Garden of the Year' award in 1987. The features include the Double Herbaceous Border, one of the earliest to be established in England 1846, unique avenue of clipped Quercus Ilex, collection of Shrub Roses, fine Yew hedges, Herb Garden, Walled Garden, Woodland Garden with exotic trees, Shrubs, Azaleas and a collection of over 200 varieties of Rhododendrons.

CONTACT

Eric Ransome
Arley Hall and Gardens
Northwich
Cheshire
CW9 6NA

Tel: (0565) 777353
Fax: (0565) 777465

LOCATION

5 miles from Knutsford
5 miles from Northwich
5 miles from M6
Motorway Junct. 19/20.
5 miles from M56
Motorway Junct. 9/10.

Air: Manchester Airport
16 mls.

SUITABILITY FOR OTHER EVENTS

Business Meetings & Conferences, Corporate Activity Events, Receptions & Dinner Parties, Concerts, Filming.

EXTRA FACILITIES

100 acres parkland, grass, cricket pitch. Grand piano in Gallery.

ADVICE TO COURIERS & DRIVERS

Free entry and refreshments for courier and coach driver. Photography only in the gardens.

FACILITIES FOR THE DISABLED

Disabled and elderly visitors may alight at the entrance to the Hall, before parking in the allocated areas. Toilets for the disabled.

PARKING FOR COACHES & CARS

Unlimited parking for cars, 250 yds from Hall and 6 coaches may be parked 100 yds away. Special arrangements can be made for function parking 50 yds from the Hall.

CATERING

The Restaurant/Tea Room seats up to 100 people for light refreshments, lunches and evening meals. Prices range from £1.00 to £10.00.

GUIDED TOURS

Tours of up to 25 people per guide are conducted round the Hall. Guided tours of the Gardens can be arranged for a minimum of £30 per party. Average time taken for a tour of the Hall 1 hour, and for the gardens 1 1/2 hours.

GIFT SHOP/SPECIALIST PLANT NURSERY

Open when the Gardens are open to the public, also at other selected times.

GUIDE BOOKS

Colour Guide Books on House and Gardens.

CONFERENCE AND FUNCTION FACILITIES

ROOM	DIMENSIONS	CAPACITY	LAYOUT	POWER POINTS	SUITABLE FOR A/V
Drawing Room	38'x22'	110	Theatre	Ample	✓
		70	Schoolroom		
		22	Boardroom		
		100	Finger Buffet		
		70	Lunch/Dinner		
Gallery	41'x25'	100	Finger Buffet	Ample	✓
Front Hall	35'x22'	22	Boardroom	Ample	✓
		22	Lunch/Dinner		
Tudor Barn	56'x22'+	200	Theatre	6	✓
		120	Finger Buffet		
		100	Lunch/Dinner		

CAPESTHORNE HALL
Macclesfield, Cheshire

CAPESTHORNE HALL has been the home of the Bromley-Davenport Family and their ancestors since Domesday times when the appointment of Chief Forester carrying the responsibility of law and order in the Forests of Macclesfield and Leek was granted to them. Since then many generations have served in Parliament, the Bromley side providing both a Chancellor and Speaker. The present owner is H.M. Lord Lieutenant for Cheshire.

The existing Hall dating from 1719 was originally designed by the Smiths of Warwick, then altered by both Blore in 1837 and Salvin in 1861, the latter rebuilding the centre section following a disastrous fire.

The Hall contains a great variety of paintings, sculptures, furniture and tapestry including a collection of Colonial furnishings brought over by the late Lady Bromley-Davenport from her former American home in Philadelphia.

The park and gardens extend to some 60 acres and feature a beautiful Georgian Chapel dating from 1720 where services are still held, a chain of man-made lakes the central one being spanned by a multi-arch brick bridge. A pair of 18th Century Milanese gates, and a nature trail and woodland walk where an old Ice House and Water Cascade can be seen.

CONTACT

Jacquie Caldwell
Capesthorne Hall
Siddington
Macclesfield
Cheshire
SK11 9JY

Tel: (0625) 861221 or
861779
Fax: (0625) 861619

LOCATION

30 mins South of
Manchester on A34
Near M6, M63 and M62.

Air: Manchester
International 20 mins.
Helicopter: (051) 427
1609.

Rail: Macclesfield 5mls
(2hrs from London).

Taxi: (0625) 611600.
Air Taxi: (061) 499 1447.

SUITABILITY FOR OTHER EVENTS

Capesthorne's situation makes it the ideal venue for functions aimed at the Manchester and North West corporate sector. Facilities are available for clay pigeon shooting, product launches, filming, still photography, shows, wedding receptions, fishing, caravanning and camping, equestrian events (own cross-country course), garden parties, rallies, barbecues, survival games, murder mystery evenings, firework displays, son et lumière etc.

EXTRA FACILITIES

The Theatre is used as a Lecture Room and seats up to 150 people. Cost of hire of the room, audio-visual facilities and lecture negotiable.

ADVICE TO COURIERS & DRIVERS

Rest Room and free meal provided for drivers. No photography in the Hall. Dogs in Park only.

FACILITIES FOR THE DISABLED

Compacted paths, ramps and toilet facilities available.

PARKING FOR COACHES & CARS

Parking for 100 cars/20 coaches on hard-standing and for 2,000 in the park, 50 yds from the house.

CATERING

Capesthorne has its own in-house catering staff providing a wide variety of meals from afternoon tea to banquets. Garden Restaurant, Bromley Room and the ornate Saloon and Queen Anne Rooms available. Special arrangements for corporate functions.

GUIDED TOURS

Can be arranged for up to 50 people at any one time Also available in Italian. The owner can meet tours visiting the house. Average time taken for tour 1 hour.

GIFT SHOP/GUIDE BOOKS

Open when Hall is open and by request at other times. Various brochures on the house, park and garden are available.

CONFERENCE AND FUNCTION FACILITIES

ROOM	DIMENSIONS	CAPACITY	LAYOUT	POWER POINTS	SUITABLE FOR A/V
Theatre	120'x25'	155	Theatre	Ample	✓
Garden Restaurant	100'x20'	100	Theatre	Ample	✓
		80	Schoolroom		
		50	Boardroom		
		100	Buffet		
		80	Lunch/Dinner		
Saloon	40'x25'	100	Theatre	Ample	✓
		80	Schoolroom		
		50	Boardroom		
Queen Anne Room	38'x26'	80	Schoolroom	Ample	✓
		100	Theatre		

LYME PARK
Stockport, Cheshire

CONTACT

Angela Stead
Marketing Manager
Lyme Park
Disley
Stockport
Cheshire
SK12 2NX

Tel: (0663) 762023
Fax: (0663) 765035

LOCATION

From Chester 56 mls on M56, M63 and A6. Main entrance on Manchester-Buxton road ½ mile west of Disley village.

Rail: Regular trains from Stockport to Disley.

LYME PARK is one of the National Trust's most spectacular country estates featuring herds of red and fallow deer. Lyme has been the home of the Legh family for 600 years. The magnificent house is the largest in Cheshire, Part of the Elizabethan house survives today. Giacomo Leoni transformed the house into a Palladian mansion with an internal Italian courtyard and Classic portico in 1720. Lewis Wyatt also left his mark in the 19th century with the Wyatt tower and a beautiful Orangery. The house contains outstanding rooms from every period of history including an Elizabethan Long Gallery. The Saloon contains magnificent Grinling Gibbons carvings and the Drawing Room contains some historic stained glass. There is a a comprehensive collection of English clocks.

The 17 acres of historic gardens have many features including formal Victorian flower beds a sunken Dutch garden with fountain a rose garden, a reflection lake, and the wild beauty of Killtime. Wyatt's Orangery contains two beautiful Camellias over 150 years old.

The estate itself is set in stark wild moorland scenery with magnificent views over the Cheshire Plain and the Derbyshire Peaks. Woodland walks and nature trails enable the visitor to enjoy the park to the full. From Lyme's famous landmark, the Cage, once a hunting tower, six counties can be seen.

SUITABILITY FOR OTHER EVENTS

Corporate Entertaining of all types, including Clay Target Shooting, Country Pursuit Days, Receptions, Balls and Marquee Events up to 800. Available for Conferences, Product Launches, Weddings, Filming etc.

EXTRA FACILITIES

Other Facilities Include: A Visitor Centre, Countryside Centre, Information Centre, Pitch & Putt Course, Adventure Playground.

EVENTS

Lyme has a full programme of events, please ring for details.

ADVICE TO COURIERS & DRIVERS

Drop off point and pick up area in front of Hall. Please note that all vehicles are required to park in the official coach park. No ice cream, photographs or dogs (except guide dogs) allowed in the Hall. Parking for 1,000 cars and coaches, 100yds from house

FACILITIES FOR THE DISABLED

Disabled and elderly visitors may alight at the Hall. Vehicles can then be parked in the allocated areas. Tearoom and shop accessible. Parts of the Hall, Gardens and Park accessible. Suitable WC for Hall visitors and by lakeside for park visitors. Booster scooter (free) to enable enjoyment of the Park and gardens. Special trail and picnic area. Access to Hall and gardens is difficult, please phone for details. Limited parking for badge holders hear to Hall.

CATERING

The Tea Room can cater for 40 with additional seating for 50. Groups can book in advance for tea and other meals. Menus available on request. Buffets, lunches and dinners can be arranged for special functions. Refreshment kiosk in car park.

GUIDED TOURS

Private and theme tours can be arranged anytime either in or outside normal opening hours. Min. size of private tour 20, average time taken 1 hour. Themed and special interest tours include: The ghosts of Lyme, Below Stairs, Child's Eye View etc.

GIFT SHOP

Open at the same time as the Hall. Items include souvenirs, confectionery and local crafts.

GUIDE BOOKS

Colour guide book £1.00. Childrens' Activity Guide 50p. National Trust Guide Book £1.50.

SCHOOLS/EDUCATION SERVICE

Extensive education programme tailored to national curriculum in term time with trained staff. Other activities in holidays

OPENING TIMES

HALL
From 1st April, Good Friday. For details and times and days, open, please telephone information line 0663 766492

GARDENS
April-Sept. incl. open daily 10.30am-5pm
Oct.-March incl.
Tues.to Sundays 10.30am-4pm
Closed Mondays
Closed Dec. 25th and 26th

ESTATE
Open every day of the year 8am - Dusk.

TEAROOMS
April-Sept. daily 11.30am-5pm
Oct.-Dec. Sundays only 12noon-4pm
Jan-March Closed

REFRESHMENT KIOSK
Open weekends and school holidays (Stockport) and June & July. Daily from 11am.

SHOP
April-Sept. 12noon-5pm
Oct.-Dec. Sundays only 1pm-4pm
Jan-March Closed

ADMISSION

1994 charges under review.

Please ring : 0663 766492

CONFERENCE AND FUNCTION FACILITIES

ROOM	DIMENSIONS	CAPACITY	LAYOUT	POWER POINTS	SUITABLE FOR A/V
Entrance Hall		140	Various	✓	✓
Servants Hall		74	Various	✓	✓
Joseph Watson Room		74	Various	✓	✓

DUNHAM MASSEY
Altrincham, Cheshire

DUNHAM MASSEY, home of the Stamford family for over 200 years, owes its special character to George Booth, the second Earl of Warrington 1675-1758. His formal parkland with its radiating avenues of oak, beech and lime remains much as intended, and the 250 acres are still grazed by a herd of fallow deer. The park is open to the public all year round.

The 18th Century House encasing an earlier Tudor building was renovated at the beginning of this century by the father of the 10th and last Earl of Stamford, who died in 1976. It contains a collection of Huguenot silver, a library of some 2,500 leather-bound books, souvenirs of the Grand Tour collected by the 5th and 6th Earls of Stamford, as well as a fine collection of furniture and paintings dating back to the 17th Century.

GARDENS

The 30 acre formal garden has an 18th Century Orangery, canal borders planted with moisture loving plants, extensive lawns, a large woodland area underplanted with late flowering azaleas and a formal parterre. The Elizabethan mount overlooks the original moat which provides water for the working sawmill.

CONTACT

The Administrator
The National Trust
Dunham Massey Hall
Altrincham
Cheshire
WA14 4SJ

Tel: 061-941 1025

Restaurant and Shop:
061-941 2815

LOCATION

3 miles south west of Altrincham on the B5160, off the A56. Signposted from junct. 7 of the M56 and close to junct. 19 of M6.

Bus: North Western/GM Buses 38.

Rail: Altrincham station 3 miles, Hale 3 miles.

SUITABILITY FOR OTHER EVENTS

Garden parties, concerts in the Great Gallery, Craft Fairs, workshops and also a film location.

ADVICE TO COURIERS & DRIVERS

Coach parking free, refreshments free for drivers. The usual National Trust restraints apply within the House.

PARKING FOR COACHES & CARS

Car park £2 per car. Spaces for 600 cars. 250 yards from House.

FACILITIES FOR THE DISABLED

Manual wheelchairs and Batricar available. Limited facilities for disabled visitors to drive to House. Adapted lavatory cubicles. Steps at entrance to and throughout House. Park and garden fully accessible. A Braille Guide is available. Leaflet giving full details of facilities is available on application to the Administrator.

CATERING

Restaurant on first floor of Stable Block seats 120. Elderly or disabled visitors may have trays brought down to them. Separate room and party menu available for parties of up to 50 booked in advance. Telephone the Catering Manager on 061-941 2815.

GIFT SHOP

Large range of quality goods.

GUIDED TOURS

Price includes cassette audio tour. Guided tours in evening by arrangement.

GUIDE BOOKS

Selection available priced from 50p to £2.50.

SCHOOL VISITS/CHILDREN

Living History and Environmental Education programmes related to National Curriculum and a school room available. Contact Education Co-ordinator for details and booking 061-941 4986. A children's guide and quiz are available.

OPENING TIMES

Summer
HOUSE
2 April - 30 October
Sat - Wed   12noon-5pm.
Last admission 4.15pm.

GARDEN
1 April-30 October
Daily   11am-5.30pm.

RESTAURANT AND SHOP
1 April-30 October
Daily   11am-5.00pm.

Winter
3 Nov - 18 Dec
Thurs - Sun 12noon-4pm

ADMISSION

HOUSE & GARDEN*	
Adult	£4.50
Child	£2.00
HOUSE ONLY*	
Adult	£3.00
Child	£1.50
GARDEN ONLY	
Adult	£2.00
Child	£1.00

*Prices include audio tour: N.T. members Audio tour £1.00.

Party rates available on application to the Administrator

CONFERENCE AND FUNCTION FACILITIES

PRIVATE AND CORPORATE FUNCTIONS CAN BE ARRANGED. PLEASE CONTACT THE ADMINISTRATOR.

TATTON PARK
Knutsford, Cheshire

CONTACT

Corporate incentives, trade/outdoor events
David Hardman
Marketing Manager
Conferences, functions, party visits, catering
Sheila Wych or
Sylvia Williams
Tatton Park
Knutsford
Cheshire
WA16 6QN
Tel: (0565) 654822
Fax: (0565) 650179

LOCATION

From M56, junct. 7, follow signs.
From M6, junct. 19, signed on A56 and A50.

Rail: Knutsford or Altrincham Stn, then taxi.

TATTON is one of the most complete historic estates in Britain. Five separate features, special events and private functions attract around 700,000 visitors each year.

A STORY FOR EVERY AGE, the new interpretive theme, describes the development of the noble English Country Estate, bringing history alive.

Man's occupation of Tatton began 10,000 years ago. The landscape History Trail guides walkers through time from a prehistoric camp to the wartime dropping zone for new recruits to the 1st Parachute Regiment, based at Ringway (now Manchester International Airport). The trail's explanatory boards are also in the reception barn at Old Hall. Visitors are taken on an authentic journey through four centuries from the smokey shadows of the 15th century great hall lit by flickering candles. The tour ends with a visit to the home of a 1950's estate employee. The Old Hall was leased to his cousin by Thomas Egerton, Lord Chancellor of England during the reign of Queen Elizabeth I and James I.

At the other side of the park the Palladian Mansion by Wyatt is the jewel in Tatton's crown. The Egerton family collection of fine paintings, porcelain and furniture is found in the splendid setting of the magnificent staterooms.

In stark contrast, the Victorian kitchens and cellars give a fascinating insight into life "downstairs".

Much of the wealth to provide such a grand home and surroundings was created by agriculture.

The Home Farm is still working with traditional breeds of animals. Estate workshops, a steam engine and regular demonstrations all assist in telling the story, together with "Horses at Tatton" which explain the use of horses for work and pleasure.

GARDENS

These are immaculately maintained by a staff of 12. The superb gardens are full of delightful surprises from all parts of the globe. Successive generations expanded the range of features and specimen plants according to their own taste and style of the times. Extending to 50 acres, including the arboretum, the gardens are considered to be amongst the most important in England. Attractions include the famous Japanese garden with a tea house and Shinto temple, orangery, New Zealand tree fernery, Italian terraced garden and maze. There's also an African hut and a Greek monument.

Alongside man, deer have roamed the landscape since 8000 BC. Roughly 800 red and fallow deer can still be seen when walking or driving in the Parkland.

Tatton Park is maintained, managed and financed by Cheshire County Council on lease from the National Trust to whom the Mansion and Gardens were bequeathed in 1958 by the late Right Honourable Maurice, Baron Egerton of Tatton, "for the benefit of the Nation".

SPECIAL ATTRACTIONS

Theme "A story for every age".
Largest collection of Gillow furniture
Paintings and porcelain
Servants rooms, cellars
Maurice Egerton's colonial collection
Coaches and vehicles
Pinetum, Arboretum

OPENING TIMES

Summer
1 April - 30 September
and October half-term.
Closed on Mondays,
except Park.
Park   10.30am-7pm
Gardens   10.30am-6pm
Last Admission   5pm
Mansion, Old Hall & Farm
           12pm-5pm
Last Admission   4pm
Groups advised to book early visit to Old Hall (from 10am) at no extra charge.
Winter
1 October-31 March
Closed Mondays.
Park: 11am-5pm
Gardens: 11am-4pm
Farm: Sun   12-4pm
Restaurant, Shop:
weekends 11.30am—4pm
All attractions open weekends in Oct. Mansion, Farm open weekends in Dec before Xmas.

ADMISSION

All Year

	Single	Group*
ALL ATTRACTIONS		
Adult	£6.00	£5.00
Child**	£4.20	£4.00
ANY 2 ATTRACTIONS		
Adult	£4.00	£4.00
Child	£2.50	£2.50
OAP	£4.00	£3.20
MANSION		
Adult	£2.50	£2.00
Child**	£1.50	£1.50
GARDEN		
Adult	£2.50	£2.00
Child**	£1.50	£1.50
OLD HALL		
Adult	£2.00	£1.60
Child**	£1.30	£1.30

FARM & HORSES same rates as Old Hall
*Min 12 People.
** Aged 5-15
*** Mansion and Gardens only £4.00
OAP rate as Adult unless specified.*

SUITABILITY FOR OTHER EVENTS

A new reception building provides Tatton with a purpose designed service area and bar for conferences, trade exhibitions, presentations and product launches in the Tenants Hall. Entry is still possible via the Mansion staterooms and Gardens. A total of 8000 sq ft is now available for hire in the Tenants Hall Event Wing. Other uses include dinners, dances, receptions, concerts, fashion shows, weddings and computer training workshops. Syndicate rooms are nearby.

Special family days can be arranged to run alongside conferences and exhibitions.

For smaller functions Lord Egertons' Apartment has been converted for meetings, dining and receptions. From the covered balcony delegates enjoy an unrivalled view of the Italian garden and Parkland with its lakes to the peaks of Derbyshire beyond. The apartment, like the Tenants Hall, is self contained and away from the envious eyes of day visitors. The Entrance Hall is available for champagne receptions.

Over 50 public special events are held annually outside in the Park and Gardens, from the Halle with Fireworks to large gatherings of vintage cars.

EXTRA FACILITIES

Spotlights, catwalk, dance floor, full public address system, sailing, parkland, shuttle service and marquee hire. The pillarless Tenants Hall has 2 sources of 3 phase power, a scaffold tower and can seat up to 400 for lectures. Projector and screens can be provided. Independent telephones throughout.

ADVICE TO COURIERS & DRIVERS

Visitors now benefit from recent investment in major new services and facilities. Additions and conversions include new lavatories, shops, group dining room, restaurant and a reception/information point adjacent to the coach park. The Privilege Coach Club scheme entitles members and passengers to vouchers.

PARKING FOR COACHES & CARS

Parking for 4,000 cars, 300yds from the Mansion and for 50 coaches, 200yds from the Mansion.

VOUCHERS

These are accepted and invoices sent after the visit has been made.

CATERING

There is a newly refurbished self-service restaurant with new caterers,tuck shop for snack and ice-cream.

Less comprehensive catering facilities at Old Hall May-Aug. Prices range from £3.50 special rates apply to groups. Lunches and dinners in Lord Egerton's apartment from £17, max. 40.

Booked groups in Harness Room., capacity 80. Menus include pork with cider, beef bordelaise, venison masterchef, buffets. Enquire for availability of Tenants Hall bar.

GUIDED TOURS

Everyone is taken on a guided tour of Old Hall where "A story for every Age" begins. Tours of other attractions can be arranged during and outside normal opening times from £1,40 per person. Tours available in Japanese, German, French, Spanish, Italian. Average time taken 1 hour per attraction.

GIFT SHOP/GARDEN SALES

Open 11.30am-5.30pm. Local crafts, books, children's souvenirs, film, home grown plants, farm produce.

GUIDE BOOKS

Colour guide books from £1. Paying visitors receive free leaflets at each attraction.

ROOM	DIMENSIONS	CAPACITY	LAYOUT	POWER POINTS	SUITABLE FOR A/V
Tenants Hall (Excluding new reception and walled garden)	125'x45'	330-400	Various	34	✓
Tenants Hall Event Wing – total of 8,000 Sq Feet available					✓
Servants Hall	22'x15'	30-50	Various	4	✓
Lord Egerton's Apartment	20'x16' 24'x18'	16-30 19-35	Various Various	4 4	✓ ✓
Stables Block Function Room	31'x20'	80	Various	4	✓
Dining Room	50'x40'	120	Various	4	✓

SCHOOL VISITS/CHILDREN

Tatton's award-winning educational programmes are available all year round by prior arrangement with the Education Department. Environmental days with the Rangers in the Park, scrubbing pigs down on the farm or scrubbing floors as a Victorian servant in the Mansion are just some of the activities available. You can even spend the day as an Anglo-Saxon! Flexibility and imagination are the watchwords at Tatton - we can also arrange fishing tuition, sailing instruction, orienteering, photo safaris or any combination of exciting activities suitable for all ages (including adults!) and tastes. An adventure playground is also available.

SPECIAL EVENTS 1994

April	2-4	Crafts on the Farm
May	1-2	Tatton May Fair
	6-8	19th & 20th Century Paintings Fair
	7	Brass Band Competition
	26-27	Flower Arranging Show
	28-30	Country Crafts Festival
June	4-5	Classic Car Spectacular with Autojumble
	10-12	Book Fair
	12	Orchid Show
	18-19	Carriage Driving Trials & Country Fair
	25-26	Vintage Stationary Engine Rally
July	2-3	American Cars Weekend
	7-9,11	Shakespeare at Old Hall
	16-17	Medieval Fair
	24(Sun)	Halle' Orchestra with Fireworks
August	5 (Sun)	Concert in the Italian Gardens
	21	Models & Miniatures Exhibition
	27-29	Tatton Festival of Crafts
Sept.	3-4	Vintage Vehicle Show
	14-18	Quality Antiques Fair
October	1-2	Wood Weekend
	21-23	14th National Craft and Design Show
Nov.	11-13	World of Oriental Carpets
	26	Theatre Organ Concert
Dec.	3-18	Christmas Festival
	6-8	Street Fair and Candlelit Mansion

✿ **Beeston Castle**
(0829) 260464 2 miles west of Bunbury, 11 miles south east of Chester.

Cholmondeley Castle Gardens, Malpas
(0829) 720383/720203 Off A41 Chester/Whitchurch Road.

🏛 **Dorfold Hall,** Nantwich
(0270) 625245 1 mile west of Nantwich on A534.

Gawsworth Hall, Macclesfield
(0260) 223456 3 miles south of Macclesfield on the A536.

Handforth Hall, Handforth, Wilmslow
1/2 mile east of Handforth on B5358.

✿ **Hare Hill Garden,** Over Alderley, Macclesfied.
Between Alderley Edge and Prestbury off B5087.

✿ **Little Moreton Hall**, Congleton.
(0260) 272018 4 miles south west of Congleton off A34.

✿ **Nether Alderley Mill,** Nether Alderley
(0625) 523012 1 1/2 miles south of Alderley Edge on east side of A34.

Norton Priory Museum, Runcorn.
(0928) 569895 From M56 junct. 11, turn towards Warrington and follow road signs.

Peover Hall, Over Peover, Knutsford.
(0565) 722656 4 miles south of Knutsford off A50 at Whipping Stocks Inn.

✿ **Quarry Bank Mill,** Styal
(0625) 527468 1 1/2 miles north of Wilmslow off B5166, 1 mile from exit 5 M56.

Woodhey Chapel, Faddiley, Nantwich
(027074) 215 1 mile south west of Faddiley off A534

TABLEY HOUSE

MOUNT EDGCUMBE
Torpoint, Cornwall

MOUNT EDGCUMBE HOUSE stands above its tree-lined avenue overlooking Plymouth Sound, as it has done for the past 500 years.

It was the ancestral home of the Mount Edgcumbe family, and following severe World War II damage was rebuilt by the architect Adrian Gilbert Scott. The interior follows the 16th Century design, but is light and airy, and has recently been renovated using 18th century techniques and design.

GARDENS

The garden surrounding the House is a delightful mixture of the formal, with its Victorian beds, and the informal. It includes a rare example of an 18th Century grotto, the Shell Seat.

The 18th century Formal Gardens designed by the family in the English, French and Italian styles have recently been complemented by New Zealand and American gardens.

CONTACT

Mrs Cynthia Gaskell Brown
Mt Edgcumbe House
Cremyll
Torpoint
Cornwall
PL10 1HZ

Tel: (0752) 822236
Fax (0752) 822199

LOCATION

From Plymouth via Torpoint Ferry, follow A374 to Antony then B3247. 1 hr approx. From Cornwall, A38 to Trerulefoot Roundabout, A374, B3247. From London, M4, M5 via Bristol to Exeter, then A38 to Plymouth. (3-4 hours).

Foot: From Plymouth (Royal Parade) bus to Cremyll Ferry at Admirals Hard, Durnford St. Ferry crossing 7 minutes.

Bus: Bus from Royal Parade to gate via Torpoint Ferry.

Air: Plymouth Airport.

Taxi: (0752) 822196.

SUITABILITY FOR OTHER EVENTS

Fashion shows, photography, archery, garden parties, shows, filming, hot air ballooning, commercial product launching. Any idea considered.

EXTRA FACILITIES

Also available for use: parkland, helipad, cricket pitch and good coastal walking. Lectures can be arranged on the property, its gardens and history for up to 60 people. A room, seating about 35, can be hired by prior arrangement. A projector and screen are available. Baby changing facility.

ADVICE TO COURIERS & DRIVERS

Grounds include Formal Gardens so allow plenty of time. Free entry to house for familiarisation visit and free meal when accompanying party on production of appropriate identification. No unaccompanied children, no dogs - this applies to the House and Earl's Garden only. No photography in House.

FACILITIES FOR THE DISABLED

Restaurant, Formal Gardens, House and part of Park area suitable for the disabled. Disabled and elderly visitors may alight by entrance to the House. Lift in House to first floor. There are toilet facilities for the disabled in the Orangery Restaurant and in the House. Two wheelchairs are available.

PARKING FOR COACHES & CARS

Car park for 50 cars and 6 coaches 400 yds from House. Other car parks at Cremyll, Maker and Rame.

CATERING

'The Orangery' in the Formal Gardens has a capacity of 120. Parties can book in advance and special rates are given to groups of more than 25 people. Menus are available on request. Cream Teas from £2.60; Luncheon from £4.50.

GUIDED TOURS

These are available, by prior arrangement and at no extra cost, for groups of up to 60 people (split into groups of 20). Room Stewards are normally on duty. The Park Manager will meet groups visiting the House. Tours in other languages may be arranged. Average time taken to see the House 1 1/2 hours.

It is sometimes possible to provide tours of the Formal Gardens on Weekdays. Please enquire for charges.

GIFT SHOP

The Cremyll Lodge Gift Shop is open 10am-5.30pm from 1st April to the end of October, and sells many locally-made souvenirs and gifts. There is also a Gift Shop in the House: House opening times apply.

GUIDE BOOKS

New colour guide book, £2.95. Souvenir booklet £1.00, text available in Japanese, French, Spanish, German, Dutch, Polish and Russian.

SCHOOL VISITS/CHILDREN

School visits welcome. A guide and schoolroom can be provided. Areas of interest: tree trail, seashore, Parkland and Armada Diorama.

OPENING TIMES

All Year
Park and Formal Gardens open daily . Free

Summer
1 April - 31 October

House and Earl's Garden
Mon   Bank Hols only
       11.00am-5.30pm
Tues   Closed
Wed ⎫
Thur ⎪
Fri ⎬ 11.00am-5.30pm
Sat ⎪
Sun ⎭

Winter
House open only by appointment.

ADMISSION

HOUSE AND EARL'S GARDEN

Adult	£3.00
Child*	£1.50
OAP	£2.15
Student	£2.15
Concessions**	£2.15

* Aged 5-16

**NACF members, Friends of Plymouth City Museums and Art Gallery, Unemployed, Disabled.

GROUPS
Any booking made in advance with a value of £30.00 or more attracts a 20% discount, which can be passed to the booking agent to be used at his discretion.

Winter

Full normal admission is charged to groups visiting outside normal hours by special arrangement.

PRIDEAUX PLACE
Padstow, Cornwall

Tucked into the shelter of the busy little port of Padstow lies Prideaux Place, for four hundred years the home of the Prideaux family. Surrounded by gardens and wooded grounds, Prideaux Place overlooks an ancient deerpark and the Camel estuary to the moors beyond.

Completed in 1592 for Sir Nicholas Prideaux, and embellished and extended by successive generations, the house still retains its Elizabethan 'E' shape front, family treasurers and a homely atmosphere. The house, grounds and impressive outbuildings have been the subject of extensive

repair and restoration in recent years, not only has a magnificent 16th century plaster ceiling in the Great Chamber been uncovered for the first time since 1760 but considerable work has also transformed the overgrown gardens to reveal their Georgian and Victorian origins.

During the year, and especially during the summer, Prideaux Place is the setting for a host of events, from grand opera, concerts and candlelit suppers, to art exhibitions and 'day schools' on subjects ranging from genealogy to garden design.

CONTACT

Janet Hughes
Administrator
Prideaux Place
Padstow
Cornwall
PL28 8RP

Tel: (0841) 532945/
532411

LOCATION

250 miles (approx 5 hrs) from London via M4/M5 or M3, A303 to Exeter then Okehampton, Bodmin, Padstow.

5 miles from A39 on A389 Newquay/Wadebridge link road. Clearly signposted by brown Historic House signs.

Rail: Bodmin Parkway Station 18 miles

Bus: Limited local service.

SUITABILITY FOR OTHER EVENTS

Ideal venue for concerts, art exhibitions, car enthusiasts' meetings fashion shows, lectures, filming. Wedding receptions, balls etc may be held in a marquee on the lawn. Conferences.

EXTRA FACILITIES

Two Grand Pianos, croquet lawn, owners often able to meet pre-booked groups.

ADVICE TO COURIERS & DRIVERS

Groups may book morning, afternoon or early evening tours. No photography inside house. Dogs welcome in grounds on leads.

FACILITIES FOR THE DISABLED

Ramps to toilets but cubicles standard size.

PARKING FOR COACHES & CARS

Parking for cars and Minibuses 50 yards from House. (Coach passengers may alight at Main Gates, a short walk of 100 yards).

CATERING

Tearoom seating 30 (waitress service) serving coffee, teas, cakes etc. Candlelight suppers in the Dining Room for private parties. Light lunches for pre-booked parties.

GUIDED TOURS

Guided tours inclusive in admission charge, approx 45-60 minutes duration.

GUIDE BOOKS

Guide book with colour photographs £1.50. Plan and brief history of Grounds and Deer Park.

GIFT SHOP

Reasonably priced souvenirs of the House.

SCHOOL VISITS/CHILDREN

Groups are welcome. Specially trained guides, also literature to help teachers' and pupils' interpretation. Questionnaire for interior of House; fun "Golden Hind Treasure Trail" Quiz Book for better enjoyment of Grounds and Deer Park.

OPENING TIMES

Summer
Easter to end September

Sun	
Mon	
Tues	1.30-5pm
Weds	
Thurs	
Fri	Closed
Sat	

Easter, Late Spring and August Bank Holidays. 11am-5pm

Winter
1st October - Easter

Open by arrangement for groups of 10+.

ADMISSION

All Year

HOUSE & GARDEN
Adult	£3.50
Child	£1.00
OAP	£3.50
Grounds only	£1.50
Groups:	
Adult	£3.25
Child	By arrangement
OAP	£3.25

TREWITHEN
Probus, Cornwall

TREWITHEN means 'house of the trees', and the name truly describes this fine early Georgian House in its splendid setting of wood and parkland. Country Life described the house as "one of the outstanding West Country houses of the 18th Century."

The origins of the house go back to the 17th Century, but it was the architect Sir Robert Taylor, as well as Thomas Edwards of Greenwich who was responsible for the fine building we see today. The rebuilding was commissioned by Philip Hawkins, who bought the house in 1715, and was completed only some 40 years later. The house has been lived in by the same family for over 250 years.

Behind Trewithen's facade of quiet elegance hides a fascinating history. The Hawkins family were eminent landowners, they encouraged tin, copper and china clay mining in Cornwall and they built a railway and a harbour (Pentewan). The most notable member was Christopher Hawkins, created a baronet in 1799, who was MP for Grampound and, later, Father of the House of Commons. All Hawkins were great collectors and much of their contribution to both county and national life is reflected inside the house.

GARDENS

The gardens at Trewithen, (some 12 hectares) are outstanding and of international fame. Created since the beginning of the century by George Johnstone - a direct Hawkins descendant - they contain a wide and rare collection of flowering shrubs. Many of the plants here are unique to Trewithen: they were sent in seed form during the 1920s from Tibet, China and Nepal, and now flower spectacularly in the mild Cornish climate. Some of the Magnolias and Rhododendron species in the garden are known throughout the world. Plants and Shrubs are available for sale. The gardens, impressive throughout the year, are particularly attractive between March and the end of June, and again in the Autumn. They are one of the two attractions in this county to be awarded three stars by Michelin.

CONTACT

Mrs I Norman
Trewithen
Grampound Road
Nr Truro
Cornwall
TR2 4DD

Tel: (0726) 882763/
882418

LOCATION

From London (4-5 hrs)
M4, M5, A30, A390.
Via A390, St Austell 20
mins; Truro 20 mins;
Newquay-St Mawgan 20
mins.

Taxi: (0726) 73153.

ADVICE TO COURIERS & DRIVERS

Please book in advance to visit the House. No dogs or photography in The House. Dogs on leads in the Garden.

FACILITIES FOR THE DISABLED

There are toilet facilities for the disabled.

PARKING FOR COACHES & CARS

There is parking for up to 150 cars and 7 coaches 50 yards from the House.

CATERING

Tea shop at Trewithen for light refreshments.

GUIDED TOURS

These are available for groups of up to 10 people for the House only. There is no additional cost for this. Average time taken to see the House 1/2 hour. There is a new video room: a 25 minute video showing the history of the House and Garden is shown free of charge.

GARDEN SHOP

The Garden Shop is open for the same hours as the Gardens themselves. The shop sells guide books, postcards and a substantial range of plants and shrubs, many of which are rare, highly prized or famous Trewithen hybrids. There is a picnic area and exciting childrens' play corner.

GUIDE BOOKS

Colour guide books, 80p.

OPENING TIMES

Summer

GARDENS
1 March-30 September
Mon - }
Sat   } 10am-4.30pm
Sun   Closed

HOUSE
April-July and Aug Bank
Holiday Monday
Mon &
Tues   2 - 4.00pm
NB Please book

Winter
30 Sept - 1 March
Closed

All Year
NURSERY
Mon - }
Sat   } 9am - 4.30pm

ADMISSION

Summer

HOUSE ONLY
Adult   £2.80
Child   £2.80
OAP   £2.80
Student   £2.80

GARDENS
March-June
 Adult   £2.20
 Child*   £1.20
July-September
 Adult   £2.20
 Child*   £1.20

* Aged 5-15; under 5s free

Antony Woodland Garden, Torpoint.
5 miles west of Plymouth via Torpoint car ferry. 2 miles north west of Torpoint off A374

ANTONY

OPEN
30 March-31 October

Tues, Wed, Thurs & Bank Hol. Mondays plus Sundays in June, July & August.
1.30pm-5.30pm.

Last adm. 4.45pm.

ANTONY, TORPOINT TEL: 0752 812191
(The National Trust)

Antony - a superb example of an early eighteenth century mansion. The main block is faced in silver grey stone, with red brick wings. Set in parkland and fine gardens overlooking the Lynher River, home of the great Cornish family of Carew. Antony contains a wealth of paintings, tapestries, furniture and embroideries, many linking the great families of Cornwall. An unusual Bath House in the grounds can be viewed by arrangement.

Location: 5 miles west of Plymouth via Torpoint Car Ferry, 2 miles north west of Torpoint.
Admission: £3.40. Pre-arranged parties £2.60

Chysauster Ancient Village
(0736) 61889 2¹/₂ miles north west of Gulval, near Penzance.

COTEHELE

OPEN
30 March-31 Oct.
House:
12 - 5.30pm
Restaurant & Mill
11am - 5.30pm
daily except Fri.
(Open Good Fri)

Gardens, Shop, Tea Room daily 11.00am-5.30pm

Closes 5pm in October.

COTEHELE, CALSTOCK TEL: 05779 50434
(The National Trust)

Cotehele - Enchantingly remote, perched high above the wood banks of the Tamar, Cotehele was home to the Edgcumbe family for nearly six centuries. The manor house, so gracefully evolved from its early origins, gives the impression of having been woven through time. It retains a remarkably medieval atmosphere and contains a fascination of contemporary furnishings and objets d'art.,

Location: On west bank of Tamar, 1 mile west of Calstock by footpath (6 miles by road), 8 miles south west of Tavistock, 14 miles from Plymouth via Saltash Bridge.
Admission: House, Gardens, Grounds £5, Garden & Mill £2.50, Pre-arranged parties £4.

Godolphin House, Helston.
(07360 762409   5 miles north west of Helston between Townshend and Godolphin Cross.

Glendurgan Garden, Mawnan Smith.
(0326) 250906   4 miles south west of Falmouth.

LANHYDROCK

OPEN
30 March-31 October
Daily except Mondays, when the House only is closed (open Bank Hol. Mons)

11.00am-5.30pm

Closes 5pm in October.

LANHYDROCK, BODMIN TEL: 0208 73320
(The National Trust)

Lanhydrock - The grandest and most welcoming house in Cornwall. Lanhydrock is superbly set in 450 acres of woods and parkland and encircled by a garden of rare shrubs and trees, lovely in all seasons. Although dating from the seventeenth century, Lanhydrock was largely rebuilt after a fire in 1881 and now exemplifies the great Victorian country house.

Location: 2 ¹/₂ miles south east of Bodmin, follow signposts from either A38 or B3268.
Admission: House, Garden & Grounds £5.00. Garden & grounds £2.50. Pre-arranged parties £4.00.

Launceston Castle, Launceston.
(0566) 772365 In Launceston.

PENCARROW

OPEN
Easter-15 Oct.
1.30-5.00pm
Sun-Thurs.

1 June-10 Sept & Bank Holiday Mondays opens 11am.

PENCARROW, BODMIN TEL: 020884 368
(Molesworth-St.Aubyn family)

Still owned and lived in by the family. Georgian house and grade II listed gardens. Superb collection of pictures, furniture and porcelain. Marked walks through 50 acres of beautiful formal and woodland gardens, Victorian rockery, Italian gardens, lake and ice house. Craft centre, tearooms, children's play area and plant shop. Facilities for the disabled, Dogs welcome in the grounds.

Location: 4 miles north wests of Bodmin off A389 and B3266 at Washaway.
Admission: Adults £3.50. Children £1.50.

Pendennis Castle, Falmouth.
(0326) 316594 Pendennis Head, 1 mile south east of Falmouth.

Restormel Castle, Lostwithiel.
(0208) 872687 1¹/₂ miles north of Lostwithiel.

St Mawes Castle, St Mawes.
(0326) 270526 In St Mawes.

ST MICHAELS MOUNT

OPEN
30 March - 31 October
Mon - Fri 10.30am-5.30pm Last Adm. 4.45pm
1 November - 29 March
Guided tours as tide, weather and circumstances permit.

**ST MICHAEL'S MOUNT,
MARAZION TEL: 0736 710507**
(The National Trust)

St. Michael's Mount - This magical island is the jewel in Cornwall's crown, a national treasure which is a must for every visitor to the far West. The great granite crag which rises from the waters of Mount's Bay is surmounted by an embattled 14th century castle. home of the St. Aubyn family for over 300 years. The Mount's flanks are softened by lush sub tropical vegetation and on the water's edge there is a harbourside community, an ancient trading place for tin and other Cornish goods which today features shops and restaurants.

Location: At Marazion there is access on foot over Causeway at low tide. In summer months there is a ferry at high tide.
Admission: £3.20 Family Ticket £8. Pre-arranged parties £2.80.

⚘ **Tintagel Castle,** Tintagel.
(0840) 770328 ½ mile north west of Tintagel.

TINTAGEL OLD POST OFFICE

OPEN
30 March-31 October
Daily
11.00am-5.30pm

Closes 5.00pm in October.

TINTAGEL OLD POST OFFICE, TINTAGEL TEL: 0840 770024
(The National Trust)

Tintagel Old Post Office - One of the most characterful buildings in Cornwall, and a house of great antiquity, this small 14th century manor is full of charm and interest. Tumble roofed and weathered by the centuries, it is restored in the fashion of the Post Office it was for nearly 50 years.

Location: In centre of Tintagel.
Admission: £1.90

Tregrehan, St Austell.
(0726) 814389/812438 2 miles east of St Austell on A390.

🌿 **Trelissick Garden,** near Truro.
(0872) 862090 5 miiles south of Truro on both sides of B3289 overlooking King Harry Ferry.

🏛 **Trelowarren House and Chapel,** Mawgan-in-Meneage, Helston.
(032622) 366 6 miles south of Helston off B3293.

🌿 **Trengwainton Garden,** Penzance.
(0736) 63021 2 miles north west of Penzance ½ mile west of Heamoor on B3312.

TREBAH

OPEN
Every day of the year.

10.30am-5.00pm
(Last admission).

TREBAH, MAWNAN SMITH TEL: 0326 250448
(Major & Mrs J A Hibbert)

Trebah Gardens merit so many superlatives that, outside the 65,000 visitors each year, no-one who has not seem them would believe a word..

Do we exaggerate? Why not go and see for yoursellf, or write for a leaflet.

Locationa: 1 mile west of Mawnan Smith. 4 miles south west of Falmouth..
Admission: Adults £2.50, Under 16's and disabled £1.00 Party rates.

TRERICE

OPEN
30 March-31 October
Daily except Thursdays
11.00am-5.30pm

Closes 5.00pm in October

TRERICE, NEWQUAY, TEL: 0637 875404
(The National Trust)

Trerice is an architectural gem and something of a rarity - a small Elizabethan manor house hidden away in a web of narrow lanes and still somehow caught in the spirit of its age. An old Arundell house, it escaped the common fate of material alteration over the centuries and has what is possibly the earliest Dutch-style gabled façade in the country to survive.

Location: 3 miles south east of Newquay via A392 and A3058 (turn right at Kestle Mill).
Admission: £3.60. Pre-arranged parties £3.00.

TRESCO ABBEY GARDENS

OPEN
All Year Round

10.00am-4.00pm

TRESCO ABBEY GARDENS, ISLES OF SCILLY TEL: 0720 22849
(Mr R A and Mrs L A Dorrien-Smith)

Tresco Abbey built by Augustus Smith has been the family home since 1834. The garden here flourishes on the small island. Nowhere else in the British Isles does such an exotic collection of plants grow in the open. Agaves, Aloes, Proteas and Acacia's from such places as Australia, South Africa, Mexico and the Mediterranean grow within the secure embrace of massive Holm Oak hedges. Valhall Ships Figurehead Museum.

Location: Isles of Scilly. Isles of Scilly Steamship 0736 62009. B.I.H. Helicopters 0736 63871 Details of day trips on application.
Admission: Adults £3.50. Children £1. Weekly ticket £6. Guided tours for groups available.

BRANTWOOD
Coniston, Cumbria

BRANTWOOD is the most beautifully situated house in the Lake District. It enjoys the finest lake and mountain views in England, and no other house in the district has such diverse literary and artistic associations.

The home of John Ruskin from 1872 until 1900, Brantwood became an intellectual powerhouse and one of the foremost cultural centres in Europe. Tolstoy, Mahatma Gandhi, Proust and William Morris can all be counted amongst Ruskin's disciples.

Ruskin was one of the greatest figures of the Victorian age. Poet, artist and critic, he was also a social revolutionary who challenged the moral foundations of 19th Century Britain. Ruskin's ideas came to shape much of our thinking today, and his words are as relevant now as ever they were in his own lifetime.

Brantwood today contains a glorious collection of Ruskin drawings and watercolours, and the house still retains that special feeling which has given inspiration to so many.

GARDENS

In the oakwoods and beside the lake-shore Ruskin created a garden which is under active and imaginative restoration. It is a special place, a true lakeland paradise. The woods in springtime are carpeted with bluebells and the heavy scent of the yellow "azalea luteum" fills the air.

CONTACT

J B C Hanson Esq
Brantwood
Coniston
Cumbria
LA21 8AD

Tel: (05394) 41396

LOCATION

Road: M6 Junct. 36, 25 miles, London 5 hours, Edinburgh 3 hours, Chester 2¹/₂ hours.

Rail: Windermere Station 14 miles.

Water: Steam Yacht "Gondola" sails regularly to Brantwood from Coniston Pier. New Ferry Service M.V. "Ruskin" sails hourly. (30 mins past the hour).

Taxi: Coniston Taxis (05394) 41683

SUITABILITY FOR OTHER EVENTS

The house is spectacularly situated, with magnificent lake and mountain views and lends itself particularly to photographic or film use, but is suitable for a variety of events. Ruskin's wonderful Dining Room has potential for groups of up to 12.

EXTRA FACILITIES

³/₄ mile Lakeshore with large pier. 250 acre estate, woodland and moorland. Grand Piano.

ADVICE TO COURIERS & DRIVERS

Coaches have access to Brantwood but the last 1¹/₂ miles are a little slow. Parties can come by water from Coniston Pier a delightful approach with good access for coaches. New Ferry service from Coniston. Dogs not allowed in the House.

FACILITIES FOR THE DISABLED

Disabled visitors may alight at the entrance to the property. There are special toilet facilities available.

PARKING FOR COACHES & CARS

75 cars and 2 coaches within 100 yards of the property.

GIFT SHOP

Bookshop and high quality craft gallery.

SCHOOL VISITS/CHILDREN

School visits are welcomed but special facilities are not yet available. Nature and Woodland Walks are of special interest.

GUIDE BOOKS

Colour guide book, £2.50.

CATERING

'Jumping Jenny' Tearooms & Restaurant seating 60. Groups can book in advance but the total capacity cannot be booked during normal opening hours. Menus available on request and prices are very flexible according to requirements, special rates available for groups. Catering facilities available for special functions, conferences etc.

GUIDED TOURS

Visitors are usually free to tour the property at leisure but guided tours can be arranged. The Administrator will meet groups visiting the House. Lectures on the property can be arranged.

OPENING TIMES

Summer
Mid March-Mid Nov.

Mon	
Tues	
Wed	
Thur	11am-5.30pm
Fri	
Sat	
Sun	

Winter
Mid Nov.-Mid March

Wed	
Thur	
Fri	11am-4pm
Sat	
Sun	

ADMISSION

All Year

Adults	£3.00
Child*	FREE

*Under 18

GROUP	
Adults	£2.40

CONFERENCE AND FUNCTION FACILITIES

Rooms are available but only during the evening in Summer or all day Monday or Tuesday in Winter. The Administrator will participate in Functions and meet groups if required. Full details available upon request.

DALEMAIN
Near Penrith, Cumbria

DALEMAIN is a fine mixture of Medieval, Tudor and Early Georgian architecture. The imposing Georgian facade strikes the visitor immediately but in the cobbled courtyard the atmosphere of the North Country Tudor Manor is secure. The present owners family have lived at Dalemain since 1679 and have collected china, furniture and family portraits. Visitors can see the grand Drawing Rooms with 18th Century Chinese Wallpaper and fine oak panelling also the Nursery and Housekeeper's Room. The Norman Pele Tower contains the regimental collection of the Westmoreland and Cumberland Yeomanry. The House is full of the paraphernalia of a well established family House which is still very much lived in by the family.

The 16th Century Great Barn holds a collection of agricultural bygones and a Fell Pony Museum.

GARDENS

The Garden has a long history stretching back to the medieval Herb Garden. Today a Knot Garden remains with a fine early Roman fountain and box hedges enclose herb beds.

The imposing terrace wall supports a full and colourful herbaceous border during the summer months. The late Mrs McCosh revitalised the gardens replanting many of the borders introducing rare and exotic plants. Visitors can enjoy the fine views of the park and the woodland and riverside walks.

The gardens have been featured on television's 'Gardeners World' and also in 'Country Life'.

SUITABILITY FOR OTHER EVENTS

Fashion shows, archery, clay pigeon shooting, garden parties, rallies, filming, caravan rallies, antique fairs and childrens' camps. Business Meetings and Conferences with limited numbers during closed season.

EXTRA FACILITIES

Grand piano, parkland and Lake District National Park are available for use. Lectures on the House, contents, gardens and history can be arranged for up to 60 people. Cost for hire of room and lecture on request. Deer Park

ADVICE TO COURIERS & DRIVERS

Parties of 20 or more must pre-book. Allow 2 hours to see Dalemain. No dogs. Parking for 100 cars and 30 coaches, 50 yards from the House. No photography in the House.

FACILITIES FOR THE DISABLED

Disabled or elderly visitors may alight at the entrance prior to parking in the allocated areas. There are toilet facilities for the disabled. Free admission for disabled visitors in wheelchairs

GUIDED TOURS

German and French translations in every room. Tours take 1 hour approx. Garden Tour for parties extra.

CATERING

Licensed Restaurant/Tea Room seats 60. Prices and menus on request. Groups should book in advance for lunches and high teas. Catering available for special functions/conferences.

GIFT SHOP

Items include local crafts, House souvenirs, postcards stamps etc. Surplus plants on sale in the courtyard.

GUIDE BOOK

Colour guide £2.00.

SCHOOL VISITS/CHILDREN

School groups are welcome and guides can be provided. Military, Country Life, Agricultural and Fell Pony Museums. Adventure playground.

CONTACT

R Hasell-McCosh
Dalemain Estate Office
Dalemain
Penrith
Cumbria
CA11 0HB

Tel: (07684) 86450 or
(0899) 20208

Fax: (07684) 86223

LOCATION

From London, M1, M6 exit 40: 4 hours.
From Edinburgh, A73, A74, M6 exit 40: 2¹/₂ hrs

Rail: Penrith 3 miles.

Taxi: Walkers Taxis, Penrith 62349.

OPENING TIMES

Summer
27 March - 2 October

Mon	
Tues	11.15am-5pm
Wed	
Thurs	
Fri	
Sat	Closed
Sun	11.15am-5pm

NB Parties of 20 or more should pre-book.

Winter
Mid-October - Easter

Open by special arrangement.

ADMISSION

HOUSE & GARDEN

Adult	£4.00
Child*	£3.00
Family	£11.00
Disabled**	FREE
Groups***	
Adult	£3.80
Child*	£2.80

GARDEN ONLY

Adult	£3.00
Child*	FREE
Disabled**	FREE

* Under 16 years.
**Disabled in wheelchair.
*** Min. 12 Adults

CONFERENCE AND FUNCTION FACILITIES

ROOM	DIMENSIONS	CAPACITY	LAYOUT	POWER POINTS	SUITABLE FOR A/V
Dining Room		40	Theatre	3	✓
		15	Boardroom	3	✓
Old Hall		50	Buffet	4	✓
		50	Lunch/Dinner	4	✓

HOLKER HALL
Grange-over-Sands, Cumbria

HOLKER HALL, home of Lord and Lady Cavendish, shows the confidence, spaciousness and prosperity of Victorian style on its grandest scale. The New Wing, built by the 7th Duke of Devonshire (1871-4), replaced a previous wing totally destroyed by fire. Workmanship throughout is of the highest quality, particularly the detailed interior carving and linenfold panelling.

Despite this grand scale, Holker is very much a family home. Visitors can wander freely throughout the New Wing. Photographs, beautiful floral displays and bowls of scented pot pourri create the warm and friendly atmosphere so often remarked upon by visitors. Varying in period and style, Louis XV pieces happily mix with the Victorian. Pictures range from an early copy of the famous triple portrait of Charles I by Van Dyck to a modern painting by Douglas Anderson.

GARDENS

Christies/HHA Garden of the Year (1991), includes formal and woodland areas covering 24 acres. Designated "amongst the best in the world in terms of design and content" by the Good Gardens Guide. This wonderful Italianate-cum-English Garden includes a limestone cascade, a fountain, a rose garden and many rare and beautiful plants and shrubs.

CONTACT

Mrs Carolyn Johnson
Holker Hall & Gardens
Cark-in-Cartmel
Grange-over-Sands
Cumbria
LA11 7PH

Tel: (05395) 58328
Fax: (05395) 58776

LOCATION

From Kendal, A6, A590, B5277, B5278: 16 mls.

Bus: From Grange-over-Sands.

Rail: To Cark-in-Cartmel.

Motorway: M6 Junct 36.

Taxi: Parkers Motors, Grange-over-Sands. Nelsons Garage, Cark-in-Cartmel.

SUITABILITY FOR OTHER EVENTS

Filming and still photography. Promotion venues include: limestone escarpments and quarries.

EXTRA FACILITIES

Deer Park and Discovery Walks. Lakeland Motor Museum, adventure playground and exhibitions.

ADVICE TO COURIERS & DRIVERS

No dogs in Gardens or Hall. No video cameras in Hall.

FACILITIES FOR THE DISABLED

Disabled and elderly visitors may be dropped at the entrance. There are unisex toilet facilities for the disabled. Ramps where necessary.

PARKING FOR COACHES & CARS

Capacity of the car park, 50+ cars and 12 coaches, 100-150 yards from Hall. Plus grass car parking.

CATERING

The Clocktower Cafeteria (capacity 120), is a self-service café, selling salads, hot and cold sandwiches, home made cakes and beverages (including wine by the glass and canned beer and lager).

GUIDED TOURS

Tours of Hall available at additional cost of 25p per person: must be pre-booked.

GIFT SHOP

Open 10.30am-5.30pm, same days as the Hall, wide range of gifts from toys to fine china.

GUIDE BOOKS

Colour guide book, £2.00. Translations available in French, Spanish and German. Childrens Guide 75p. Guide to the Woodland Gardens by Lord Cavendish.

SCHOOL VISITS/CHILDREN

Environmental study day for primary school children, cost per child from £2.00. Holker is the holder of two Sandford Awards for Heritage Education. Holker provides a wide range of educational opportunities for primary aged children to fit in with curriculum requirements i.e: Houses & Home; Technology & Design; Structures; Victorians.

OPENING TIMES

Summer
1 April - 31 October

Mon	
Tues	
Wed	10.30am-6pm
Thur	
Fri	
Sat	Closed
Sun	10.30am-6pm

NB Last admission 4.30pm

Winter
1 November - 31 March

Closed

ADMISSION

Summer

93 prices

HOUSE & GARDEN
Adult	£4.50
Child	£2.70

GROUP
Adult	£3.10
OAP	£2.75
Child	£2.35

Winter

Closed

MUNCASTER CASTLE
Ravenglass, Cumbria

MUNCASTER CASTLE has been owned by the Pennington family since 1208. It has grown from the original pele tower built on Roman foundations to the impressive structure visible today. Outstanding features are the Great Hall and Salvin's octagonal library and the Drawing Room with its barrel ceiling.

The Castle contains many treasures including beautiful furniture, exquisite needlework panels, tapestries and oriental rugs. The family silver is mostly by Paul Storr and is accompanied in the Dining Room by the Ongley Service, the most ornamental set of porcelain ever created by the Derby factory, Florentine 16th Century bronzes and an alabaster lady by Giambologna can be

seen. The Castle has 3 ghosts. All the rooms open to the public are lived in by the family who are actively involved in entertaining their many visitors.

The woodland gardens cover 77 acres and command spectacular views of the Lakeland Fells, with many delightful walks. From mid March to June the rhododendrons, azaleas, camellias and magnolias are at their best.

The Owl Centre boasts a fine collection of owls from all over the world. 'Meet the Birds' occurs daily at 2.30pm (20th March to 30th October), when a talk is given on the work of the centre. Weather permitting the birds fly.

CONTACT

Peter Frost-Pennington
Muncaster Castle
Ravenglass
Cumbria
CA18 1RQ

Tel: (0229) 717614
Fax: (0229) 717010

LOCATION

From London 6 hrs,
Chester 2 1/2 hrs
Edinburgh 3 1/2 hrs
M6 exit 36, A590,A595
(from south).
M6 exit 40, A66, A595
(from east).
Carlisle, A595 (from
north).

Rail: Ravenglass (on
Barrow-in-Furness-
Carlisle Line) 1 1/2 mls.

SUITABILITY FOR OTHER EVENTS

Muncaster provides a backdrop for fashion shoots, garden parties, filming, clay pigeon shooting and wedding receptions.

EXTRA FACILITIES

Lectures can be arranged on the property, its contents, gardens and history. By prior arrangement a grand piano can be hired.

ADVICE TO COURIERS & DRIVERS

For groups, please apply for information pack and book in advance to qualify for discounts. No photography or filming inside castle. Free parking for 200 cars and 5 coaches, 800 yds from the House.

FACILITIES FOR THE DISABLED

Toilets, wheelchair for loan. Special tapes available for walkman tour for the partially sighted or those with learning difficulties. Disabled and elderly visitors may alight near to Castle.

OWL CENTRE

Home of the British Owl Breeding and Release Scheme (BOBARS) run by TV naturalist Tony Warburton.

GIFT SHOPS & PLANT CENTRE

Open daily 20th March to30th October 11am to 5pm selling a wide variety of gifts and plants. Colour guide book available.

GUIDED TOURS

All castle visitors are offered a Sony Walkman individual tour narrated by the family that lasts 40 mins included in the entry price. Private tours with a personal guide (option family member) can be organised for a small additional fee.

CATERING

The Stable Buttery caters for up to 80 with a full menu. Groups may book meals in advance (0229) 717432. Catering in the Castle can also be arranged (0229) 717614.

SCHOOL VISITS/CHILDREN

School visits are welcome and guides are provided if required. Cost per child £2.00. Historical subjects from the Romans to W.W.II. Special work sheets available.

CONFERENCE AND FUNCTION FACILITIES

ROOM	DIMENSIONS	CAPACITY	LAYOUT	POWER POINTS	SUITABLE FOR A/V
Drawing Room		120	Theatre	6	✓
		100	Lunch/Dinner		
Dining Room		30/70	Various	2+	✓
Family Dining Room		20	Boardroom/Dinner	4	
		40	Theatre		
Great Hall		110	Various	6	✓

CUMBRIA

Abbot Hall Art Gallery and Museum of Lakeland Life & Industry, Kirkland, Kendall.
(0539) 722464 Off Kirkland, near Kendal Parish Church. Exit 36, M6.

Acorn Bank Garden, Temple Sowerby, Penrith.
(07683) 61893 Just north of Temple Sowerby, 6 miles east of Penrith on A66.

Brough Castle.
091 261 1585 (Area Office) 8 miles south east of Appleby.

Brougham Castle, Penrith
(0768) 62488 1½ miles east of Penrith.

Carlisle Castle, Carlisle.
(0228) 591922 North of town centre.

Castletown House, Rockcliffe, Carlisle.
(0228 74) 205 5 miles north west of Carlisle on Solway coast.

Conishead Priory, Ulverston.
(0229) 584029 2 miles from Ulverston.

Furness Abbey
(0229) 23420 1½ miles north of Barrow- in- Furness.

HUTTON-IN-THE-FOREST

OPEN
House 1-4pm
Easter Sun.,
4--8 April incl.
May1 to Oct.2
Thurs., Fri., Sun.
Wednesdays in
August plus
Bank Hol. Mons.
Gardens &
Grounds
11am-5pm
Every day except
Sats. and
Christmas Day.

HUTTON-IN-THE-FOREST, PENRITH TEL: 07684 84449
(The Lord Inglewood)

The home of Lord Inglewood's family since the beginning of the 17th century. Built around a medieval pele tower with 17th, 18th and 19th century additions. Fine English furniture and pictures, ceramics and tapestries. Outstanding gardens and grounds with terraces, walled garden, dovecote, lake and woodland walk through magnificent specimen trees.

Location: 7 miles north west of Penrith and 2 ½ miles from exit 41 M6 on B5305
Admission: House, Gardens, Grounds Adults £3.00.,childlren £1.50 . Gardens and Grounds adults £1,50, children free.

Lanercost Priory
(06977) 3030 2 miles north east of Brampton.

LEVENS HALL

OPEN
3 April-30 Sept.
Sunday-
Thursday
11am-5pm
Last Admission
4.30pm

Steam Collection
2pm-5pm.

LEVENS HALL, KENDAL TEL: 05395 60321
(C H Bagot Esq)

This Elizabethan mansion contains a fine collection of Jacobean furniture, panelled interiors, plasterwork, Cordova leather wall coverings and the earliest English patchwork. The world famous topiary garden was laid out in 1694 by Monsieur Beaumont. To mark the three hundredth anniversary, a new garden feature has been specially created. In addition there is a working collection of model steam engines.

Location: 5 miles south of Kendal on the A6 (M6 exit 36).
Admission:

MIREHOUSE

OPEN
30 March-30 Oct.
Grounds,
Playgrounds &
Tearoom
Daily: 10.30am-
5.30pm
House: Suns.,
Weds., (also Fri.
in August)
2.00-4.30
Groups welcome
at other times by
appointment.

MIREHOUSE, KESWICK TEL: 07687 72287
(John Spedding Esq)

17th century central Lakeland manor house, not sold since 1688. Many literary connections: Tennyson, Wordsworth, Southey, Carlyle, Bacon. Live music in house on regular opening days. Children welcomed. Adventure playgrounds. Home made food in teaaroom. Lakeside walk. Access to ancient Lakeside Church of St. Bega.

Location: 3½ miles north of Keswick on A591 (Carlisle) road. Regular bus service.
Admission: (1994 rates) Grounds: Adults £1, child 80p. House and Grounds, Adult £3.00. child £1.50.

Naworth Castle, Brampton.
(06977) 3666 12 miles east of Carlisle near Brampton off A69.

RYDAL MOUNT

OPEN
Open Daily
Summer:
House & Garden
9.30am-5.00pm

Winter:
House & Garden
Closed Tuesdays
10.00am-4.00pm

RYDAL MOUNT, AMBLESIDE TEL: 05394 33002
(Peter & Marian Elkington)

Once the home of the poet William Wordsworth 1813-1850 now the family home of his direct descendants. It contains portraits, furniture, memorabilia, first editions and displays about the poet, his life and works. The garden is still kept as the poet landscaped it and is one of the most beautiful and interesting small gardens in the country.

Location: Situated 300 yards off main A59 1½ miles north of Ambleside and 2½ milse south of Grasmere.
Admission: House & Garden: Adult £2, Child 80p. Group (min. 10) adult £1.70, child 80p.

Sizergh Castle and Gardens, Kendal
(05395) 60070 3½ miles south of Kendal, 2 miles from Levens Hall.

Stott Park Bobbin Mill, Finsthwaite.
(05395) 31087 2 miles north of A590 Kendall/Barrow-in-Furness road at Newby Bridge.

Townend, Troutbeck
(05394) 32628 Troutbeck village, 3 miles south east of Ambleside.

Wordsworth House, Cockermouth.
(0900) 824805 In Main Street, Cockermouth.

CATTON HALL
Catton, Swadlincote, Derbyshire

CATTON, first mentioned in the Domesday Book in 1085 and purchased by ancestors of the Neilson family in 1405, stands on the banks of the River Trent, surrounded by 100 acres of its own traditional and private parkland.

This classic Georgian house, which is not open to the public, has remained unspoilt since it was built in 1745 and still contains most of its original collection of antique furniture and fine 17th and 18th century paintings. It is lived in by the Neilson family as their private home and has a wonderful relaxed and friendly atmosphere which makes all visitors feel welcome whether they are guests for a formal dinner or enjoying activities in the park from a marquee.

Catton is perfectly situated in the centre of England and within 100 miles of half the population of the country, and with easy access to all the main motorways. London, Bristol, Liverpool and York are all about 2 hours by car. Birmingham or East Midlands airports, The Belfry Golfing Centre, National Exhibition Centre and the International Conference Centre are within half an hour by road.

CONTACT

Robin & Katie Neilson
Catton Hall
Catton
Swadlincote
Derbyshire
DE12 8LN

Tel: (0283) 716311
Fax: (0283) 712876

LOCATION

Catton lies 1/2 hour north of Birmingham, half way between Lichfield and Burton on Trent and 5 minutes to the East of the A38.

Railway: Lichfield 10 minutes.

Rail and Airport: Birmingham 1/2 hour.

OPENING TIMES

Open throughout the year for private functions, activities or events.

The House is not open to the General Public.

RATES

As each day is organised differently we suggest you telephone to discuss your individual requirements.

SUITABILITY FOR EVENTS

Outside there are 100 acres of flat, permanent grassland which are ideal for clay shooting, motorised activities, ballooning, falconry, archery, shows, fairs, fireworks and marquees to suit every possible occasion.

We are specialists at arranging tailor made events at Catton in a personal and professional way and inside we offer exclusive facilities to enjoy concerts, conferences, business meetings, lunches or dinners, whether formal or informal, or special evenings which might include murder, magic or music.

EXTRA FACILITIES

A small chapel which can accommodate up to 100 people for a wedding or concert.
Seven miles cross country ride with 36 optional jumps
Pheasant and partridge shooting
Fishing

ACCOMMODATION

Extremely comfortable en suite accommodation is available in three 4 poster rooms and five twin bedded rooms.

FACILITIES FOR THE DISABLED

There is access only to the grounds and ground floor of the house but no other special facilities are available.

PARKING FOR COACHES AND CARS

Unlimited parking for cars and coaches within 50 yards of the house.

CATERING

Excellent in-house catering is arranged for most functions although outside caterers are welcome.

GUIDED TOURS

Group tours can be arranged by appointment.

CONFERENCE AND FUNCTION FACILITIES

ROOM	DIMENSIONS	CAPACITY	LAYOUT	POWER POINTS	SUITABLE FOR A/V
Morning Room	20'x26'	40	Various	6	
Dining Room	28'x30'	80	Various	6	
Drawing Room	20'x26'	40	Various	6	

CHATSWORTH
Bakewell, Derbyshire

THE GREAT TREASURE HOUSE of Chatsworth is everything a palace should be but still maintains the sympathetic proportions of a family home. The first house was built by Bess of Hardwick in 1552 and it has been lived in by the Cavendish family, Dukes of Devonshire ever since. The House today owes its appearance to the 1st Duke who remodelled the building at the end of the 17th Century, while the 6th Duke added a North Wing by Sir Jeffry Wyatville 200 years later. Visitors see 24 rooms including the run of 5 virtually unaltered 17th Century State Rooms and Chapel. There are painted ceilings by Verrio, Thornhill and Laguerre, furniture by William Kent and Boulle, tapestries from Mortlake and Brussels, a library of over 17,000 volumes, sculpture by Cibber and Canova, old master paintings by Rembrandt, Hals, Van Dyck, Tintoretto, Giordano, Lely as well as Landseer and Sargent; the collection of classical sculpture, Oriental and European porcelain and the dazzling silver collection including an early English silver chandelier. The present Duke is a collector like his ancestors and the sculptures by Angela Conner and paintings by Lucien Freud bring the treasures up to date.

GARDEN

The garden was the creation of the 6th Duke and his gardener Sir Joseph Paxton, who later built the Crystal Palace. Together they devised a system of cascades, fountains and pools culminating in the 290ft jet of the Emperor Fountain. They planted rare trees and specimen shrubs and placed naturalistic rocks, buildings and statuary to enhance the design. More recent additions include the Maze and the now famous serpentine beech hedge. From bulbs in Spring to rich colours in Autumn Chatsworth's vast garden provides a worthy setting for the great House.

SPECIAL ATTRACTIONS

Maze in Garden; collection of paintings, drawings, sculpture, silver and porcelain; cascade; Capability Brown landscape; farmyard; adventure playground.

ADVICE TO COURIERS & DRIVERS

Allow a minimum of 2 hours to see Chatsworth. There is a coach drivers' rest room. Unlimited parking for cars, 100 yards from the House, and for coaches, 25 yards from the House.

FACILITIES FOR THE DISABLED

Unfortunately it is not possible for people in wheelchairs to tour the House due to the number of stairs, They are most welcome in the garden and two wheelchairs are available at the entrance. There are toilet facilities for the disabled. A leaflet specially designed for our disabled visitors is available.

CATERING

The Restaurant serving home-made food can cater for up to 300 for afternoon tea and other meals. Menus available on request.

GUIDED TOURS

Tours of house and/or greenhouses available at extra charge (£12 per person) by arrangement. Average time taken 1½ hrs.

GUIDE BOOKS

There are two colour guide books for sale: Chatsworth and Chatsworth Garden. French, German and Japanese translations available of The House Guide Book. Special guide for children.

GIFT SHOP

There are two shops open at the same time as the House. Items chosen for the shops by the Duchess of Devonshire.

AUDIO TOURS

A cassette with a tape recorded tour can be hired at the Entrance Hall. Group bookings must be made in advance.

SCHOOL VISITS/CHILDREN

Guided tours, packs, trails and schools room are now available for a school visit. Teachers are welcome to arrange a free preliminary visit and discuss their requirements with the Schools Liaison Officer, who can give talks in school. For further details telephone Simon Seligman on Baslow (0246) 582204.

CONTACT

Eric Oliver
Chatsworth
Bakewell
Derbyshire
DE45 1PP

Tel: (0246) 582204
Fax: (0246) 583536

LOCATION

From London 3 hours, M1 Junction 29, signposted via Chesterfield.

Rail: Chesterfield Station, 9 miles.

Bus: Chesterfield - Bakewell, 1½ miles.

OPENING TIMES

Summer
23 March - 31 October

Mon	
Tues	
Wed	
Thur	11am-4.30pm
Fri	
Sat	
Sun	

Winter
1 November - Easter

Closed

ADMISSION

Summer

HOUSE & GARDEN
Adult	£5.50
Child	£2.75
OAP/Student	£4.75
Family	£14.00

Pre-booked parties
Adult	£5.00
Schools	£2.50
OAP/Student	£4.25

GARDEN ONLY
Adult	£3.00
Child	£1.50
OAP	£2.50
Student	£2.50
Family	£8.00

SCOTS SUITE
Adult	£1.00
Child	£0.50

Car Park	£1.00

HADDON HALL
Bakewell, Derbyshire

THIS WONDERFULLY ROMANTIC house, the most complete surviving medieval manor house in the Country, is situated in the heart of the Peak District. Built over a period of 400 years, it's architecture progresses from Norman, through Medieval and Tudor, to Elizabethan, thereby displaying every aspect of domestic life from the past. Natural, rather than formal, Haddon is wrapped in an an atmosphere of homeliness and is a truly 'understandable' house.

Since the 12th century, Haddon has been the home of the Vernon and Manners families. It was the Vernons, owners from 1170 to 1567, who were largely responsible for the construction of the house as we see it today. The House changed ownership in 1567, through the marriage of Dorothy Vernon to John Manners, 2nd son of the 1st Earl of Rutland. In 1703, the Dukedom of Rutland was conferred upon the Manners family and Haddon was abandoned in favour of Belvoir Castle, the Ducal seat in Rutland for 200 years. Haddon was uninhabited, until the 9th Duke of Rutland returned early this century to make the house's restoration his life's work.

The terraced Rose Gardens, stepping down to the fast-flowing River Wye, are planned for year-round colour. Over 150 varieties of rose and clematis, many over 70 years old, provide colour and scent throughout the summer.

CONTACT

The Comptroller
Estate Office
Haddon Hall
Bakewell
Derbyshire
DE45 1LA

Tel: (0629) 812855
Fax: (0629) 814379

LOCATION

From London 3 hours,
Sheffield 1/2 hour,
Derby 3/4 hour.
Haddon is on the A6,
1 1/2 miles south of
Bakewell.

M1 Junct. 29/30, M6
Junct. 17/18/19, 1 hour.

SUITABILITY FOR OTHER EVENTS

Fashion shows archery, garden parties and filming. Haddon is able to provide the finest facilities for clay pigeon shooting in the North of England, with the shooting ground adjacent to the Hall which provides magnificent backdrops. A full clay pigeon shooting package, with tutoring by olympic coaches, is available, accompanied by excellent catering facilities. Please write for further details and dates.

CONFERENCE FACILITIES

This Medieval House is able to offer restricted facilities for conferences and functions in the Main Banqueting Hall and Long Gallery. Please contact the Estate Office with any enquiries, and we should be delighted to assist.

EXTRA FACILITIES

There is provision for helicopters if required. Lectures on the property, its contents, gardens and history can be arranged for up to 35 people. Projector and screen can be provided.

ADVICE TO COURIERS & DRIVERS

Owing to the age of the House, and its uneven, worn stone floors and staircases, Haddon is not entirely suitable for large groups of elderly people. No dogs are allowed in the House or Grounds, except guide dogs.

FACILITIES FOR THE DISABLED

Disabled and elderly people may alight at the entrance and vehicles then parked in the allocated area. A courtesy vehicle is available to help disabled visitors from the coach park to the Hall. Please advise us of your requirements.

PARKING FOR COACHES & CARS

Parking for 400 cars and 20 coaches, 500 yards from the House.

CATERING

The Restaurant/Tea Room seats up to 75 people. Prices range from £2-3 for tea and other meals. For special functions, buffets lunches and dinners can be arranged.

GUIDED TOURS

£10.00 extra for groups of 20. 7 days notice required.

GUIDE BOOKS

Colour guide book, £2.00, also in French and German.

SCHOOL VISITS/ CHILDREN

School groups are welcome, price £2.10 per child. School's pack is available, enabling children to follow interesting project work. There is an in-school introductory talk by the guide who will take the children round the house on the day if their visit. Schoolroom available. Special guide books can be purchased

OPENING TIMES

Summer
1 April - 30 September

Mon	Closed (except Bank Hol Mons 11am - 6pm)
Tues	
Wed	
Thurs	11am-6pm
Fri	
Sat	
Sun	

Last entry 5.15pm

NB Also closed on Sundays in July & August, except Bank Holiday weekends

Winter
October - 30 March

Closed to the public.

ADMISSION

Summer

Adult	£4.00
Child*	£2.50
OAP	£3.00
Family Ticket	£11.00
2 adults/2 children	

GROUPS**

Adult	£3.00
Child*	£2.10
OAP	£3.00

* Aged 5-16
** Min 20 people

DERBYSHIRE

- **Bolsover Castle,** Bolsover.
  (0246) 823349 6 miles east of Chesterfield on A632.

- **Calke Abbey and Park,** near Derby.
  (0332) 863822 9 miles south of Derby on A514 at Ticknall.

EYAM HALL

OPEN
3 April - 30 Oct
Weds., Thurs.,
Suns., Bank Hol
Mons.
11am-5pm, last
tour 4.30pm.
Pre-booked
parties: as
above.
Schools:
Tuesdays Open
10am last tour
4pm. Also 14
March-Easter.

EYAM HALL, EYAM TEL: 0433 631976
(R H V Wright Esq)

Built by the Wright family in 1671 and still their family home, Eyam Hall is a cosy and intimate house, only recently opened to the public. All visitors receive a guided tour at no extra cost, including the Jacobean staircase, tapestry room "wallpapered" with tapestries and impressive old kitchen. Family portraits, furniture, china, glass, silver, embroidery, costumes and clocks.

Location: 100 yards west of Church in centre of village. Eyam is off A623 between Baslow and Chapel-en-le-Frith.

Admission: Adults £3.25, children £2.25, concessions £2.75. Family (2 adults + 4 children) £9.50. Party rates available.

- **Hardwick Hall,** near Chesterfield.
  (0246) 850430 2 miles south Chesterfield/Mansfield road A617.

- **Kedleston Hall,** Derby.
  (0332) 842191 4 miles north west of Derby.

MELBOURNE HALL

OPEN
Hall
Aug. (not first 3
Mondays)
2.00pm-5.00pm
Gardens
2 April-28 Sept.
Weds., Sats.,
Suns.
Bank Hol Mons.
2.00pm-6.00pm

MELBOURNE HALL AND GARDENS, DERBY TEL: 0332 862502
(Lord and Lady Ralph Kerr)

This beautiful house of history, in its picturesque poolside setting, was once the home of victorian Prime Minister William Lamb. As 2nd Viscount Melbourne, William gave his name to the famous city in Australia. The fine gardens, in the French formal style, contain Robert Bakewell's intricate wrought iron arbour and a fascinating yew tunnel.

Location: 8 miles south of Derby. On M1 from London exit 24 follow signs to East Midlands Airport.

Admission: Hall only: Adults £2, OAP's £1.50, children 75p. Gardens only: Adults £2, OAP's and children £1. Hall & Gardens (Aug. only) Adults £3, OAP's £2.50. children £1.75 These rates may increase in 1994,

- **Old House Museum,** Bakewell.
  (0629) 813647 Above the church in Bakewell.

- **Peveril Castle,** Castleton.
  (0433) 20613 In Castleton on A625, 15 miles west of Sheffield.

RENISHAW HALL

OPEN
April 4th, May
30th, Aug. 29th
and every
Sunday
afternoon in
May, June, July
and August also
Sept. 4th, 11th
and 18th.

12noon-5pm.

RENISHAW HALL, SHEFFIELD TEL: 0246 432042
(Sir Reresby Sitwell, Bt., DL)

George Sitwell built in 1625 a small H-shaped manor house to which his descendant Sitwell Sitwell, later 1st baronet, added vast additions, also the Georgian Stables (now containing a small museum) and various follies in and around the Park. The beautiful Italianate garden, park and lake were the creation of the eccentric Sir George Sitwell 4th baronet (1860-1943) father of the literary "trio" (Edith, Osbert and Sacheverell) and grandfather of the present owner.

Location: 6 miles equidistant from Sheffield and Chesterfield, 3 miles junct.. 30 of M1.

Admission: House: Open by written application only £7 per head. Garden: £3 for adults, £2 for OAP's, £1 for small children.

- **Sudbury Hall and Museum of Childhood,** near Derby.
  (0283) 585305 At Sudbury, 6 miles east of Uttoxter off A50.

- **Winster Market House,** near Matlock.
  (033529) 245 4 miles west of Matlock on south side of B5057.

CHATSWORTH

KEDLESTON HALL

48

KILLERTON HOUSE
Broadclyst, Devon

KILLERTON HOUSE is set in a 7,000 acre estate of rolling parkland, forest, woodland and fields. The house was built by the Acland family as a temporary residence but the permanent house was never started. Now owned by the National Trust, visitors today feel as if they have come to a comfortable country home; they are invited to play the organ or piano in the music room, tour the splendid dining room and cosy library, or visit the laundry with its 'wet' and 'drying' areas.

The first floor rooms contain displays of costumes from the last three centuries shown in room tableau and changed every year. The theme for 1994 is "Fame and Fashion", showing the style of clothes that such famous figures from the past as Jane Austen would have worn.

GARDENS

Killerton's 15 acre garden is a garden for all seasons with choice plants from around the world brought back by Victorian plant collectors who used Killerton as a trial ground. Flowering bulbs carpet the garden slopes in winter and spring, banks of rhododendrons and azaleas flare into colour in May, while the summer herbaceous borders and autumn reds and oranges are spectacular. Children are fascinated by the bear hut, a wooden summer house decorated with wicker and pine cones which was home to the Acland's pet bear, and the ice house where forty tons of ice were stored in Victorian times. Visitors to Killerton can also enjoy extensive walks around the estate, browsing around the produce and gift shops and the plant centre, and the special events organised for all ages.

CONTACT

Mrs Denise Melhuish
The Administrator
Killerton House
Broadclyst
Exeter
Devon
EX5 3LE

Tel: (0392) 881345

LOCATION

On west side of B3181, entrance off B3185. From M5 northbound, exit 29 via Broadclyst and B3181. From M5 southbound, exit 28.

Rail: Pinhoe (not Sunday) 4½ miles; Exeter St Davids and Exeter Central both 7 miles.

SUITABILITY FOR OTHER EVENTS

Business meetings and conferences. Filming, concerts and plays.

EXTRA FACILITIES

Orienteering route. Special events such as activities for children, concerts and demonstrations organised through the year.

ADVICE TO COURIERS & DRIVERS

Pre-booking essential. Reductions for pre-arranged parties of 15 or more. Please book with the Administrator. No photography in the house. Dogs welcome in park but not in house or garden. Please allow at least two hours for house and garden visiting. Visitors should avoid wearing sharp-heeled shoes.

FACILITIES FOR THE DISABLED

Special parking. Motorised buggies with driver to take visitors to the house and on a garden tour. Lavatories. Wheel chairs available. Free admission is given on request to the necessary companion of a visitor with a physical or visual disability.

PARKING FOR COACHES & CARS

Ample parking for cars. Space for 4 coaches.

CATERING

Restaurant in the house with waitress service (capacity 90). Self-service tea room in the old stables. Visitors may picnic throughout the grounds.

GUIDED TOURS

Occasionally available outside normal opening hours. Contact the Administrator.

GIFT SHOP/GUIDE BOOK

Gift shop, plant centre with stock reflecting the plants in the garden and food shop selling local produce. Main guide £1.50.

SCHOOL VISITS/CHILDREN

Pre-booked school groups are welcome. Killerton is ideal for National Curriculum studies in history, geography, environmental education, science and technology, and art. Activity room with handling collection and books, teachers' pack and environmental educational activities, including walks with the warden and pond dipping. Teachers planning a visit are encouraged to make a free preliminary visit. Entrance is free for National Trust School Corporate Members. Children's guide book available.

OPENING TIMES

Summer
30 March - 30 October
Daily   11am - 5.30pm
Last admissions 5pm
Closed Tuesdays

Garden only:
Daily   10.30am - dusk

Winter
31 October - April 1995
House closed.

Garden only:
Daily   10.30am - dusk

Shop, plant centre and produce shop, also tea room tel (0392) 881912 for opening times, which vary during winter.

ADMISSION

Summer
Adult	£4.60
Child	£2.30
Pre-booked groups	
Adult	£3.50
Child	£1.75

GARDEN ONLY	
Adult	£2.80
Child	£1.40

Winter
Nov. - Feb.

GARDEN ONLY	
Adult	£1.00
Child	£0.50

CONFERENCE AND FUNCTION FACILITIES

ROOM	DIMENSIONS	CAPACITY	LAYOUT	POWER POINTS	SUITABLE FOR A/V
Study		50	Theatre	3	✓
		80	Standing		
		60	Buffet		
Restaurant		45	Lunch/Dinner		
		80	Buffet		

POWDERHAM CASTLE
Kenton, Devon

Historic family house of the Earl of Devon, Powderham Castle was built between 1390 and 1420 by Sir Philip Courtenay. The present Earl is his direct descendant. The Castle was extensively damaged during the Civil War and fell to the Parliamentary Forces after a protracted siege. When the family returned to the Castle 70 years later they embarked on a series of rebuilding and restoration which continued into the 19th Century.

The Castle contains a large collection of portraits by many famous artists, including Reynolds, Kneller and Hudson as well as some charming paintings by gifted members of the family. The 14ft high Stumbels Clock and the magnificent rosewood and brass inlaid bookcases by John Channon are particularly fine.

One of the most spectacular rooms on view to visitors is the Music Room, designed for the 3rd Viscount by James Wyatt. It contains an exceptional Axminster Carpet upon which sits recently commissioned carved gilt wood furniture.

GARDENS

The Castle is set within an ancient deer park beside the Estuary of the River Exe and the Gardens and grounds are informally laid out. The Rose Garden is planted mostly with older sweet scented varieties and enjoys fine views from its terraces across the Park. Timothy, a 150 year old tortoise, lives here and keeps the lawns weed free.

CONTACT

Mr Tim Faulkner
The Estate Office
Powderham Castle
Kenton
Exeter
Devon
EX6 8JQ

Tel: (0626) 890243
Fax: (0626) 890729

LOCATION

6 miles south west of Exeter, 4 miles Junct 30, M5.

Air: Exeter Airport 9 miles.

Rail: Starcross Station 2 miles.

Bus: Devon General Nos 85, 85A, 85B to Castle Gate.

SUITABILITY FOR OTHER EVENTS

Antique and Craft Fairs, conferences, dinners, charity balls, filming and wedding receptions, car launches including 4WD, vehicle rallies, clay pigeon shoots etc.

EXTRA FACILITIES

Grand piano in Music Room, 3800 acre Estate, Tennis Court, cricket pitch Horse Trials Course.

ADVICE TO COURIERS & DRIVERS

Complimentary drinks and meals for drivers in the Courtyard Tea Rooms. Advance warning of group bookings preferred but not essential. Unlimited parking.

FACILITIES FOR THE DISABLED

Suitable for disabled visitors, disabled toilets opening 1994.

CATERING

Home made lunches and proper Devon Cream Teas.

GIFT SHOP

There is a gift and souvenir shop with a variety of quality items.

GUIDE BOOKS

Guide books are available in English with French, Dutch and German translations.

GUIDED TOURS

All visits to the House is by guided tour which lasts about 1 hour.

SCHOOL VISITS/CHILDREN

Schools and children of all ages very welcome. Guided tour is a fascinating and useful insight into the life of one of England's Great Houses over the centuries.

CONFERENCE AND FUNCTION FACILITIES

ROOM	DIMENSIONS	CAPACITY	LAYOUT	POWER POINTS	SUITABLE FOR A/V
Music Room	56'x25'	130	Theatre		
		130	Seated		
		150	Buffet		
Dining Room	42'x22'	65	Seated		
		90	Buffet		
		80	Theatre		
Ante Room	28'x18'	25	Theatre		
Library 1	32'x18'	50	Seated		
		75	Buffet		
		50	Theatre		
Library 2	31"x18'	As Library 1			

A La Ronde, Exmouth.
(0395) 265514 2 miles north of Exmouth on A376.

Arlington Court, Barnstaple.
(0271) 850296 8 miles north east of Barnstaple.

Avenue Cottage Gardens, Asprington, Totnes.
(0803) 732769 3 miles south east of Totnes. 300 yards from Asprington Church.

BICKLEIGH CASTLE

OPEN
Easter Week (Good Fri to Fri.) then Weds., Suns and Bank Hols to late May Bank Hol, then to early Oct, daily. (closed Sats.) 2.00-5.30pm Groups of 20+ welcome by prior arrangement.

BICKLEIGH CASTLE, TIVERTON TEL: 0884 855363
(O N Boxall Esq)

Royalist stronghold: 900 years of history and architecture. 11th century detached Chapel; 14th century Gatehouse comprising Armoury (with Cromwellian arms and armour), Guard Room - tudor furniture and fine oil paintings, Great Hall - 52' long and 'Tudor' Bedroom, massive fourposter.   17th century Farmhouse: inglenook fireplaces, bread ovens, oak beams. Museum: Maritime exhibitions: 'Mary Rose', 'Titanic' and model ships, World War II spy and escape gadgets. Spooky Tower, The Great Hall and picturesque moated garden make Bickleigh Castle and Garden a favoured venue for functions, particularly wedding receptions.

Location: Off the A396 Exeter-Tiverton road. Follow signs from Bickleigh Bridge.
Admission: Adults £3.20, children (5-15) £1.60, Fam. Tickets £8.80

BICTON PARK GARDENS

OPEN
March/October 10.00am-4.00pm

April-September 10.00am-6.00pm

BICTON PARK GARDENS, BUDLEIGH SALTERTON
TEL: 0395 68465
(Bicton Park Charitable Trust)

Over 60 acres of Parkland and Gardens, including Italian, American, Oriental, Hermitage and Alpine Gardens: Palm House and specialist greenhouses: Countryside Museum housing nationwide collection of farm and country implements, machinery and vehicles. "Fabulous Forest". Large indoor play area for under teens plus acres of Adventure Playground. 25 minute woodland Railway Ride. Full catering facilities. Plant and Gift Shop.

Location: 2 miles north of Budleigh Salterton on B3178.
Admission: Adults £3.75, OAP/Child £2.75, Fam. Tkt. £12. Group and school rates available.

Buckland Abbey, Yelverton.
(0822) 853607 11 miles north of Plymouth, 6 miles south of Tavistock.

Cadhay, Ottery St Mary.
(0404) 812432 1 mile north west of Ottery St Mary on B3176

Castle Drogo, near Chagford.
(064743) 3306 4 miles north east of Chagford.

Coleton Fishacre Garden, Coleton.
(0803) 752466 2 miles from Kingswear, follow garden signs.

Compton Castle, near Paignton.
(0803) 872112 1 mile north of Marldon off A381.

Dartmouth Castle, Dartmouth
(0803) 833588 1 mile south east of Dartmouth.

Endsleigh House, Milton Abbot, near Tavistock.
(0822) 87248 4 miles west of Tavistock on B3362.

FURSDON HOUSE

OPEN
Easter-End of September.

Thurs. & Bank Hol. Mons.

2.00-4.00pm

FURSDON, CADBURY TEL: 0392 860860
(Mr and Mrs E D Fursdon)

The Fursdon family has lived here for over 700 years. Extensively altered in the 1730's but evidence of the medieval dwelling exists - an oak screen was recently uncovered. There is a wonderful family costume collection with fine examples from 18th and 19th century. Fursdon is set in parkland with a small walled and terraced garden.

Location: On A3072 between Tiverton and Crediton, nine miles north of Exeter near Cadbury.
Admission: £2.75 House & Garden. £1 under 16 (under 10 free) £2.50 in party of 20+.

KEY TO SYMBOLS

  Historic Houses Association Member

  National Trust Property

  Property in care of English Heritage

  National Trust for Scotland Property

HARTLAND ABBEY

OPEN
Wednesdays
May-Sept (incl.)
Sundays, July,
August and Sept.
Plus Suns and
Bank Hol Mons
from Easter to
September
inclusive.

2.00pm-5.30pm

HARTLAND ABBEY, BIDEFORD TEL: 02374 41264
(Sir Hugh Stucley Bt.)

An Augustinian Abbey founded in the 12th century . Finally dissolved by Henry VIII in 1539 and handed to the Captain of his wine cellar, William Abbott. Descended to the present day through a series of marriages to the Stucley family, but never sold. Pictures, furniture and porcelain collected over many generations. Document collection dating from 1160AD and Victorian and Edwardian photographic exhibition. Shrub gardens and woodland walk to remote Atlantic cove.

Location: Between Bideford and Bude - 4 miles off the A39. North west corner of Devon.
Admission: Adults £3.00. children £1.50. Parties £2.50.

Marwood Hill, near Barnstaple.
   4 miles north of Barnstaple. Opposite church in Marwood.

Okehampton Castle, Okehampton.
   (0837) 522844 1 mile south west of Okehampton.

Overbecks Museum and Garden, Sharpitor, Salcombe.
   (054884) 2893 1½ miles south west of Salcombe.

Rosemoor Garden, Great Torrington.
   1 mile south east of Great Torrington on B 3220.

Saltram House, Plymouth.
   (0752) 336546 2 miles west of Plympton, 3½ miles east of Plymouth.

Sand, Sidbury, Sidmouth.
   (0395) 7230 ¾ mile north east of Sidbury, 400 yards from A375.

Shute Barton, Shute, near Axminster.
   (0297) 34692 3 miles south west of Axminster.

Tiverton Castle, Tiverton.
   (0884) 253200 Next to St Peters Church.

Torre Abbey, Torquay.
   (0803) 293593 On Torquay sea front.

Totnes Castle, Totnes.
   (0803) 864406

Ugbrooke House, Chudleigh
   (0626) 852179 Chudleigh.

Yarde, Marlborough, Kingsbridge.
   (054884) 2367 On A381 ½ mile east of Marlborough.

Hemerdon House, Plympton.
   (0752) 223816 2 miles from Plympton.

Kingshayes Court, near Tiverton.
   (0884) 254665 2 miles north of Tiverton, turn off A396 at Bolham.

SALTRAM

ABBOTSBURY
Weymouth, Dorset

Swannery
Tel: (0305) 871684

Gardens
Tel: (0305) 871387

Tithe Barn
Tel:(0305) 871817

LOCATION

Located on B3157 coastal road between Weymouth and Bridport. From Bournemouth and South A36 via Dorchester.

Rail: Weymouth 9 miles.

SHELTERED from the sea by the mighty Chesil Bank and nestling beneath rolling green hills, Abbotsbury is the embodiment of everyone's idea of a typical English village. The charming thatched village with its cottages of warm yellow sandstone attracts thousands of visitors from all over the world.

Tucked away at the reed fringed western end of the Fleet lagoon, the Swannery is home for the only managed colony of Mute Swans in the world and retains a wildness seldom found elsewhere, Visitors can wander freely amongst nesting swans and marvel as parents and cygnets mingle with the public. The reedbed walk takes the visitor past the ancient duck decoy, the oldest of its kind still in operation in Britain. Viewing hides offer a chance to view the birdlife on the Fleet lagoon and the information centre help the visitor to understand and appreciate the 600 year history of the Swannery.

The Sub-Tropical Gardens are a mecca for plant lovers. Set in a sheltered leafy hollow where cold winds do not penetrate, many rare and delicate plants more usually confined to the greenhouse thrive happily in the open. There are winding walks beneath enormous trees and throughout the Gardens palm trees abound. Many of the plants found in the Gardens can be purchased at the country Gift and Plant Centre.

The magnificent 15th Century Tithe Barn, one of the largest of its kind in England, is virtually all that remains of the former Abbey of St Peter. The interior of the Barn, spectacular in its own right, now houses the Croker Collection of agricultural bygones. This beautiful collection carefully reconstructs the scenes of a bygone age. The Farmworkers Kitchen, Gamekeeper, Reaper, Animal Doctor and Blacksmith are just a few of the many exhibits that vividly portray the ingenuity and hardships of the days before.

SPECIAL ATTRACTIONS

Sub-tropical gardens, Swannery and Fleet Nature Reserve, Tithe Barn Museum, Chesil Beach, Iron Age Hill Fort, St Catherine's Chapel, Monastery remains, Abbotsbury village.

SUITABILITY FOR OTHER EVENTS

Music Concerts (in the Tithe Barn), garden parties, filming and television, garden tours for Horticultural Clubs, summer music festivals, conference facilities.

ADVICE TO COURIERS & DRIVERS

Free coach parking. Setting down and picking up points directly opposite attractions. There is a sharp left hand turn to the Swannery and Tithe Barn when approaching from Weymouth. Drivers are advised to turn at the Sub-Tropical Gardens car park and approach this junction head on.

Guided tours of the Swannery for all pre-booked coach parties.

FACILITIES FOR THE DISABLED

All paths at Swannery, and most at the Gardens, negotiable by wheelchair. Wheelchair available for loan free of charge. Disabled toilets are available at Swannery and Gardens.

PARKING FOR COACHES & CARS

Free car parking and coach parking at all attractions.

GUIDED TOURS

Guided tours are available by arrangement.

CATERING

Teas, light lunches etc at Gardens. Many cafés, inns and tea rooms in the village.

GIFT SHOP

Our shops offer a large selection of quality gifts and the Gardens Plant Centre stocks many rare and unusual specimens.

GUIDE BOOKS

Colour brochures are available.

SCHOOL VISITS/CHILDREN

School visits are welcome by prior arrangement. Teacher packs

Summer
SWANNERY
Easter - End October
GARDENS
All Year.
TITHE BARN
Easter - End October

Winter
SWANNERY
Tours by arrangement
TITHE BARN
Sundays only

ADMISSION

Summer
SWANNERY
Adult	£3.50
OAP/Student	£3.00
Child	£1.00

GARDENS
Adult	£3.50
OAP/Student	£3.00
Child	FREE

TITHE BARN
Adult	£2.00
OAP/Student	£1.50
Child	FREE

GROUPS
Reduced rates for parties.

Winter
Swannery: Group Rates
Gardens: Reduced Rates
Tithe Barn: Summer Rates

PARNHAM
Beaminster, Dorset

PARNHAM is a jewel of a Dorset manor dating from 1540 and embellished and enlarged by Nash in 1810. It is a working and friendly house, imaginatively restored and lived in by John and Jennie Makepeace. Built of golden hamstone in a river valley of wooded parkland, this noble house is surrounded by fourteen acres of landscaped gardens; grand terraces, balustrading and courtyards with twin gazebos overlook fifty topiaried yews, bisected by water rills, to a small Lake with many grand old trees. To the north there are herbaceous borders and everywhere distinctive and unusual plant combinations reflect the personal style of Jennie Makepeace, who has restored and replanted much of the garden in recent years. Inside, the rooms relate to the growth of the house over centuries; their many fine features, stained glass, panelling and beautiful ceiling - provide the perfect setting for the superb Makepeace furniture shown in them. The Workshop is an essential part of a visit and provides an opportunity to see unique pieces in the making.

In 1954, Parnham's remaining estates were sold and by 1976 the house faced an uncertain future. The internationally-recognised furniture-designer and seminal force in the newly-emerging crafts movement in Britain, John Makepeace, bought the house and moved his workshops here. Parnham was given a new and exciting future and has become unique as a Mecca for modern design where superlative craftsmanship flourishes. Furniture made at Parnham is collected worldwide by private clients, corporations and museums.

The Parnham Trust, an educational charity, administers two schools: Parnham College teaches young people design, business management and craftsmenship in wood; four miles away is Hooke Park College, remarkable for its innovative approach to the education of entrepreneurs in sustainable design and manufacturing, on a campus where the already-famous buildings are being constructed out of thinnings from the surrounding woodland.

CONTACT

The House Manager
Parnham House
Beaminster
Dorset
DT8 3NA

Tel:(0308) 862204
Fax: (0308) 863494

LOCATION

On A3066, 5 miles north of Bridport, half-a- mile south of Beaminster.

6 miles from Crewkerne Station (Waterloo-Exeter St. Davids line).

Taxi: Greenhams (0308) 862493

Nearest airports - Bristol, Exeter, Bournemouth.

SUITABILITY FOR OTHER EVENTS

Parnham is available for wedding receptions, conferences, filming and private parties.

EXTRA FACILITIES

Excellent restaurant. Lawns for any-size marquees.

ADVICE TO COURIERS & DRIVERS

The use of cameras and camcorders is not permitted inside. Dogs on leads welcome in grounds only. Parking for 2 coaches & 120 cars.

FACILITIES FOR THE DISABLED

Wheelchair access to workshop, ground floor of house and most of gardens. Toilet.

CATERING

Excellent licensed restaurant serving teas, coffees. hot and cold lunches, daily "specials".

GUIDED TOURS

For Groups only on **Tuesdays** and **Thursdays** (see opening times). On **Sundays, Wednesdays** and **Bank Holidays**; workshop and house are manned by voluntary stewards.

GIFT SHOP

Parnham's shop in the old Library is not a souvenir shop but sells books, postcards and exciting contemporary craftwork in wood, textiles and ceramics.

GUIDE BOOKS

Full-colour guide book £2.50.

SCHOOL VISITS/CHILDREN

School visits are welcomed and can be guided if required.

OPENING TIMES

Summer
1 April - 28 October

Suns, Weds, Bank Hols.
10am - 5pm
Public and Groups.

Tues and Thurs
Groups only.

N.B. All groups, on whatever days, must be pre-booked.

CLOSED ON ALL OTHER DAYS

Winter

Closed from November to March inclusive

ADMISSION

Summer

Adult (inc. OAP)	£4.00
Child(10-16)	£2.00
Under 10	FREE
Other (student with card)	£2.00

GROUPS
Suns., Weds, Bank Hols
As Above
Tues. & Thurs.
Adult	£4.50
Child (10-15)	£2.00

CONFERENCE AND FUNCTION FACILITIES

ROOM	DIMENSIONS	CAPACITY	LAYOUT	POWER POINTS	SUITABLE FOR A/V
Gt. Hall	40'x20'	120	Concert-style	8	✓
Pine Room	30'x18'	80	Concert-style	4	✓
Oak Room	30'x18'	60	Concert-style	6	

ATHELHAMPTON HOUSE & GARDENS

OPEN
27 March-30 Oct.
Weds., Thurs.,
Sundays & Bank
Hols.
Also Tues. May
to Sept.
and Mons & Fris
in July and
August.
12 - 5pm
Craft Fairs Easter
& Aug. Bank Hol
weekends.

ATHELHAMPTON HOUSE & GARDENS, DORCHESTER
TEL: 0305 848363
(Patrick Cooke Esq)

Athelhampton is one of the finest examples of the 15th century domestic architecture in the Kingdom. Enjoy the lived in family house with its Great Hall, Great Chamber, Wine Cellar and Kings Room - all exquisitely furnished. Wander through 20 acres of beautiful grounds including 8 walled gardens with fountains, pavilions and topiary pyramids, all encircled by the River Piddle. Home made Cream Teas, Gift Shop and free Car park.

Location: On A35 5 miles east of Dorchester.
Admission: House/Garden Adults £4.20, child £1.70. Garden only Adult £2.50, child Free.

Chettle House, Chettle, Blandford
(025889) 209 6 miles north east of Blandford on A354.

Clouds Hill, near Wool.
1 mile north of Bovington Camp.

Corfe Castle, near Wareham.
(0929) 481294 In village of Corfe Castle on A351.

Cranborne Manor Gardens, Cranborne.
(07254) 248 18 miles north of Bournemouth on B3078.

Edmondsham House and Gardens, Cranborne, near Wimborne.
(0725) 517207 Between Cranborne and Verwood off the B3081.

Forde Abbey, Chard, Somerset
(0460) 220231 **See full details under Somerset page 137**

Hardy's Cottage, Higher Bockhampton.
(0305) 262366 3 miles north east of Dorchester.

Highbury, West Moors
(0202) 874372 In Woodside Road off B3072.

Horn Park, Beaminster.
(0308) 862212 1½ miles north of Beaminster on A3066.

Ilsington, Puddletown, Dorchester.
(0305) 848454 4 miles from Dorchester on A35.

Kingston Lacy, near Wimborne Minster.
(0202) 883402 On B3082 1½ miles west of Wimborne.

MAPPERTON

OPEN
Gardens.
1 March-31 Oct.
Daily
2.00-6.00pm

House:
Open only to
groups by
appointment
(times as above)

MAPPERTON, BEAMINSTER TEL: 0308 862645
(Mr and Mrs John Montagu)

Jacobean 1660's manor with Tudor features and classical north front. Italianate upper garden with orangery, topiary and formal borders descending to fish ponds and shrub gardens. All Saints Church forms south wing opening to courtyard and stables. Area of outstanding natural beauty with fine views of Dorset hills and woodlands.

Location: 1 mile off B3163, 2 miles off B3066, 2 miles Beaminster, 5 miles Bridport.
Admission: £2.50 for gardens, £2.50 house (tour). Under 18 £1.50, under 5 free.

MacPennys, Bransgore, Christchurch.
(0425) 72348 4 miles north east of Christchurch.

Minterne, Dorchester.
(0300) 341370 On A352 2 miles north of Cerne Abbas.

Portland Castle, Portland.
(0305) 820539 Overlooking Portland Harbour, adjacent to RN helicopter base.

Priest's House Museum and Garden, 23 High Street, Wimborne Minster
(0202) 882533 Centre of Wimborne Minster.

Purse Caundle Manor, near Sherborne.
(0963) 250400 4 miles east of Sherborne.

Sandford Orcas Manor House, Sandford Orcas, Sherborne.
(0963) 220206 2½ miles north of Sherborne.

Shaftesbury Abbey Ruins and Museum, Shaftesbury.
(0747) 52910 100 metres west of Shaftesbury town centre.

SHERBORNE CASTLE

OPEN
Easter Sat-end
Sept.
Thurs., Sats.,
Suns and Bank
Hol. Mons.

Castle:
2.00-5.30pm

Grounds & Tea
Room
12noon-5.30pm

SHERBORNE CASTLE, SHERBORNE TEL: 0935 813182
(Mr Simon Wingfield Digby)

A fully furnished Historic House built by Sir Walter Raleigh in 1594 and home of the Digby family since 1617, reflecting various styles from the Elizabethan Hall to the Victorian Solarium. Splendid collections of art, furniiutre and porcelain. Well informed guides are happy to answer questions. Set in beautiful parkland with lawns, wooded walks and a 50 acre lake.

Location: ³/₄ mile south east of Sherborne town centre. Follow brown signs from A30 or A352
Admission: Grounds & Castle £3.60 Adults, £3 OAP, £1.80 child. Grounds only £1.50 Adult/OAP , child 80p.

Sherborne Old Castle, Sherborne.
(093581)2730 ¹/₂ mile east of Sherborne.

SMEDMORE HOUSE

OPEN
May 1st & 29th
Sept. 18th

Garden only
May 15th

2.00-5.00pm

Groups by
arrangement

SMEDMORE, KIMMERIDGE, WAREHAM TEL: 0929 480719
(Dr Philip Mansel)

The home of the Mansel family for nearly 400 years nestles at the foot of the Purbeck hills looking across Kimmeridge Bay to Portland Bill. Originally built in 1620 by the present owner's ancestor William Clavell, the imposing Georgian front was added in the 1760s. Beautiful walled garden which contains many special and interesting plants.

Popular for Holiday lets, Weddings, Business and Private functions.

Location: 15 miles south west of Dorchester.
Admission: full details from the Warden

Wolfeton House, Dorchester
(0305) 263500 1¹/₂ miles from Dorchester on Yeovil road A37.

LORD BARNARD

RABY CASTLE
Staindrop, Darlington, Co. Durham

RABY CASTLE, home of Lord Barnard's family for over 360 years, is set in a 200 acre Deer Park. The Castle was mainly built in the 14th Century, on the site of an earlier Manor House, by the powerful Neville family, who owned it until the Rising of the North in 1569, when Raby was seized by the Crown. It remained Crown property until 1626, when it was bought from Charles I by the eminent statesman and politician Sir Henry Vane, Lord Barnard's ancestor.

Despite its appearance, Raby was intended to be a fortified home rather than a fortress, although it played an important part in the Wars of the Roses and the English Civil War. In the 18th Century,

the Castle was transformed from a rugged stronghold to an elegant country residence, with further alterations in the mid 19th Century. Despite this, much of the original exterior remains, with important medieval rooms, notably the Great Kitchen (used for over 600 years until 1952), with its vast ranges and collection of Victorian copper utensils, and the original Garrison of the Castle now the Servants' Hall.

Today, serene in its tranquil setting, Raby still conveys the sense of its historic past, enhanced by its elegant furnishings and renowned collection of Meissen porcelain. Raby is living history, not a dead museum.

CONTACT

Mrs E A Steele
Raby Castle
Staindrop
Darlington
Co Durham
DL2 3AH

Tel: (0833)
660202/660888

LOCATION

From Edinburgh, 170
miles via A1 or A68.
From London, 250 miles
via M1 and A1.

Rail: Darlington Station,
12 miles.

Air: Teeside Airport,
20 miles.

SUITABILITY FOR OTHER EVENTS

By arrangement, though Raby is unsuitable for meetings, conferences or corporate catering.

EXTRA FACILITIES

These include: Picnic tables, 200 acres of parkland and $3^1/2$ acres of gardens. Lectures can be provided on the Castle, its contents, gardens and history.

ADVICE TO COURIERS & DRIVERS

No photography or video filming is permitted in the Castle: slides are on sale. No dogs allowed in the Castle (except guide dogs). Dogs must be on leads in the park. Unaccompanied children are not admitted to the Castle or park. Unlimited parking on the grass car park and coaches will find hard standing nearby.

FACILITIES FOR THE DISABLED

Disabled or elderly visitors may alight at the entrance to the Castle. The vehicles should then return to the car park. There are two toilets specially adapted for the disabled, near the Car Park and Tearoom. Doors to Tearoom (1 step) are wide enough for wheelchairs.

CATERING

Stables converted to self-service Tearooms, offering light refreshments, seating 60. For other requirements, please contact Curator.

GUIDED TOURS

Tours with experienced guides available at no extra cost, guides posted in most rooms on general open days, when no guided tours are available. Tours last about $1^1/2$ hours. For special interest groups, in-depth tours with the Curator may be arranged, for an additional fee. Garden tours with the Head Gardener can also be organised.

GIFT SHOP

There are two gift shops, one in the Castle, the other in the gardens. Open from 1pm-5pm. A wide variety of gifts are available. Venison, game and soft fruits available in season.

GUIDE BOOKS

Colour guide book currently reprinting. Full text available.

SCHOOL VISITS/CHILDREN

Raby welcomes school parties of up to 60 children, who must be accompanied in a ratio of 1:20. Experienced guides available for school visits. Raby is suitable for several educational purposes: Social history, architecture, art and natural history. Schools are welcome to use the picnic tables, space for supervised games nearby. Room available for picnics when weather inclement.

JARROLDS/NEIL JINKERSON

OPENING TIMES

Summer

EASTER AND ALL BANK
HOLIDAY WEEKENDS
Saturday - Wednesday

MAY - JUNE
Mon } Closed
Tues }
Wed   1pm - 5pm
Thurs
Fri } Closed
Sat }
Sun   1pm - 5pm

JULY - SEPTEMBER
Mon
Tues
Wed } 1pm - 5pm
Thurs
Fri
Sat   Closed
Sun   1pm - 5pm
Garden and Park open
11am - 5pm on above days

PARTIES BY ARRANGEMENT
Easter - end June
Mon-Fri   10am - 4.30pm
July - end September
Mon-Fri Mornings only

Winter
October -Easter
Closed

ADMISSION

Summer

HOUSE & GARDEN
Adult   £3.30
Child*   £1.50
OAP   £3.00
Bulmer's Tower   50p
(when open)

GARDEN ONLY
Adult   £1.00
Child*   £0.75
OAP   £0.75

GROUPS**
By arrangement

* Aged 5-16
** Min 25 people

Auckland Castle, Bishop Auckland.
(0388) 601627 Market Place, Bishop Auckland.

Barnard Castle, Barnard Castle, Durham.
(0833) 38212 In Barnard Castle.

Botanic Garden, University of Durham, Durham.
(091 3742671) 1 mile from Durham along Hollingside Lane.

Brancepeth Castle, near Durham.
091 378 0628   4 miles, Durham.

Durham Castle, Durham.
In the centre of the city next to the Cathedral.

Rokeby Park, near Barnard Castle.
(0833) 27268

BRANCEPETH CASTLE

RABY CASTLE

AUDLEY END HOUSE & PARK
Saffron Walden, Essex

James I is said to have remarked that Audley End was too large for a king but not for his Lord Treasurer, Sir Thomas Howard, who built it.

The house was so large in fact that early in the 18th century about half of it was demolished as being unmanageable, but this still leaves a very substantial mansion. The interior contains rooms decorated by Robert Adam, a magnificent Jacobean Great Hall, a picturesque "Gothic" chapel and a suite of rooms decorated in the revived Jacobean style of the early 19th century.

SUITABILITY FOR OTHER EVENTS

Suitable for various events.

ADVICE TO COURIERS & DRIVERS

Coaches to book in advance.

FACILITIES FOR THE DISABLED

Grounds and most of ground floor suitable for visitors in wheelchairs.

PARKING FOR COACHES & CARS

Car parking is available, Coaches to book in advance.

CATERING

Restaurant facilities available.

GUIDED TOURS

Please telephone for details,

GIFT SHOP

The gift shop contains a large selection of souvenirs and postcards.

GUIDE BOOKS

Souvenir Guide available.

SCHOOL VISITS/CHILDREN

Visits by schools are free if booked in advance. `Please contact the administrator.

CONTACT

The Administrator
Audley End House
Saffron Walden
Essex
CB11 4JF

Tel: (0799) 522842
Fax: (0799) 521276

LOCATION

1 mile west of Saffron Walden on B1383, M11 exits 8 and 9 northbound , exit 10 southbound.

Rail: Audley End - 1 mile

OPENING TIMES

Summer
April - September

Wed	
Thurs	
Fri	1pm-6pm
Sat	
Sun	

Bank Holidays 1pm-6pm
Last admission 1 hour before closing,

Grounds open 12 noon

ADMISSION

Summer

Adult	£5.20
Child	£2.60
OAP/Students/ UB40 holders	£3.90

Grounds only	
Adult	£2.85
Child	£1.40
Concessions	£2.15
GROUPS	

15% off groups of 11 or more.

LAYER MARNEY TOWER,
Colchester, Essex

LAYER MARNEY TOWER, built in the reign of Henry VIII, is the tallest Tudor gatehouse in Great Britain.

Lord Henry Marney clearly intended to rival Wolsey's building at Hampton Court, but he died before his masterpiece was finished. His son John died two years later, in 1525, and building work stopped.

Layer Marney Tower has some of the finest terracotta work in the country, most probably executed by Flemish craftsmen trained by Italian masters. The terracotta is used on the battlements, the windows and most lavishly of all, on the tombs of Henry and John Marney.

Visitors may climb The Tower, passing through the recently restored History Room, and enjoy the marvellous views of the Essex countryside. There are fine outbuildings, including the Long Gallery with its magnificent oak roof and the medieval barn which now houses some of the Home Farm's collection of Rare Breed Farm animals.

CONTACT

Nicholas and Sheila
Charrington
Layer Marney Tower
Colchester
Essex
CO5 9US

Tel: 0206 330784
Fax: 0206 330784

LOCATION

Layer Marney Tower is 5 miles south west of Colchester.

Road: From London A12 53 miles

Rail: Kelvedon Station 3½ miles signposted off the B1022 (Colchester-Maldon road).

SUITABILITY FOR OTHER EVENTS

Film locations, clay pigeons, archery, jousting, banquets, concerts, opera.

ADVICE TO COURIERS & DRIVERS

Parking and refreshments free for drivers.

FACILITIES FOR THE DISABLED

Tower excepted, there is reasonable access and a "disabled loo".

PARKING FOR COACHES & CARS

Free parking on hard standing.

CATERING

Teas, coffee and cakes available. Parties of 20 and more may book in advance for morning coffee, lunch, full tea or an evening meal.

GUIDED TOURS

By arrangement for parties of 20 and over. The tour lasts about 1½ hours. Price £4.00 per person.

GIFT SHOP

Small gift shop with adjoining Farm Butchery specialising in venison.

GUIDE BOOKS

Colour guide £1.65, walkabout guide 50p.

SCHOOL VISITS/CHILDREN

School visits are welcomed throughout the year, with Basic classroom facilities offered, price £1.20 per child, with one adult free with every 10 children.

OPENING TIMES

Summer
1 April-30th September

Daily except Saturdays
2 - 6pm
Bank Holidays
11am - 6pm

Winter
1 October-31 March
Closed

Open by arrangement for guided tours and school visits.

ADMISSION

Summer
Adult	£3.00
Child	£1.50
OAP	£3.00
Family	£8.00

GROUPS*
Adult	£2.50
Child	£1.50
Guided Tour	£4.00

* 20 or more

The Long Gallery

CONFERENCE AND FUNCTION FACILITIES

ROOM	DIMENSIONS	CAPACITY	LAYOUT	POWER POINTS	SUITABLE FOR A/V
Long Gallery	75'x19'	120	Seated	2	
		200+	Buffet		
		200	Theatre		
Carpenters Shop	46'x24'	80	Seated	10	✓
		120	Buffet		
		150	Theatre		

MOYNS PARK
Birdbrook, Essex

LOCATION

London - 1 hour
Cambridge - 30 minutes
Newmarket - 30 minutes

15 minutes from Junct. 9 off the M11, just 2 miles south of Haverhill. For details Location Map, please ring for Colour Brochure.

Home of Lord Ivar Mountbatten, younger son of the 3rd Marquess of Milford Haven, Moyns Park is one of the country's finest examples of an Elizabethan manor house, set in 250 acres of classical rolling parkland.

Situated on the Essex/Suffolk border, within one hour's drive of London, and 30 minutes from Cambridge and Newmarket, the Estate takes it's name from the Le Moign family, who owned the lands from the time of the Norman Conquest in 1066. During the reign of Henry VII the manor passed to the Gent family, who retained ownership until 1880, when Moyns was sold to General St Ives, Silver-Stick-in-Waiting to Queen Victoria and grandfather of the late Ivar Bryce,

previous owner and uncle to Lord Ivar Mountbatten.

Moyns Park is not only steeped in its own fabulous history, but reflects the fascinating history of the Mountbatten and Milford Haven family and their relationship to every Royal household in Europe.

Ian Fleming based the exploits of James Bond on those of his great friend, the late Ivar Bryce, who was an OSS Agent during the second world war.

Moyns Park is not open to the public, but available on an exclusive use basis for guests seeking complete privacy in relaxed, elegant and traditional surroundings.

OPENING TIMES

Available throughout the year.

RATES

Day Delegate Rate
from £35 per person.

24 hour Delegate Rate
from £125 per person.

Private Dinner Party/ Banquet
from £25.00 per head.

Venue Hire Fee
from £500.

For full Tariff and Terms of Business, please contact the Sales Office.

FACILITIES

The House is available for Conferences, Seminars, Incentive Programmes, Corporate Hospitality Events, Wedding Receptions, Private Parties and Banquets.

A full range of outdoor activities can be organised within the Estate and located close to the House. Multi-Activity Events are particularly well suited.

Moyns Park Stud Farm was famous for breeding Loose Cover, the world recorder holder for the mile. There is ample stabling and also horses available for riding through the Estate.

There is plenty of space for Marquee or Steel Framed Structures including utilisation of the Stables and Courtyards for additional Exhibitions and Product Launchs.

CATERING

An exceptionally highs standard of in-house catering is guaranteed, matched with professional and friendly service. Clients are treated as guests and leave as friends.

ACCOMMODATION

9 Principle Suites currently available, with an additional 6 bedrooms from mid-1994. Lord Ivar Mountbatten believes in maintaining the Moyns Park tradition of style and service rarely offered nowadays, including Maid Service and breakfast in bed for the Ladies.

CONFERENCE AND FUNCTION FACILITIES

ROOM	DIMENSIONS	CAPACITY	LAYOUT	POWER POINTS	SUITABLE FOR A/V
Great Hall	41'x30'	130	Theatre	6	✓
		70	Boardroom		
Drawing Room	22'x24'	24	Boardroom	6	✓
		18	U-Shaped		
		36	Theatre		
		30	Dining		
Library	22'x16'	8	Boardroom	3	✓
		8	Dining		
Dining Room	22'x19'	20	Boardroom	5	✓
		16	U-Shaped		
		34	Theatre		
		40	Dining		

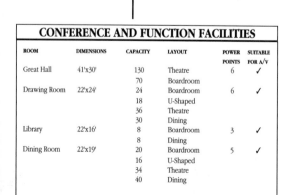

HEDINGHAM CASTLE

OPEN
Easter-31 Oct.
10.00am-5.00pm
Castle and grounds open daily
(House closed)

**HEDINGHAM CASTLE,
CASTLE HEDINGHAM
TEL: 0787 460261**
(The Hon. Thomas and Mrs Lindsay)

Magnificent Norman Keep built 1140 by the famous medieval family the de Veres, Earls of Oxford. Visited by King Henry VII, King Henry VIII and Queen Elizabeth I and beseiged by King John. See the Banqueting Hall with Minstrels' Gallery and the lovely Tudor bridge. Beautiful grounds ideal for family picnics with peaceful woodland and lakeside walks. Light refreshments, home made cakes. Cream teas/talks/ guided tours by arrangement.

Location: On B1058, 1 mile off A604 between Cambridge and Colchester. Easy reach London, M25, M11, A12.
Admission: Adults £2.50. Children £1.50, Family ticket £7.00.

INGATESTONE HALL

OPEN
2 April-25 Sept.
Fri., Sat, Sun &
Bank Holidays
also
Jul 13-Sept 1
Wed. & Thurs.

1.00pm-6.00pm

INGATESTONE HALL, INGATESTONE TEL: 0277 353010
(The Lord Petre)

16th century mansion, set in 11 acres of grounds (formal garden and wild walk), built by Sir William Petre, Secretary of State to four tudor monarchs, which has remained in the hands of his family ever since. The 2 Priests' hiding places can be seen, as well as the furniture, portraits and family memorabilia accumulated over the centuries.

Location: Off the A12 between Brentwood and Chelmsford. Take Station Lane at the London end of the High Street, cross level crossing and continue for 1/2 mile.
Admission: Adults £3, OAP £2.50, children £2, under 5 Free. Group discount (50p.) for 20+. Family Ticket £9 (admits 5 including up to 3 adults.)

Sir Alfred Munnings Art Museum, Castle House, Dedham.
(0206) 322127 3/4 mile Dedham village.

Paycocke's, Coggeshall.
(0376) 561305 On A120 south side of West Street, Coggeshall next to Fleece Inn. 5 1/2 miles east of Braintree.

St Osyth Priory, St. Osyth.
(0255) 820492 8 miles from Frinton.

Saling Hall, Great Saling, Braintree.
6 miles north west of Braintree

Tilbury Fort, Tilbury.
(0375) 858489 1/2 mile south east of Tilbury.

AUDLEY END

BERKELEY CASTLE
Berkeley, Gloucestershire

NOT MANY can boast of having their private house celebrated by Shakespeare nor of having held it in the possession of their family for nearly 850 years, nor having a King of England murdered within its walls, nor of having welcomed at their table the local vicar and Castle Chaplain, John Trevisa (1342-1402), reputed as one of the earliest translators of the Bible, nor of having a breach battered by Oliver Cromwell, which to this day it is forbidden by law to repair even if it was wished to do so. But such is the story of Berkeley.

This beautiful and historic Castle, begun in 1117, still remains the home of the famous family who gave their name to numerous locations all over the word, notably Berkeley Square in London, Berkeley Hundred in Virginia and Berkeley University in California. Scene of the brutal murder of Edward II in 1327 (visitors can see his cell and nearby the dungeon) and besieged by Cromwell's troops in 1645, the Castle is steeped in history but twenty-four generations of Berkeleys have gradually transformed a Norman fortress into the lovely home it is today.

The State Apartments contain magnificent collections of furniture, rare paintings by primarily English and Dutch masters, and tapestries. Part of the world-famous Berkeley silver is on display in the Dining Room. Many other rooms are equally interesting including the Great Hall upon which site the Barons of the West Country met in 1215 before going to Runnymede to force King John to put his seal to the Magna Carta.

The Castle is surrounded by lovely terraced Elizabethan Gardens with a lilypond, Elizabeth I's bowling green, and sweeping lawns.

CONTACT

The Custodian
Berkeley Castle
Gloucestershire
GL13 9BQ

Tel: (0453) 810332

LOCATION

Midway between Bristol and Gloucester, just off the A38.

From motorway M5 use exit 14 (5 miles) or exit 13 (9 miles).

Bus: No 308 from Bristol and Gloucester

SUITABILITY FOR OTHER EVENTS

Wedding receptions, fashion shows, corporate entertainment, receptions, filming.

ADVICE TO COURIERS & DRIVERS

Please advise your passengers that no photography is allowed inside the Castle. No dogs admitted beyond car park. Evening parties accepted by arrangement. GROUP VISITS MUST BE BOOKED.

FACILITIES FOR THE DISABLED

In exceptional circumstances disabled and elderly visitors may alight in the Outer Bailey. There are no toilet facilities for the disabled.

PARKING FOR COACHES & CARS

Free Car Park: 150 yds from the Castle. Up to 15 coaches can be parked 250 yds from the Castle.

CATERING

Tea Rooms serving light lunches and home-made teas. Separate room available for up to 60 people (advance booking required for groups).

GUIDED TOURS

Guided tours available at no extra charge. Max. size 120. Minimum time taken for a tour 1 hour.

GIFT SHOP

Open at the same time as the Castle. It is well-stocked with quality gifts for adults and children.

GUIDE BOOKS

Colour guide book by Vita Sackville West £1.50. Special children's guide book.

SCHOOL VISITS/CHILDREN

School groups are welcome. The Castle has much of interest for all age groups, in particular general history, social history and architecture. School groups visiting the Castle have free admission to Butterfly Farm.

OPENING TIMES

Summer
April - September

Mon	Bank Hol Mons 11am - 5pm
Tues	
Wed	April: 2 - 5pm
Thurs	May - Sept:
Fri	11am - 5pm
Sat	
Sun	2pm - 5pm

Winter
October
Sun   2 - 4.30pm
November - March
Closed

NB Groups must book

ADMISSION

Summer

HOUSE & GARDEN
Adult	£3.80
Child*	£1.90
OAP	£3.00
Groups**	
Adult	£3.30
Child*	£1.70
OAP	£2.80

BUTTERFLY HOUSE
Adult	£1.00
Child*	£0.50
OAP	£0.50

* Aged 5-16
** Min 25 people

CHAVENAGE
Tetbury, Gloucestershire

CHAVENAGE is a wonderful Elizabethan house of mellow grey Cotswold stone and tiles which contains much of interest for the discerning visitor.

The approach aspect of Chavenage is virtually as it was left by Edward Stephens in 1576. Only two families have owned Chavenage; the present owners since 1891 and the Stephens family before them. A Colonel Nathaniel Stephens, M.P. for Gloucestershire during the Civil War was cursed for supporting Cromwell giving rise to legends of weird happenings at Chavenage since that time.

Inside Chavenage there are many interesting rooms housing tapestries, fine furniture, pictures and many relics of the Cromwellian period. Of particular note are the Main Hall, where a contemporary screen forms a minstrel's gallery and two tapestry rooms where it is said Cromwell was lodged.

Recently Chavenage has been used as a location for T.V. and film productions including 'Barry Lyndon', a Hercule Poirot story 'The Mysterious Affair at Styles Manor', many episodes of the sequel to 'Are you Being Served' now called 'Grace & Favour' and 'The Noel Edmunds House Party'.

Chavenage is especially suitable for those wishing an intimate, personal tour, usually conducted by the owner, or for small groups wanting a change from large establishments. It also provides a charming venue for small conferences and functions.

CONTACT

D Lowsley - Williams
Chavenage
Tetbury
Gloucestershire
GL8 8XP

Tel: (0666) 502329
Fax: (0453) 832700

LOCATION

Off M4 at Chippenham turn-off. Signed from Tetbury (1¾ mls) on the B4104. Signed from the A46 (Stroud-Bath road).

Rail: Kemble Station, 7 miles.

Taxi: Tetbury Cars, Tetbury 503393

SUITABILITY FOR OTHER EVENTS

Corporate entertaining. Clay pigeon shooting, archery, crossbows, pistol shooting, A.T.V. driving, weddings, dinners, lunches, small fashion shows, concerts, plays, seminars, filming, product launching, photography.

ADVICE TO COURIERS & DRIVERS

Coaches only by appointment. Stop at the front gates for instructions as to parking.

PARKING

Up to 100 cars and 2-3 coaches.

FACILITIES FOR THE DISABLED

Ground floor accessible to 'chairs'. There are toilet facilities for the disabled.

CATERING

In-house catering available for Weddings, functions, lunches, teas, dinners and picnics by arrangement.

GUIDED TOURS

Normally the owner gives a guided tour to all visitors. Larger groups are given a talk about the house prior to viewing on their own but with the owner present to answer questions. (No extra charge for the above services). Couriers and group leaders should arrange the format required prior to the visit.

GUIDE BOOKS

New colour guide book available.

SCHOOL VISITS/CHILDREN

Groups are welcome at £1.00 per head. Chairs can be arranged for lecturing. Tour of working farm, modern dairy and corn facilities can be arranged at £1.00.

OPENING TIMES

Summer

May - Sept, Easter Sun & Mon and Bank Holidays

Mon	Bank Hols only 2pm - 5pm
Tues } Weds }	Closed
Thurs	2pm - 5pm
Fri } Sat }	Closed
Sun	2pm - 5pm

NB Open at other times by prior arrangement for groups.

Winter

October - March

By appointment only for groups.

ADMISSION

Summer

Adult	£2.50
Child*	£1.25
Friend of HHA	FREE

CONCESSIONS
By prior arrangement, concessions may be given to groups of 20+ and also to disabled and to exceptional cases.

Winter

Groups only: Rates by arrangement.

* Aged 0-16

CONFERENCE AND FUNCTION FACILITIES

ROOM	DIMENSIONS	CAPACITY	LAYOUT	POWER POINTS	SUITABLE FOR A/V
Ballroom	70'x30'	100	Theatre	8	
		120	Schoolroom		
		70	U-shape		
		26	Boardroom		
		100	Dinner/Dance		
		100	Lunch/Buffet		
Oak Room	25'x20'	30	Schoolroom	4	
		16	U-shape		
		12	Boardroom		

STANWAY HOUSE
Cheltenham, Gloucestershire

STANWAY, home of Lord Neidpath, is a jewel of Cotswold Manor houses, very much lived in rather than a museum. All rooms visited are used daily and there is an atmosphere of stepping back in time. Most of the furniture has been in the house since it was built. The paintings, nearly all family portraits give a vivid impression of Stanway's often colourful owners and their relatives over five centuries - for instance one was a gunpowder plotter, two died in "drinking match", one was sentenced to death for rape and one sat in Parliament for a (record) 72 years.

Visit the Audit Room where Estate tenants still assemble every quarter day to pay their rent in person; the Great Hall with its funeral hatchments and 23ft shuffleboard table; the drawing room with its Chippendale Chinese Day Beds.

The evocative landscape includes a typical village cricket field (with a pavilion built by Sir James (Peter Pan) Barrie - a frequent guest). The mellow Jacobean architecture, the exquisite Gatehouse, the old Brewery, the Medieval Tithe Barn, the Pyramid and formal landscape contribute to the timeless charm of one of the most romantic and beautiful houses in England.

CONTACT

Liz Foley
Stanway House
Stanway
Cheltenham
Gloucestershire
GL54 5PQ

Tel: (038 673) 469

LOCATION

From London M40, A40 to Burford, A424 to Stow, B4077 towards Tewkesbury. Stanway is 9 miles past Stow. London, 2 hours.

Motorway: M5 Exit 9, approx 8 miles. (Take A438 towards Stow).

SUITABILITY FOR OTHER EVENTS

Stanway House is suitable for fashion shows, archery, clay pigeon shooting, equestrian events, garden parties, rallies, shows, filming and wedding receptions.

EXTRA FACILITIES

These include: Piano, parkland, farm, fields, cricket pitch, arboretum and old mill.

ADVICE TO COURIERS & DRIVERS

No unaccompanied children. No dogs or photography. Morning coffee and biscuits or afternoon tea with sandwiches and cakes can be provided for pre-booked groups on days when the house is not open to the public.

FACILITIES FOR THE DISABLED

There are no toilet facilities for the disabled.

PARKING FOR COACHES & CARS

Capacity of the car park: 200 cars and 5 coaches, 20 yds from the House.

CATERING

For special functions/conferences, buffets, lunches and dinners can be arranged. Teas are available during opening hours, at the Old Bakehouse in the village from June - August.

GUIDED TOURS

Tours can be arranged for up to 70 people. During winter cost per tour £4.00 per head. Tea or coffee and tour £5.50 per head. Tours are available in French. If requested, the owner may meet groups visiting the House. Average time taken for tour $1^1/4$ hours.

GUIDE BOOKS

A guide book can be purchased, price £1.00.

SCHOOL VISITS/CHILDREN

Groups of children are welcome. Cost per child £1.00. If requested a guide can be provided. There are nature walks.

OPENING TIMES

Summer
June - September

Mon   By appointment
Tues   2pm - 5pm
Wed   By appointment
Thurs 2pm - 5pm
Fri
Sat } By appointment
Sun

Winter
Open by appointment for guided tours only.

ADMISSION

Summer
Adult	£3.00
Child*	£1.00
OAP	£2.50
Student	£2.00

GROUPS**
Adult	£2.00
Child*	£1.00
OAP	£2.00
Student	£2.00

** Min payment £50.00

Winter (Tours only)

HOUSE & GARDEN
Adult	£4.00
Child*	£3.50
OAP	£4.00
Student	£4.00

HOUSE & GARDEN WITH TEA
Adult	£5.50
Child*	£4.00
OAP	£5.50
Student	£5.50

* Under 16

CONFERENCE AND FUNCTION FACILITIES

ROOM	DIMENSIONS	CAPACITY	LAYOUT	POWER POINTS	SUITABLE FOR A/V
Great Hall	40'x25'	100	Buffet	5	✓
		50	Boardroom		
		40	Lunch/Dinner		
Dining Room	25'x20'	25	Boardroom	3	✓
		20	Lunch/Dinner		
Tithe Barn	90'x30'	300	Various	4	✓

SUDELEY CASTLE
Winchcombe, Gloucestershire

SUDELEY CASTLE, one of England's most charming and unusual Country Houses, was the inspiration for 'Blandings' in P.G. Wodehouse's novels. Surrounded by the dramatic scenery of the Cotswolds escarpment, the house has inspired many artists.

Sudeley has a 1,000 year history of royal connections and has, on many occasions, been in the hands of the crown. In the 15th Century it came into the possession of Richard, Duke of Gloucester, later Richard III, who built the splendid Banqueting Hall, now in spectacular ruin. It was also the home of Queen Katherine Parr, who lived here with the young Lady Jane Grey after the death of Henry VIII and is buried in the Chapel. During the Civil War, Sudeley was garrisoned by both Royalists and Parliamentarians and withstood several sieges.

For art enthusiasts, works by Rubens, Turner and Van Dyck are shown amongst the unusual array of exhibits collected by the Dent family during the years of restoration.

Sudeley is the home of Lord and Lady Ashcombe and their family. Many visitors appreciate the friendly atmosphere and warm welcome of a 'lived in' Castle.

Special events planned for 1994 include Craft Fayres, Game Fair, Open Air Theatre, Classical concerts.

CONTACT

James Doherty
Sudeley Castle
Winchcombe
Nr Cheltenham
Gloucestershire
GL54 5JD

Tel: (0242) 602308
Fax: (0242) 602959

LOCATION

8 Miles Northeast of Cheltenham on B4632. From Bristol or Birmingham M5, Exit 9. Take A438 towards Stow-on-the-Wold.

Bus: Castleways to Cheltenham.

Rail: Cheltenham Station 8 miles.

GARDENS

The centrepiece of the gardens at Sudeley is the Queens Garden, named after Queen Katherine Parr, reconstructed from traces of a Tudor Knot Garden on the site. The garden is flanked by fifteen-foot high double yew hedges which are fashioned into corridors with connecting doorways.

SUITABILITY FOR OTHER EVENTS

Wedding receptions, filming, concerts, product launches, exclusive banquets, corporate entertainment, fashion shows.

EXTRA FACILITIES

A full programme of corporate events, such as a vintage car treasure trail, clay pigeon shooting and archery can be arranged. Projector and screen can be provided.

ACCOMMODATION

The Estate offers 16 superb holiday cottages, each accommodating 2-7 people.

ADVICE TO COURIERS & DRIVERS

Coach operators: meal vouchers plus rest room with TV. No dogs, photography or video cameras in the Castle. Colour guide book available, £2.50. Parking for 1,000 cars and 50 coaches.

CASTLE SHOP

Gift shop and specialist plant centre open 11am-5.30pm.

CATERING

The Stableyard Restaurant/Tea Room can cater for up to 90 people for afternoon tea and other meals. Meals can be booked using a party booking form. Menus are available on request. Catering facilities for special functions/conferences can be arranged. Receptions and dinner within the Castle apartments can be arranged.

GUIDED TOURS

By prior arrangement only. Guide Book £2.50

SCHOOL VISITS/CHILDREN

Worksheets are available on request. For a small fee a preliminary talk can be given in the Chapel. A guide can be provided on request. Areas of particular interest include: Rustic adventure playground, working crafts exhibition and wildfowl..

OPENING TIMES

Summer
1 April - 31 October

CASTLE
Mon $\Big\}$ 11am - 5pm
Sun

GROUNDS, CRAFT CENTRE, CHAPEL, RESTAURANT
Mon $\Big\}$ 10.30am - 5.30pm
Sun

Winter
1 November - 1 April

Sudeley Castle Roses open Mid Feb-End Nov.

ADMISSION

Summer

HOUSE & GARDEN
Adult	£4.90
Child*	£2.75
OAP	£4.50
Family	£13.00

Groups**
Adult	£3.80
Child*	£2.00
OAP	£3.50

GROUNDS ONLY
Adult	£3.30
Child*	£1.60
OAP	£2.90

SEASON
Adult	£19.00
Child	£9.50
Family	£36.00
Grounds	£12.00

* Under 16 years
** Min 20 people

CONFERENCE AND FUNCTION FACILITIES

ROOM	DIMENSIONS	CAPACITY	LAYOUT	POWER POINTS	SUITABLE FOR A/V
Chandos Hall	1,200 sq ft		Meeting Room		
		100	Theatre		
		35	Schoolroom		

GLOUCESTERSHIRE

BARNSLEY HOUSE GARDENS

OPEN
Garden only
Every Mon.,
Wed., Thurs.,
Sat. all year
round.

10.00am-6.00pm

Nursery open
Mon-Sat.

BARNSLEY HOUSE GARDEN, CIRENCESTER TEL: 0285 740281
(Charles Verey Esq)

Mature 4 1/2 acre garden designed by Rosemary Verey with interesting collection of trees and shrubs; spring bulbs and autumn colour, mixed borders, knot garden, herbs, laburnam walk (late May to early June). Decorative vegetable garden. Garden furniture by Charles Verey. Fountain and statues by Simon Verity. 18th century wall and summerhouses. Winner (1988) HHA/Christies award.

Location: In Barnsley village - 4 miles north east of Cirencester on B4425.
Admission: £2.00, OAP's £1, children free. No charge in December and January..

BATSFORD ARBORETUM

OPEN
March- mid Nov.

Daily

10.00am-5.00pm

BATSFORD ARBORETUM, MORETON-IN-MARSH
TEL: 0608 650722 OR WEEKENDS 0386 700409
(The Batsford Foundation)

50 acres of private gardens containing well over 1,000 different species of trees and shrubs. Carpets of snowdrops and daffodils with the blossom of magnolias and flowering cherries in the spring. Garden Centre, refreshments in the Apple Store, Falconry Centre, Free car park.

Location : Entrance off A44 Evesham Road, Moreton-in-Marsh.
Admission: Adult £2.50, OAP's/children/groups of 12 or more £1.50

BURNT NORTON

OPEN
Garden Only

By Arrangement

BURNT NORTON, CHIPPING CAMPDEN TEL: 0386 840162
(The Earl and Countess of Harrowby)

"Time past and time future...." The inspiration for the first of T S Eliot's "Four Quartets" - BURNT NORTON - written after a visit to the garden by the poet in the 1930's Twelve acres, mostly semi-wild, especially beautiful in daffodil and primrose times, on the Cotswold escarpment overlooking the Vale of Evesham. Visits by prior arrangement with Mr J Izod, Gardener's Cottage, Burnt Norton, Chipping Campden, Gloucestershire GL55 6PR

Location: Detailed directions from Mr Izod.
Admission: £2.00 per head with discounts for large parties, OAP's and children

Bourton House Garden, Bourton-on-the Hill
(0386) 700121

Chedworth Roman Villa, Yanworth, near Cheltenham.
(0242) 890256 3 miles north west of Fossebridge on A429.

Hailes Abbey.
(0242) 602398 2 miles north east of Winchcombe.

Hardwicke Court, near Gloucester.
(0452) 720212 5 miles south of Gloucester and A38.

HIDCOTE MANOR GARDENS

National Trust/K Statham

OPEN
April-end Oct.
Daily except
Tues & Fri
11.00am-7.00pm

Last admission
6pm or 1 hour
before sunset if
earlier).

Closed Good
Friday.

HIDCOTE MANOR GARDEN, CHIPPING CAMPDEN
TEL: 0386 438333
(The National Trust)

One of the most delightful gardens in England, created this century by the great horticulturist Major Lawrence Johnston; a series of small gardens within the whole separated by walls and hedges of differencet species; famous for rare shrubs, trees, herbaceous borders, 'old' roses and interesting plant species.

Location: 4 miles north east of Chipping Campden, 1 mile east of B4632 (orginally A46) off B4081 [151:SP176429].
Admission: Adult £4.80, child £2.40, Family Tkt £13.20 (2 adults + up to 4 children).

Kiftsgate Court, near Chipping Campden.
3 miles north east of Chipping Campden, 1 mile east of A46 and B4081.

Lydney Park, Lydney.
(0594) 842844 1/2 mile west of Lydney on A48.

MISARDEN PARK GARDENS

OPEN
5 April-29 Sept.
Tuesdays,
Wednesdays,
Thursdays

9.30am-4.30pm

MISARDEN PARK, STROUD TEL: 0285 821303
(Major M T N H Wills)

Noted in the spring for its bulbs and flowering trees and in mid summer for the large double herbaceous borders. Fine topiary throughout and a traditional rose garden (recently refurbished). Outstanding position, standing high overlooking the "Golden Valley". Garden nurseries open daily (except Mondays). Garden featured in Country Life 1992.

Location: 6 miles north west Cirencester. Follow signs off A417 from Gloucester or Cirencester or B4070 from Stroud.

Admission: £2.00 children free. 10% reduction for groups (20 or more) who book in advance.

OWLPEN MANOR

OPEN
3 April-30 Sept
Tues., Thurs.,
Sun. & Bank
Hol. Mons.
2.00-5.00pm

Also Wed., in
July and August.
2.00-5.00pm

OWLPEN MANOR, DURSLEY TEL: 0453 860261
(Mr and Mrs Nicholas Mander)

Romantic Tudor manor house, 1450-1616, with some Cotswold Arts and Crafts restoration. Remote wooded valley setting, with 16 and 17th century formal terraced gardens and magnificent yews. Contains unique painted cloth wall hangings, family collections. Mill (1726), Court House (1620); licensed restaurant in medieval tithe barn. Fine Victorian estate church. Nine period holiday cottages. Corporate events.

"Owlpen - ah, what a dream is there!" - Vita Sackville-West

Location: 3 miles east of Dursley, 1 mile east of Uley, off B4066, by Old Crown pub.
Admission: Adults £3.00, children £1.50.

PAINSWICK ROCOCO GARDENS

OPEN
1st February-mid December
Wed-Sun and Bank Hols.
11am-5pm

PAINSWICK ROCOCO GARDEN, PAINSWICK
TEL: 0452 813204
(Painswick Rococo Garden Trust)

Unique 18th century garden restoration situated in a hidden 6 acre Cotswold combe. Charming contemporary buildings are juxtaposed with winding woodland walks and formal vistas. Famous for its early spring show of snowdrops. Coffee, light lunches and teas.

Location: ½ mile outside village of Painswick on B4073
Admission: Adults £2.50. senior citizens £2.10, child £1.25.

Newark Park, Wotton under Edge.
(0453) 842644 1½ miles east of Wotton under Edge. 1½ miles south of Junction of A4135 and B4058.

Sezincote, Moreton-in-Marsh.
1½ miles west of Moreton-in-Marsh on A44 to Eversham.

SNOWSHILL MANOR

National Trust/K. Statham

OPEN
April & Oct.
Sat, Sun & Easter
Mon closed
Good Friday
May to end Sept.
Daily except
Tuesday.
1.00-6.00pm
Last admission
to house 30
mins. before
closing.

SNOWSHILL MANOR, BROADWAY TEL: 0386 852410
(The National Trust)

A Tudor house with a c.1700 facade; 21 rooms containing Charles Paget Wade's collection of craftsmanship, including musical instruments, clocks, toys, bicycles, weavers' and spinners' tools, Japanese armour; small formal garden and Charles Wade's cottage.

Location: 3 miles south west of Broadway, turning off the A44. [150:SP096339].
Admission: Adult £4.20, child £2.10, Family ticket £11.60 (2 adults + up to 4 children).

WESTBURY COURT GARDEN

OPEN
April-end Oct.
Wed. to Sun. and
Bank Hol. Mons
11.00am-6.00pm

Closed Good
Friday.

Other months by
written
appointment
only

WESTBURY COURT GARDEN, GLOUCESTER TEL: 0452 760461
(The National Trust)

A formal water garden with canals and yew hedges, laid out between 1696 and 1705; the earliest of its kind remaining in England. Restored in 1971 and planted species dating from pre 1700 including apple, pear and plum trees.

Location: 9 miles south west of Gloucester on A48 [162: SO718138]
Admission: Adult £2.20. Child £1.10

Whittington Court, Whittington, Cheltenham.
(0242) 820218 4½ miles east of Cheltenham on A40.

Woodchester Park Mansion, Nympsfield.
(0453) 860531 ½ mile from the village of Nympsfield on the B4066.

BEAULIEU
Beaulieu, Hampshire

BEAULIEU, in the beautiful New Forest between Bournemouth and Southampton, has been Lord Montagu's family home since 1538, when it was purchased by Lord Montagu's ancestor, Thomas Wriothesley, 1st Earl of Southampton. Palace House and gardens have been open to the public since 1952, when the present Lord Montagu inherited.

Beaulieu Abbey was founded in 1204 and, although most of the buildings were destroyed during the Dissolution, much of beauty and interest remains. The Domus, a fine remaining building, houses an exhibition which takes the visitor back to the ages of King John and medieval monastic life.

The inclusive admission to Beaulieu covers entry to the National Motor Museum, Palace House and Gardens, Beaulieu Abbey and Exhibition of Monastic Life.

CONTACT

Lesley Ann Harnett
John Montagu Building
Beaulieu
Hampshire
SO42 7ZN

Tel: (0590) 612345

LOCATION

From London, M3 West, M27, M271, A35 then B3056 from Lyndhurst.

Bus: Bus stops within complex.

Rail: Stations at Brockenhurst and Beaulieu Rd both 7 miles away.

SUITABILITY FOR OTHER EVENTS

Rallies, product launches, promotions, banquets, filming, outdoor events, exhibitions. Most requests considered.

EXTRA FACILITIES

Helicopter landing point, audio-visual facilities, lectures, private dining room of Palace House available for receptions, dinners, lunches etc., hardstanding exhibition arena adjacent to Motor Museum, veteran and vintage cars and buses available to transport guests.

ADVICE TO COURIERS & DRIVERS

During the season the very busy period is from 11.30am to 1.30pm. It is advisable to allow 2 hours or more for visits. Last admission 40 minutes before closing. On arrival at the Information Centre, admission warrants should be presented at the Information Desk, where hostesses are on hand to welcome and assist you. Coach drivers should sign in at the Information Desk. Free admission is given to coach drivers and they receive a voucher which can be exchanged for food, drink and souvenirs. No dogs in the buildings.

FACILITIES FOR THE DISABLED

Disabled and elderly visitors may be left at the entrance to the Palace House, before parking in the allocated areas. There are toilets for the disabled. There are some concessions for handicapped parties. Wheelchairs are available at the Information Centre for use within the grounds.

PARKING FOR COACHES & CARS

Parking for 1,500 cars and 30 coaches.

CATERING

The Brabazon seats 300 in a self-service Restaurant and Bar. Open daily when House open. Prices from £4 for tea and £7 for lunch. Groups can book in advance. Further details and menus available from Catering Manager (0590) 612102.

GUIDED TOURS

Attendants on duty in Palace House and National Motor Museum. Guided tours by prior arrangement.

GIFT SHOP

Information Centre Shop, open as property. Palace House Shop, Kitchen Shop, Herb Shop, Abbey Shop open Summer only. Gifts include motoring items, books, comestibles and toiletries.

GUIDE BOOKS

Colour guide books available.

SCHOOL VISITS/CHILDREN

Beaulieu offers an extensive education service to student groups of all ages. Professionally qualified staff are available to assist in planning of visits to all attractions. Services include introductory talks, films, guided tours, role play and extended projects.

In general, educational services incur no additional charges, and publications are sold at cost. Starter sets of material are available free of charge to pre-booked parties. Full information pack available from Education at Beaulieu, John Montagu Building, Beaulieu, Hampshire. SO42 7ZN.

Responsible behaviour is expected at all times.

OPENING TIMES

Summer
Easter - October

Mon	
Tues	
Wed	
Thurs	10am - 6pm
Fri	
Sat	
Sun	

Winter
October - Easter

Mon	
Tues	
Wed	
Thurs	10am - 5pm
Fri	
Sat	
Sun	

ADMISSION

All Year
Individual rates upon application.

GROUPS**
Adult	£6.00
Child*	£4.00
OAP	£5.00
Student	£5.00

* Aged 4-16
** Min 15 people.

CATERING/FUNCTIONS

Please send for our new conference and function brochure.

The Brabazon and Domus (pictured above) banqueting halls can be hired all year round. For a fee Lord Montagu may meet groups and participate in functions.

Groups can be booked in advance for buffets, lunches, dinners and Royal Feasts. Please contact the Catering Manager for further details and menus. Tel: (0590) 612102.

CONFERENCE AND FUNCTION FACILITIES

ROOM	DIMENSIONS	CAPACITY	LAYOUT	POWER POINTS	SUITABLE FOR A/V
Brabazon (3 sections)	40'x40'(x3)	120(each)	Theatre	3	✓
		70	Schoolroom		
		40	U-shape		
		40	Boardroom		
		100	Buffet		
		300	Dinner/Dance		
		80 (each)	Lunch/Dinner		
Domus	69'x27'	170	Theatre	3	✓
		60	Schoolroom		
		40	U-shape		
		40	Boardroom		
		120	Lunch/Dinner		
Classic Car Theatre		200	Tiered Theatre Style Seating	3	✓

THE NATIONAL MOTOR MUSEUM

When Lord Montagu inherited Beaulieu, he displayed a handful of early vehicles in the Front Hall as a memorial to his father, one of the leading pioneers of motoring in Britain. From this beginning the now famous National Motor Museum grew.

The Museum traces the story of motoring from 1894 to the present day, with many special displays and 250 cars, commercial vehicles and motorcycles. It is especially proud to have four World Land Speed Record Breaking Cars (see left).

'Wheels - The Legend of the Motor Car', is a major feature in the Museum. This spectacular ride-through display is a tribute to man's motoring achievements. 'Wheels' transports visitors in space-age 'pods' through 100 years of motoring, from the early pioneers and their problems, to fantasies of the future, and shows how the motor vehicle has revolutionised our lives.

A monorail transports visitors to the Motor Museum, entering the building at roof level. There are rides on a 1912 open-topped London Bus or in Miniature Veteran Cars; Remote Controlled Model Cars; and a superb Model Railway, one of the largest layouts of its kind in the world.

Entry to the museum is included in the inclusive admission price.

BROADLANDS
Romsey, Hampshire

BROADLANDS is a fine example of 18th Century architecture. The House and grounds are the work of Lancelot 'Capability' Brown. The House contains many fine works of art, including several Van Dycks and furniture by Mayhew and Ince.

Lord Mountbatten lived here until his tragic death in 1979. It is now the home of his grandson, Lord Romsey and his family

The life stories of Lord and Lady Mountbatten are told in the Mountbatten Exhibition and in 'The Life and Times of Lord Mountbatten', a spectacular 30 minute audio-visual presentation housed in the William and Mary stable block.

The large Japanese artillery gun seen in the courtyard was brought home by Lord Mountbatten as a souvenir and reminder of his role as Supreme Allied Commander in South East Asia during World War II. Also on display is his 1924 Silver Ghost Rolls Royce.

Around the grounds and the park visitors will be able to spot many trees planted by famous personalities, including members of the Royal Family. The tradition of tree planting started in the early 17th Century is perpetuated today.

CONTACT

A Hughes-Onslow
Broadlands
Romsey
Hampshire
SO51 9ZD

Tel: (0794) 517888
Fax: (0794) 516878

LOCATION

Road: From London M3, M27 exit Junction 3, A3057, entrance A31 Romsey by-pass.

Rail: Romsey station 1 mile.

Bus: Bus station 3/4 mile.

Taxi: Rotax (0794) 513108

SUITABILITY FOR OTHER EVENTS

Filming on the Estate is by arrangement with the General Manager. Ideal venue for open air concerts, shows and air displays.

ADVICE TO COURIERS & DRIVERS

Allow at least $2^1/2$ hours. Free admission, and a gift voucher incentive for coach drivers together with a £4.00 restaurant voucher which is also available to couriers leading groups of 15 or more paying visitors. No dogs.

FACILITIES FOR THE DISABLED

Disabled visitors may alight in the stable yard, 100 yards from the house, by arrangement with the car park staff. Toilet facilities for the disabled.

PARKING FOR COACHES & CARS

Parking for 750 cars and 20 coaches, 300 yards from the House.

BOOKING ARRANGEMENTS

Pre-booking of group visits is desirable but not essential. Organised groups will always be welcome at any time during advertised opening hours.

CATERING AND TEAROOM

Self-service with capacity of 60 inside and 100 outside. Menus on request .

GUIDED TOURS

Guided tour of House only. Exhibition self guiding.

GIFT SHOP

Two gift shops open during opening hours.

GUIDE BOOKS

Colour guide book available, £2.00.

SCHOOL VISITS/CHILDREN

Educational groups are welcome. Work-sheets are available. Links with CSU5.

OPENING TIMES

Summer
31 March - 25 September

Mon Tues Wed Thurs	12noon - 5.30pm
Fri	Good Friday & August only. 12noon - 5.30pm
Sat & Sun	12noon - 5.30pm

Last admissions 4pm, but we recommend that coach parties arrive before 3pm in order to have enough time to see everything without hurrying.

Winter
October - End March

Closed

ADMISSION

Prices on application

HIGHCLERE CASTLE
Newbury, Berkshire

Designed by Charles Barry in the 1830s at the same time as he was building the Houses of Parliament, this soaring pinnacled mansion provided a perfect setting for the 3rd Earl of Carnarvon one of the great hosts of Queen Victoria's reign. The extravagant interiors range from church Gothic through Moorish flamboyance and rococo revival to the solid masculinity in the long Library. Old master paintings mix with portraits by Van Dyck and 18th Century painters. Napoleon's desk and chair rescued from St. Helena sits with other 18th and 19th Century furniture.

The 5th Earl of Carnarvon, discovered the Tomb of Tutankhamun with Howard Carter. The castle houses a unique exhibition of some of his discoveries which were only rediscovered in the castle in 1988. The current Earl is the Queen's Horseracing Manager. In 1993 to celebrate his 50th year as a leading owner and breeder "The Lord Carnarvon Racing Exhibition" was opened to the public, and offers a fascinating insight into a racing history that dates back three generations.

GARDENS

The magnificent parkland with its massive cedars was designed by Capability Brown. The walled gardens also date from an earlier house at Highclere but the dark yew walks are entirely victorian in character. The glass Orangery and Fernery add an exotic flavour. The Secret Garden has a romance of its own with a beautiful curving lawn surrounded by densely planted herbaceous gardens. A place for poets and romantics.

CONTACT

T Howland
HMH Management
The Field House
Highclere Park
Near Newbury
Berkshire
RG15 9RN

Tel: (0635) 253210
Fax: (0635) 254051

LOCATION

Highclere Castle is approx 4¹/₂ miles out of Newbury on A34 towards Winchester. From London: M4 Junct 13; A34, Newbury-Winchester 20 mins. M3 Junct. 5 approx 15 miles.

Air: Heathrow M4 45 mins.

Rail: Paddington-Newbury 45 mins.

Taxi: 4¹/₂ miles(0635) 40829.

SUITABILITY FOR OTHER EVENTS

Ideal for conferences, exhibitions, receptions, dinners, activity days, filming, concerts and corporate hospitality.

OUTDOOR EVENTS

Stunning backdrop for concerts, (cap. 8000) Fairs and displays.

ADVICE TO COURIERS & DRIVERS

No dogs are permitted in the house or gardens. No photography in the house. Ample Parking.

FACILITIES FOR THE DISABLED

Disabled and elderly visitors may alight at the entrance to the house. There are toilet facilities for the disabled.

CATERING

Exceptional catering for corporate events. During public openings the tea rooms can accommodate 60. Lunches for parties of 24+ can be booked in advance.

GIFT SHOP

The Gift Shop is open throughout the Castle open season..

GUIDED TOURS

They are available for visits outside normal opening hours. Average time taken to see the house is 2 hours.

GUIDE BOOKS

Colour guide book, £2.50.

SCHOOL VISITS/CHILDREN

Groups welcome by prior arrangement. Areas of interest: The Egyptian collection discovered at the Tomb of Tutankhamun by the 5th Earl. Nature walks, beautiful old follies.

OPENING TIMES

Summer

1 July - 30 September
Mon   Closed
Tues   Closed
Wed ⎫
Thur ⎪
Fri ⎬ 2pm-6pm
Sat ⎪
Sun ⎭

Bookings Only:
11am-1pm

Winter

October-July
By appointment only.

ADMISSION

Summer

Adult	£5.00
Child	£3.00
OAP	£4.00
Gardens only	£3.00
Family(2 + 2)	£13.00
GROUPS*	
Adult	£4.50
Child	£2.50
OAP	£3.50

*For 30 or more people.

CONFERENCE AND FUNCTION FACILITIES

ROOM	DIMENSIONS	CAPACITY	LAYOUT	POWER POINTS	SUITABLE FOR A/V
Library	43'x21'	120	Theatre	✓	✓
Saloon		150	Reception	✓	✓
Dining Room		70	Lunch/Dinner Seated	✓	
Library, Saloon, Drawing Room Music Room, Smoking Room		400	Reception	✓	

ROTHERFIELD PARK
East Tisted, Alton

ROTHERFIELD stands on a fine site on which a House has stood since Tudor times. There are magnificent views to the East across carefully landscaped parkland.

James Scott, bought Rotherfield from the Marquis of Winchester in 1808 and his descendants still live in the house he rebuilt by 1821 to the design of Joseph Parkinson - new cottages were built and in 1840 the Church was enlarged with a Tower now a key feature in the landscape.

Additional work in the 1880s romanticised the house with turrets and towers and large windows which provide light reception rooms.

The Central Hall is indeed imposing yet friendly. This is now a good example of increasingly rare Victorian Gothic architecture made interesting with many contemporary contents and furnishings.

GARDENS

The ten acre garden provides a rare mixture of lovely old trees and some younger ones replacing the many lost in the severe storms of 1987 and 1990. There is a walled garden full of trained fruit trees, herbaceous borders and young shrubs. These are examples of plants raised for sale. There is a well stocked greenhouse, rose garden and pond. There are seats on which visitors may rest and enjoy the peace and quiet.

CONTACT

Lady Scott
Rotherfield Park
East Tisted
Alton
Hampshire
GU34 3QL

Tel: (0420) 58204
Fax: (0420) 587312

LOCATION

In village of East Tisted 4¹/₂ miles south of Alton on A32 (exit 5 off M3 or, from Guildford, the A31 to Alton).

70 minutes from Central London - non rush hour.

OPENING TIMES

Summer

HOUSE & GARDENS
Sundays & Mondays of all Bank Holidays and 1/7June, 1/7 July and 1/7 August.
2.00 - 5.00pm

Groups at other times by appointment.

GARDENS ONLY

April - September

Sun   } 2.00-5.00pm
Thur

ADMISSION

Summer

HOUSE & GARDEN
Adults   £2.50
Children*   FREE

GARDEN ONLY
Adults   £1.00
Children*   FREE

* Under 14

EXTRA FACILITIES

Clay pigeon shooting.

ADVICE TO COURIERS & DRIVERS

No cameras or smoking in the House.

FACILITIES FOR THE DISABLED

Access for wheelchairs, gentle steps.

CATERING

Teas when House and Garden open. Buffet meals or luncheons for groups by appointment.

GUIDED TOURS

Guided tours at no extra charge.

GIFT SHOP

No shop - small articles for sale. Plants for sale.

GUIDE BOOKS

Colour guide book, £1.00. Leaflets free.

SCHOOL VISITS/CHILDREN

School groups are welcomed but there are no special facilities.

CONFERENCE AND FUNCTION FACILITIES

ROOM	DIMENSIONS	CAPACITY	LAYOUT	POWER POINTS	SUITABLE FOR A/V
Dining Room	24'x55'	14	Boardroom	3	
		50	Buffet		
		50	Lunch/Dinner		

SOMERLEY
Ringwood, Hampshire

To visit Somerley, even briefly, is to taste the elegant lifestyle. The architectural grandeur, the elegance of its interiors and its magnificent setting on the edge of the New Forest combine to make it one of Britain's finest houses. The house was designed by Samuel Wyatt in the mid 1700s and has been the residence of the Normanton family for almost 200 years. The sixth Earl and Countess live here today with their three children.

The house is not open to the public; the magnificently proportioned rooms with high gilded ceilings house a treasure trove of fine antique furniture, porcelain, paintings and objets d'art, and can be enjoyed by guests who visit to conduct business meetings, conferences, concerts, receptions, product launches and top level corporate hospitality. The house is 1½ miles from the nearest road and although easily accessible, provides privacy for meetings demanding security and complete confidentiality. The 7,000 acres of parkland can be used for incentive fun days, promotions and Polo and Golf events. The high standard of service and cuisine (much of the food comes from the Estate and gardens) and the warm friendly atmosphere are very rarely found in a house of this size. The peace and tranquillity of the grounds are a sheer delight.

CONTACT

Pamela Benton
Somerley
Ringwood
Hampshire
BH24 3PL

Tel: (0425) 480819
Fax: (0425) 478613

LOCATION

Off the M27 to Bournemouth, A31 1ml. London 1¾ hrs via M3, M27, A31.

Air: Bournemouth International Airport, 5miles.

Rail: Bournemouth Station 12 miles.

Taxi: A car can be arranged from the House if applicable.

SUITABILITY FOR OTHER EVENTS

Specialising in game and clay pigeon shooting, filming, archery, polo and golf instruction. Large scale events, fashion shows, air displays, equestrian events, garden parties, shows, rallies, wedding receptions.

EXTRA FACILITIES

Also available for use: Grand Piano, organ, billiard room, parkland, formal gardens, croquet, tennis, polo ground, and golf driving range and teaching course, outdoor pool, salmon fishing, clay shoot. Picture Gallery includes work by Reynolds, Canaletto, Gainsborough, Murillo and Etty. Furniture mainly Louis XIV and XVI.

ACCOMMODATION

Somerley offers 1 single and 8 twin/doubles with bathrooms. All rooms to be taken by house party. Smaller numbers negotiable.

ADVICE TO COURIERS & DRIVERS

Liaise with Pamela Benton or the Earl of Normanton: 0425 480819. No individual visits. All uses of Somerley are on an exclusive basis, by application only.

FACILITIES FOR THE DISABLED

Disabled and elderly visitors may alight to the Front Entrance of the House.

PARKING FOR COACHES & CARS

There is parking for up to 200 cars and 20+ coaches adjacent to the house.

CATERING

The Dining Room is available for private parties (capacity 50 people). Parties must book in advance and menus are available on request. Meals from £23.00 per head. Outside caterers may be used in the Grounds if requested.

BROCHURES

A colour brochure is complimentary, given to conference/function enquirers

OPENING TIMES

Privately Booked Functions only.

ADMISSION

Upon application for privately booked functions only.

CONFERENCE AND FUNCTION FACILITIES

ROOM	DIMENSIONS	CAPACITY	LAYOUT	POWER POINTS	SUITABLE FOR A/V
Picture Gallery	80'x30'	150	Reception	8	
Drawing Room	38'x30'	50	Various	6	
Dining Room	39'x19'	50	Various	4	
East Library	26'x21'	20	Boardroom	4	
		20	Lunch/Dinner		
		30	Reception		

HAMPSHIRE

Jane Austen's House, Chawton.
  (0420) 83262 In Chawton, 1 mile south west of Alton.

Avington Park, Winchester.
  (0962) 779260 4 miles north east of Winchester just south of B3047 in Itchen Abbas.

Basing House, Basingstoke.
  (0256) 467294 2 miles from Basingstoke Town Centre.

Bishop's Waltham Palace, Bishops Waltham.
  (0489) 892460 In Bishop's Waltham.

Bramdean House, Bramdean, Alresford.
  (0962) 771214 In Bramdean on A272.

Breamore House, Fordingbridge.
  (0725) 22468 3 miles north of Fordingbridge.

Calshot Castle
  (0703) 892023 On Spit 2 miles south east of Fawley off B3053.

Exbury Gardens, near Southampton .
  (0703) 899422 Exbury village 15 miles south west of Southampton close to New Forest.

Fort Brockhurst, Portsmouth.
  (0705) 581059 Off the A32 in Elson on the north side of Gosport.

HILLIER GARDENS

OPEN
Open All Year
Every Day

1 April-31 Oct.
10.30am-6.00pm

1 Nov.-31 March
10.30am-5.00pm
or Dusk

Closed
Dec. 25th, 26th
and Jan. 1st.

THE SIR HAROLD HILLIER GARDENS AND ARBORETUM,
ROMSEY TEL: 0794 368787
(Hampshire County Council)

A Plantsman's paradise , these 160 acre gardens contain one of the finest collections of trees and shrubs in the British Isles. Begun in 1953 by Sir Harold Hillier and given to Hampshire County Council in 1977. It is truly 'A Garden for all Seasons', with something of interest providing colour and fragrance throughout the year, even in deepest winter.

Location: 9 miles south west of Winchester, 3 miles north east of Romsey signposted off A31 Romsey to Winchester Road and from A3057.
Admission: £3.00 adult, £2.50 OAP, £1.00 child up to 15. Groups of 30+ £2.50per person.

Hinton Ampner, near Alresford.
  (0962) 771305 1 mile west of Bramdean Village on A272.

Hurst Castle.
  (0590) 642344 Approach by ferry from Keyhaven.

ABOVE: AVINGTON PARK

BELOW: BREAMORE

Jenkyn Place, Bentley.
  In Bentley 400 yards north of cross roads. Signs on A31.

HOUGHTON LODGE

OPEN
Garden
March-Sept.
Sats. & Suns.
10.00am-5.00pm

Mon, Tues, Fri
2.00-5.00pm
Other times by
appointment,

House by
appointment
ony.

HOUGHTON LODGE GARDEN, STOCKBRIDGE
TEL: 0264 810177/810502
(Captain M W Buck)

Perhaps among the most 'picturesque' of 18th century gothic "cottages ornees" with its architectural fantasy and perfect garden setting overlooking the tranquil beauty of the Test valley. The kitchen garden surrounded by rare chalkcob walls contains The Hydrooponicum, a living exhibition of horticulture without soil, demonstrating its application worldwide and in space.

Location: 1¹/2 miles south of Stockbridge (A30) on minor road signposted Hoghton village.
Admission: £2.50. Discounts for parties. House prices on application.

The Manor House, Upton Grey, Basingstoke.
  (0256) 862827 6 miles south east of Basingstoke in Upton Grey on hill immediately above the church.

Medieval Merchants House, 58 French Street, Southampton.
  (0703) 221503 Between Castle Way and Town Quay.

Mottisfont Abbey Garden, Mottisfont.
  (0794) 41220 4¹/2 miles north west of Romsey.

Netley Abbey, Netley.
  (0703) 453076 In Netley, 7 miles south east of Southampton facing Southampton Water.

Porchester Castle, Portchester.
  (0705) 378291 South side of Portchester.

Sandham Memorial Chapel, Burghclere, Newbury.
  (063527) 292 In village of Burghclere, 4 miles south of Newbury.

The Vyne, Basingstoke.
  (0256) 881337 4 miles north of Basingstoke.

Wolvesey: Old Bishop's Palace, Winchester.
  (0962) 54766 ¹/4 mile south east of Winchester Cathedral, next to Bishop's Palace.

GILBERT WHITE'S HOUSE

OPEN
26 March-31 Oct.
Daily

11.00m-5.00pm

Nov.-Dec.
Weekends

Groups by
appointmennt in
evenings.

GILBERT WHITE'S HOUSE & GARDEN, THE WAKES, SELBORNE
TEL: 0420 511275
(Oates Memorial Trust)

Historic House with furnished rooms and glorious tranquil 5 acre garden. Home of famous 18th century naturalist Rev. Gilbert White, author of 'The Natural History of Selborne': also museum devoted to the Oates family and in particular Lawrence Oates of Antarctic fame. Weekend of Events 25th and 26th June.

Location: On B3006 in village of Selborne close to A3.
Admission: Adults £2.50, OAP's £2.00, children £1.00. First child free.

EASTNOR CASTLE
Ledbury, Herefordshire

This magical castle in its fairytale setting attracts ever-increasing visitors and interest. Here's why:

***The atmosphere.** Everyone is struck by it. The vitality of a young family brings the past to life and the sense of warmth and optimism is tangible. Eastnor, however grand is a home.

*"**Sleeping**" for the past fifty years, the Castle has recently undergone a triumphant renaissance - 'looking better than it probably ever has' Country Life 1993.

***Hidden** away in attics and cellars since the war, the castle's treasures are now revealed for the first time. Early Italian Fine Art, 17th century Venetian furniture and Flemish tapestries, Mediaeval armour and paintings by Van Dyck, Reynolds, Romney and Watts, photographs by Julia Margaret Cameron.

*'**The princely and imposing pile**' as it was described

in 1812 when it was being built to pitch the owner into the aristocracy remains the home of his descendants. The Castle contains two hundred years of possessions, letters diaries, clothes and furnishing belonging to friends   and relations who include: Horace Walpole, Elizabeth Barret Browning, Tennyson, Watts, Julia Margaret Cameron and Virginia Woolf.

***Encircled** by the Malvern Hills, the mediaeval beauty of the estate remains unchanging.

GARDENS

Castellated terraces descend to a 21 acre lake with a newly opened lakeside walk. An arboretum holds a famous collection of mature specimen trees. There are spectacular views of the Malvern hills across a 900 acre deer park, once part of a mediaeval chase and now designated a Site of Special Scientific Interest.

CONTACT

The Administrator
Eastnor Castle
Ledbury
Herefordshire
HR8 1RN

Tel: (0531)633160/
632302

Fax: (0531)631776/
631030

LOCATION

London 2½ hours
Birmingham 1 hour
Gloucester 25 minutes
Cheltenham 35 minutes
Worcester 30 minutes
Hereford 25 minutes
Please ring for directions

Meredith Taxis: (0531)
632852
Redline Taxis:
(0432) 890313

OPENING TIMES

Summer/Winter
12.00 - 5.00pm
Bank Holiday Mondays
Sundays from Easter to
End September
August:
Sunday to Friday
Other times and dates
throughout the year by
appointment.
NB Parties must pre-book.
Groups by appointment at
any time, including
evenings, when the Castle
is closed to casual visitors.

ADMISSION

Summer

HOUSE & GROUNDS
Adult   £3.50
Child*   £1.75
Group**   £3.00

GROUNDS ONLY
Adult   £1.75
Child*   £0.75

*Age 5 - 14
** Min. payment £60 for 20 people.

Winter
Closed except by appointment.

SUITABILITY FOR OTHER EVENTS

The Castle is at the centre of an unspoilt 5,000 acre estate, used with great success for off-road driving, clay pigeon shooting, quad bikes, archery and falconry. The varied terrain ideal for team building activity days and survival training. for which accommodation is available. The impressive interior of the castle makes an original setting for product launches, corporate hospitality, fashion shows, concerts, weddings, charity events, craft fairs, television and feature films.

EXTRA FACILITIES

Exclusive off-road driving on the "Land Rover" test track with qualified instructors.
Luxury Accommodation within the castle for small exclusive groups.
Meeting Room/Dormitory for Survival/Team Building days with showers and kitchen.
Chapel for small Weddings/Christenings.

ADVICE TO COURIERS & DRIVERS

Please telephone in advance to arrange parking space near the Castle and any catering requirements.   Free meal for drivers..
No smoking in the house

FACILITIES FOR THE DISABLED

Disabled and elderly visitors may alight at the Castle entrance. Priority for nearby parking.

PARKING FOR COACHES & CARS

Capacity of the car park: 70 cars and a few coaches. 10-100 yds from the Castle.

GIFT SHOP

Eastnor souvenirs, books, gifts and toys. All excellent value

GUIDE BOOKS

Guide Book, £2.00. Additional room notes in every room.

CATERING

Excellent country house cooking within the Castle for booked events. Home-made light lunches, teas and ice-cream in the Tea Room. Menus on request. Groups please book in advance..

GUIDED TOURS

Throughout the year by appointment

SCHOOL VISITS/CHILDREN

School parties welcome £1.50 per child. Guides available if required. Nature walks in the grounds by experienced warden to complement the national curriculum.

CONFERENCE AND FUNCTION FACILITIES

ROOM	DIMENSIONS	CAPACITY	LAYOUT	POWER POINTS	SUITABLE FOR A/V
Library		120	Various	✓	✓
Great Hall		160	Various	✓	✓
Dining Room		120	Various	✓	✓
Gothic Room		50	Various	✓	✓
Octagon Room		50	Various	✓	✓

BERRINGTON HALL

Open
26 Mar-end Sept.
Daily except
Mon & Tues.
(open Bank Hol.
Mons, closed
Good Fri.)
1.30pm-5.30pm
Oct. Wed to Sun
1.30-4.30pm
Last admissions
30 mins before
closing.
Grounds open
from 12.30. Park
Walk open Jul.
Aug. Sept & Oct.
times as house.

BERRINGTON HALL LEOMINSTER TEL: 0568 615721
(The National Trust)

An elegant late 18th century house, designed by Henry Holland and set in a 'Capability' Brown park: the formal exterior belies the delicate interior with beautifully decorated ceiling and fine furniture and a restored bedroom suite, nursery, Victorian laundry and pretty tiled Georgian dairy. Attractive garden with interesting plants and historic apple orchard in walled garden.

Location: 3 miles north of Leominster, 7 miles south of Ludlow on west side of A49.
Admission: Adult £3.50, child £1.75. Family ticket £9.60 (2 adults + up to 4 children). Grounds only £1.60.

Burton Court, Eardisland.
(05447) 231 5 miles west of Leominster between A44 and A4112.

CROFT CASTLE

OPEN
April & October
Sat & Sun.
2.00.--5.00-pm
Easter Sat, Sun &
Mon 2.00-
6.00pm
Closed Good Fri.
May to end Sept.
Wed. to Sun. &
Bank Hol Mons.
2.00-6.00pm
Last admission
30 mins. before
house closing.

CROFT CASTLE, LEOMINSTER TEL: 0568 780246
(The National Trust)

Home of the Croft family since Domesday (with a break of 170 years from 1750); walls and corner towers date from 14th and 15th centuries; interior mainly 18th century when the fine Georgian-Gothic staircase and plasterwork ceilings were added; splendid avenue of 350 year old Spanish chestnuts. Iron Age fort (Croft Ambrey) may be reached by footpath.

Location: 5 miles north west of Leominster, 9 miles south west of Ludlow; approach from B4362.
Admission: £3.00 adult, £1.50 child, £8.25 Family ticket (2 adults + up to 4 children).

Cwmmau Farmhouse, Brilley, Whitney-on-Wye.
(0497) 831251 4 miles south west of Kington between A4111 and A438.

Goodrich Castle, Ross on Wye.
(0600) 890538 3 miles south west of Ross-on-Wye.

Hellens, Much Marcle.
(0531) 84440 In the village of Much Marcle on Ledbury/Ross road.

HERGEST CROFT GARDENS

OPEN
April 1-Oct. 30
1.30pm-6.30pm

Winter
By appointment
only.

HERGEST CROFT GARDENS, KINGTON TEL: 0544 230160
(W L Banks and R A Banks)

From spring bulbs to autumn colour this is a garden for all seasons. One of the finest collections of trees and shrubs developed over 130 years by four generations of the Banks family. An old fashioned kitchen garden has spring and summer borders. Park wood is a hidden valley with Rhododendrons up to 30 feet tall.

Location: Situated on the west side of Kington. 1/2 mile off A44 turn left at Rhayader end of bypass. Turn right and gardens are 1/4 mile on left. Signposted from bypass.
Admission: Adult/OAP £2.30, Child under 15 Free. Groups: Adult/OAP £1.80, Child Free.

Hill Court Gardens and Garden Centre, Hom Green, Ross-on-Wye
(0989) 763123 B4234 from Ross-on-Wye.

How Caple Court Gardens, How Caple.
(098986) 626 B4224 Ross-on-Wye 4 1/2 miles.

Kentchurch Court, Hereford.
(0981) 240228 Off B4347, 3 miles south east of Pontrilas.

Kinnersley Castle, Kinnersley.
(05446) 407 4 miles west of Weobley on A4112.

Lower Brockhampton, Bromyard.
(0885) 488099 2 miles east of Bromyard.

Moccas Court, Moccas.
(0981) 500381 10 miles east of Hay on Wye. 1 mile off B4352.

The Weir, Swainshill, near Hereford.
(0684) 850051 (Regional Office) 5 miles west of Hereford on A438.

EASTNOR CASTLE

MOCCAS COURT

HATFIELD HOUSE
Hatfield, Hertfordshire

This celebrated Jacobean house, which stands in its own great park, was built between 1607 and 1611 by Robert Cecil, 1st Earl of Salisbury and Chief Minister to King James I. It has been the family home of the Cecils ever since.

The main designer was Robert Lyminge helped, it is thought, by the young Inigo Jones. The interior decoration was the work of English, Flemish and French craftsmen, notably Maximilian Colt. The State Rooms are rich in world-famous paintings including The Rainbow Portrait of Queen Elizabeth I, and The Ermine Portrait by Nicholas Hilliard. Other paintings include works by Hoefnagel, Mytens, John de Critz the Elder and Sir Joshua Reynolds. Fine furniture from the 16th,

17th and 18th Centuries, rare tapestries and historic armour can be found in the State Rooms.

Within the delightful gardens stands the surviving wing of The Royal Palace of Hatfield (1497) where Elizabeth I spent much of her girlhood and held her first Council of State in November 1558. Some of her possessions can be seen in the House.

GARDENS

The West Gardens contain a formal garden, a scented garden with a herb garden at its centre, and a knot garden, planted with plants and bulbs which would have grown there in the 15th, 16th and 17th Centuries.

CONTACT

Col D McCord
Hatfield House
Hatfield
Hertfordshire
AL9 5NQ

Tel: (0707) 262823
Fax: (0707) 275719

LOCATION

21 miles North of London, A1(M), 8 miles North of M25 on A1000.

Bus: Local bus services from St Albans, Hertford, Hitchen and Barnet.

Rail: From Kings Cross and Moorgate every 30 minutes. Hatfield BR Station is immediately opposite entrance to Park.

SUITABILITY FOR OTHER EVENTS

Archery, equestrian events, shows, filming, wedding receptions, lunches and dinners up to 250 people.

EXTRA FACILITIES

The National Collection of Model Soldiers, 3,000 models in panoramic display. William IV Kitchen Exhibition. Nature Trails with supporting handbook or leaflet. Small children's Venture Play Area. Indoor and outdoor picnic areas.

ADVICE TO COURIERS & DRIVERS

Hardstanding for coaches. No dogs in House or gardens, and only in Park on leads. No photography is allowed in the House.

FACILITIES FOR THE DISABLED

Disabled and elderly visitors may alight at the entrance to the House, before parking. Toilet and lift facilities for the disabled.

PARKING FOR COACHES & CARS

Unlimited free parking for cars and coaches.

CATERING

The Old Palace Yard Restaurant/Coffee Shop seats up to 120. Prices from £2.00 to £6.00. Pre-booked lunch and tea available for parties of 10 or more: (0707) 262030. Special rates offered

for groups. Catering facilities for special functions can be arranged Elizabethan Banquets held in the Old Palace throughout the year: (0707) 262055.

GUIDED TOURS

Groups of 40 or more are split into two, no extra charge for tour. Available in French, German, Italian or Spanish, by prior arrangement. Garden tours may be booked in advance: price £10.00 per tour. Hours Tours can be tailored to special interests.

GIFT AND GARDEN SHOPS

Open one hour before the House, selling items such as pot pourri made at Hatfield. Open six weekends prior to Christmas

GUIDE BOOKS

House Guide Book £1.20, Garden Guide Book £1.70. Leaflets available in French, German, Spanish, Italian and Japanese

SCHOOL VISITS/CHILDREN

Groups are welcome. 1 teacher free per 15 children. A guide is provided. Areas of interest include: kitchen exhibition, model soldier collection, adventure playground and picnic trails.

OPENING TIMES

Summer
25 March - 9 October

PARK
Daily   10.30am - 8pm

GARDENS
Daily   11am - 6pm
Last entry 5pm

March to July:
Closed Sundays

HOUSE
Mon   Closed
Tues
Wed   12 noon - 5pm
Thurs   Last admission
Fri   4.00pm
Sat
Sun   1.30 - 5.00pm

NB Open Easter, May Day, Spring and August Bank Hol Mondays.
11am - 5pm
Closed Good Friday

Winter
10 October - 24 March
Closed.

ADMISSION

EXHIBITION, HOUSE & GARDENS
Adult   £4.70
Child*   £3.10
OAP   £3.90
Group**
  Adult   £3.90
  Child*   £2.60

EXHIBITION, PARK & GARDENS
Adult   £2.60
Child*   £2.00
OAP   £2.40
Group**
  Adult   £2.40
  Child*   £1.80

* Aged 5-15
** Min 20 people

CONFERENCE AND FUNCTION FACILITIES

ROOM	DIMENSIONS	CAPACITY	LAYOUT	POWER POINTS	SUITABLE FOR A/V
The Old Palace	112'x33'	300	Theatre	3	✓
		240	Schoolroom		
		100	U-shape		
		250	Buffet		
		250	Dinner/Dance		
		250	Lunch/Dinner		

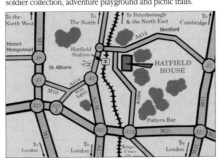

KNEBWORTH HOUSE
Knebworth, Hertfordshire

Knebworth House has been the home of the Lytton family for over 500 years. Originally a Tudor Manor House, it was transformed 150 years ago with spectacular High Gothic decoration by Victorian romantic novelist Edward Bulwer-Lytton. There are many beautiful rooms, important portraits and furniture. The magnificent Jacobean Hall, where Charles Dickens acted in private theatricals and Winston Churchill painted at his easel, recently underwent restoration work which revealed an unknown early 17th Century hand-painted archway under the original panelling, now on permanent display to the public. Knebworth was the home of Constance Lytton, the suffragette, and Robert Lytton, Viceroy of India. Lord Lytton's Viceroyalty and the Great Delhi Durbar of 1877 are commemorated in a fascinating exhibition and audio-visual display.

GARDENS

The elaborate formal gardens of the Victorian era were simplified by Sir Edwin Lutyens. The unique quincunx pattern Herb Garden was designed for Knebworth in 1907 by Gertrude Jekyll and contains a delightful mixture of many herbs. The House stands in 250 acres of parkland, with herds of Red and Sika Deer, Fort Knebworth, (a large Adventure Playground) Miniature Railway and is the setting for many Special Events

CONTACT

John Hoy
The Estate Office
Knebworth House
Knebworth
Hertfordshire
SG3 6PY

Tel: (0438) 812661
Fax: (0438) 811908

LOCATION

Public entrance direct from A1(M) at Junct. 7, 30 miles North of Central London and 12 miles North of M25.

Rail: Stevenage Station 2 miles (from Kings Cross).

Coach: 797 from Victoria.

Air: Luton Airport 8mls.

Taxi: (0438) 811122.

Landing facilities

SUITABILITY FOR OTHER EVENTS

Fashion shows, air displays, archery, clay pigeon shooting, equestrian events, garden parties, shows, rallies and filming. Marquees and semi-permanent structures can be erected for a variety of requirements. Knebworth Park holds the Corporate Hospitality Association's 'Non-Sporting Venue of the Year' Award for 1992.

EXTRA FACILITIES

Evening House tours available by prior arrangement. Parkland, cricket pitch, helicopter landing facilities and Knebworth Barns (capacity 450) are all available for use. Speciality evenings, incorporating full use of all Knebworth facilities, can be arranged to suit your requirements. These include Indian Raj Evenings and Elizabethan Banquets with jousting.

ADVICE TO COURIERS & DRIVERS

All group visits must be booked in advance with Estate Office. In the House no dogs, pushchairs, photography, smoking or drinking are allowed. Wheelchairs are welcome in the House. Dogs on leads are allowed in the Park.

FACILITIES FOR THE DISABLED

Disabled and elderly visitors may be driven to the entrance to the House, before parking in the allocated areas. The ground floor of the House is accessible to wheelchairs.

PARKING FOR CARS & COACHES

Parking for coaches and cars is unlimited.

CATERING BY LYTTON CATERING

Restaurant in 400 year old tithe barn. Special rates are available for groups who can book in advance. Menus available on request. Lytton Catering offers a full catering service in the Park as well as an extensive high quality outside catering service.

GUIDED TOURS

Guided tours operate on Tuesday - Friday, at approx 30 minute intervals, or at specifically booked times up to 4.30pm. Tours at other times, including evenings, are available by prior arrangement. Average time taken for tour 1 hour. Shorter tours by arrangement. Room Wardens on duty at weekends. A special 'Gothick Visions' tour is now available.

GIFT SHOPS

Open when the House is open to the public. Colour Guide Book £2.50 (1993 price).

SCHOOL VISITS/CHILDREN

National Curriculum based worksheets and children's guide available, covering a variety of topics ranging from the Tudors to the Victorians.

OPENING TIMES

Summer

PARK & FORT KNEBWORTH
Daily
26 March-17 April and 28 May-4 Sept.
Plus: Weekends and Bank Hols from 23 April-22 May; and weekends only from 10 Sept-2 Oct.

HOUSE AND GARDENS
As above but closed Mondays, except Bank Holiday Mondays.

HOURS
Park & Fort Knebworth
11am - 5.30pm
House and Gardens
12noon - 5.00pm

Pre-booked Parties
26 March - 2 October
(Subject to special events)

Winter
Closed, except to pre-booked parties.

ADMISSION

All Year

HOUSE, GARDEN, PARK & FORT KNEBWORTH
Adult	£4.50
Child*	£4.00
OAP	£4.00
Group**	
Adult	£3.60
Child*	£3.20
Sen.Citizen	£3.20

PARK & PLAYGROUND ONLY
Adult/Sen.Citizen	£3.00
Child*	£3.00
GROUP**	£2.40

* Age 3-16
**Minimum payment 20 people

CONFERENCE AND FUNCTION FACILITIES

ROOM	DIMENSIONS	CAPACITY	LAYOUT	POWER POINTS	SUITABLE FOR A/V
Banqueting Hall	26'x41'	45-80	Various	2	
Dining Parlour	21'x38'	25-50	Various	3	
Library	32'x21'	20-40	Various	2	
In Knebworth Barns Conference & Banqueting Centre, adjacent to Knebworth House:					
Manor Barn	70'x25'	50-300	Various	8	✓
Lodge Barn	75'x30'	30-250	Various	6	

ROSSWAY PARK
Berkhamsted, Hertfordshire

ROSSWAY PARK is probably the finest example of a privately-owned family estate within the green belt. It lies just south of Berkhamsted and has good access from the north and London.

The house itself is an excellent example of a mid-19th Century residence, retaining many of its original architectural and domestic features. It has been meticulously restored and the use of authenticated colours, fabrics and materials have re-created its high Victorian splendour.

Guests are assured of complete privacy and the exclusive use of the house's facilities whilst at Rossway. Apart from the usual conference and catering requirements, a full range of outdoor activities can be organised in the extensive parkland.

The Hadden-Patons work very hard to create an atmosphere that is at once business-like and professional, yet warm and friendly. Clients are very much treated as guests, with personalised service and attention to detail being their hallmark.

OPENING TIMES

All Year for Corporate Events, Conferences, Functions,etc.

RATES

CONFERENCES

From £47.50 per person inclusive of venue hire and full catering.

ACTIVITY DAYS

from £52.50 per person inclusive of venue hire and full catering.

CONTACT

Nigel Hadden-Paton
Rossway Park
Berkhamsted
Hertfordshire
HP4 3TZ

Tel: (0442) 865160
Fax: (0442) 863697

LOCATION

Road: Just south of Berkhamsted (A41 By-Pass) with good access from M1 (exit 12 from North, exit 8 from London), M25 (exit 20) and M40 (exit 2)

Rail: Berkhamsted Station (Euston).

Taxi: Gates
Tel: 0442 870223.

SUITABILITY FOR OTHER EVENTS

Wedding Receptions, Dances, Lunch and Dinner parties. Large-scale Corporate events with full Event Management available. Film and still photography location work.

EXTRA FACILITIES

Outdoor heated swimming-pool. Trout fishing. Tennis Court. Six mile Riding Course with jumps. Croquet Lawn, Cricket Pitch..

ADVICE TO COURIERS & DRIVERS

Note that the A41 By-Pass from M25 (Exit 20) is now open. Use A416 Chesham exit.

Guests to use main entrance, sub-contractors use Farm entrance.

FACILITIES FOR THE DISABLED

The toilets are not specially built but are able to accommodate disabled guests.

CATERING

In-house catering of the highest quality is available. Three outside caterers are used on a regular basis.

ACCOMMODATION

May sometimes be available in connection with events. Please enquire for further details.

CONFERENCE AND FUNCTION FACILITIES

ROOM	DIMENSIONS	CAPACITY	LAYOUT	POWER POINTS	SUITABLE FOR A/V
Drawing Room	30'x18'	36	Schoolroom	8	✓
		18	U-Shape		
		22	Boardroom		
		40	Theatre		
Library	15'x15'	8	Boardroom	4	✓
Dining Room	26'x18'	60	Buffet		
		40	Lunch/Dinner		

Ashridge, Berkhamsted.
(0442) 843491 3¹/₂ miles north of Berkhamsted A41.

BENINGTON LORDSHIP GARDENS

OPEN

Gardens only
April-August
Weds & Bank
Hold Mons.
12noon-5.00pm
Sundays
2.00-5.00pm

Weds. only in
September.

House closed

BENINGTON LORDSHIP GARDENS, STEVENAGE
TEL: 0438 869668
(C H A Bott Esq)

Terraced garden on the spectacular site of a Norman castle ruins, fine folly, double herbaceous borders, roses, rockery, kitchen garden with unusual vegetables grown in raised beds and small nursery surround Queen Ann manor overlooking lakes and parkland..

Location: In village of Benington next to the church.
Admission: Adults £2.20. Children Free. Disabled and wheelchairs Free.

BENINGTON LORDSHIP GARDENS

Cromer Windmill, Ardley, Stevenage.
(0438) 861293 Adjoins B1037 between Walkern and Cottered.

The Gardens of the Rose, Chiswell Green, St. Albans.
(0727) 50461 Off B4630 (formerly A412).

Gorhambury, St Albans.
(0727) 54051 2 miles west of St Albans.

Moor Park Mansion, near Rickmansworth.
(0923) 776611 1 mile south east of Rickmansworth.

Scott's Grotto, Ware.
(0920) 464131 Scott's Road, Ware off A119 Hertford Road.

HATFIELD

OSBORNE HOUSE
East Cowes, Isle of Wight

This was Queen Victoria's seaside residence built at her own expense in 1845. The Prince Consort played a prominent part in the design of the house, it was his version of an Italian villa, and the work was carried out by Thomas Cubitt, the famous London builder. The Queen died here in 1901 and her private apartments have been preserved more or less unaltered. Crowded with furniture and bric-a-brac they epitomise the style we call "Victorian". also see the Queen's bathing machine. There is a carriage drawn by horse running from House to the Swiss Cottage Gardens and Museum. This is included in the admission price.

CONTACT

The House Administrator
Osborne House
Royal Apartments
East Cowes
Isle of Wight
PO32 6JY

Tel: (0983) 200022

LOCATION

1 mile south east of East Cowes.

Isle of Wight ferry terminal: East Cowes.

SUITABILITY FOR OTHER EVENTS

No conference facilities available. Events held in the grounds

ADVICE TO COURIERS & DRIVERS

Allow plenty of time for visitors to view the house and grounds.

FACILITIES FOR THE DISABLED

The exterior and ground floor are suitable for visitors in wheelchairs.

PARKING FOR COACHES & CARS

Plenty of car and coach spaces available.

CATERING

There is a Restaurant. Groups should book in advance.

GUIDED TOURS

These are available, telephone in advance for information.

GIFT SHOP

The gift shop contains a large selection of souvenirs and postcards.

GUIDE BOOK

Souvenir Guide available.

SCHOOL VISITS/CHILDREN

Visits by schools are free if booked well in advance. An education room is available for schools. Please contact House Administrator for details.

OPENING TIMES

Summer

April - October

Daily   10am-5pm

ADMISSION

Summer

Adult	£5.50
Child	£2.75
OAP/Students/ UB40 Holders	£4.10

Grounds only	
Adult	£2.60
Child	£1.30
OAP/Students/ UB40 Holders	£1.95

GROUPS

15% off groups of 11 or more.

Appuldurcombe House, Wroxall
(0983) 852484 1½ mile west of Wroxall.

Carisbrooke Castle.
(0983) 522107 1½ miles south west of Newport.

The Needles Old Battery, West Highdown, Totland Bay.
(0983) 754772 At Needles Headland, west of Freshwater Bay.

Newtown Old Town Hall, Newtown.
(0983) 741052 In Newtown midway between Newport and Yarmouth.

Nunwell House and Gardens, Brading.
(0983) 407240 1 miles from Brading, turning off A3055. 3 miles south of Ryde.

Yarmouth Castle, Yarmouth.
(0983) 760678

OSBORNE HOUSE, ISLE OF WIGHT

BOUGHTON MONCHELSEA PLACE
Nr Maidstone, Kent

A BATTLEMENTED MANOR HOUSE of Kentish Ragstone, situated above its own landscaped deer park. The house was built in 1576 by Robert Rudston. The home of the late Michael Winch, the house has been in the Winch family since 1903. Standing in a prominent position 310 feet above sea level with the 'reputed' finest view of the Weald of Kent.

The interior is still that of an inhabited home, and contains fine examples of period furniture and works of art to which successive generations have added. Displays of dresses and agricultural bygones.

GARDENS AND GROUNDS

The 60 acre Deer Park has a herd of fallow deer - records of which go back as far as 1669. Two walled gardens: the lower contains a fine mixture of unusual herbaceous plants and shrubs, the top older varieties of fruit trees and unusual shrubs.

SUITABILITY FOR OTHER EVENTS

Wedding Receptions, fashion shows, product launches, conferences, seminars, clay pigeon shoots, archery, quad biking, fly fishing casting, garden parties, fetes, filming. Exquisite site for marquees.

EXTRA FACILITIES

Deer Park.

ADVICE TO COURIERS & DRIVERS

Free refreshments for coach drivers and couriers. No photography or dogs in the House.

FACILITIES FOR THE DISABLED

Disabled toilets available. Disabled and elderly visitors may alight at the rear entrance to the House. Access for disabled into Tea Room and lower floor of the House.

PARKING FOR COACHES & CARS

Unlimited parking for cars and coaches 300 yards from House.

CATERING

Afternoon Teas in Tudor Tea Room, or Inner Courtyard (weather permitting). Lunches, Suppers, Dinners available, menus on request.

PRIVATE DINING

Luncheons, Suppers and Dinners in House (Max. formal seating 45 in either Red Dining Room, Drawing Room or Courtyard Room; informal (buffets) 140 in House, 55 in Courtyard Room.

GIFT SHOP

The Gift Shop is open whenever house is open.

GUIDED TOURS

Visitors are always guided. Average time taken to see the House 55 minutes.

GUIDE BOOKS

Colour guide book available.

SCHOOL VISITS/CHILDREN

Educational Booklet available. Discounted admission. Any day during open season, by prior arrangement. Groups of 20 or more.

GROUP VISITS

By prior arrangement. On days of the week morning or afternoon, during open season. Discounted admission. Groups of 20 or more).

CONTACT

C W Gooch
Boughton Monchelsea Place
Boughton Monchelsea
Maidstone
Kent
ME17 4BU

Tel: (0622) 743120

LOCATION

Junction 8 off M20, take B2163 through Leeds to A274. Cross A274 on to B2163. Boughton Monchelsea Place is 3 miles on left. 4½ miles south of Maidstone. A229 from Maidstone at Linton on B2163. London 1 hour, 10 mins.

Rail: Maidstone Station

OPENING TIMES

Summer

Easter - 9 October
Sun   2.00pm - 6pm

June, July & August
Wed   2.00pm - 6pm

Bank Holiday Mondays & Sundays
      2.00 - 6.0pm

Last Tour 5.15pm

Groups by appointment at any time.

Winter
October - Easter

Closed

ADMISSION

HOUSE & Grounds
Adult	£3.75
Child*	£2.50
OAP/Disabled	£3.50
Group**	
Adult	£3.25
Child*	£2.25
OAP/Disabled	£3.25

GROUNDS ONLY
Adult	£2.25
Child*	£1.50
OAP/Disabled	£2.50
Group**	
Adult	£2.25
Child*	£1.75
OAP/Disabled	£2.25

* Aged 0-14
** Min 20 people.

CONFERENCE AND FUNCTION FACILITIES

ROOM	DIMENSIONS	CAPACITY	LAYOUT	POWER POINTS	SUITABLE FOR A/V
Red Dining Room	31'3"x19'6"	25-60	Various	3	✓
Drawing Room	31'3"x19'6"	25-60	Various	5	✓
Courtyard Room	36'9"x13'5"	25-75	Various	8	✓
Entrance Hall	26'x19'	50-60	Buffet	2	✓

CHILHAM CASTLE GARDENS
Chilham, Kent

CHILHAM CASTLE has a continuous history of nearly 1,000 years behind it, for beneath the Castle Keep, built by Henry II in 1170, lies an earlier hall which must have been standing when William the Conqueror passed through Kent on his way to London to be crowned in Westminster Abbey on Christmas Day. Now beside the old Castle, overlooking the valley of the River Stour, stands a magnificent Jacobean Manor House built by Sir Dudley Digges in 1616.

GARDENS

A garden of terraces, trees and a lake have been made on the slope down to the river. The garden was originally laid out by Tradescant for Sir Dudley Digges but in the late 18th Century this was all but destroyed by Capability Brown who landscaped the Park. This can still be admired with its clumps of trees and distant views. The garden was gradually recreated in the 19th and 20th Centuries so that today there are terraces, a tiny woodland, a rose garden and a 3½ acre lake with a walk round it approached by a delightful rock and water garden with trees and shrubs of many sorts.

SUITABILITY FOR OTHER EVENTS

Fashion shows, archery, clay pigeon shooting, equestrian events, garden parties, wedding receptions, concerts, operas, dinners/dances, filming and corporate hospitality.

EXTRA FACILITIES

Clay pigeon shooting. Archery. Exhibitions, either open air or in marquees.

ADVICE TO COURIERS & DRIVERS

Groups admitted at party rate. Tudor village of Chilham with antique and gift shops, and friendly local pub should also be visited.

FACILITIES FOR THE DISABLED

Disabled and elderly visitors may alight at the entrance to the Castle, before parking. No disabled toilets or ramps provided.

PARKING FOR COACHES & CARS

Capacity of the car park: 300 cars, 100 yards from the Castle, and 24+ coaches, 150 yards away.

CATERING

The Tea Room/Restaurant can cater for 50-60 people. Prices range from £1.70 - £7.00. Groups must book in advance for meals. Menus are available on request. Catering facilities are available for special functions and conferences when buffets, lunches, dinners, dances and wedding receptions can be booked. Medieval Banquets a speciality.

GIFT SHOP

The shop is open daily from 12 noon - 5pm.

GUIDE BOOKS

Colour guide book, price 70p.

SCHOOL VISITS/CHILDREN

Items of particular interest include birds of prey which are flown daily except Mondays and Fridays.

OPENING TIMES

Summer
House open by appointment only.

27 March - 16 October
Garden Open

Mon		
Tues		
Wed	11am - 6pm	
Thurs	Last entry 5pm	
Fri		
Sat		
Sun		

Winter
17 October - 8 April

Closed

ADMISSION

Summer
GARDEN ONLY
Adult	£3.00
Child*	£1.50
OAP	£2.50
Group**	
Adult	£2.50
Child*	£1.25
OAP	£2.50

* Aged 5-15
** Min 20 people.

Winter
Closed

CONFERENCE AND FUNCTION FACILITIES

ROOM	DIMENSIONS	CAPACITY	LAYOUT	POWER POINTS	SUITABLE FOR A/V
Gothic Hall	60'x20'	220	Theatre	8	✓
		103	Schoolroom		
		125	Buffet		
		125	Dinner/Dance		
		125	Lunch/Dinner		
Red Room	30'x15'	88	Theatre	4	✓
		40	Schoolroom		
		45	Dinner/Dance		
		45	Lunch/Dinner		

COBHAM HALL
Cobham, Kent

"One of the largest, finest and most important houses in Kent" Cobham Hall is an outstandingly beautiful, red brick mansion in Elizabethan, Jacobean, Carolean and 18th Century styles.

It yields much of interest to the student of art, architecture and history. The Elizabethan wings were begun in 1584 whilst the central section contains the Gilt Hall, wonderfully decorated by John Webb, Inigo Jones' most celebrated pupil, 1654. Further rooms were decorated by James Wyatt in the 18th century.

Cobham Hall, now a girls' school, has been visited by several of the English monarchs from Elizabeth I to Edward VIII, later Duke of Windsor. Charles Dickens used to walk through the grounds from his house in Higham to the Leather Bottle Pub in Cobham Village. In 1883, the Hon Ivo Bligh, later the 8th Earl of Dranley, led the victorious English cricket team against Australia bringing home the "Ashes" to Cobham.

GARDENS

The gardens, landscaped for the 4th Earl by Humphry Repton, are gradually being restored by the Cobham Hall Heritage Trust. Extensive tree planting and clearing have taken place since the hurricanes of the 1980s. The Gothic Dairy and some of the classical garden buildings are being renovated. The gardens are particularly delightful in Spring, when they are resplendent with daffodils and a myriad of rare bulbs.

CONTACT

Mrs Sue Anderson
Cobham Hall
Cobham
Kent
DA12 3BL

Tel: (0474)
824319/823371
Fax: (0474) 822995

LOCATION

Cobham Hall is situated adjacent to the A2/M2, 8 miles east of Junc. 2 on M25, between Gravesend and Rochester.
London - 25 miles
Rochester - 5 miles
Canterbury 30 miles

Rail: Meopham 3 miles.
Gravesend 5 miles.
Taxi rank at both stations.

Air: Gatwick 45 mins.
Heathrow 60 mins,
Stansted 50 mins.

SUITABILITY FOR OTHER EVENTS

Cobham Hall is a unique venue for any function, business or social. Providing for residential (250 beds) or non-residential courses. A wide choice of period or modern rooms, including the magnificent 1,200 sq.m .Gilt Hall, to suit every occasion. 150 acres of parkland ideal for sports events and open air concerts.

EXTRA FACILITIES

New multi-purpose sports centre and indoor 25m swimming pool. Use of Art Studios, Music Wing, Tennis Courts. Helicopter landing area, field study area, nature conservation. Lectures on the property, gardens and history can be arranged in the Gilt Hall for up to 180 people.

ADVICE TO COURIERS & DRIVERS

Pre-booked coach parties are welcome outside advertised opening times. Coffee, teas, lunch (cap. 200). Special events days. No smoking. Large free parking area.

FACILITIES FOR THE DISABLED

Disabled and elderly visitors should be aware that the house tour involves two staircases. Limited access for wheelchairs, ground floor only.

CATERING

Excellent in-house catering team for private and corporate events (cap. 200). Afternoon Teas served when open to public. Other meals by arrangement.

GUIDED TOURS

All tours guided: Historical guided tours of house for up to 25 people; time taken 1¹/2 hours. Tours of garden by arrangement.

GIFT SHOP

Open as House. Guide books of house and garden, £1 each.

SCHOOL VISITS/CHILDREN

Guide provided, £2.00 per child: special guide book and worksheets for 1994..

CONFERENCE AND FUNCTION FACILITIES

ROOM	DIMENSIONS	CAPACITY	LAYOUT	POWER POINTS	SUITABLE FOR A/V
Gilt Hall	41'x34'	180	Theatre	4	✓
		90	Banquet		
Wyatt Dining Room	49'x23'	135	Theatre	6	✓
		85			
Clifton Dining Room	24'x23'	75	Theatre	3	✓
		50	Banquet		
Activities Centre	119'x106'	300	Theatre	10	✓
		250	Banquet		

HEVER CASTLE
Nr Edenbridge, Kent

HEVER CASTLE dates back to 1270, when the gatehouse, outer walls and the inner moat were first built. 200 years later the Bullen (or Boleyn) family added the comfortable Tudor Manor house constructed within the walls. This was the childhood home of Anne Boleyn, Henry VIII's second wife and mother of Elizabeth I. A costume exhibition in the Long Gallery includes all of the familiar characters from this royal romance. The Castle was later given to Henry VIII's fourth wife, Anne of Cleves.

In 1903, the estate was bought by the American millionaire William Waldorf Astor, who became a British subject and the First Lord Astor of Hever. He invested an immense amount of time, money and imagination in restoring the castle and grounds. Master craftsmen were employed and the castle was filled with a magnificent collection of furniture, tapestries and other works of art.

This year a new miniature model houses exhibition has been opened in the grounds of the castle focusing on life in country houses through the ages.

GARDENS

Between 1904-8 over 30 acres of formal gardens were laid out and planted, these have now matured into one of the most beautiful gardens in England. The unique Italian garden is a four acre walled garden containing a superb collection of statuary and sculpture exhibited amongst the flowers and shrubs. Other areas include the rose garden, Anne Boleyn's Tudor style garden, a traditional yew maze and some unusual topiary. The grounds contain many water features, along with a 30 acre lake there are fountains, cascades, grottoes and an inner and outer moat. fountains cascades and pools - and some fine topiary. The yew-hedge maze is open to the public.

SUITABILITY FOR OTHER EVENTS

Filming, product launches and wedding receptions. Dinner dances in Pavilion Restaurant.

EXTRA FACILITIES

Lectures on the property, its contents, gardens and history for up to 70 people in summer and 250 in winter. Prices on application. Projectors, and screen can be provided. Additional facilities for clients using the Tudor Village include outdoor heated pool, tennis court, billiard room, gardens/grounds.

ADVICE TO COURIERS & DRIVERS

Free coach parking. Free admission for driver and tour leader. Voucher for driver. Advisable to book in advance. Group rates for 15+. Allow 2 hours for visit.

FACILITIES FOR THE DISABLED

There are toilets for the disabled. Gardens mostly accessible, but ground floor only of Castle. No ramps into castle so can be difficult. Access to restaurants, gift shop and book shop. Some additional wheelchairs available.

PARKING FOR COACHES & CARS

Capacity of car park - approx 1000 cars, 100 yards from the Castle and 30 coaches, 200 yards from the Castle.

CATERING

Two self-service restaurants offer visitors lunch, tea and refreshments. Supper is provided during Open Air Theatre season. Special rates are offered to groups and menus/prices on request. Catering facilities for special functions/conferences include buffets, lunches and dinners.

SCHOOL VISITS/CHILDREN

School groups are welcome at a cost of £2.40.per child. A guide can be provided for groups of 20 at £4.00. per person. Areas of particular interest: Kent and Sharpshooters Museum, torture instruments, exhibition on Anne Boleyn, adventure playground and maze. 1 teacher/adult free per 10/12 children. Free preparatory visits for teachers within normal opening hours.

GUIDED TOURS

Pre-booked guided tours can be arranged outside normal opening hours. 25 people per guide. Basic £7.70 per head, £9.70 with guide book, £12.45 Connoisseurs including coffee, sherry, and guide book. Tours in French, German, Dutch, Italian, Spanish and Japanese for a small additional premium.

GIFT SHOP/GUIDE BOOKS

The Gift Book and Garden Shops are all open at the same times as the Gardens Castle Guide £2.00 Garden Guide £1.70.

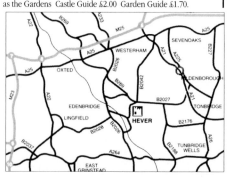

CONTACT

Claire Prout
Hever Castle
Hever
Edenbridge
Kent
TN8 7NG

Tel: (0732) 865224
Fax: (0732) 866796

LOCATION

M25 Junct. 5 and 6
M23 Junct. 10,
A21 North Tonbridge
exit, follow signs.

Rail: Hever Station 1 mile (no taxis), Edenbridge Town 3 miles (taxis).

Taxi: Relyon Car Services, Edenbridge 863800, Beeline Taxis Sevenoaks 456214

OPENING TIMES

Summer
15 March-6 November

DAILY
Gardens Open	11am
Castle Open	12 noon
Last admission	5pm
Closes	6pm

Winter
7 November-Easter

Last admission	4pm
Closes	5pm

Open for pre-booked private guided tours only.

ADMISSION

CASTLE & GARDEN
Adult	£5.20
Child*	£2.60
OAP	£4.70
Family (2+2)	£13.00
Group**	
Adult	£4.60
Child*	£2.40
Student***	£3.40

GARDEN ONLY
Adult	£3.80
Child*	£2.20
OAP	£3.30
Family (2+2)	£9.80
Group**	
Adult	£3.20
Child*	£2.00
Student***	£3.00

*Group = 15 plus people total must be paid in one amount
**Age 5-16
***Age 17-19

Winter
Private guided tour of house & garden
Adults - Min.20
£7.70	Basic Tour
£9.70	Tour & Guide Book
£12.45	Connoisseur Tour.

The Tudor Village was built for William Waldorf Astor in the style of the Tudor period, but with every modern comfort and luxury.

All twenty, individually decorated, rooms have private bathrooms, colour televisions, direct dial telephones, tea/coffee making facilities and hair dryers. Guests can enjoy a Billiard Room, outdoor heated swimming pool, tennis court and croquet lawn.

The village is available year round for groups requiring high standards of accommodation and service, delicious foods and wines and top-level conference facilities. There are three interconnecting reception rooms which can be used for conferences, dining or meetings. There are also a number of smaller syndicate rooms.

The Hever Castle Estate includes Stables House, an imposing five bedroomed property overlooking the River Eden. This is an ideal venue for smaller groups, which can also make use of the Tudor Village amenities.

In addition the magnificent Dining Hall (see picture to the right) in the Castle is available for a truly memorable dinner. Guests can enjoy a private guided tour of the Castle and a Tudor Banquet with minstrels.

Laser Clay Pigeon Shooting, Archery, Fishing, Riding, Golf and other pursuits can be arranged on or near the estate.

In all, the Tudor Village provides a unique and unusual venue for private meetings, receptions, product launches or corporate hospitality.

Hever Castle/Tudor village offers the following accommodation (see picture below):

    4 singles with bath

    10 twins with bath

    6 doubles with bath

    4 twins and 1 double (in the
    Stables House)

CONFERENCE AND FUNCTION FACILITIES

The Dining Hall, Breakfast Room and Sitting Room (which together form the Tudor Suite) are available throughout the year. Smaller seminar rooms are also available. The Pavilion can be hired between November and March.

Overhead projector, carousel projector and screen can be provided and audio-visual equipment hired.

Catering facilities for special functions and conferences include buffets, lunches and dinners.

ROOM	DIMENSIONS	CAPACITY	LAYOUT	POWER POINTS	SUITABLE FOR A/V
Dining Hall	35'x20'	70	Theatre	5	✓
		32	Schoolroom		
		25	U-shape		
		32	Boardroom		
		70	Lunch/Dinner		
Breakfast Room	22'x15'	20	Theatre	3	✓
		16	Schoolroom		
		16	Boardroom		
		16	Lunch/Dinner		
Sitting Room	24'x20'	12	Boardroom	4	✓
		12	Lunch/Dinner		
Pavilion	96'x40	250	Theatre	24	✓
		200	Schoolroom		
		250	Buffet		
		250	Dinner/Dance		
Moat Restaurant	25'x60'	75	Dinner/Dance	6	

LEEDS CASTLE
Maidstone, Kent

Surrounded by 500 acres of magnificent parkland and gardens, and built on two small islands in the middle of a natural lake, Lord Conway christened Leeds "the loveliest Castle in the world."

The site of a manor of the Saxon royal family in the 9th Century, it was then re-built in stone by the Normans and later converted into a Royal Palace by Henry VII.

For some 300 years, the Castle was home to the Kings and Queens of medieval England. Now lovingly restored and beautifully furnished, it contains a magnificent collection of medieval furnishings, tapestries and paintings.

The Castle was purchased in 1926 by the late the Hon Olive, Lady Baillie, whose American Whitney inheritance helped restore the Castle and cement strong Anglo-American links. The Leeds Castle Foundation now preserves the Castle for the nation, hosts important medical conferences and supports the Arts.

A unique collection of Dog Collars can be viewed in the Castle Gate House.

Popular attractions within the Castle grounds include the colourful Culpeper Garden, Wood garden, Duckery, Castle greenhouses and vineyard. An aviary houses rare and endangered species from around the world, beyond which can be found a traditional maze and underground grotto. A challenging nine hole golf course surrounds the Castle, whose moat occasionally comes into play!

CONTACT

Joanna Oswin
Marketing Manager
Leeds Castle
Maidstone
Kent
ME17 1PL

Tel: (0622) 765400
Fax: (0622) 735616

LOCATION

From London, A20/M20, Exit 8, 40 miles, 1 hour .

Rail: BR combined train & admission, London Victoria - Bearsted.

Coach: Nat Express/ Invictaway coach & admission from Victoria.

Air: Gatwick 45 miles, Heathrow 65 miles.

Channel Tunnel: 25 miles.

SUITABILITY FOR OTHER EVENTS

Residential conferences and corporate hospitality (including large scale marquee events); exhibitions, wedding receptions, sporting days with clay shooting, falconry, field archery, hot air ballooning, war games and golf.

EXTRA FACILITIES

Parkland, golf course, croquet lawn, swimming pool and heli-pad. Talks given by specialist staff can be arranged for horticultural, viticultural, historical and cultural groups.

ADVICE TO COURIERS & DRIVERS

Pre-booking is advisable but not essential. Couriers/guides and coach drivers admitted free. Voucher for refreshments. Shuttle transport for the elderly and disabled. No dogs, or radios.

FACILITIES FOR THE DISABLED

Accessible mini-bus, wheelchairs on loan, wheelchair lift in Castle, purpose-built toilets. Special rates-leaflet available.

PARKING FOR COACHES & CARS

5,000 cars and 20 coaches, 800 yds from the Castle. For special functions/tours parking nearer the Castle can be arranged.

CATERING

17th Century tithe barn restaurant offers full range of hot meals, salads and cream teas. Group lunch menus available. For special functions, conferences, buffets and dinners can be arranged.

GUIDED TOURS

Guides in every room except winter mid-week when there are regular guided tours outside normal hours, by appointment.. French, Spanish, Dutch and German. Italian and Russian guides. Average time taken 1 hour.

GIFT SHOPS

Castle Shop, Book Shop, Park Shop and Special Christmas Shop (Nov - Dec).

GUIDE BOOKS

Illustrated Guide available in English, French, German Dutch, Spanish, Italian and Japanese, £3.00. Aviary Guide and Children's Activity Book 95p.

SCHOOL VISITS/CHILDREN

Educational groups welcome, outside normal opening hours private tours can be arranged. Teachers Resource Pack including Fact Sheets and Discovery Sheets on 6 different topics.

OPENING TIMES

Summer
1 March - 31 October

Open Daily .10am-6pm
NB Last Entry 5pm

Winter
November - End February

Open Daily
10am - 4pm
(except Christmas Day)
NB Last Entry 3pm

Also special private tours for pre-booked groups at any other time by appointment

ADMISSION

1994 Rates - from 1 March
CASTLE & PARK

Adult	£7.00
Child*	£4.80
OAP/Student	£6.00
Family (2+2)	£19.50
Disabled Visitors	
Adult	£4.00
Child*	£2.80
Group**	
Adult	£5.50
Child*	£3.80
OAP/Student	£4.50
Disabled Visitors	
Adult	£4.00
Child*	£2.80

PARK & GARDENS

Adult	£5.50
Child*	£3.30
OAP/Student	£4.50
Family (2+2)	£15.00
Disabled Visitors	
Adult	£3.00
Child*	£1.80
Group**	
Adult	£4.50
Child*	£2.80
OAP/Student	£3.50
Disabled Visitors	
Adult	£3.00
Child*	£1.80

* Aged 5-15
** Min 20 people.
Leeds Castle Privilege Card - season pass.

CONFERENCE AND FUNCTION FACILITIES

ROOM	DIMENSIONS	CAPACITY	LAYOUT	POWER POINTS	SUITABLE FOR A/V
Fairfax Hall	64'6"x36'	50-250	Various	✓	✓
Gate Tower	34'x20'	16-120	Various	✓	✓
Culpeper	20'8"x25'	8-30	Various	✓	✓

PENSHURST PLACE
Nr Tonbridge, Kent

PENSHURST PLACE is one of England's greatest family-owned stately homes with a history going back six and a half centuries.

In some ways time has stood still at Penshurst; the great House is still very much a mediaeval building with improvements and additions made over the centuries but without any substantial rebuilding. Its highlight is undoubtedly the mediaeval Baron's Hall, built in 1341, with its impressive 60ft-high chestnut beamed roof.

A marvellous blend of paintings, tapestries and furniture from the 15th, 16th and 17th Centuries can be seen throughout the House, including the helm carried in the state funeral procession to St Paul's Cathedral for the Elizabethan courtier and poet, Sir Philip Sidney, in 1587. This is now the family crest.

The Gardens, first laid out in the 14th Century, have been developed over successive years by the Sidney family who first came to Penshurst in 1552. A twenty-year restoration and re-planting programme undertaken by the late Viscount De L'Isle has ensured that they retain their historic splendour. He is commemorated with a new Arboretum, planted in 1991. The Gardens are divided by a mile of yew hedges into "rooms", each planted to give a succession of colour as the seasons change. There is also a Venture Playground, Nature and Farm Trails for children.

CONTACT

Adrian Gilpin
Penshurst Place
Penshurst
Nr Tonbridge
Kent
TN11 8DG

Tel: (0892) 870307
Fax: (0892) 870866

From London M25 Junct. 5 then A21 to Tonbridge North, B2027 via Leigh; from Tunbridge Wells A26, B2176.

Bus: Maidstone & District 231, 232, 233 from Tunbridge Wells.

Rail: Charing Cross/ Waterloo-Hildenborough, Tonbridge or Tunbridge Wells; then taxi

SUITABILITY FOR OTHER EVENTS

Private Banqueting, product launches, wedding receptions, garden parties, photography, filming, fashion shows.

EXTRA FACILITIES

Archery, clay pigeon shooting. Parkland available for hire for public events, fairs, product launches. Lectures on the property, its contents and history can be arranged for up to 60. Specialist garden tours can be arranged.

ADVICE TO COURIERS & DRIVERS

No access to bus park by double decker buses; these to be parked in village. Entrance arrangements for morning booked parties notified in advance to organisers. No dogs. No photography in the House. Parking for 250 cars and 10 coaches, 25 yds from the House. Further parking for 200 cars and 10 coaches 250 yds from the house.

GUIDED TOURS

Tours available (mornings only) by arrangement. Adult £4.95, child £2.50. Lunch/Dinner can be arranged in Private Dining Room Out of season, tours by appointment: adult £4.95, minimum charge £150.00. Guided tours of the gardens also available at £5.95.

CATERING

Self-service Restaurant for light refreshments, lunches and teas. Restaurant and waitress service can be booked by groups of 20+.

FACILITIES FOR THE DISABLED

Wheelchair-bound visitors' access limited due to age/architecture of buildings. Disabled and elderly visitors may be left at entrance while vehicles are parked in allocated area.

GIFT SHOP

Open seven days a week, hours as House.

GUIDE BOOKS

Colour Guide Book, £2.50. Room Guides available in French, German, Dutch and Japanese.

SCHOOL VISITS/CHILDREN

Visits all year by appointment. Discount rates. Education room and packs available.

OPENING TIMES

Summer
26 March - 2 October

HOUSE
Mon
Tues
Wed
Thurs } 12pm - 5.30pm
Fri
Sat
Sun
Last Entry 5pm

GROUNDS
11.00am - 6pm

Winter
3 October - 26 March

Open to Groups by appointment only (see Guided Tours).
House and Grounds only open weekends in March and October 1994.

ADMISSION

Summer

HOUSE & GARDEN
Adult £4.95
Child* £2.75
Concessions** £4.50
Group***
  Adult £4.50

GARDEN ONLY
Adult £3.50
Child* £2.25
Concessions** £3.00

Wheelchairs Welcome

* Aged 5-16; under 5s FREE.

** Concessions:
OAP/Students/UB40

*** Min 20 people, afternoons only. Special rates for morning Guided Tours

CONFERENCE AND FUNCTION FACILITIES

ROOM	DIMENSIONS	CAPACITY	LAYOUT	POWER POINTS	SUITABLE FOR A/V
Sunderland Room	45'x18'	100	Various	6	✓
Baron's Hall	64'x39'	250	Theatre	4	✓

PHOTOGRAPH: JEREMY WHITAKER

SQUERRYES COURT
Westerham, Kent

SQUERRYES COURT has been the home of the Wardes for over 250 years and is still lived in by the family. It was built in 1681 and is a typical William and Mary Manor House. Formerly owned by the Earl of Jersey, from whom John Warde bought it in 1731, the mellow red brick house stands in a parkland setting. Although only 22 miles from London and easily accessible from the M25, it is in a rural position with a view over the lake to one of the oldest lime avenues in England.

The house is filled with an important collection of Old Master paintings collected by the family in the 18th Century including works by Ruysdael, Breughel, Van Goyen and Van Dyck. There are also pictures by Stubbs, Wootton, Romney and other paintings commissioned from leading English artists of the period. A large still life of fruit and flowers by Peter de Ring has been described as being among the finest of all Dutch still lifes of its scale.

The furniture and porcelain has been in the house since the 18th Century and the Tapestry Room contains a fine set of Soho tapestries made c.1720.

General Wolfe of Quebec was a friend of the family and there are items connected with him in the Wolfe Room.

GARDENS

These were originally laid out in the formal style but were re-landscaped in the 18th Century; fortunately the original lime trees remain. The Victorians planted many fine specimen trees and the family are restoring the formal garden.

CONTACT

Curator or Mrs Warde
Squerryes Court
Westerham
Kent
TN16 1SJ

Tel: (0959)
562345/563118

LOCATION

Off the M25, Junct. 6, 6
`miles, 1/2 mile west of
Westerham.
London 1-1 1/2 hours.

Rail: Oxted Station 4
miles.
Sevenoaks 6 miles.

Air: Gatwick, 30 minutes.

SUITABILITY FOR OTHER EVENTS

Fashion shows, archery, clay pigeon shooting, garden parties, promotions, shows, wedding receptions (marquee in garden).

EXTRA FACILITIES

Grand Piano, Parkland, Lake for fly fishing.

ADVICE TO COURIERS & DRIVERS

Groups welcome any day. Please book in advance. No photography in the House. Dogs on leads in grounds. Free teas for drivers and couriers.

FACILITIES FOR THE DISABLED

Disabled and elderly visitors may alight at the entrance to the property. Toilets for the disabled.

PARKING FOR COACHES & CARS

Parking for up to 60 cars and 2 coaches on the gravel forecourt.

CATERING

Teas are served in the Old Library (capacity 53 people). Parties must book advance for lunch/tea/supper. Menus are available upon request. Teas from £2.20. Lunch/Supper from £5.00. Facilities for buffets, lunches and dinners.

GUIDED TOURS

Available for groups of up to 55 people, small additional charge payable. The owner will meet groups visiting the house, by prior arrangement. Average time to see the house 3/4 hour.

GIFT SHOP

The small Gift Shop is open at the same time as the House.

GUIDE BOOKS

Colour guide book, £1.50.

SCHOOL VISITS/CHILDREN

Groups are welcome, cost £1.50 per child. A guide is provided. Areas of interest include: Nature Walk, ducks and geese.

OPENING TIMES

Summer
March: Sundays only
1 April - 30 September

Mon	Bank Hols only 2pm - 6pm
Tues	Closed
Wed	2pm - 6pm
Thurs	Closed
Fri }	
Sat }	2pm - 6pm
Sun }	

NB Pre-booked groups welcome any day.

Winter
October -end February

Closed

ADMISSION

HOUSE & GARDEN
Adult	£3.50
Child*	£1.60
OAP/Student	£3.20
Groups**	
Adult	£3.00
Child*	£1.50
OAP	£3.00

HOUSE ONLY
Adult	£3.50
Child*	£1.60
OAP	£3.20
Groups**	
Adult	£3.00
Child*	£1.50
OAP	£3.00

GARDEN ONLY
Adult	£2.00
Child*	£1.00
OAP	£1.80
Groups**	
Adult	£1.80
Child*	£0.90
OAP	£1.80

* Aged 0-14
** Min 20 people.

CONFERENCE AND FUNCTION FACILITIES

ROOM	DIMENSIONS	CAPACITY	LAYOUT	POWER POINTS	SUITABLE FOR A/V
Hall	32'x32'	80	Buffet U-shape Boardroom Lunch/Dinner	4	✓
Old Library	20'x25'6"	40	Buffet Boardroom	5	✓

Bedgebury National Pinetum, near Goudhurst.
(0580) 211044 On B2079, 1 mile from A21.

Belmont, near Faversham.
(0795) 890202 4 miles south south west of Faversham.

Black Charles, near Sevenoaks.
(0732) 833036 3 miles south of Sevenoaks off A21.

Chartwell, Westerham.
(0732) 866368 2 miles south of Westerham off B2026.

Chiddingstone Castle, near Edenbridge.
(0892) 870347 In Chiddingstone village off the B2027.

Deal Castle, Deal.
(0304) 372762 Near town centre.

Doddington Place Gardens, near Sittingbourne.
(079586) 385 4 miles from A2 and A20. 5 miles from Faversham.

Dover Castle, Dover.
(0304) 201628 East side of Dover.

Emmetts Garden, near Brasted.
(0732) 750367 1½ miles south of A25 on Sundridge/Ide Hill Road.

Great Maytham Hall, Rolvenden.
½ mile east from Rolvenden villlage.

GREAT COMP GARDENS

OPEN

March 1-Oct.31

Open Daily

11.00am-6.00pm

GREAT COMP GARDEN, BOROUGH GREEN TEL: 0732 886154
(R Cameron Esq)

One of the finest gardens in the country, comprising ruins, terraces, tranquil woodland walks and sweeping lawns with a breathtaking collection of trees, shrubs, heathers and perennials, many rarely seen elsewhere. The truly unique atmosphere of Great Comp is further complemented by its Festival of Chamber Music held in July/September. Unusual plants for sale. Teas most days.

Location: 2 miles east of Borough Green, B2016 off A20. First right at Comp crossroads. ½ mile on left.
Admission: Adults £2.50, children £1.00. Parties of 20+ adults £2.00. Annual tickets £7.50.. OAP's £5.00.

FINCHCOCKS

OPEN

Easter Sunday-
25 Sept.
Suns & Bank Hol
Mons.
Daily in August
except Mons &
Tues.
2.00-6.00pm

April-October.
By appointment
most days

FINCHCOCKS, GOUDHURST TEL: 0580 211702
(Mr and Mrs Richard Burnett)

Fine early Georgian house, facade attributed to Thomas Archer, in beautiful garden and park, containing magnificent collection of early keyboards in full concert condition. Music whenever house is open. Many musical events. Fully licensed cellar restaurant . Newly restored wall garden suitable for outside events.

Location: Off A262, 1 mile from Goudhurst, 10 miles from Tunbridge Wells.
Admission: From £4.50

Gad's Hill Place, Rochester.
(047482) 2366 On A226, 3 miles from Rochester.

Godinton Park, Ashford.
1 mile west of Ashford off Maidstone Road A20.

Goodnestone Park, near Canterbury.
(0304) 840107 8 miles south east of Canterbury.

GROOMBRIDGE PLACE

OPEN

Gardens only
April & May
Weekends &
Bank Holidays

1 June-30 Sept.
Daily (except
Thurs & Fri)

October
First & second
weekends only

2.00-6.00pm

GROOMBRIDGE PLACE, TUNBRIDGE WELLS TEL: 0892 863999
(Mr Andrew de Candole)

The setting for Peter Greenaway's smash hit film "The Draughtsman's Contract". Surrounded by breathtaking parkland, ancient and mystical woodland with spring fed pools and dramatic views over the weald, this medieval site contains the famous Grade I listed 17th century walled gardens and moated Groombridge Place which have enchanted and inspired writers, artists and connoisseurs of beauty for hundreds of years.

Location: Groombridge is 4 miles south west of Tunbridge Wells.
Admission: Gardens & Woodland £3.00, child under 17/OAP £2.00. Group tours (Min 20) special rates by prior arrangement.

BELMONT

Haxted Mill and Museum, Haxted near Edenbridge.
Summer (0732) 865720 Winter (0306) 887979 1½ miles west of Edenbridge.

Ightham Mote, Ivy Hatch.
(0732) 810378 3 miles south of Igtham off A227.

Knole, Sevenoaks.
(0732) 450608 At the Tonbridge end of Sevenoaks.

Ladham House Gardens, Goudhurst.
11 miles east of Tonbridge Wells, off A262.

Lullingstone Castle, Eynsford.
(0322) 862114 In the Darenth valley via Eynsford on A225.

Lullingstone Roman Villa, Eynsford.
(0322) 863467 ½ mile south west of Eynsford.

Lympne Castle, near Hythe.
(0303) 267571 3 miles north west of Hythe off B2067.

Mount Ephraim Gardens, Hernhill, near Faversham.
(0227) 751310 6 miles west of Canterbury.

New College of Cobham, Cobham
(0474) 814280 4 miles west of Rochester.

South Forelands Lighthouse, Dover.
On cliff top between Dover and St Margaret's Bay.

Stoneacre, Otham.
(0622) 862871 3 miles south east of Maidstone.

Tonbridge Castle, Tonbridge.
(0732) 770929 In town centre, off High Street, Tonbridge.

NORTHBOURNE COURT GARDENS

OPEN
Groups by
appointment at
any time.

Also Sundays
May 1, 29,
June 12, 26,
July 10, 24,
Aug. 14,28,
Sept. 11,25.

2.30 - 5.30pm

NORTHBOURNE COURT GARDENS, DEAL TEL: 0304 611281
(Hon. Charles James)

Northbourne Court was originally the site of a Saxon Palace. It was given to St Augustines Abbey in 618, taken by Henry VIII and later given to Sir Edwyn Sandys. The beautifully preserved Tudor terraced gardens which can be seen today are cared for by the Northbourne family, who have owned Northbourne Court since 1895.

Location: Village of Northbourne signposted from A256/A258. Nearest Railway Sandwich/Deal.
Admisson: Adults £2.50, children/OAP's £1.50. Parking for cars/coaches is free. Parties/tours by prior arrangement.

WALMER CASTLE

OPEN
1 April-31 Oct.
Daily
10am-6pm

1 Nov-31 March
Wed-Sun
10am-4pm

WALMER CASTLE & GARDENS TEL: 0304 364288
(English Heritage)

One of the coastal castles built by Henry VIII and the official residence of The Lords Warden of The Cinque Ports including Queen Elizabeth, the Queen Mother and the Duke of Wellington who died at Walmer and whose furnished rooms have been preserved unaltered (The original 'Wellington Boot' may be seen here).

Location: On coast south of Walmer .
Admission: Adult £3.00. child £1.50, Concessions £2.25.

Willesborough Windmill, Ashford.
2 miles east of Ashford town centre off A292.

Owl House Gardens, Lamberhurst.
8 miles south east of Tunbridge Wells.

Port Lympne Zoo Park, Mansion & Gardens, Lympne, Hythe.
(0303) 264646 3 miles west of Hythe, 6 miles west of Folkestone.

Quebec House, Westerham.
(0959) 62206 At Junction of A25/B2026.

Quex House, Quex Park, Birchington.
(0843) 42168 In Birchington. 13 miles east of Canterbury.

Richborough Castle, Sandwich
(0304) 612013 1 ½ miles north of Sandwich.

Riverhill House, Sevenoaks.
(0732) 452557 2 miles south of Sevenoaks on A225

Rochester Castle, Rochester.
(0634) 402276 By Rochester Bridge.

St. Augustine's Abbey, Canterbury.
(0227) 767345 In Canterbury, near the Cathedral.

Scotney Castle Garden, Lamberhurst.
(0892) 890651 1½ miles south east of Lamberhurst on A21.

Sissinghurst Garden, Sissinghurst.
(0580) 712850 1 mile east of Sissinghurst village on A262.

Smallhythe Place, Tenterden.
(05806) 2334 2½ miles south of Tenterden on B2082.

HOGHTON TOWER
Nr Preston, Lancashire

HOGHTON TOWER, home of the 14th Baronet Sir Bernard de Hoghton, is one of the most dramatic looking houses in Lancashire. The symmetrical fortified front castellated gatehouse and flanking towers is reached by steep straight avenue over half a mile long.

The present House was built almost entirely by Thomas Hoghton in 1562 - 1565, though stylistically it could date from 100 years earlier. In 1617, King James I visited the house and knighted the Loin of Beef hence 'Sirloin'. During the Civil War, Sir Richard's son Gilbert held Lancashire for the Crown and the keep of Hoghton was blown up and never replaced.

In the late 17th Century the 4th Baronet repaired and modernised the House.

Sir Henry Hoghton Bt, in 1862 started restoration of the House. This was completed in 1901 under a London architect R D Oliver, who designed the Ballroom and grand chimney pieces. The King's Ante-chamber, the King's Bed-Chamber and the Buckingham Room all retain their 17th Century interiors.

GARDENS

The grounds are sited on the hill commanding extensive views to the sea, the Lakes, and North Wales. Walled gardens

CONTACT

The Administrator
Hoghton Tower
Hoghton
Lancashire
PR5 OSH

Tel: (025 485) 2986

LOCATION

M6 Junct. 28 (10 minutes), 3½ hours to London. M61 (10 minutes), 30 minutes Manchester

Rail: Preston Station 15 minutes: 3 hours, London

Bus: Ribble Bus Co. buses to the bottom of drive.

Taxi: Preston Railway Station and locals.

SUITABILITY FOR OTHER EVENTS

Hoghton Tower provides a suitable setting for fashion shows, archery, clay pigeon shooting, equestrian events, garden parties, shows, rallies and filming, wedding receptions, corporate functions.

EXTRA FACILITIES

Lectures can be arranged, or a video can be shown, in the Conference Room for up to 100 people. Facilities such as projectors and screens can be provided. When the weather is wet indoor facilities can be offered for picnicking (Gt Barn). Hire and/or use of a grand piano, parkland, cricket pitch, golf course and airstrip can be arranged; cost negotiable.

ADVICE TO COURIERS & DRIVERS

Please telephone in advance to seek advice as to where to park prior to releasing the party or parties. Please ask visitors to treat the grassland with respect and advise the ground staff of any damage created. No interior photography, no dogs, no fires in the woods and no unaccompanied children.

PARKING FOR COACHES & CARS

Parking available for 300 cars or 200 cars and 20 coaches. Further parking by arrangement.

FACILITIES FOR THE DISABLED

Although disabled visitors are welcome to enjoy the extensive views from outside the House, there are no special facilities (toilets etc.) provided for them.

CATERING

A Tea Room is available for up to 80 people at any one time. Banqueting Hall available for max 120 persons. Groups can book in advance and menus are available upon request. Special rates for groups are negotiable.

GUIDE BOOKS

Colour guide book is available giving a detailed history of the family and the estate. Translations are available in French, German, Italian, Spanish and Swedish.

GUIDED TOURS

Tours are available and in some cases the owner may meet the group. Duration of the tour is approx 1½ hours. Minimum 25 persons.

OPENING TIMES

Summer
Easter Sat - End October

Mon	Closed *
Tues	11am - 4pm
Wed }	July and
Thur }	Aug only
Fri	Closed
Sat }	
Sun	1pm-5pm

* Except for some Bank Hol Mons.

NB Group visits may be arranged all year round by contacting The Administrator.

Winter
31 Oct - Good Friday

Open for private events and functions.

ADMISSION

Summer
GARDENS, SHOP & TEAROOM
Adult £1.00
Child £1.00

HOUSE TOURS
Adult £2.50
Child (under 5) FREE
Child* £1.25
OAP/Student £2.00
Family (4) £6.00
*Age 5-16

PRIVATE TOURS
Adult £3.50
Child £1.75

Winter

Negotiable

CONFERENCE AND FUNCTION FACILITIES

ROOM	DIMENSIONS	CAPACITY	LAYOUT	POWER POINTS	SUITABLE FOR A/V
Banqueting Hall	45'x26'	150	Various	✓	✓
Ballroom	41'x20'	70	Various	✓	✓
Smoking Room	41'x20'	70	Various	✓	✓
Billiards	48'x20'6"	70	Various	✓	✓

The Banqueting Hall, Ballroom, Smoking Room and Billiards Room are all available throughout the year subject to availability. If requested the owner may meet the group visiting the House and when invited may participate in these functions. Slide and overhead projectors, screens and audio-visual equipment can be hired if required.

PLEASE TELEPHONE FOR FURTHER DETAILS AND RATES

LEIGHTON HALL
Carnforth, Lancashire

OPENING TIMES

Summer
1 May-30 September
Mon   Bank Hol Mons
       2pm-5pm

Tues ⎫
Wed ⎬ 2pm-5pm
Thur ⎪
Fri ⎭
Sat   Closed
Sun   2pm-5pm

NB Pre-booked parties of 25 or more at any time by appointment

Winter
1 October-30 April

Open to parties of 25 or more which must be pre-booked.

LEIGHTON HALL is one of the most beautifully sited houses in the British Isles, situated in a bowl of parkland, with the whole panorama of the Lakeland Fells rising behind. The Hall's neo-Gothic facade was superimposed on an 18th century house, which, in turn, had been built on the ruins of the original mediaeval house. The present owner is descended from Adam d'Avranches who built the first house in 1246.

The whole house is lived in by the Reynolds family and emphasis is put on making visitors feel welcome in a family home.

Connoisseurs of furniture will be particularly interested in the 18th Century pieces by Gillow of Lancaster. Mr Reynolds is directly descended from the founder of Gillow and Company, hence the strong Gillow connection with the house. Also on show are some fine pictures, clocks, silver and objets d'art.

GARDENS

The main garden has a continuous herbaceous border and rose covered walls, while the Walled Garden contains flowering shrubs, a herb garden, an ornamental vegetable garden and a maze. Beyond is the Woodland Walk, where wild flowers abound from early Spring.

A varied collection of Birds of Prey is on display in the adjoining parkland.

CONTACT

Mrs C S Reynolds
Leighton Hall
Carnforth
Lancashire
LA5 9ST

Tel: (0524) 734474
Fax: (0524) 720357

LOCATION

9 miles North of Lancaster,
10 miles South of Kendal,
3 miles from M6/A6,
Junct. 35, signed from
Junct. 35A.

Lancaster Station 9 miles.

Manchester Airport, 65 miles.

Carnforth Radio Taxis
Carnforth 732763.

SUITABILITY FOR OTHER EVENTS

Product launches, small seminars, filming, garden parties, wedding receptions, rallies, overland driving and archery. The existing clay pigeon layout can be hired on a daily basis.

EXTRA FACILITIES

Lectures on the property, its contents, gardens and history can be arranged . Grand piano.

ADVICE TO COURIERS & DRIVERS

Photography is allowed in both the House and grounds. Please leave sufficient time (2hrs) for both tour of House and flying display. No dogs in the gardens. By appointment, parties of 25 and over may visit the Hall in the evening and out of season.

FACILITIES FOR THE DISABLED

Disabled and elderly visitors may alight at the entrance to the property, before parking in the allocated areas.

PARKING FOR COACHES& CARS

100 cars and 6 coaches, 150 yards from the Hall

CATERING

The Restaurant/Tea Room can cater for 55 people. Prices range form £2.75 for afternoon tea to £6.00 for other meals. Groups must book in advance and menus are available on request. For special functions/conferences buffets, lunches and dinners can be arranged.

GIFT SHOP

Open at the same time as the Hall. Items include small souvenirs. Colour guide book, £1.00.

GUIDED TOURS

Parties are taken round in groups. There is no additional cost for the facility. By prior arrangement the owner may meet the groups. Average time taken for a tour 45 minutes/1 hour.

SCHOOL VISITS/CHILDREN

Groups of children are welcome. School Programme from 10am-2pm daily May-Sept. except Mondays and Saturdays. Birds of prey flown for schools at midday. Cost per child £1.70. The Schools Visit Programme won the Sandford Award for Heritage Education in 1983 and again in 1989.

During the afternoon when the house and grounds are open to the general public a large collection of birds of prey are on display, some of which fly at 3.30pm - weather permitting.

ADMISSION

Summer
HOUSE & GARDEN
Adult   £3.20
Child*   £2.00
OAP   £2.70

Group**
 Adult   £2.70
 Child*   £1.70
 OAP   £2.70

*Age 0-16
**Minimum payment £62.50.

Winter
As above but groups by appointment only.

CONFERENCE AND FUNCTION FACILITIES

ROOM	DIMENSIONS	CAPACITY	LAYOUT	POWER POINTS	SUITABLE FOR A/V
Music Room	24'x21'6"	80	Theatre	6	✓
		50	Dinner		
		60	Buffet		

ASTLEY HALL

OPEN
April 1-Oct 31
11am-noon
1.00pm-5.00pm
(Last adm. noon
& 4.30pm)
Nov.1-March31
Fri., Sat., Sun.
11am-noon
1.00pm-4.00pm
(Last adm. noon
& 3.30pm)

ASTLEY HALL, CHORLEY TEL: 0257 262166
(Chorley Borough Council)

Set in beautiful parkland, this delightful Tudor/Stuart building retains a comfortaable and 'lived in' atmosphere. It houses fine pieces of furniture, ceramics and interesting pictures. The plasterwork ceilings are very possibly the best example of their kind in England. Here you will also find a small room full of touching mementos of the local "Pals" Battalion of the First World War.

Location: 5 minutes drive south west from Junction 8 of M61. 10 mins drive south east from Junc. 28 of M6. 2 miles west of Chorley Town Centre off A581.
Admission: Adults £2.00, Concessionary £1.00. Fam. Tkt. £4.00 (2 x 2). Special Rates for school and party bookings.

Browsholme Hall, Clitheroe.
(0254) 826719 5 miles north west of Clitheroe.
Croxteth Hall & Country Park, Liverpool.

051 228 5311 5 miles north east of Liverpool city centre.

Gawthorpe Hall, Padiham
(0282) 778511 On eastern outskirts of Padiham.

Hall I 'th' Wood, Green Way, Bolton.
(0204) 301159 2 miles north east of town centre off A58.

Martholme, Great Harwood, Blackburn.

Meols Hall, Southport.
1 mile north of Southport.

Rufford Old Hall, Rufford, Ormskirk.
(0704) 821254 7 miles north of Ormskirk on A59.

Smithills Hall, Smithills Dean Road, Bolton.
(0204) 841265 1½ miles north west of town centre off A58.

Speke Hall, Liverpool.
051 427 7231 8 miles from city centre, 1 mile off A561 on west side of Liverpool Airport.

Stonyhurst College, Hurst Green.
(0254) 826345 Just off the B6243 on outskirts of Hurst Green.

Townley Hall Art Gallery & Museum and Museum of Local Crafts & Industries, Burnley.
(0282) 24213 ½ mile south east of Burnley on A671.

GILLOW FURNITURE AT LEIGHTON HALL

NOSELEY HALL
Billesdon, Leicestershire

NOSELEY HALL, is one of the most friendly and successful locations in the East Midlands for all types of function. The house is not open to the public, but is available for private and corporate hire. It is especially suitable for outdoor activities and country pursuits.

The tranquillity of the setting, and the marvellous views, just 15 minutes from Leicester, make Noseley one of the nicest and most central locations for film and photographic work, board meetings, business seminars, conferences, product launches and private parties. Noseley's extensive parkland is ideal for outside events such as Multi-Activity Days. The five acres of lawn, immediately in front of the house, provide the perfect fully-serviced marquee site. All functions are personally overseen by the owner and his wife.

The present house, which dates from 1728, enjoys panoramic views over unspoilt parkland and has a very beautiful 13th Century chapel on the lawn. The well preserved interior includes an exceptionally fine two storey Hall, in which guests are greeted on arrival, a panelled Dining Room and an elegant Drawing Room. The house has been the seat of the Hazlerigg family since 1419. The most famous Hazlerigg was one of the five members of parliament who led the rebellion against King Charles I in 1642. He was later Cromwell's general in the North East.

CONTACT

The Hon Arthur or Mrs Hazlerigg
Noseley Hall
Billesdon
Leicestershire
LE7 9EH

Tel: (0533) 596606
/596322
Fax: (0533) 596774

LOCATION

From London M1 Junct. 15, A508 through N'hamton to Mkt Harborough, A6, B6047. 12 miles east of Leicester.

Rail: Market Harborough or Leicester.

Air: Leicester (private).

Helicopters: may land on lawn.

EXTRA FACILITIES

All activities can be arranged. The chapel has excellent acoustics for concerts. 4 wheel drive course. Lawn for marquees. Noseley regularly holds multi-activity and other corporate days.

ACCOMMODATION

Can occasionally be arranged within the House in connection with functions held therein.

FACILITIES FOR THE DISABLED.

Disabled and elderly visitors may alight at the entrance to the property, before parking in the allocated areas. There are no special toilets for the disabled.

PARKING FOR COACHES & CARS

100 cars within 50 yards. 10 more acres can be made available.

CATERING

The House is available for Corporate Entertainment functions only. Delicious Cordon Bleu menus.

RATES

Noseley Hall is not open to the public. As a guide to rates for conferences and corporate entertainment, the following are given, but please contact the owners for full details and a quotation.

Conferences: Daily delegate rate to include morning coffee, lunch, afternoon tea: From £37.50 + VAT.

Activity Days: Average £60 + VAT per head fully catered.

Lunches & Dinners: please apply for prices.

Facility Fee: Exclusive use of grounds and facilities will be based on £800 + VAT per day but each event will be quoted for individually.

OPENING TIMES

Not open to the public. Available for corporate events, conferences, filming, etc. throughout the year.

ACTIVITIES

Clay Pigeon Shooting
Archery
Pistols
Fly Casting
Quad Bikes
Pilot Buggies
Trials Cars
Argocat
Hovercraft
Land Rovers
Reverse Steer Car
Blind Driving
2CV Autotest
4x4 Troop Transporter
Karts
Radio Controlled Minitrux
Autotest Driving Game
Tractor Driving Test
Laser Clay Shooting
Video Activities
Falconry
Scalextric
Mobile Skittle Alley
Golf Swing Analyser
Croquet
Virtual Reality

CONFERENCE AND FUNCTION FACILITIES

ROOM	DIMENSIONS	CAPACITY	LAYOUT	POWER POINTS	SUITABLE FOR A/V
Stone Hall	28'x21'	60	Buffet	5	
Drawing Room	42'x22'	70	Theatre	4	✓
		40	Schoolroom		
		30	U-shape/Boardroom		
Dining Room	45'x22'	70	Theatre	4	✓
		70	Schoolroom		
		100	Buffet		
		40-80	Lunch/Dinner		
Library	34'x18'	50	Theatre	8	✓
		30	Schoolroom/Boardroom		
		25	U-shape		
Marquee on Lawn			Dinner/Dance		

STANFORD HALL
Lutterworth, Leicestershire

STANFORD has been the home of the Cave family, ancestors of the present owner, Lady Braye, since 1430. In the 1690s, Sir Roger Cave commissioned the Smiths of Warwick to pull down the old Manor House and build the present Hall, which is an excellent example of their work and of the William and Mary period.

As well as over 5000 books, the handsome Library contains many interesting manuscripts, the oldest dating from 1150. The splendid pink and gold Ballroom has a fine coved ceiling with four trompe l'oeil shell corners. Throughout the house are portraits of the family and examples of

furniture and objets which they collected over the centuries. There is also a collection of Royal Stuart portraits, previously belonging to the Cardinal Duke of York, the last of the male Royal Stuarts. An unusual collection of family costumes is displayed in the Old Dining Room, which also houses some early Tudor portraits and a fine Empire chandelier.

The Hall and Stables are set in an attractive Park on the banks of Shakespeare's Avon. There is a walled Rose Garden behind the Stables. An early ha-ha separates the North Lawn from the mile-long North Avenue.

CONTACT

Lt Col E H L Aubrey-Fletcher
Stanford Hall
Lutterworth
Leicestershire
LE17 6DH

Tel: (0788) 860250

LOCATION

M1 Juncts 18/20, 6 miles,
M6 Junct. 1, 9 miles,
A14, 1½ miles.

Follow Historic House signs.

Rail: Rugby Stn 7½mls.

Air: Birmingham Airport 27 miles.

Taxi: Fone-A-Car. (0788) 543333

SUITABILITY FOR EVENTS

Clay pigeon shoots, corporate incentive days, lunches, dinners, wedding receptions, filming and photography, fashion shows, car launches. Motor Car and Motorcycle Club Rallies held in the Park most Sundays from early May to end September. Further details on application.

EXTRA FACILITIES

These include parkland, Bluthner piano, helicopter landing area, river for fishing, raft races, canoe parties. Lecture Room available for up to 60 people. Cost for hire of the room £70.

ADVICE TO COURIERS & DRIVERS

Free meals for coach drivers. Coach parking on gravel in front of house. Dogs on leads in the park. No dogs or photography inside the house. Parking for 1,000 cars, 100 yds from the house and 6 to 8 coaches 25yds from the house.

CATERING

Groups of up to 70 can book in advance for homemade afternoon tea, lunches, high teas and suppers. Outside Catering facilities are available for special functions/conferences.

FACILITIES FOR THE DISABLED

Disabled and elderly visitors may alight at the entrance to the house. There is a toilet for the disabled.

GUIDED TOURS

Duration of tour approx ¾ hour in groups of 25 people.

GIFT SHOP

Souvenir Shop opens 2.30pm (12 noon on Bank Holidays and Event Days). Craft Centre (most Sundays) from 11.00am.

SCHOOL VISITS/CHILDREN

Groups are welcome, price per child £1.30. By prior arrangement a guide can be provided. There is a nature trail with special guide book and map. The Motorcycle Museum is of particular interest.

OPENING TIMES

Summer
Easter - End September

Mon	}	Bank Hols &
Tues	}	Tues following: 2.30pm - 6pm
Wed		
Thurs	}	Closed
Fri		
Sat	}	2.30 - 6pm
Sun	}	

Last admission 5.30pm

NB On Bank Holidays and Events Days, open at 12 noon (House at 2.30pm). Open any day or evening for pre-booked parties.

Winter
October - Easter
Closed to public.
Open during October for Corporate Events.

ADMISSION

HOUSE & GROUNDS
Adult	£3.20
Child*	£1.50
Group**	
Adult	£2.90
Child*	£1.30
OAP	£2.70

GROUNDS ONLY
| Adult | £1.80 |
| Child* | £0.70 |

MOTORCYCLE MUSEUM
Adult	£1.00
Child*	£0.30
School Group	
Adult	FREE
Child*	£0.20

* Aged 4-15
** Min payment £58.00.

CONFERENCE AND FUNCTION FACILITIES

ROOM	DIMENSIONS	CAPACITY	LAYOUT	POWER POINTS	SUITABLE FOR A/V
Ballroom	39'x26'	70	Theatre	4	✓
		60	Schoolroom		
		40	U-shape		
		100	Buffet		
		64-80	Lunch/Dinner		
Old Dining Room	30'x20'	50	Theatre	4	✓
		30	Schoolroom		
		25	U-shape/Boardroom		
		70	Buffet		
		30	Lunch/Dinner		
Crocodile Room	39'x20'	60	Theatre	1	✓

⬡ **Ashby De La Zouch Castle,** Ashby De La Zouche.
(0530) 413343 In Ashby De La Zouche.

Belgrave Hall, Church Road, Belgrave.
Off Thurcaston Road in Leicester.

Bosworth Battlefield Visitor Centre & Country Park, Market Bosworth.
(0455) 290429 15 miles west of Leicester.

⬡ **Kirby Muxloe Castle**, Leicester.
(0533) 386886 4 miles west of Leicester.

⬡ **Lyddington Bede House,** Lyddington.
(057282) 2438 6 miles north of Corby.

The Manor House, Donnington-le-Heath.
In Donnington-le-Heath, Hugglescote near Coalville.

Oakham Castle, Market Place, Oakham.
(0572) 723654 In Oakham

Wygston's House, Museum of Costume, Applegate, Leicester.
(0533) 554100 St Nicholas Circle, Leicester.

STANFORD HALL

BELVOIR CASTLE
Grantham, Lincolnshire

BELVOIR CASTLE, home of the Duke and Duchess of Rutland, commands a magnificent view over the Vale of Belvoir. The name, Belvoir, meaning beautiful view, dates back to Norman times, when Robert de Todeni, Standard Bearer to William the Conqueror, built the first Castle on this superb site. Destruction caused by two Civil Wars and by a catastrophic fire in 1816 have breached the continuity of Belvoir's history. The present building owes much to the inspiration and taste of Elizabeth, 5th Duchess of Rutland and was built after the fire.

Inside the Castle are notable art treasures including works by Poussin, Holbein, Rubens, and Reynolds, Gobelin and Mortlake tapestries, Chinese silks, furniture, fine porcelain and sculpture.

The 17th/21st Lancers Museum at Belvoir has a fascinating exhibition of the history of the 'Death or Glory Boys', as well as a fine collection of weapons, uniforms and medals.

GARDENS

The Statue Gardens are built into the hillside below the Castle and take their name from the collection of 17th Century sculptures on view. The garden is planted so that there is nearly always something in flower.

The Duchess' private Spring Gardens are available for viewing throughout the year by pre-booked groups of 10 persons or more. Details from the Estate Office.

CONTACT

Richard Fenn
Castle Estate Office
Belvoir Castle
Grantham
Lincolnshire
NG32 1PD

Tel: (0476) 870262
Fax: (0476) 870443

LOCATION

A1 from London (110mls), York (100mls) & Grantham (7mls). A607 Grantham-Melton Mowbray.

Air: East Midlands Int'l.

Rail: Grantham Stn 7mls

Bus: Melton Mowbray - Vale of Belvoir via Castle Car Park.

Taxi: Grantham Taxis 63944/63988.

SUITABILITY FOR OTHER EVENTS

Ideal location for banquets, exhibitions, product launches and conferences. Filming welcomed.

EXTRA FACILITIES

Any activity or event is a possibility and we would be delighted to discuss requirements, regardless of size.

ADVICE TO COURIERS & DRIVERS

Coaches should report to the Main Car Park and Ticket Office on arrival. Photography welcomed (permit £1.00).

FACILITIES FOR THE DISABLED

Ground floor of Castle is easily accessible for disabled people, including the Restaurant and Toilet Facilities. Further access to Castle is restricted for wheelchairs. Please telephone for advice.

GUIDED TOURS (BY APPOINTMENT)

Guided tours available by prior arrangement. £7.50 per group (up to 20 persons). Duration approx 1¼ hours.

PARKING FOR COACHES & CARS

150 cars, next to the Castle and a further 500 spaces, 500 yds from the Castle. Up to 40 coaches can be parked. Coaches can take passengers to entrance by arrangement..

CATERING

Extensive choice of hot and cold home-made food available throughout the day in the 100-seat Licensed Restaurant. Groups and parties catered for, from afternoon tea to a set three-course meal. Private room available.

GIFT SHOP

Open when Castle is open to the public, offering many quality gifts and souvenirs. There is also an unusual plant stall open at the Castle on Sundays in Season.

GUIDE BOOKS

Pictorial guide with details of the Castle and contents. Price £2.00. Translations in French, German, Italian and Spanish. Braille guide book available.

SCHOOL VISITS/ CHILDREN

Guided tours available to all schools parties, along with a private room for education or packed lunch purposes, subject to availability. Picnic area and Adventure Playground.

OPENING TIMES

Summer

1 April - 30 September
Mon   Bank Hols only
        11am - 6pm
Tues
Wed   } 11am - 5pm
Thurs
Fri   Closed
Sat   11am - 5pm
Sun   11am - 6pm
NB Open Good Friday
        11am - 6pm

October
Sun only   11am - 6pm

Winter

Groups welcome by appointment.

ADMISSION

All Year

Adult	£4.00
Child	£2.50
OAP	£2.75
GROUP*	
Adult	£3.00
Child**	£2.00

* 20 or more adults.
** School or Youth groups.

CONFERENCE AND FUNCTION FACILITIES

ROOM	DIMENSIONS	CAPACITY	LAYOUT	POWER POINTS	SUITABLE FOR A/V
State Dining Room	52'x31'	100	Schoolroom	8	✓
		60	U-shape		
		80	Boardroom		
		150	Buffet		
		130	Theatre		
		100	Lunch/Dinner		
Regents Gallery	131'x16'6"	300	Reception		✓
Old Kitchen	45'x22'6"	120	Buffet	4	✓
		80	Lunch/Dinner		

BURGHLEY HOUSE
Stamford, Lincolnshire

BURGHLEY HOUSE, home of the Cecil family for over 400 years, was built as a country seat during the latter part of the 16th Century by Sir William Cecil, later Lord Burghley, principal adviser and Lord Treasurer to Queen Elizabeth.

The House was completed in 1587 and there have been few alterations to the architecture since that date thus making Burghley one of the finest examples of late Elizabethan design in England.

The interior was remodelled in the late 17th Century by John, 5th Earl of Exeter who was a collector of fine art on a huge scale, establishing the immense collection of art treasures at Burghley.

Burghley is truly a 'Treasure House', containing one of the largest private collections of Italian art, unique examples of Chinese and Japanese porcelain and superb items of 18th Century furniture. The remodelling work of the 17th Century mean that examples of the work of the principal artists and craftsmen of the period are to be found here at Burghley: Antonio Verrio, Grinling Gibbons and Louis Laguerre all made major contributions to the beautiful interiors.

GARDENS

The House is set in a 300 acre Deer Park landscaped by Capability Brown under the direction of the 9th Earl. As was usual with Brown's designs a lake was created and delightful avenues of mature trees feature largely. The park is home to a herd of Fallow Deer and is open to the public at all times of the year. The gardens surrounding the House are only open on certain weekends, usually Bank Holidays. Please telephone for details.

CONTACT

J Culverhouse
Burghley House
Stamford
Lincolnshire
PE9 3JY

Tel: (0780) 52451
Fax: (0780) 480125

LOCATION

Burghley House is 1 mile north of Stamford.

From London A1, 2 hours.

Rail: Stamford Station 1½ mls.

Taxi: Merritt (0780) 66155.

SUITABILITY FOR OTHER EVENTS

Burghley is suitable for a wide variety of events.

EXTRA FACILITIES

Large park, golf course, helicopter landing area, cricket pitch.

ADVICE TO COURIERS & DRIVERS

Parking and refreshments free for drivers. No dogs within the House. Please advise clients that there is no photography inside.

FACILITIES FOR THE DISABLED

Disabled and elderly visitors may alight at the entrance, before parking in the allocated areas. Toilets for the disabled. Chair lift to the Orangery Coffee Shop. Disabled visitors should be aware that the house tour involves two staircases.

PARKING FOR COACHES & CARS

Capacity of the Car Park, 500 cars, 100 yards from the House, and 20 coaches, 120 yards from the House.

GUIDE BOOKS

Colour guide book, £2.50.

CATERING

Restaurant/Tea Room seating up to 100/120 people. Groups can book in advance for afternoon tea and lunch. Prices from £2.50 for afternoon tea to £7.00 for lunch (three course).

GUIDED TOURS

Tours lasting approximately 1½ hours start at 15 minute intervals. Maximum size of each party taken round is 25.

SCHOOL VISITS/CHILDREN

School visits are welcome, a guide will be provided. Cost per child, £2.50. A children's guide book can be obtained.

Summer
1 April - 2 October

Mon	
Tues	
Wed	
Thurs	} 11am - 5pm
Fri	
Sat	
Sun	

NB Closed 3 September

Winter
2 October - 1 April

Closed to the general public.

ADMISSION

Summer

Adult*	£5.10
Child**	£2.50
OAP	£4.80

GROUPS***	
Adult	£3.75
Child*	£2.50

* One child (under 14) admitted FREE per paying adult.
** Aged up to 14.
*** Min 20 people

CONFERENCE AND FUNCTION FACILITIES

ROOM	DIMENSIONS	CAPACITY	LAYOUT	POWER POINTS	SUITABLE FOR A/V
Great Hall	70'x30'	180	Theatre	2	
		90	Schoolroom		
		60	U-shape		
		42	Boardroom		
		100	Dinner		
Orangery	100'x20'	120	Buffet	6	✓

Aubourn Hall, Lincoln.
In Aubourn Village, 7 miles south of Lincoln.

Belton House, Grantham.
(0476) 66116 3 miles north east of Grantham on A607.

Bishop's Palace, Lincoln.
(0522) 27468 On south side of Lincoln Cathedral.

Elsham Hall Country and Wildlife Park, Brigg.
(0652) 688698 Near Brigg, M180 junction 5.

Fulbeck Hall, Grantham.
(0400) 72205 On A607, 14 miles from Lincoln.

Grantham House, Grantham.
In Castlegate, immediately east of Grantham Church.

Grimsthorpe Castle and Gardens, Bourne
(0778) 32205 4 miles north west of Bourne on A151.

Gunby Hall, Burgh-le-Marsh.
2¹/₂ miles north west of Burgh-le-Marsh..

Lincoln Castle, Castle Hill, Lincoln.
(0522) 511068

Marston Hall, Grantham.
(0400) 50225

Tattershall Castle, Lincoln.
(0526) 342543 12 miles north east of Sleaford on A153.

Thornton Abbey.
(0469) 40357 2 miles north east of Thornton Curtis.

Woolsthorpe Manor, near Grantham.
(0476) 860338 7 miles south of Grantham, 1 mile west of A1.

DODDINGTON HALL

OPEN
2.00-6.00pm
Early Spring
Garden days
Easter Bank Hol.
Mon.
May to Sept.
Weds., Suns &
Bank Hol Mons.

August
Daily except
Saturdays.

DODDINGTON HALL, LINCOLN TEL: 0522 694308
(Mr & Mrs Antony Jarvis)

Magnificent Smythson mansion completed in 1600 and standing complete with contemporary walled gardens and Gatehouse. The Hall has an elegant Georgian interior with fine collections of porcelain, furniture, paintings and textiles representing 400 years of unbroken family occupation. Wild garden, nature trail and gift shop. Fully licensed restaurant open from 12.00 noon. Sandford award winning schools project.

Location: 5 miles west of Lincoln on the B1190, clearly signposted off the A46 Lincoln Bypass.
Admission: £3.50 adult, £1.75 children. Gardens half price. Family Ticket

FULBECK HALL

THE QUEENS HOUSE
Greenwich, London

At the centre of a group of splendid historical buildings lies The Queens's House, a royal palace designed by Inigo Jones. The house has been sumptuously restored to show the vibrant colours of the decoration when occupied by Queen Henrietta Maria in 1662, wife of Charles I. The Great Hall, a 40' cube, has a ceiling by Gentileschi (reproduction) and the house displays a fine collection of Dutch marine art. The vaults now house a Treasury of trophies, swords and plate.

In the park is the famous Old Royal Observatory by Sir Christopher Wren incorporating apartments for the first Astronomer Royal, The Meridian Line dividing East and West is marked in the courtyard. The Time Ball drops at one o'clock to mark Greenwich Time, on which the world time zone system is based. Adjoining the Queen's House, the National Maritime Museum displays gilded Royal barges; dramatic paintings of great 17th Century sea battles; unusual river craft from distant lands; ships models; charts and plans, and special features on Nelson.

The Passport ticket includes admission to The Queens House, Observatory, Museum and Cutty Sark clipper ship.

CONTACT

Robin Scates
National Maritime
Museum
Romney Road
Greenwich
London
SE10 9NF

Tel: (081 858) 4422
Fax: (081 312) 6632

LOCATION

On the South Bank of the Thames at Greenwich. A2/A206 from London. From elsewhere M25, Junct. 2.

Rail: From Charing Cross, Waterloo East or London Bridge to Maze Hill or Greenwich.

River: Cruises from Central London to Greenwich.

Air: London City Airport 4 miles.

SUITABILITY FOR OTHER EVENTS

Corporate hospitality, prestigious functions, fashion photography, filming, small balls.

EXTRA FACILITIES

Parkland and grounds. Lecture room in adjacent museum.

ADVICE TO COURIERS & DRIVERS

Set down only at property. Free coach parking on Blackheath. Pay and display at the Cutty Sark. Guides and drivers admitted free. Childrens groups must be pre-booked for admission to the Queen's House.

FACILITIES FOR THE DISABLED

Queens House 30% accessible for wheelchairs. Signed and Touch tours for groups by prior arrangement. Advisory leaflet available. Disabled groups welcome.

PARKING FOR COACHES & CARS

There is car parking for 50 cars within 100 yards and for 25 coaches within 600 yards. Coaches can set down nearby prior to parking.

CATERING

Restaurant seating 150 in adjoining museum. Function catering from approved and recommended caterers.

GIFT SHOP

A Gift Shop, open as the House, is in adjoining building.

GUIDED TOURS

By prior arrangement. Tel. 081-312-6647. Cost approx £33 per group.

GUIDE BOOK

Colour guide book, £1.95. Handouts are also available in French, German, Italian, Spanish and Japanese.

SCHOOL VISITS/CHILDREN

Special educational services linked to National Curriculum available with gallery talks from experienced teaching staff. Education enquiries 081-312-6608.

OPENING TIMES

Summer
April - September

| Mon Tues Wed Thurs Fri Sat | 10am - 6pm |
| Sun | 12 noon - 6pm |

Winter
October - March

| Mon Tues Wed Thurs Fri Sat | 10am - 5pm |
| Sun | 2pm - 5pm |

Last tour 3.30pm Oct-Feb.

Closed 24th, 25th, 26th December and 5th-28th January.

ADMISSION

Applicable until 31.3.93

All Year

HOUSE ONLY
Adult   £3.75
Concessions*   £2.75

4 SITE TICKET
Adult   £7.45
Concessions*   £5.45

GROUPS
A discount of 20% for groups of 10 or more.

* Concessions for OAPs, Children (7-16), students, UB40, Disabled.

CONFERENCE AND FUNCTION FACILITIES

ROOM	DIMENSIONS	CAPACITY	LAYOUT	POWER POINTS	SUITABLE FOR A/V
Great Hall	40'x40'	250*	Buffet	3	✗
		150*	Dinner		
Orangery		170*	Buffet	3	✓
		125*	Dinner		

* Includes ante-rooms.

ROYAL SOCIETY OF ARTS
London

The House of the RSA (Royal Society for the encouragement of Arts, Manufacturers and Commerce) was designed specially for the Society by Robert Adam in the early 1770's. Today the RSA's terrace of five 18th Century houses is the finest and historically most interesting remaining section for the Adam brothers' development known as the Adelphi. A complex £4,500,000 building and refurbishment programme has brought the RSA's magnificent vaults into full use for receptions and private dining.

The Great Room. The jewel in the RSA's crown is the Great Room, one of the most spectacular and delightful Lecture Halls in the country. It's walls are decorated by the celebrated sequence of allegorical paintings - The Progress of Human Knowledge - by James Barry, together with portraits by Gainsborough and Reynolds.

A perfect setting for any gathering from Annual General Meeting to concert recital, the Great Room's unique atmosphere allows an audience from 50 to 200 to feel at ease and involved.

Benjamin Franklin Room: The classic Benjamin Franklin Room is a specious assembly room with its chandelier and Adam Fireplaces yet with a controlled ventilation system, ideal for meetings, receptions and banquets for 30-150 persons.

The Vaults: Beneath the Society's house lies the largest remaining part of the Adelphi arches. Originally built for storage and more recently used as wine cellars, the vaults have now been restored and converted to provide a unique venue for all forms of event. They feature the original 18th Century brickwork, and can be dressed to enhance product launches, parties, themed events and private exhibitions.

CONTACT

Ms Christine Bond
Conference Manager
RSA
8 John Adam Street
London
WC2N 6EZ

Tel: 071 930 5115
Fax: 071 321 0271

LOCATION

Near to 2 mainline stations: Charing Cross, Waterloo.

Nearest underground stations: Embankment, Charing Cross, Covent Garden

SUITABILITY FOR OTHER EVENTS

Product launches, themed parties, corporate announcements, film previews, dinner dances, private concerts, exhibitions.

EXTRA FACILITIES

Lectures can be arranged on the history of the house in the Great Room. There is a Steinway Baby Grand piano, which is available for private recitals in the Great Room.

ADVICE TO COURIERS AND DRIVERS

All visits are by prior arrangement. Coaches may only set down and pick up on John Adam Street or the Strand.

FACILITIES FOR THE DISABLED

There is wheel chair access to all the main rooms of the house via a lift. A disabled cloakroom is located on the 1st floor. Unfortunately Westminster Council does not permit disabled parking in restricted parking zones.

PARKING FOR COACHES AND CARS

The closest Coach parking area is at Vauxhall. Meters in John Adam Street. Car parks in Savoy Place and St Martin's Lane.

CATERING

Catering can be arranged for groups in a private room Rooms may be hired for lunches, dinners, receptions. We regret we do not have facilities for individuals.

GUIDED TOURS

Tours of the house for groups of up to 25 people may be arranged in advance. All visitors to the house must pre-book.

OPENING TIMES

Summer
Closed during the last 2 weeks of August.

9.00am - 8.00pm

Winter
Closed 24th December - 2nd January 1995

9.00am - 8.00pm

ADMISSION

For Room Hire Prices, please contact the RSA Conference Office direct for a brochure.

CONFERENCE AND FUNCTION FACILITIES

ROOM	DIMENSIONS	CAPACITY	LAYOUT	POWER POINTS	SUITABLE FOR A/V
Great Room	42x36	200	Theatre	✓	✓
Durham St Auditorium	36x30	60	Theatre	✓	✓
B. Franklin Room	42x36	150	Reception	✓	✓
Tavern Room	40x17	70	Reception	✓	✓
Folkestone Room	20x20	30	Reception	✓	✓
Gallery	40x20		Reception	✓	✓
THE VAULTS					
Vault 1	55x28	100	Reception	✓	✓
Vault 2	36x18	50	Reception	✓	✓
Vault 3	20x18	30	Reception	✓	✓
Vault 4	37x11	75	Reception	✓	✓

The Dining Room, Spencer House

SPENCER HOUSE
London

CONTACT

Stephen Jones
Director
Spencer House
27 St James's Place
London
SW1A 1NR

Tel: 071 409 0526
Fax: 071 493 5765

LOCATION

Central London: off St James's Street, overlooking Green Park.

Nearest tube: Green Park.

SPENCER HOUSE, built 1756-66 for the 1st Earl Spencer, an ancestor of Her Royal Highness The Princess of Wales, is London's finest surviving eighteenth-century town house. The magnificent private palace has regained the full splendour of its late eighteenth century appearance, after a painstaking seven-year restoration programme.

Designed by John Vardy and James 'Athenian' Stuart, the nine state rooms are amongst the first neo-classical interiors in Europe. Vardy's Palm Room, with its spectacular screen of gilded palm trees and arched fronds, is a unique Palladian setpiece, while the elegant mural decorations of Stuart's Painted Room reflect the eighteenth-century passion for classical Greece and Rome. Stuart's superb gilded furniture has been returned to its original location in the Painted Room by courtesy of the V&A and English Heritage. Visitors can also see a fine collection of eighteenth century paintings and furniture, specially assembled for the house, including five major Benjamin West paintings, graciously lent by Her Majesty The Queen.

The state rooms are open to the public for viewing on Sundays. They are also available on a limited number of occasions each year for private and corporate entertaining during the rest of the week.

SUITABILITY FOR OTHER EVENTS

Cocktail receptions, lunches, dinners, board meetings, theatre style meetings, contract signings, wedding receptions, private parties.

ADVICE TO COURIERS & DRIVERS

No children under 10. No dogs admitted. No photography inside House.

FACILITIES FOR THE DISABLED

Ramps, lifts and accessible toilets available.

PARKING FOR COACHES & CARS

No parking facilities. Coaches can drop off at door.

CATERING

Excellent in-house catering team for private and corporate events. However, no catering for Sunday visitors.

GUIDE BOOKS

Comprehensive colour guide book £2.95.

GUIDED TOURS

All visits are by guided tour.

OPENING TIMES

**All Year
(except Jan and Aug)**

Sundays
11.30am-5.30pm.
Last tour
4.45pm.

Tours begin approx every 15 minutes and last 1 hour. Maximum number on each tour is 15.

Advance reservations: 071-499-8620 (Tues-Fri, 10am-1pm only).

Open for corporate hospitality except during January and August.

ADMISSION

To end March 1994.

Adults   £6.00
Concessions*   £5.00

* Senior citizens, students, NT members, Friends of V&A, Tate Gallery (all with cards), children under 16 (no under 10's admitted).

Prices include guided tour.

CONFERENCE AND FUNCTION FACILITIES

ROOM	DIMENSIONS	CAPACITY	LAYOUT	POWER POINTS	SUITABLE FOR A/V

Cocktail receptions for up to 400 (500 if using the Terrace). Lunches and dinners (from 2 - 120). Board meetings (max 40, theatre style meetings (max 12).

Ashburnham House, Westminster.
071 222 3116

The Banqueting House, Whitehall.

❀ **The Blewcoat School,** 23 Caxton Street, Westminster.
071 222 2877

Boston Manor, Boston Manor Road, Brentford.
081 862 5805

Burgh House, Hampstead.
071 431 0144

Carew Manor and Dovecote, Church Road, Beddington.
081 773 4555

❀ **Carlyle's House,** 24 Cheyne Row, Chelsea
071 352 7087

Carshalton House, St Philomena's School, Pound Street, Carshalton.
081 773 4555

⌗ **Chapter House and Pyx Chamber of Westminster Abbey.**
071 222 5897

Chelsea Physic Garden, 66 Royal Hospital Road, Chelsea.
071 352 56646s

CHISWICK HOUSE

OPEN
Summer
1 April-31 Oct.
Daily   10.00am-6.00pm
Winter
1 Nov-31 March
Wed.-Sun.   10.00am-4.00pm

CHISWICK HOUSE, CHISWICK TEL: 081 995 0508
(English Heritage)

Architect and Patron of the arts the third Earl of Burlington set a fashion with this Italian-style villa, built to house his library and art collections. The gardens were landscaped by William Kent.

Location: Burlington Lane ½ mile north east Chiswick Station.
Admission: Adults £2.30, Concessions £1.70. Child £1.15.

College of Arms, Queen Victoria Street, City of London.
071 248 2762

De Morgan Foundation, Old Battersea House, 30 Vicarage Crescent, Battersea.
081 788 1341

The Dickens House Museum, 48 Doughty Street.
071 405 2127

❀ **Fenton House,** Hampstead Grove, Hampstead.
071 435 3471

Fulham Palace Gardens, Bishop's Avenue, Fulham.
071 736 5821

Gunnersbury Park Museum, Gunnersbury Park.
081 992 1612

Hall Place, Bexley.

❀ **Ham House,** Ham, Richmond.
081 940 1950   Near Junction of A2 and A223

Hampton Court Palace, Hampton Court.
081 977 8441

Heritage Centre, Honeywood Walk, Carshalton.
081 773 4555

Hogarth's House, Hogarth Lane, Great West Road, Chiswick.
081 994 6757

Keats House, Wentworth Place, Keats Grove, Hampstead.
071 435 2062

Kensington Palace, Kensington Gardens.
071 937 9561

KENWOOD

OPEN
Summer
1 April-31 Oct
Daily   10.00am-6.00pm
Winter
March-Nov.
Daily   10.00am-4.00pm

THE IVEAGH BEQUEST, HAMPSTEAD TEL: 081 348 1286
(English Heritage)

Adam mansion, once the seat of Lord Mansfield. The Iveagh Bequest of Old Master and British paintings, including works by Rembrandt, Vermeer, Hals, Gainsborough, Turner and Reynolds. Fine collection of neo-classical furniture.

Location: Hampstead Lane, NW3. Bus; London Transport 210. Rail: Finsbury Park, Golders Green. Underground: Highgate 1 mile.
Admission: Free admission

Kew Gardens, Kew.
071 940 1171

Kew Palace, Kew.
081 781 9540

🏛 **Leighton House Museum,** 12 Holland Park Road, Kensington.
071 602 3316

Linley Sambourne House, 18 Stafford Terrace, Kensington.
081 994 1019

Little Holland House, 40 Beeches Avenue, Carshalton.
081 773 4555

Museum of Garden History, Lambeth Palace Road, Lambeth.
071 261 1891

KEW PALACE

THE MUSEUM OF ST JOHN

OPEN
Mon-Fri   10.00am-5.00pm
Saturdays   10.00am-4.00pm
Closed Bank Holidays
Tours: Tues., Fri. & Sats at 11am, 2.30pm
Ref. Library: Open by appointment.

ST JOHN'S GATE, LONDON
TEL: 071 253 6644
(The Order of St John)

Headquarters of the Order of St John in England, the 16th century Gatehouse contains the most comprehensive collection of items relating to the Knights Hospitaller. Together with the nearby Priory Church and 12th century Crypt it now forms the headquarters of the modern Order whose charitable foundations include St Johns Ambulance and the Ophthalmic Hospital in Jerusalem. The collection includes Maltese silver, furniture, paintings and pharmacy jars.

Location: St John's Lane, London EC1M 4DA. Nearest tube; Farringdon, Barbican.
Admission: Free but donations are welcome.

THE RANGERS HOUSE

OPEN
Summer
1 April-31 Oct
Daily   10.00am-6.00pm
Winter
March-Nov.
Wed - Sun   10.00am-4.00pm

THE RANGERS' HOUSE,
BLACKHEATH
TEL: 081 853 0035
(English Heritage)

A Gallery of English Portraits in the 4th Earl of Chesterfield's house, from the Elizabethan to the Georgian period. Dolmetsch Collection of musical instruments in period rooms on restored first floor.

Location : Chestfield Walk. London S.E. 10
Admission: £2.00 adult,
£1.50 concessions,
£1.00 child

The Octagon, Orleans House Gallery, Riverside, Twickenham.
081 892 0221

The Old Palace, Old Palace Road, Croydon
081 680 5877

Old Royal Observatory, Greenwich.
081 858 4422

Osterley Park, Isleworth, Middlesex.
081 560 3918

Pitshanger Manor Museum, Mattock Lane, Ealing.
081 567 1227

Queen Charlotte's Cottage, Kew Gardens, Kew.
081 781 9540

R.I.B.A. Drawings Collection and Heinz Gallery, 21 Portman Square.
071 580 5533

Sir John Soane's Museum, 113 Lincoln's Inn Fields.
071 430 0175

Southside House, Wimbledon Common.
081 947 2491

HM Tower of London, Tower Hill.
071 709 0765

Whitehall, 1 Malden Road, Cheam.
081 643 1236

BUCKINGHAM PALACE FROM ST JAMES PARK

PICTURE: JEREMY WHITTAKER (0428 712292)

SYON PARK
Brentford, Middlesex

SYON takes it's name from a monastery founded in 1415 by Henry V. After the dissolution it was given to the Protector Somerset who re-built it much as it is seen today. On his death Syon reverted to the crown until granted by James I to the Percy family, now Dukes of Northumberland, who own and live in it to this day. In 1762 the First Duke of Northumberland retained Robert Adam to remodel the house, resulting in a set of state rooms, probably his finest work. From the classic Great Hall, the unique scagliola floor, Cipriani ceiling and spectacular Long Gallery, the visitor sees a collection of great paintings and 17th Century furniture, some of which was designed by Adam for the House.

GARDENS

The Gardens were transformed in the 1760s by Capability Brown. Syon is thought to be the first garden where trees were used purely for ornament and there is a fine and rare collection. In the gardens stands The Great Conservatory, a beautiful glass and steel structure, designed in 1820 by Charles Fowler.

A new attraction is the Syon Park Miniature Railway.

CONTACT

Prue Turnbull
Syon Park Ltd
Brentford
Middlesex
TW8 8JF

Tel: (081 560) 0881
Fax: (081 568) 0936

LOCATION

In London, off A310 and A315.

Rail: Southern Region: Waterloo to Kew Bridge, then bus. Nearest Station Syon Lane.

Underground: District or North London Line to Gunnersbury Station, then bus.

Bus: Gunnersbury or Kew Bridge to Brent Lea Gate, 237 or 267.

SUITABILITY FOR OTHER EVENTS

Fashion shows, archery, garden parties, shows, rallies, filming, and wedding receptions.

CONFERENCE FACILITIES

The Conference and Banqueting Centre offers 5 individual suites capable of seating between 10 and 200 people. Each Suite has its own patio area which overlooks the Gardens of Syon House. Syon Park is ideal for wedding receptions, dinner dances, conferences and exhibitions. Further information can be obtained by phoning 081 568 0778.

ADVICE TO COURIERS & DRIVERS

No dogs in Syon House or Park and no photography permitted in the House.

FACILITIES FOR THE DISABLED

There are toilet facilities for the disabled. Induction loop for the hard of hearing in House.

CATERING

PATIO RESTAURANT A self-service restaurant with ample seating is situated adjacent to the Gardens. A selection of hot food, sandwiches, cakes and pastries are offered daily. Coach parties are welcome and may book in advance. Phone 081-568 0778 for further information..

GUIDED TOURS

Tours are given at no additional cost. Average time taken 1¼ hours. (Not Sundays). Free Sound Alive tours for all visitors.

NATIONAL TRUST GIFT SHOP

Open all year.

GUIDE BOOKS

Several colour guide books.

SCHOOL VISITS/CHILDREN

Groups are welcome. Areas to visit include: the butterfly house. Cost per child for guided tour varies according to venue. The formal Gardens provide a safe and enjoyable environment for school picnics.

OPENING TIMES

Summer
1 April - 30 September

HOUSE
Mon — Tues } Closed
Wed
Thurs
Fri } 11am - 5.pm
Sat
Sun
*Open Bank Holiday Mondays

Steam Railway Weekends and Bank HOliday Monday, and by arrangement.

Winter
HOUSE
October
Sun   11.00am - 5pm
November - March
By appointment only.
GARDENS & GREAT CONSERVATORY
Open   10am-6pm/dusk
Every day except Xmas Day and Boxing Day.
Season Ticket available
STEAM RAILWAY - By arrangement only.

ADMISSION

HOUSE & GARDEN
Adult   £4.75
Concession   £3.50

HOUSE ONLY
Adult   £3,25
Concession   £2.50

GARDEN ONLY
Adult   £2.25
Concession   £175

STEAM RAILWAY
Adult   £0.75
Concession   £0.50

SCHOOL PARTIES ONLY
House only   £1.00
Gardens only   £0.75p
House & Gardens £1.50

CONFERENCE AND FUNCTION FACILITIES

ROOM	DIMENSIONS	CAPACITY	LAYOUT	POWER POINTS	SUITABLE FOR A/V
Garden	14.95 x 11.47m	200	Various		
Lakeside	18.50 x 10.75m	150	Various		
Gunters	10.74 x 12.34m	110	Various		
Terrace	11.94 x 9.40m	80	Various		
Conservatory	12.34 x 6.1m	50	Various		

CAPEL MANOR

OPEN
April-October
Daily
10.00am-5.30pm
(last entry
4.30pm)
Nov.-March
Weekdays only
10.00am-4.30pm
Please check
Xmas/N.Year
arrangements.
House not open
to the public.

CAPEL MANOR GARDENS, ENFIELD TEL: 0992 763849
(Capel Manor Corporation)

These extensive, richly planted gardens are delightful throughout the year offering inspiration, information and relaxation. The gardens include various themes - historical, modern, walled, rock, water, sensory and disabled and an Italianate Maze, Japanese Garden and "Gardening Which?" demonstration and model gardens. Capel Manor is a college of Horticulture and runs a training scheme for heritage gardeners in conjunction with the Historic Houses Association.

Location: Minutes from exit 25 of the M25. Tourist Board signposted (AA signs in summer).
Admission: Adults £3.00, Concessions £2.00, Children £1.50, Family Ticket £7.50.
Please note charges alter at special Show Weekends.

MARBLE HILL HOUSE

OPEN
Summer
1 April-31 Oct.
Daily
10.00am-6.00pm

Winter
1 Nov-31 March
Wed.-Sun.
10.00am-4.00pm

MARBLE HILL HOUSE, TWICKENHAM TEL: 081 892 5115
(English Heritage)

A complete example of an English Palladian Villa. Early Georgian paintings and furniture.

Location: Richmond Road. Stations: St Margarets 1/2 mile, Twickenham 1 mile or Richmond 2 miles.
Admission: Free

SYON PARK

BLICKLING HALL
Blickling, Norfolk

Blickling Hall is one of the most spectacular country houses in East Anglia. The 17th century red brick house is flanked by two immense Yew hedges and has an extensive colourful garden.

Sir Henry Hobart, Chief Justice of the Common Pleas to James I, purchased Blickling in 1616 taking possession of a medieval moated house. The present house was built between 1619 and 1626. From 1765, Sir Henry's descendant, the 2nd Earl of Buckinghamshire, carefully rebuilt parts of the house preserving the original design. Blickling remained the principal seat of the Hobarts until the death of the 2nd Earl in 1739, passing to the The Marquis of Lothian. In 1940 the house and estate were left to The National Trust by Philip Kerr, the 11th Marquis.

The furniture and other collections were assembled mainly in the 18th and 19th centuries, and the Library of more than 12,000 books is one of the most distinguished. The 2nd Earls Drawing Room is dominated by the colossal tapestry of Tsar Peter the Great given to him by the Empress Catherine.

GARDENS

The garden includes an extensive parterre with large herbaceous borders, a Secret Garden, an 18th century Orangery and dry moat. The Park was extensively replanted in the 18th century, its centrepiece is the long crescent shape lake. The Park offers several miles of footpaths and unusual buildings like the pyramidal mausoleum of the 2nd Earl.

SUITABILITY FOR OTHER EVENTS

Conference and corporate entertainment, open air concerts, marquee events, receptions, prestigious functions.

EXTRA FACILITIES

Picnic site, Plant Centre, House and Garden History Tours, Parkland and Estate walks. Fishing during season, Village Hall for hire. Baby-change Rooms.

ADVICE TO COURIERS & DRIVERS

Free admission for drivers. No dogs or photography in House. Booking advisable. Free Parking.

FACILITIES FOR THE DISABLED

House, Gardens, Shop, Tearoom and some Parkland accessible. Toilets, ramps, lift wheelchairs. Braille Guide.

PARKING FOR COACHES & CARS

Coach park adjacent to Hall. All cars to Main Car Park next to ticket office.

GIFT SHOP

Wide selection of gifts. Open same days as Garden. Also Thursdays to Sunday in November and December. Saturday and Sunday in January to March.

CATERING

Blickling Restaurant opens 11am for coffee same days as Garden. Lunch and afternoon teas. Parties advised to book.

GUIDED TOURS

Available during closed times only. Apply to Administrator.

GUIDE BOOKS

Main Guide, Short Guide, Childrens Guide, Park Walk Guide.

SCHOOL VISITS/CHILDREN

Are welcome, wet weather indoor picnic site for school parties. Teacher familiarization visit is complimentary. Special guided tours can be arranged.

CONTACT

The Administrator
Blickling Hall
Blickling
Norfolk
NR11 6NF

Tel: (0263) 733084
Fax: (0263)734924

LOCATION

1 mile west of Aylsham on B1354 signposted off A140 Cromer/Norwich Road.

From Norwich: 25 minutes

Rail: Norwich Station

Air: Norwich Airport 20 minutes.

Bus: Norwich Bus Station, 758/759

OPENING TIMES

Summer
26 March - 30 October

House closed Monday and Thursday.
Garden closed Monday and Thursday except July and August when open daily.

House	1pm - 5pm
Garden	Noon - 5pm

House and Garden open Bank Holiday Mondays

ADMISSION

HOUSE AND GARDEN

Sun, B.Hol Mons	£5.50
Tues Weds Fri Sat	£4.90
Groups	
Suns B.Hol Mons	£4.50
Other days	£3.90

GARDEN ONLY

Sun, B.Hol Mons	£2.75
Tues Weds Fri Sat	£2.50

Children half-price

CONFERENCE AND FUNCTION FACILITIES

ROOM	DIMENSIONS	CAPACITY	LAYOUT	POWER POINTS	SUITABLE FOR A/V
Garden Room	31x20	60	Various	✓	✓
Dining Room	26x24	40seated	Various	✓	✓
Board Room	20x19	15		✓	
Syndicate Room		8		✓	✓

HOLKHAM HALL
Wells-next-the-Sea, Norfolk

HOLKHAM HALL has been the home of the Coke family and the Earls of Leicester for almost 250 years. Built by William Kent between 1734 and 1762 it is a fine example of 18th Century Palladian style. Constructed mainly of local yellow brick with a magnificent Entrance Hall of English Alabaster, the House reflects Thomas Coke's natural appreciation of Classical Art developed during the Grand Tour.

The State Rooms occupy the first floor and contain antique statuary, paintings by Rubens, Van Dyck, Claude, Poussin and Gainsborough and original furniture.

The visitors on leaving the House pass the Pottery started by Elizabeth, Countess of Leicester in 1951 and today supervised by Viscountess Coke. A highly skilled team produce a fine range of pottery.

Beyond are the 19th Century stables and the Holkham Bygones Collection. Some 4,000 items range from working steam engines, vintage cars and tractors to craft tools and kitchen ware.

The House is set in a 3,000 acre Park with 600 head of fallow deer. On the lake, 1 mile long, can be seen many species of wildfowl. Two walks encircle either the Lake or Agricultural buildings.

The Holkham Garden Centre occupies the 18th Century walled Kitchen Garden and a large range of stock is on sale to the public

CONTACT

The Administrator
Holkham Hall
Estate Office
Wells-next-the-Sea
Norfolk
NR23 1AB

Tel: (0328) 710227
Fax: (0328) 711707

LOCATION

From London 120mls,
Norwich 35mls, Kings
Lynn 30mls.

Rail: Norwich Stn 35mls,
Kings Lynn Stn 30mls.

Air: Norwich Airport
32mls.

Taxi: Lavender Taxi
Services, Fakenham.
(0328) 862906.

SUITABILITY FOR OTHER EVENTS

Fashion shows, air displays, archery, clay pigeon shooting, equestrian events, shows, rallies and filming.

ADVICE TO COURIERS & DRIVERS

No smoking, dogs or flash photography in the Hall.

FACILITIES FOR THE DISABLED

Disabled and elderly visitors may be left at the entrance to the property, before parking in the allocated areas. There are toilets for the disabled.

PARKING FOR COACHES & CARS

Capacity of the car park: over 1,000 cars and 20 coaches, 150 yards from the Hall.

CATERING

The Tea Room can cater for up to 100 people. Menus are available on request.

GUIDED TOURS

When the Hall is open to the public, guides are posted in each room. At other times guided tours can be arranged. Average time taken for a tour 1 hour.

GIFT SHOP

Open 10.00am-5.30pm Mon-Fri, 12.00-5.30pm Sundays. Items include books and pamphlets on the local area and wildlife, gifts and souvenirs for children.

GUIDE BOOKS

Colour guide book, £1.75

SCHOOL VISITS/CHILDREN

Groups of children are welcome. Price per child £1.50. Areas of interest: 2 nature walks, deer park, lake and wild fowl. Bygones collection, including dolls house and toy collection.

OPENING TIMES

Summer
29 May - 29 September

Mon	
Tues	1.30pm - 5pm
Wed	
Thurs	
Fri	Closed
Sat	
Sun	1.30pm - 5pm

Last admission 4.40pm

Open Sun/Mon on Easter, May, Spring & Summer Bank Hols:
11.30am - 5pm

Winter
October - May

Open by appointment.

ADMISSION

Summer

HALL	
Adult	£3.00
Child*	£1.50
BYGONES	
Adult	£3.00
Child*	£1.50
ALL INCLUSIVE	
Adult	£5.00
Child*	£2.50

* Ages 5-15
Discounts on Parties of 20+

Winter

By arrangement

RAINTHORPE HALL
Tasburgh, Norfolk

RAINTHORPE HALL is a half-timbered Tudor house which was modernised in 1579 by Thomas Baxter, an eminent barrister, who added wings to form the fashionable E-shape.

The house survived without further alteration until it was bought in 1853 by the Hon. Frederick Walpole M.P. who believed it to be the birthplace of Amy Robsart. Walpole carried out much work on it, installing much collected carving, from the middle ages to the 17th Century, Spanish leather wall-coverings, and a Tudor chimney-piece from a house demolished by his great-great-grandfather. After his death the house was sold to another antiquary, Sir Charles Harvey Bt, who built a nursery wing to match the original house and collected much stained and painted glass.

GARDENS

The lawns run down to the River Tas, which flows on both sides of the conservation lake, with its three islands. There are Yew hedges, ancient trees, a nuttery, a collection of bamboos and an Elizabethan knot-garden. In the old Kitchen Garden is a plant sales centre, with display gardens to demonstrate different styles of design and planting.

CONTACT

G F Hastings
Rainthorpe Hall
Tasburgh
Norwich
Norfolk
NR15 1RQ

Tel: (0508) 470 618/191

LOCATION

From London, M11, A11, A45, A143, A140 to Newton Flotman; Flordon Road, gates 1 mile on left.

Rail: Norwich Stn 8miles (15 mins).

Bus: Newton Flotman 1 mile

Taxi: Norwich 623333

SPECIAL ATTRACTIONS

Carved panelling, doors and overmantels; 12th-19th Century Stained Glass; 16th Century plaster ceiling; 17th Century Spanish embossed leather wallcovering; 17th Century Dutch Tiles; Elizabethan Knot Garden.

LOCAL PLACES OF INTEREST

Tasburgh Church with Saxon Tower, Somerleyton Hall, Norwich Cathedral.

SUITABILITY FOR OTHER EVENTS

Rainthorpe is suitable for such events as fashion shows, archery, garden parties, filming and wedding receptions.

ADVICE TO COURIERS & DRIVERS

The gate at the end of Tasburgh drive is 16' wide, and best approached from the South. Please advise visitors that children must be accompanied and dogs kept on leads.

FACILITIES FOR THE DISABLED

Disabled and elderly visitors may alight at the door of the property, before parking in the allocated areas. There are toilets for the disabled.

PARKING FOR COACHES & CARS

Capacity of the Car Park: 60 cars, 40 yards from the House. Includes an area for coaches.

CATERING

Home-made teas. Other catering available by prior arrangement.

GUIDED TOURS

All tours are guided. The cost is £2.50 per person (minimum £50 per tour). Duration of a tour is approximately 1 hour.

GUIDE BOOKS

Colour guide books, £1.50.

SCHOOL VISITS/CHILDREN

School visits can be arranged. The cost per child is £2.50 for the House and garden and 75p for the Gardens only. A guide would be provided for a tour of the House.

OPENING TIMES

Summer
Easter - 31 October

Gardens open:
Sun
Bank
Hol }10am - 5pm
Mons

Mon
Tues
Wed
Thurs } House open
Fri   by appointment
Sat
Sun

Winter

House open by appointment.

ADMISSION

All Year

HOUSE & GARDEN
Adult	£2.50
Child*	£2.50
OAP	£2.50

GARDEN ONLY
Adult	£1.50
Child*	£0.75
OAP	£0.75

* Aged 0-14.
(Tours of House unsuitable for small children).

SANDRINGHAM
King's Lynn, Norfolk

The private country retreat of Her Majesty The Queen, Sandringham House is at the heart of the beautiful estate which has been owned by four generations of Monarchs. King George V described his home in the picturesque West Norfolk countryside as "dear old Sandringham, the place I love better than anywhere else in the world".

The neo-Jacobean house was built in 1870 for Albert Edward, Prince of Wales and his wife, Princess Alexandra, later King Edward VII and Queen Alexandra. A grand and imposing building, where all the main rooms used by The Royal Family when in residence are open to the public, Sandringham House has the warmth and charm of a well-loved family home. Visitors see portraits of The Royal Family, collections of porcelain, jade, quartz, enamelled Russian silver, gold and bronze set amongst fine furniture.

GARDENS

Sixty acres of glorious grounds surround the House and offer beauty and colour throughout the seasons with a rich variety of flowers, shrubs and magnificent trees, informally planted round lawns and lakes to provide a multitude of tranquil views.

Sandringham Museum, situated within the grounds, contains fascinating displays of Royal memorabilia ranging from family photographs to vintage Daimlers, and an exhibition of the Sandringham Fire Brigade.

CONTACT

Mrs Gill Pattinson
The Estate Office
Sandringham
King's Lynn
Norfolk
PE35 6EN

Tel: (0553) 772675
Fax: (0485) 541571

LOCATION

Sandringham is 8 miles north east of Kings Lynn off A148.
3 hours from London
1½ hours from Stansted Airport via M11 and A10.

Rail: King's Lynn 8 miles.

SUITABILITY FOR OTHER EVENTS

Grounds for open-air concerts/theatre. 140 acre private park for rallies, fairs etc.

EXTRA FACILITIES

600 acre Country Park with Tractor and Trailer tour.

ADVICE TO COURIERS & DRIVERS

Parking, admission and refreshments free to drivers. Please advise no dogs inside grounds. No photography inside House.

FACILITIES FOR THE DISABLED

Wheelchair access throughout. Parking and lavatories for disabled persons.

PARKING FOR COACHES & CARS

Parking area for 600 cars/150 coaches close to Visitor Centre, 300 yards from Grounds entrance.

CATERING

A major re-development of the Sandringham Visitor Centre opens at Easter 1994 with air-conditioned restaurant seating up to 200 visitors. Traditional waitress-service tea room seating 60 also available and may be booked by groups. Open Easter to end of October.

GUIDED TOURS

Guided tours may be arranged for groups of up to 25 people at certain times of the season.

GIFT SHOP

Large gift shop at Visitor Centre stocking a large range of quality gifts, books, foods and souvenirs open Easter to end of October.

GUIDE BOOKS

A guide book with colour photographs is available.

SCHOOL VISITS/CHILDREN

School visits are welcome. Educational sheets/questionnaires available for House and Museum. Field study room for up to 70 children available in Country Park.

OPENING TIMES

Summer
1 April - 2 October

House Closed
19 July -4 Aug
Grounds and Museum Closed
19 July -3 Aug

Grounds open
10.30am-5pm. (11.30am Good Friday and Sundays)

House and Museum
11.00am-4.45pm. (12noon Good Friday and Sundays)

Winter
3 October - Spring 1995

Closed

ADMISSION

HOUSE, GROUNDS & MUSEUM

Adult	£3.50
Child*	£2.00
Student	£2.50
Sen. Citizen	£2.50

GROUNDS & MUSEUM ONLY

Adult	£2.50
Child*	£1.50
Student	£2.00
Sen. Citizen	£2.00
Season Ticket	£10.00

GROUPS
Discount of 10% for pre-booked, pre-paid parties of 20 or more.

* Aged 5-15.

Winter

Closed

CONFERENCE AND FUNCTION FACILITIES

ROOM	DIMENSIONS	CAPACITY	LAYOUT	POWER POINTS	SUITABLE FOR A/V
Restaurant	35'x50'	300	Reception/ Buffet	8	✓
		150	Dinner		
		200	Theatre		
		50	Boardroom		

✿ **Berney Arms Windmill,** north bank of River Yare, Reedham.
(0493) 700605 3¹/₂ miles north east of Reedham. Accessible by boat or ¹/₂ mile walk.

BRESSINGHAM GARDENS

OPEN

1 April-31 Oct.
10.00am-5.30pm
7 days a week

NEW FOR 1994
Gardeners
Mondays
every Monday
the Dell Garden
and Adrian
Bloom's "Foggy
Bottom Garden"
open.

BRESSINGHAM GARDENS, DISS TEL: 037988 382
(Alan Bloom)

Enjoy Alan Bloom's world famous "Dell" Garden. Some 47 island beds devoted mainly to perennials and alpine plants, and with over 5,000 species and varieties it is one of the widest collections of hardy perennials in the world. Mature trees, lovely walks and adjacent Plant Centre and Steam Museum make a visit to Bressingham totally enjoyable.

Location: On A1066 2¹/₂ miles west of Diss
Admission: Rates upon application,

Castle Acre Priory, Swaffham.
(07605) 394   3¹/₂ miles north of Swaffham.

Castle Rising Castle, King's Lynn.
(055387) 330 4 miles north of King's Lynn.

The Fairhaven Garden Trust, Norwich.
(060549)449 9 miles north east of Norwich on B1140.

❧ **Felbrigg Hall,** Cromer
(0263) 837444 2 miles south west of Cromer on A148.

✿ **Grimes Graves,** Brandon.
(0842) 810656 2³/₄ miles north east of Brandon.

⌂ **Houghton Hall,** King's Lynn.
(0485) 528569 13 miles east of King's Lynn.

⌂ **Mannington Gardens and Countryside,** Saxthorpe.
(026387) 4175 2 miles north of Saxthorpe near B1149.

Norwich Castle, Norwich.
(0603) 222222

❧ **Oxburgh Hall.** Swaffham.
(036621) 258 7 miles south west of Swaffham.

Raveningham Hall Gardens, Norwich.
(0508) 548222 4 miles from Beccles off the B1136.

Trinity Hospital, Castle Rising.
4 miles north east of King's Lynn on A149.

Wolterton Park, Erpingham.
(026387) 4175 Signposted from A140.

ALTHORP HOUSE, NORTHAMPTON

ALTHORP HOUSE
Althorp, Northampton

ALTHORP, home of the Earl and Countess Spencer and their young family, was built in its original, red brick form by Sir John Spencer in 1508. Remodelled in 1660 by Anthony Ellis, the house's present appearance dates from 1790 when Henry Holland 'improved' both the interior and exterior, entirely facing the main house with fashionable grey brick tiles.

Inside, the main rooms show the complexity of the building's history: the Entrance Hall - a marvellous Palladian room by Morris, the Grand Staircase dating from 1650, and the breathtaking Picture Gallery - 115 feet of panelling, covered with masterpieces, culminating in Van Dyck's celebrated double portrait , 'War and Peace'.

Althorp House is available for dinners, luncheon parties, wedding, conferences and cocktail parties. The 450 acres of undulating parkland are used for product launches, open air concerts, craft fairs, car rallies, horse trials, country fairs and filming. A cricket pitch is also available for hire.

Althorp houses one of the finest art collections in England, begun in the 17th Century by Robert, 2nd Earl of Sunderland, and enlarged by nearly every successive Spencer generation. Rubens, Reynolds, Gainsborough and Lely are all well represented. The collection's quality is almost matched by that of the 18th Century furniture, and the porcelain is also outstanding, with pieces from Sevres and Meissen.

The Althorp Carriages are currently on show, with a major conservation programme in place.

GARDENS
When Holland was improving the House, he had the gardens improved by Samuel Lapidge, Capability Brown's chief assistant. The gardens seen today, however, date from 1860 and were designed by the architect W. M. Teulon. The stable block, a grand rectangle of dark, glowing ironstone built in 1732, contrasts sharply with the main house and dominates the approach to Althorp. The gardens are currently being developed with new rose beds already in place.

MUSEUM
There is a new museum housing military and other historical items connected with the Spencer family up to the present day.

CONTACT
Lisa Hanlon
Althorp House
Althorp
Northampton
NN7 4HG

Tel: (0604) 770107/770006
Fax: (0604) 770983

LOCATION
From the M1:
Exit 15A, 6 miles
Exit 16 - 7 miles
Exit 18, 10 miles
Situated on A428 Northampton-Rugby. London on average 85 minutes away.

OPENING TIMES
Summer
1-4 April (Easter) plus all Suns in April, except 24
Sat. 30 April-Mon 2 May
Tues 24, Sat 28 May
1-31 August
Every Sunday in Sept.
Sat 26, Sun 27 November
Other days to be announced please tel. 0604 770209 for details.

Opening times:
1.00pm-5.30pm.
Last tour starts:
\   4.45pm.

During events in the Park supplementary charges may be payable

Parties of over 100 people may be accepted on other days.

ADMISSION
All Year

MUSEUM, HOUSE & GARDEN	
Adult	£4.50
Child*	£2.50
OAP	£3.50

GARDEN ONLY	
Adult	£2.00
Child*	£1.00

* Aged 2-14

EXTRA FACILITIES
Helicopters can land in front of the house.

ADVICE TO COURIERS & DRIVERS
Please book in advance. No dogs, photography (in House) or unaccompanied children.

FACILITIES FOR THE DISABLED
The ground floor is suitable for the disabled and they are welcome in the grounds and tea room. Toilet for the disabled.

PARKING FOR COACHES & CARS
Parking for 40 cars and 5 coaches, 100yds from House. 120 more vehicles, 200yds from the House; limitless parking beyond this.

CATERING
There is a tea room (capacity 100 people). Parties can be booked in advance for lunch and tea. Menus available on request. Catering facilities can be arranged for dinner in the House by prior arrangement. Exclusive luncheons and dinners

are also available in the State Dining Room, which holds 20-120 people. Other rooms are ideal for conferences and presentations.

GUIDED TOURS
A free flow system may operate. Tours in French and German by appointment. Average time to see the house is 1 hour.

GIFT SHOP/GUIDE BOOKS
Open when the House is open. Many Althorp souvenirs available. A guide book with colour photographs is available. There are also guide books in Japanese

BOUGHTON HOUSE
Kettering, Northamptonshire

BOUGHTON HOUSE is the Northamptonshire home of the Duke of Buccleuch and Queensberry and has been in the family since 1528. The 500 year old Tudor monastic building was gradually enlarged around seven courtyards culminating in the french style addition of 1695, which has lead to Boughton House being described as 'England's Versailles'.

The house contains an outstanding collection of fine arts, including 17th and 18th Century French and English furniture, tapestries, 16th Century carpets, porcelain, painted ceilings and notable works by El Greco, Murillo, Caracci and 40 Van Dyck sketches. There is an incomparable armoury.

GARDENS

Boughton House is set in a 350 acre park with lakes, parklands and historic avenues of trees.

CONTACT

Gareth Fitzpatrick
Boughton House
Kettering
Northamptonshire
NN14 1BJ

Tel: (0536) 515731
Fax: (0536) 417255

LOCATION

3 miles north of Kettering on A43 - spur road from A14.

SUITABILITY FOR OTHER EVENTS

Boughton House parkland is available for film location and other events by individual negotiation.

EXTRA FACILITIES

Stables Block adjacent to House contains 120 seats. Lecture Theatre and Catering facilities.

ADVICE TO COURIERS & DRIVERS

No unaccompanied children and dogs in House and Gardens. No internal photography.

FACILITIES FOR THE DISABLED

Full disabled access and facilities - no charge for wheelchair visitors.

PARKING FOR COACHES & CARS

There is unlimited parking adjacent to the House.

CATERING

Stables Restaurant seats 100. Parties must book in advance. Varied menus of home made fayre available.

GIFT SHOP

Gift and Garden shops are open daily 2.00 - 5.00pm.

GUIDE BOOKS

New edition recently published. Also specialist book "Boughton House - The English Versailles" available - contact for further details.

GUIDED TOURS

Group visits are all guided - please contact for rates etc.

SCHOOL VISITS/CHILDREN

Heritage Education Trust Award winner. School groups admitted free, teachers information book and workbook available.

OPENING TIMES

Summer

Grounds:
1 May-30 September

Daily   1.00 - 5.00pm
(Except Fridays)

House:
1 August - 1 September

Daily   2.00 - 5.00pm

Winter

Daily by appointment for educational groups.

ADMISSION

Summer

HOUSE & GROUNDS
Adults   £4.00
Child/OAP   £2.50

GROUNDS
Adults   £1.50
Child/OAP   £0.75

Wheelchairs Free

Winter

Group Rates - contact for further details.

CONFERENCE AND FUNCTION FACILITIES

ROOM	DIMENSIONS	CAPACITY	LAYOUT	POWER POINTS	SUITABLE FOR A/V
Stables Lecture		80	Buffet	10	✓
		120+	Theatre		
		80	Lunch/Dinner		
Seminar Room		30	Schoolroom	8	✓
		20	U-Shape		
		20	Boardroom		
		20	Buffet		
		30	Theatre		

Conference facilities available in stable block adjacent to House available for Countryside and Fine Art associated themes.

CASTLE ASHBY
Northampton

LOCATION

From London via M1, 90 minutes.
From Birmingham, 50 minutes.
From Chester via M6, 2¹/₂ hours.

Rail: Northampton 7 miles; Wellingborough 8 miles.

The lands at Castle Ashby were given to the Compton family in 1512 by Henry VIII and in 1574 Queen Elizabeth I gave William, 1st Earl of Northampton, permission to demolish the derelict 13th Century Castle and rebuild on the site. The original plan of the building was the shape of an 'E' in honour of Queen Elizabeth, and about sixty years later the courtyard was enclosed by a screen designed by Inigo Jones.

One of the features of Castle Ashby is the lettering around the House and terraces. The inscriptions when translated read "The Lord guard your coming in" and "The Lord guard your going out".

Castle Ashby belongs to the 7th Marquess of Northampton, Spencer Compton, and has been in the hands of the Compton family since it was built. The family trace their history back to the 11th Century and came to Castle Ashby from Compton Wynyates in Warwickshire. The lands and titles have descended through the male line since the 11th Century. The Comptons were

created Earl of Northampton in 1618 and Marquess of Northampton in 1812.

The Compton family have played host to members of the Royal Family, at Castle Ashby, on many occasions starting with Queen Elizabeth I. James I was a regular visitor, as well as Princess Anne (later Queen Anne) and William of Orange, King George V and Queen Mary visited Castle Ashby in 1907.

GARDENS

The Extensive gardens at Castle Ashby are a combination of several styles, with a mile long avenue dating back to 1695, Victorian Terrace Gardens, the more private and romantic Italian Gardens, an elegant Conservatory, Triumphal Arch, Gloriette and Camellia House standing in a garden of its own. The carriageway continues through "Capability" Brown landscape parkland, past the Temple, round the lakes and back to the House, affording classic views on the way.

SUITABILITY FOR OTHER EVENTS

With 26 bedrooms, all with en suite bathroom, Castle Ashby is available on an exclusive basis for residential conferences, company weekends and social occasions.

There are 7 Private Function Suites available for events, for meetings for 120 people to dinners for 12. The 24 hour rate is £165 plus VAT and Day Delegate £35 plus VAT, (rates valid until Sept. 1994). Additional facilities include parkland, cricket pitch, clay shooting, archery, fishing and horse and carriage.

CATERING

All catering is provided by our team of award winning chefs. Our aim is to provide discreet service with a touch of informality. thus allowing guests to experience the complete enjoyment of using the house as if it were their own.

OPENING TIMES

Gardens

Open all year round.

House

Available throughout the year for Corporate /Private Functions.

ADMISSION

Gardens

Adults	£2.00
O.A.P	£1.00
Child	£1.00

Groups:
Prices on application,

ADVICE TO COURIERS & DRIVERS

There are 25 acres of Gardens which are open to view. Dogs on leads in gardens.

Parking is available in Castle Ashby village which can be approached via A428 to Chadstone and Castle Ashby.

GUIDED TOURS

Guided group tours of Gardens are available - bookings are required.

CONFERENCE AND FUNCTION FACILITIES

ROOM	DIMENSIONS	CAPACITY	LAYOUT	POWER POINTS	SUITABLE FOR A/V
Great Hall	48' x 26 'x 33'	40-150	Various	10	✓
Reynolds Room	47 'x 22 'x 11'	40-120	Various	12	✓
China Drawing Room	18' x 20' x 11'	15-40	Various	5	✓
Long Gallery	80 'x 14' x 12'	30-60	Various	3	
Armoury	18 'x 30' x 11'	16	Various	4	✓
Study	19 ' x 20' x 11'	12	Various	4	

There are several smaller rooms available for Syndicate Meetings

HOLDENBY HOUSE
Holdenby, Northamptonshire

"ONE of the most pleasing sites that ever I saw" (John Evelyn 1673).

Holdenby was built in 1583 by Sir Christopher Hatton, Lord Chancellor to Queen Elizabeth I. Once the largest house in England, it was sold to the crown by Sir Christopher's heirs to repay his debts. James I paid several happy visits here but King Charles I's memories were less happy. He was imprisoned here for five months in 1647 following his defeat in the Civil War. After his execution the house was largely demolished with the remains later adapted into the existing house by the present owner's Great-Great Grandmother.

Today, Holdenby House comprises both the original Elizabethan remains and a sympathetic Victorian restoration. It also provides a splendid backdrop to Holdenby's historic garden where the Elizabethan remains have been enhanced by a reconstructed Elizabethan garden and a fragrant border, both planted by Rosemary Verey. At the Falconry Centre, visitors can see birds of prey flown by experts or even try flying one themselves. Holdenby's collection of rare farm animals - some dating back to Charles I's time - wander the grounds. And for children there is a Cuddle Farm and Play Area. Holdenby is an historic house that's still lived in and shared with the public, as a family home.

SUITABILITY FOR OTHER EVENTS

Conferences, Seminars, Corporate Days, Weddings, Buffets and Dinners. Archery, Air Displays, Clay Pigeon Shoots, Equestrian Events, Garden Parties, Rallies, Filming etc.

EXTRA FACILITIES

Piano Museum, Falconry Displays, Croquet. A Lecture Room, Screen and Projector can all be provided.

FACILITIES FOR THE DISABLED

Disabled or elderly visitors can be left at the house prior to parking. There are toilet facilities for the disabled.

PARKING FOR COACHES & CARS

There is parking for 100 cars and 5 coaches.

CATERING

Special conference menus from finger buffets to silver service in the Dining Room. Victorian Tearoom/Restaurant seats 45 serving teas from £2.50, light meals from £4.50. Menus upon request.

GUIDED TOURS

Tours for groups of up to 80 at no additional cost. Average time for a tour is 45 minutes.

GIFT SHOP

The Gift Shop is open when the house and grounds are open or by prior arrangement. Local Gifts, Crafts and Souvenirs.

GUIDE BOOKS

Colour guide book, £1.50.

EDUCATIONAL VISITS/CHILDREN

Winner of The Sandford Award 1985 and 1990. Groups are welcome, a guide is provided and a school room is available. Of special interest to children is the Cuddle Farm.

CONTACT

Barbara Brooker
Holdenby House
Holdenby
Northamptonshire
NN6 8DJ

Tel: (0604) 770074
Fax: (0604) 770962

LOCATION

From London via M1, 90 mins. Leave at Junction 15, 15a or 16. Entrance 6 miles N/W of Northampton off the A428, or A50.

Rail: Northampton Station (London - Euston) 1 hour.

Taxi: Favell Cars (0604) 28177/20209.

OPENING TIMES

Summer

Open to the public:
Easter Sunday-30 Sept.

House:
Bank Holiday Mondays. except May Day. Other days by appointment

Garden:
Sundays and Bank Hol.
Mondays   2 - 6pm
Mon - Fri   1 - 5pm
(through Falconry Centre).

House and Gardens open daily by appointment to pre-booked parties.

Winter

By prior arrangement.

ADMISSION

Summer

HOUSE & GARDEN
Adult	£3.50
Child*	£1.75
OAP	£3.50
Group**	£3.50

** Min. 25 people

GARDEN ONLY
Adult	£2.50
Child*	£1.50
OAP	£2.00
Group**	£2.00

** Min. 25 people

*Aged 3-15

Winter
Same as summer rates

Open all year for conferences and corporate days.

CONFERENCE AND FUNCTION FACILITIES

ROOM	DIMENSIONS	CAPACITY	LAYOUT	POWER POINTS	SUITABLE FOR A/V
Ballroom	44'x26'	90	Theatre	3	✓
		50	Schoolroom	3	✓
		40	Boardroom	3	✓
Pytchley	24'x20'	30	Theatre	3	✓
		16	Boardroom	3	✓
Dining Room		48	Dinner	3	✓

LAMPORT HALL
Lamport, Northampton

HOME of the Isham family from 1560 to 1976. The 17th and 18th Century facade is by John Webb and the Smiths of Warwick and the North Wing of 1861 by William Burn.

The Hall contains a wealth of outstanding furniture, books and paintings including portraits by Van Dyck, Kneller, Lely and others. The fine rooms include the High Room of 1655 with magnificent plasterwork, the 18th Century library with books from the 16th Century, the early 19th Century Cabinet Room containing rare Venetian cabinets with mythological paintings on glass and the Victorian Dining Room where refreshments are served.

The first floor has undergone lengthy restoration allowing further paintings and furniture to be displayed as well as a photographic record of Sir Gyles Isham, a Hollywood actor, who initiated the restoration.

The tranquil gardens were laid out in 1655 although they owe much to Sir Charles Isham the eccentric 10th Baronet who, in the mid 19th Century, created the Italian Garden and the Rockery where he introduced the first garden gnomes to England. There are also box bowers, a rose garden and lily pond and extensive walks, borders and lawns all surrounded by a spacious park.

SUITABILITY FOR OTHER EVENTS

Wedding receptions, conferences, meetings, garden parties, company activity days, clay pigeon shoots, equestrian events, fashion shows, air displays, archery, rallies, filming, shows.

EXTRA FACILITIES

Parkland, Grand Piano, 2 exhibition rooms. Lectures can be arranged on the history of the property and gardens. Lecture/meeting rooms are available, seating a maximum of 50, with audio-visual equipment. Full details of costs on application. Free admission to the agricultural museum on Sundays from Easter to end of September.

ADVICE TO COURIERS & DRIVERS

Please use main entrance only (on A508). No unaccompanied children. No photography inside the house.

FACILITIES FOR THE DISABLED

Disabled or elderly visitors may alight at the entrance door. Access to ground floor and gardens. Toilets.

PARKING FOR COACHES & CARS

1000 cars and 3 coaches, within 20 yards of the property. Free.

GIFT SHOP

Open when the House is open and stocks a variety of items.

CATERING

The Dining/Tea Room seats 50 maximum and groups can book meals in advance. Catering available for special functions, buffets, lunches and Dinners. Guided Tours with refreshments.

GUIDED TOURS

Tours are available at no additional cost, by prior arrangement. Maximum size of party is 70, average time taken is $1^{1}/2$ hours.

GUIDE BOOKS

Colour guide book, £1.50.

SCHOOL VISITS/CHILDREN

School groups are welcome. A work room is available in the Study Centre. Groups are conducted round the house, gardens, church and village by specialist advisory teachers, who provide study packs. Further information from the Education Officer, (060 128) 508 or the Trust Office, (060 128) 272. Special guide book available for children visiting individually or with families.

CONTACT

George Drye
Executive Director
Lamport Hall
Northampton
NN6 9HD

Tel: (060 128) 272
Fax: (060 128) 224

LOCATION

From London via M1, $1^{1}/4$ hours. Leave at Junction 15. Entrance on A508, 8 miles north of Northampton at junction with B576.

Rail: Kettering Station 15 miles; Northampton 8 miles.

Bus: From Northampton and Market Harborough.

OPENING TIMES

Summer
Easter - 2 October

Suns & Bank HolMons
2.15-5.15pm

Last 2 weeks in June, weekdays
6.30pm guided tour

First 2 weeks in July, weekdays
2.30pm guided tour

Other Thurs in July &Aug
2.30pm guided tour

29th-30th October
2.15 - 5.15pm

Tours on other days by prior arrangement.

Winter

Group visits only by arrangement.

ADMISSION

Summer
HOUSE & GARDEN

Adult	£3.00
Child*	£1.50
OAP	£2.50
Group**	£POA

* Aged 5-16
*Minimum payment £100.00 inc. refreshments

Winter

Group visits only by prior arrangement.

CONFERENCE AND FUNCTION FACILITIES

ROOM	DIMENSIONS	CAPACITY	LAYOUT	POWER POINTS	SUITABLE FOR A/V
Dining Room	31'x24'6"	80	Theatre	4	✓
		48	Schoolroom		✓
		27	U-shape		✓
		34	Boardroom		✓
		60	Lunch/Dinner		✓
		60	Buffet		✓

ROCKINGHAM CASTLE
Market Harborough, Leicestershire

A ROYAL CASTLE until 1530, since then home of the Watson family, Rockingham Castle was built by William the Conqueror on the site of an earlier fortification and was regularly used by the early Kings of England until the 16th Century when it was granted by Henry VIII to Edward Watson whose family still live there today.

The house itself is memorable not so much as representing any particular period, but rather a procession of periods. The dominant influence in the building is Tudor within the Norman walls, but practically every century since the 11th has left its mark in the form of architecture, furniture or works of art. The Castle has a particularly fine collection of English 18th, 19th and 20th Century paintings, and Charles Dickens, who was a frequent visitor, was so captivated by Rockingham that he used it as a model for Chesney Wold in Bleak House.

The Castle stands in 12 acres of formal and wild garden and commands a splendid view of five counties. Particular features are the 400 year old elephant hedge and the rose garden marking the foundations of the old keep. See Special Exhibition: Castles in Northamptonshire.

CONTACT

Miss K Barton
Rockingham Castle
Market Harborough
Leicestershire
LE16 8TH

Tel: (0536) 770240

LOCATION

2 miles north of Corby; 9 miles from Market Harborough; 14 miles from Stamford on A427; 8 miles from Kettering on A6003

SUITABILITY FOR OTHER EVENTS

Buffets, concerts, conferences, fashion shows, product launches, receptions and seminars. Air displays, clay pigeon shoots, archery, equestrian events, fairs, garden parties. Filming.

EXTRA FACILITIES

Grand Piano in the Long Gallery. 250 acres of parkland, grass tennis court, cricket pitch and eventing course. Strip for light aircraft 4 miles.

ADVICE TO COURIERS & DRIVERS

No photography is allowed in the Castle.

FACILITIES FOR THE DISABLED

Disabled toilets available. Elderly or disabled visitors may alight at the Castle entrance. Ramps provided.

PARKING FOR COACHES & CARS

Unlimited parking for cars up to 100 yards from the Castle. Up to 6 coaches can be parked 100 yards from the Castle.

CATERING

Home-made afternoon teas. A maximum of 86 people can be catered for with waitress service. Other meals by arrangement.

GUIDED TOURS

All pre-booked parties are given a guided tour, except on open-days, at no additional cost. By prior arrangement, the owner may meet the groups. Duration of the tour is 45 minutes.

GIFT SHOP

Open when the castle is open to the public. Plant Stall open within Grounds.

GUIDE BOOK

Colour guide £1.60. Special children's guide.

SCHOOL VISITS/ CHILDREN

Rockingham has received 3 Sandford Awards for Heritage Education. There is much of interest for schools. A special pack has been designed with the National Curriculum in mind containing 27 booklets relating to different aspects of the Castle's history, including trails for the grounds, the village and the church. This can be obtained by post, price £7.50. Special tours for schools can be arranged and covered spaces are available for work and picnics when wet.

OPENING TIMES

Summer
Open every day by appointment for parties.

Easter Sunday - 30 Sept

Mon	Bank Hols & by appointment
Tues	*
Wed	By appointment
Thurs	1.30pm-5.30pm
Fri } Sat }	By appointment
Sun	1.30pm-5.30pm

Grounds open 12noon on Bank Hol. Suns & Mons.

*Tuesdays in August, following Bank Hols or by appointment 1.30pm-5.30pm.

Winter
Open every day by appointment for booked parties. House and garden closed to the casual visitor.

ADMISSION

All Year
HOUSE & GARDEN

Adult	£3.60
Child*	£2.20
OAP	£3.00
Group**	
Adult	£3.00
OAP	£3.00
Student	£1.45

* Up to 16 years
**Min £60, £36.25 Schools

Winter
Same as summer rates.

CONFERENCE AND FUNCTION FACILITIES

ROOM	DIMENSIONS	CAPACITY	LAYOUT	POWER POINTS	SUITABLE FOR A/V
Great Hall	37'6"x22'	100	Theatre	1	✓
Panel Room	36'x23'	100	Theatre	1	✓
Long Gallery	87'x16'6"	100	Theatre	2	
Walkers House 1	31'x17'6"	60	Buffet	2	
Walkers House 2	24'x18'	50	Buffet	2	

SULGRAVE MANOR
Banbury, Oxfordshire

SULGRAVE MANOR is the early English home of the ancestors of George Washington, first mentioned in the Domesday Book in 1086. The House was the birthplace of Reverend Lawrence Washington, whose son, Colonel John Washington, left England in 1656 to take up the land which later became Mount Vernon.

In 1914 Sulgrave Manor was presented by body of British subscribers to the peoples of Great Britain and the United States of America in celebration of the Hundred Years Peace between the two countries. Restored and refurnished, it now presents a perfect example of a small manor house and garden at the same time of Shakespeare.

Of special interest is the Washington Coat of Arms (three mullets and two bars) still clearly to be seen in a spandrel of the main doorway. This is said to have inspired the Stars and Stripes of the American National Flag.

Each room in the house is furnished in the style of its period. The Great Hall and Great Chamber above have fine collections of Tudor and Early Jacobean furniture. The Queen Anne wing, added in the year 1700, displays superb examples of 18th Century craftsmanship. However it is perhaps the magnificent Kitchen with its unique collection of utensils, its perfect range and typical furniture, that is justifiably one of the great features of the house.

GARDENS

One of the attractive features of the Manor is its garden, designed in 1921 by Sir Reginald Blomfield.

CONTACT

Martin Sirot-Smith
Sulgrave Manor
Manor Road
Sulgrave
Banbury
Oxfordshire
OX17 2SD

Tel: (0295) 76020

LOCATION

M40 5mls, M1 15mls. 10 mins from Banbury, Brackley, Towcester. 20 mins to Buckingham. 30 mins to N'hampton. 45 mins to Oxford, Warwick, Stratford. 2hrs from London.

Rail: Banbury Stn 6mls.

Bus: From Banbury/ Brackley.

Taxi: Fisher's Taxis (0295) 760797.

SUITABILITY FOR OTHER EVENTS

Craft fairs, Garden Parties, Receptions, Open Performances, Concerts.

EXTRA FACILITIES

Lectures can be arranged on the property and its history for up to 30 people.

ADVICE TO COURIERS & DRIVERS

Please book in advance as numbers and parking limited. No photography in house; dogs on leads in gardens only. No smoking in the House.

PARKING FOR COACHES & CARS

Parking for 40 cars and 4 coaches, 30 yards from House.

CATERING

'The Brew House' tea room (capacity 25/50 people). Parties can be booked in advance for tea and other meals.

GUIDED TOURS

Available for groups of up to 30 people at no additional cost. Average time taken to see the House 1-1¼ hours. There is a video of the 'Washington Trail', tracing the family links in this country.

GIFT SHOP

Gift Shop open at the same time as House.

GUIDE BOOKS

Colour guide book, £1.50.

SCHOOL VISITS/CHILDREN

Groups are welcome, cost £1.25 per child. A guide is provided. It is especially worthwhile for the young student as it is comparatively small. There is a special children's guide book and a paddock to play in. A teachers pack is available and preliminary visits are free.

OPENING TIMES

Summer
1 April - 31 October

EVERYDAY EXCEPT WEDNESDAY
10.30am to 1.00pm.
2.00pm-5.30pm (4pm Oct)

By appointment, evening parties welcome at any time.

Winter

OPEN WEEKENDS MARCH, NOVEMBER, DECEMBER
10.30am-1.00pm
2.00pm-4.00pm

Open by appointment only weekdays Feb., March, November and December.

ADMISSION

All Year

Adult	£3.00
Child*	£1.50
OAP	£3.00
Student	£1.50
Family***	£9.00
GROUP**	
Adult	£2.50
Child*	£1.25
OAP	£2.50
Student	£1.25

* Aged 5-16
** Min. 12 people.
***2 Adults + 2 or more children.

CONFERENCE AND FUNCTION FACILITIES

ROOM	DIMENSIONS	CAPACITY	LAYOUT	POWER POINTS	SUITABLE FOR A/V
Great Hall	24'x18'	50	Theatre	3	
		50	Buffet	3	
		30	Schoolroom	3	
		24	Dinner	3	

Aynhoe Park, Aynho, Banbury.
6 miles south east of Banbury on A41.

❀ **Canons Ashby House,** Canons Ashby.
(0327) 860044 13 miles from Banbury on unclassified road.

COTTESBROOKE HALL

OPEN
2.00-5.00pm
Thursdays and
Bank Holiday
Mondays from
Easter Monday
to end
September.

COTTESBROOKE HALL, NORTHAMPTON TEL: 060 124 808
(Captain and Mrs J Macdonald-Buchanan)

Architecturally magnificent Queen Anne house commenced in 1702. Renowned picture collection, particularly of sporting and equestrian subjects. Fine English and Continental furniture and porcelain. Main vista aligned on celebrated 7th century Saxon church at Brixworth. House reputed to be the pattern for Jane Austen;s "Mansfield Park". Notable gardens of great variety including fine old cedars, specimen trees and herbaceous borders.

Location: 10 miles north of Northampton near Creaton on A50, near Brixworth on A508 or Kelmarsh on A14.

Admission: £3.50 adult, Gardens only £1.50 Children half price.

Coton Manor Gardens,
(0604) 740219 10 miles north of Northampton.

Deene Park, Corby.
(078085) 278 6 miles north east of Corby on A43.

✤ **Kirby Hall,** Corby.
(0536) 203230 2 miles north of Corby.

❀ **Lyveden New Bield,** Oundle.
(08325) 358 4 miles south west of Oundle via A427

The Prebendal Manor House, Nassington.
(0780) 782575 6 miles north of Oundle.

❀ **The Priest's House,** Easton-on-the-Hill.
(0780) 62506 2 miles south west of Stamford off A43.

✤ **Rushton Triangular Lodge,** Rushton.
(0536) 710761 3/4 mile west of Rushton.

▯ **Southwick Hall,** Oundle.
(0832) 274064 3 miles north of Oundle.

Stoke Park Pavilions, Towcester.
In Stoke Bruerne village.

COTTESBROOKE

HUGH PALMER

ALNWICK CASTLE
Alnwick, Northumberland

ALNWICK CASTLE, home of the Duke of Northumberland, is the second largest inhabited Castle in England after Windsor and has been in the possession of the Percys, Earls and Dukes of Northumberland, since 1309. The earliest parts of the present Castle were erected by Yvo de Vescy, the first Norman Baron of Alnwick who became the owner of the town soon after 1096.

The rugged medieval exterior belies the richness of the interior, refurbished in the classical style of the Italian Renaissance. This replaces the Gothic decoration carried out by Robert Adam in the 18th Century.

The Castle houses an exquisite collection of art treasures, including the finest examples of Italian paintings in the north of England with works by other great artists including Van Dyck and Turner. In addition to fine English and French furniture and ornately carved wooden ceilings. The Castle also houses one of the country's most important collections of early Meissen porcelain.

GARDENS

The landscape to the north, over the River Aln, was laid out by Capability Brown, and can be enjoyed from the terrace of the Castle.

CONTACT

A Fricker
Alnwick Castle
Estate Office
Alnwick
Northumberland
NE66 1NQ

Tel: (0665) 510777
Fax: (0665) 510876

LOCATION

From London 6 hours, Edinburgh 2 hours, Chester 4 hours, Newcastle under 1 hour.

Buses from bus station in Alnwick.

Alnmouth Rail Station 5 miles.

SUITABILITY FOR OTHER EVENTS

Fashion Shows, fairs and filming. The parkland is also available for hire.

EXTRA FACILITIES

By arrangement only.

ADVICE TO COURIERS & DRIVERS

Parties are very welcome by prior arrangement if possible!. No dogs or photography indoors.

FACILITIES FOR THE DISABLED

All visitors have to walk from the car park, which is adjacent to the Castle. There are no toilet facilities for the disabled.

PARKING FOR COACHES & CARS

Parking for 70 cars and 4 coaches adjacent to the Castle. Coach and car parking facilities are also available close by in town.

CATERING

A large Tea Room offering home made food seats up to 80.

GIFT SHOP

Open at the same time as the Castle. Items include locally made pottery, small gifts and items for children.

GUIDE BOOKS

The guide book contains full colour pictures, price £2.25. Special children's guide book.

GUIDED TOURS

Are only available upon request at a cost of £5.00 per person. Up to 25 people in each party. Approx duration of the tour 1¹/₂ hours. Foreign languages tours on request

SCHOOL VISITS/CHILDREN

School visits are welcome at a cost of £1.90 per person. Educational literature on request.

OPENING TIMES

Summer
31 March -mid October

Mon	
Tues	
Wed	
Thurs	11am-5pm
Fri	
Sat	
Sun	

Last admission 4.30pm.

Winter

Special parties by arrangement only.

ADMISSION

Summer

HOUSE & GARDEN
Adult	£4.00
Child**	£2.20
OAP	£3.50
Family (2+2)	£10.00

GROUP*	
Adult	£3.50
Child**	£1.90
OAP	£3.00

*Minimum payment 12 people
**Age 5 - 16

Winter

By arrangement only.

CONFERENCE AND FUNCTION FACILITIES

ROOM	DIMENSIONS	CAPACITY	LAYOUT	POWER POINTS	SUITABLE FOR A/V
The Great Guest Hall	100'x30'	300	Silver Service/ Buffet	✓	✓

BAMBURGH CASTLE
Northumberland

CONTACT

P Bolam
R G Bolam & Son
Rothbury
Northumberland
NE65 7SP

Tel: (0669) 20314
Fax: (0669) 21236

LOCATION

42 miles north of Newcastle upon Tyne. 20 miles south of Berwick upon Tweed. 6 miles east of Belford B1342 from A1 at Belford.

Bus: Bus service 200 yards.

Taxi: R Aitchison (0668) 214392.

BAMBURGH CASTLE is the home of Lady Armstrong and her family. The earliest reference to Bamburgh shows the craggy citadel to have been a royal centre by AD 547. Recent archaeological excavation has revealed that the site has been occupied since prehistoric times. The Norman Keep has been the stronghold for nearly nine centuries, but the remainder has twice been extensively restored, initially by Lord Crewe in the 1750s and subsequently by the first Lord Armstrong at the end of the 19th Century. This Castle was the first to succumb to artillery fire - that of Edward IV.

The public rooms contain many exhibits, including the loan collections of armour from HM Tower of London, the John George Joicey Museum, Newcastle-upon-Tyne and other private sources, which complement the Castle's armour. Porcelain, China, Jade, furniture from many periods, oils, watercolours and a host of interesting items are all contained within one of the most important buildings of Britain's national heritage.

VIEWS

The views from the ramparts are unsurpassed and take in Holy Island, The Farne Islands, one of Northumberland's finest beaches and, landwards, the Cheviot Hills.

SUITABILITY FOR OTHER EVENTS

Bamburgh has been used as a location for films both interior and exterior.

ADVICE TO COURIERS & DRIVERS

No pets admitted. No cameras to be used in the interior of the building.

FACILITIES FOR THE DISABLED

Facilities for the disabled are restricted to one toilet and limited access dependant upon disability.

PARKING FOR COACHES & CARS

Capacity of the car park: approx 100 cars adjacent to the Castle. Coaches park free on tarmac drive at entrance.

CATERING

Tea Rooms for light refreshments during viewing times. Meals for organised groups can be booked in advance.

GUIDED TOURS

By arrangement at any time. Minimum charge out of hours £30.00.

GIFT SHOP

Within the Castle, offering quality merchandise. Open during public viewing hours and also for booked parties.

GUIDE BOOKS

Colour guide book, £1.30.

SCHOOL VISITS/CHILDREN

Groups of children welcome guide will be provided if requested. Of particular interest displays of arms and armour and the Armstrong naval gun. No special facilities but guides pitch tours to suit age group. Educational pack available.

OPENING TIMES

Summer

April & Sept	
Mon	
Tues	
Wed	
Thurs	1pm - 5pm
Fri	
Sat	
Sun	

May & June	
Mon	
Tues	
Wed	
Thurs	12pm - 5.30pm
Fri	
Sat	
Sun	

July & August	
Mon	
Tues	
Wed	
Thurs	12pm - 6pm
Fri	
Sat	
Sun	

October	
Mon	
Tues	
Wed	
Thurs	1pm -4.30pm
Fri	
Sat	
Sun	

Tours by arrangement at any time.

ADMISSION

Summer

Adult	£2.50
Child*	£1.10
OAP	£2.00
Group**	
Adult	£2.00
Child*	£0.90
OAP	£1.60

* Up to 16
** Min payment £30

Winter
Group rates only.

CHILLINGHAM CASTLE
Nr Alnwick, Northumberland

CONTACT

The Administrator
Chillingham Castle
Near Alnwick
Northumberland
NE66 5NJ

Tel: (06685) 359
(071) 937 7829
Fax: (06685) 463
(071) 938 3156

LOCATION

Off A1 Chatton to
Berwick road or off
B6346 Alnwick to Chatton
Road.

Rail: Alnmouth or
Berwick

THIS remarkable Castle, the home of Sir Humphry Wakefield Bt, with its alarming dungeons has, since the twelve hundreds, been continuously owned by the family of the Earls Grey and their relations. You will see active restoration of complex masonry, metalwork and ornamental plaster as the great halls and state rooms are gradually brought back to life with antique furniture, tapestries and arms and armour as of old and even a torture chamber.

At first a 12th Century stronghold, Chillingham became a fully fortified Castle in the 14th Century. Wrapped in the Nation's history it occupied a strategic position as fortress during Northumberland's bloody border feuds, often besieged and at many times enjoying the patronage of royal visitors. In Tudor days there were additions but the underlying Medieval character has always been retained. The 18th and 19th Centuries saw decorative refinements and extravagances including the lake, garden and grounds laid out by Sir Jeffrey Wyatville, fresh from his triumphs at Windsor Castle.

GARDENS

With romantic grounds the Castle commands breathtaking views of the surrounding countryside. As you walk to the lake you will see according to the season, drifts of snowdrops, daffodils or bluebells and an astonishing display of rhododendrons. This emphasizes the restrained formality of the Elizabethan topiary garden, with its intricately clipped hedges of box and yew. Lawns, the formal gardens and woodland walks are all fully open to the public.

OPENING TIMES

Summer

Easter Weekend
    1.30pm - 5pm

May - September
Mon   1.30pm - 5pm
Tues   Closed
Wed
Thurs
Fri   } 1.30pm - 5pm
Sat
Sun

August
Opens at 11.00am

Winter

Open every day by appointment for booked parties. House and garden closed to casual visitors.

ADMISSION

Summer

Adult	£3.30
OAP	£2.75
Child*	£2.00
* Up to 16 years.	
GROUP**	£2.25
20 or more, pre-booking essential	

SUITABILITY FOR OTHER EVENTS

Any form of corporate entertainment can be undertaken, we will consider any other requests in any field. Weddings welcome.

EXTRA FACILITIES

Chillingham is suitable for the use of light aircraft and helicopters. There is a pistol and rifle range. Salmon, sea trout and trout fishing available, also tuition from qualified shooting instructors, accommodation for up to 30 guests in the Castle. Must be arranged well in advance. Lunches, drinks and dinner for up to 150 people can be arranged at any time.

ADVICE TO COURIERS & DRIVERS

Avoid Lilburn route, gates wide enough to admit any coach. Coach parties welcome by prior arrangement. Telephone 06685-359 or 071 937 7829. Fax: (06685) 463. Sorry no dogs.

GUIDE BOOKS

At present there is a history of the Castle available, and a guide to the many ghosts resident at Chillingham. There shortly will be a full colour guide to the Castle and its contents.

GUIDED TOURS

These can be arranged, and the owner is frequently available to take parties around personally.

GIFT SHOP

Gift/souvenir shop, also antique and curio shop.

CATERING

Tearoom for use of public, cap. 70. Booked meals for up to 170.

CONFERENCE AND FUNCTION FACILITIES

ROOM	DIMENSIONS	CAPACITY	LAYOUT	POWER POINTS	SUITABLE FOR A/V
King James I Room		120			
Great Hall		180			
Minstrels' Hall		100			
2 x Drawing Room		60 each			
Museum		150			
Tea Room		100			
Lower Gallery		30			
Upper Gallery		40			

⌗ **Aydon Castle,** Corbridge.
(043471) 2450 1 mile north of Corbridge.

BELSAY CASTLE

OPEN
Summer
1 April-31 Oct.
Daily
10.00am-6.00pm

Winter
1 Nov-31 March
Daily
10.00am-4.00pm

BELSAY HALL, CASTLE & GARDENS, PONTELAND
TEL: 066181 636
(English Heritage)

19th century Neo-Classical mansion lies at the entrance to 30 acres of exciting gardens, which in turn lead on to the 14th century castle and ruined manor. Important collections of rare and exotic flowering trees grow in meandering deep ravines of the 'picturesque' Quarry Gardens. Massed plantings of rhododendrons. Large heather garden. Spring bulbs. Exhibition of Belsay's architectural and landscape history in stable block.

Location: 14 miles north west of Newcastle upon Tyne.
Admission: £2.40 adults, £1.80 concessions, £1.20 child.

⌗ **Berwick upon Tweed Barracks,** Berwick upon Tweed.
(0289) 304493 On the Parade, off Church Street in town centre.

⌗ **Brinkburn Priory,** near Rothbury.
(066570) 628 5 miles east of Rothbury.

✹ **Cherryburn,** Mickley.
(0661) 843276 11 miles west of Newcastle on A695.

⌗ **Chester's Roman Fort and Museum,** Chollerford.
(043481) 379 1/2 mile south west of Chollerford.

⌗ **Corbridge Roman Site,** Corbridge.
(043471) 2349 1/2 mile north west of Corbridge.

⌗ **Dunstanburgh Castle,** Alnwick.
(066576) 231 8 miles north east of Alnwick.

CRAGSIDE

OPEN
1 April-30 Oct.
(Closed Mon.,
open B.H.Mons.)
House: 1-5.30pm
(last admission
4.45pm)
Garden:
10.30am-5.30pm
Grounds:
10.30am-7pm
Visitor Centre:
(inc. Shop,
Vickers Room
Restaurant &
Armstrong
Energy Centre)
10.30am-5.30pm.

CRAGSIDE, ROTHBURY TEL: 0669 20333
(The National Trust)

Cragside was the home of the inventor and industrialist, William Armstrong. Designed mainly by Richard Norman Shaw. It was the first house in the world to be lit by electricity derived from water power. There are walks through millions of trees and rhododendrons and the Victorian Formal Garden features an Orchard House, Rose Loggia, Fernery and Italian Garden.

Location: Entrance gate 1 mile north of Rothbury, 15 miles north west of Morpeth off A697 and B6341 (Rothbury-Alnwick road).
Admission: House, Garden & Grounds £5.50, Garden & Grounds £3.40 Fam. Tkt. £14 (2+2).

⌗ **Hadrian's Roman Wall** Various sites throughout Northumberland and Tyne and Wear.

⌗ **Housesteads Roman Fort,** Bardon Mill.
(04984) 363 2 3/4 miles north east of Bardon Mill.

🏛 **Howick Hall Gardens,** Alnwick
(0665) 577285 6 miles north east of Alnwick.

Kirkley Hall Gardens, Ponteland.
(0661) 860808 3 miles north of Ponteland off A696.

✹ **Lindisfarne Castle,** Holy Island.
(0289) 89244 5 miles east of Beal across Causeway.

⌗ **Lindisfarne Priory,** Holy Island.
(028989)200 On Holy Island which can be reached by Causeway.

⌗ **Norham Castle,** Berwick.
(028982) 329 8 miles south west of Berwick.

🏛 **Preston Tower,** Chathill.
(0665) 89227 7 miles north Alnwick

⌗ **Prudhoe Castle,** Prudhoe.
(0661) 33459 In Prudhoe off A695.

🏛 **Seaton Delaval Hall**. Whitley Bay.
091 237 3040 1/2 mile from coast at Seaton Sluice.

WALLINGTON

OPEN
1 April-30 Oct.
House
1.00-5.30pm
Last adm. 5pm
(open daily
closed Tues.)
Grounds: Open
all year during
daylight hours
Walled Garden:
1 April-30 Sept.
10.30am-7.00pm
October
10.30-6.00pm
Nov.-March
10.30am-4.00pm

WALLINGTON, MORPETH TEL: 067074 283
(The National Trust)

The house was built in 1688 and greatly altered in the 1740's. Contains fine Italian plasterwork, porcelain and needlework. The central hall is decorated by William Bell Scott, Ruskin and others. Woodland walks always open and Walled Garden with Conservatory contains magnificent fuschias.

Location: 12 miles west of Morpeth (B6343) 6 miles north west of Belsay (A696) take B6342 to Cambo.
Admission: House and Grounds £4.40, Walled Garden & Grounds £2.20.

⌗ **Warkworth Castle and Hermitage.**
(0665) 711423 7 1/2 miles south of Alnwick.

BELSAY HALL

SEATON DELEVAL HALL

BLENHEIM PALACE
Woodstock, Oxford

BLENHEIM PALACE, home of the 11th Duke of Marlborough and birthplace of Sir Winston Churchill, was built between 1705-1722 for John Churchill, 1st Duke of Marlborough, in grateful recognition of his magnificent victory at the Battle of Blenheim in 1704. One of England's largest private houses, Blenheim was built in the Baroque style by Sir John Vanbrugh and is considered his masterpiece. The land and £240,000 were given by Queen Anne and a grateful nation.

Blenheim's wonderful interior reveals striking contrasts - from the lofty Great Hall to gilded State rooms and the, majestic Long Library. The superb collection includes fine paintings, furniture, bronzes and the famous Marlborough Victories tapestries. The five room Churchill Exhibition includes his birth room.

GARDENS

The Palace grounds reflect the evolution of grand garden design. Of the original work by Queen Anne's gardener. Henry Wise, only the Walled Garden remains; but dominating all is the superb landscaping of 'Capability' Brown. Dating from 1764, his work includes the lake, Park and Gardens. Achille Duchêne, employed by the 9th Duke, subsequently recreated the Great Court and built the Italian Garden on the east and The Water Terraces on the west of the Palace. Recently the Pleasure Gardens complex has been developed. This includes The Marlborough Maze, Herb Garden, Adventure Playground, Butterfly House and Putting Greens.

CONTACT

Paul F D Duffie FTS
Blenheim Palace
Woodstock
Oxon
OX20 1PX

Tel: (0993) 811091
Fax: (0993) 813527

LOCATION

From London, M40, A44 (11/2 hrs), 8 mls N of Oxford. London 63mls, Birmingham 54mls.

Air: Heathrow Airport 60mls (1hr).

Coach: From London (Victoria) to Oxford.

Rail: Oxford Stn.

Bus: Oxford (Cornmarket) - Woodstock.

SUITABILITY FOR OTHER EVENTS

Corporate hospitality, including dinners and receptions, filming, equestrian events, craft fairs. Will consider any proposals.

EXTRA FACILITIES

Lake (rowing boats for hire), motor launch trips, train rides. . Private tours may be pre-booked.

ADVICE TO COURIERS & DRIVERS

Advise Administrator of special requirements for groups over 100. Coaches/groups welcome without pre-booking. 'Notes for Party Organisers' available by post. Dogs on leash in Park. (Guide dogs only in House and Garden). Photography inside (no flash). Unlimited parking for cars and coaches.

CATERING

2 Restaurants, 2 Cafeterias. Group capacity 150. Groups can book for afternoon tea, buffets, lunches or dinners, menus available on request. Catering for private groups. Further information/bookings: Catering Manager, (0993) 811274.

FACILITIES FOR THE DISABLED

Disabled or elderly visitors may alight at the Palace entrance and vehicles then parked in allocated area. Toilet facilities in both the Palace and Park.

GUIDED TOURS

Tours included in the cost of entry. Guide Book £2.80.

GIFT SHOPS

Open 10.30am - 5.30pm also a Bookshop, Souvenir Stall and Garden Shop.

SCHOOL VISITS/CHILDREN

Welcome during normal hours. Full education service available, including visits to Palace, Park, Farm and Saw Mill. Also nature trail, lecture room and picnic hut. Holder of Sandford Award for Heritage Education since 1982 For details: Schools Liaison Officer, (0993) 811091.

OPENING TIMES

Summer
Mid March - 31 October

OPEN DAILY
10.30am-5.30pm
Last admission   4.45pm

Winter
1 November - Mid March

Park Only

The Duke of Marlborough reserves the right to close the Palace or Park or to amend admission prices without notice.

ADMISSION

Palace Tour & Churchill Exhibition, Park, Garden, Butterfly House, Adventure Play Area, Motor Launch, Train, Car or Coach Parking, but not entry to the maze or rowing boat hire.

1993 Rates

	Single	Group
Adult	£6.50	£5.30
OAP }	£4.80	£4.50
Child*}		
Child**	£3.10	£2.80

* Aged 16 & 17
** Aged 5 - 15

Blenheim Park, Butterfly House, Adventure Play Area, Train, Parking, but not entry to the Marlborough Maze or Rowing Boat Hire.

Coaches*	£16.00
Cars*	£3.50
Adult**	£0.80
Child**	£0.40

* Including occupants.
** Pedestrians.

Private visits*   £12.50
* By appointment only. Minimum charge of £250(mornings) and £375 (evenings)

CONFERENCE AND FUNCTION FACILITIES

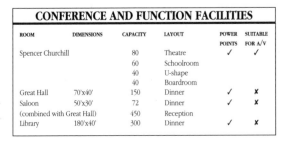

ROOM	DIMENSIONS	CAPACITY	LAYOUT	POWER POINTS	SUITABLE FOR A/V
Spencer Churchill		80	Theatre	✓	✓
		60	Schoolroom		
		40	U-shape		
		40	Boardroom		
Great Hall	70'x40'	150	Dinner	✓	✗
Saloon	50'x30'	72	Dinner	✓	✗
(combined with Great Hall)		450	Reception		
Library	180'x40'	300	Dinner	✓	✗

BROUGHTON CASTLE
Banbury, Oxfordshire

BROUGHTON CASTLE is essentially a family home lived in by Lord and Lady Saye and Sele and their family.

The original medieval Manor House, of which much remains today, was built in about 1300 by Sir John de Broughton. It stands on an island site surrounded by a 3 acre moat. The Castle was greatly enlarged between 1550 and 1600, at which time it was embellished with magnificent plaster ceilings, splendid panelling and fine fireplaces.

In the 17th Century William 8th Lord Saye and Sele, played a leading role in national affairs. He opposed Charles I's efforts to rule without Parliament and Broughton became a secret meeting place for the King's opponents.

During the Civil War William raised a regiment and he and his 4 sons all fought at the nearby Battle of Edgehill. After the battle the Castle was besieged and captured.

Arms and armour for the Civil War and from other periods are displayed in the Great Hall. Visitors may also see the Gatehouse, Gardens and Park together with the nearby 14th Century Church of St Mary, in which there are many family tombs, memorials and hatchments.

GARDENS

There are herbaceous borders, lawns reaching down to the moat and a Walled Garden filled with lavender.

CONTACT

The Administrator
Broughton Castle
Banbury
Oxfordshire
OX15 5EB

Tel: (0295) 812027

LOCATION

Broughton Castle is 2 miles west of Banbury Cross on the B4035, Shipston on Stour - Banbury Road. Easily accessible from Stratford-on-Avon, Warwick, Oxford, Burford and the Cotswolds. M40 exit 11.

Rail: From London/ Birmingham to Banbury.

Bus: Local bus service to Banbury. At busy times the approach from the South through Bloxham may be preferable.

SUITABILITY FOR OTHER EVENTS

Broughton offers a most unusual setting for filming, product launches, advertising features, corporate events in Park.

ADVICE TO COURIERS & DRIVERS

Photography permitted for personal use. No dogs inside House. At busy times avoid Banbury and bring the group via Bloxham.

FACILITIES FOR THE DISABLED

Disabled visitors allowed vehicles access to main entrance

PARKING FOR COACHES & CARS

Capacity of the car park: 60 cars with unlimited overflow and 6 coaches with ample overflow. Both areas are 300 yards from the Castle.

CATERING

Tea Room available on open days. Tea/Coffee available for guided groups if pre-booked. Other meals by arrangement.

GUIDED TOURS

Available to pre-booked groups at no extra charge. Guided tours not available on open days.

GIFT SHOP

Open on public open days and also for pre-booked guided groups.

GUIDE BOOKS

Colour guide book, £1.00. Children's guide book, 50p. Brief notes are available in French, Spanish, Dutch, Italian, Japanese and German.

SCHOOL VISITS/CHILDREN

School visits welcomed. Work sheets available and children's guide books. Children may try on armour.

OPENING TIMES

Summer
18 May - 14 September

Mon }	By appointment
Tues }	for groups
Wed	2pm - 5pm
Thurs	July & August
	2pm - 5pm
Fri	By appointment
Sat	for groups
Sun }	2pm - 5pm

Bank Hol Sundays and Mondays, including Easter (not Christmas and New Year)
2 - 5pm

Winter

Open any day and time for pre-booked groups.

ADMISSION

All Year

Adult	£3.20
Child*	£1.50
OAP	£2.70
GROUP**	
Adult	£2.70
Child*	£1.50
OAP	£2.70

5* Aged 0-16
** Min payment: adults £50 children £30p.

KINGSTONE LISLE PARK
Wantage, Oxfordshire

OPENING TIMES

11am - 5pm

10 April, 2 May, 30 May, 31 July, 29 August.

KINGSTONE LISLE is a sensational Palladian House, home of the Lonsdale Family. The house is set in 140 acres of parkland. Superb views are enjoyed up to the Lambourn Downs where the Roman Ridgeway marks the southern boundary, Three spring-fed lakes beside the house complete this very attractive landscape.

The House built in 1677, is on the site of a fortified Castle which burnt down in 1620 (the original 12th century church is all that remains), The nearby Blowing Stone which according to legend was blown by King Alfred to muster his armies on the Downs is still in the village and can be blown by visitors during daylight hours.

The hall is in the style of Sir John Soane and there is a strong impression of entering an Italian Palazzo with beautiful ornate plaster ceilings, columns and figurines. By complete contrast the inner hall becomes the classical English country house, the most exciting feature being the Flying Staircase winding its way up, totally unsupported.

A fine collection of art, furniture, clocks, glass and needlework together with the architecture inspire visitors with admiration for the craftsmanship that has existed in Britain over the centuries.

GARDENS

Twelve acres of gardens include a shrubbery, pleached limes, an avenue leading up to an ornamental pond and a replica of Queen Mary's rose garden in Regents Park. The walled garden includes a tree nursery producing 250,000 oak trees from acorns under glass each year.

ADMISSION

Summer

Adults	£5.00
Child	£2.50
Fishing only	£5.00

Groups of 20 or more 10% discount by prior arrangement only.

CONTACT

The Secretary
Kingstone Lisle Park
Wantage
Oxfordshire
OX12 9QG

Tel: (0367) 820599
Fax: (0367) 820749

LOCATION

From London 76 miles, M4 Junct. 14.
From Oxford A420, 20 miles

Heathrow Airport approx 1 hour via M4..

Rail: To Didcot where taxis are available.

SUITABILITY FOR OTHER EVENTS

Filming and, photography; shooting parties; exclusive house parties; dinner bed and breakfast by arrangement.

EXTRA FACILITIES

Dinner, Bed and Breakfast £100 per person per night. Trout fishing all year round. Coarse fishing (seasonal). Private 9 holes golf practice course.

ADVICE TO COURIERS & DRIVERS

Alternative accommodation available at the Blowing Stone Inn in the village.

FACILITIES FOR THE DISABLED

Disabled and elderly visitors may alight at the entrance to the property. There are no toilets for the disabled.

PARKING FOR COACHES & CARS

Capacity of the car park: 25 cars, 30 yards from the House, and 3 coaches, 10 yards from the House.

CATERING

Lunch and dinner parties available strictly by arrangement for up to 30 people in the superb formal dining room.

GUIDED TOURS

On the hour on open days.

GUIDE BOOKS

Colour guide book, £2.00.

MAPLEDURHAM HOUSE & WATERMILL
Nr Reading, Oxfordshire

Mapledurham, a beautiful late 16th century Elizabethan Manor House set in tranquil surroundings alongside the River Thames. has been the home of the Blount family and their descendants for over 500 years. Richard Blount purchased The Old Manor (now the Tea Rooms) in 1490 and building of the present Manor House was commenced by Sir Michael Blount, Lieutenant of The Tower of London, in 1588 and completed by his son Sir Richard in 1612.

Original plasterwork ceilings and grand oak staircases can still be admired by visitors as can the fine collection of pictures and family portraits of the 16th, 17th and 18th centuries. The family Chapel built in the late 1700's, decorated in Strawberry Hill Gothic and still in regular use is one of the rooms viewed by the public.

The great 18th century poet, Alexander Pope, spent much time visiting his friends Martha and Teresa Blount and was probably responsible for landscaping the grounds.

Mapledurham also has literary connection with John Galworthy's "Forsyte Saga" and Kenneth Graham's "Wind in the Willows". It has provided the film set for "The Eagle Has Landed" and more recently the 1994 Television series "Class Act."

A Watermill has stood at Mapledurham since saxon times, the present structure dating from 15th century. The traditional wooden machinery is fully restored and the undershot waterwheel can be seen in action powering the great french burr millstones to produce flour.

The great sense of continuing history and idyllic setting add to the pleasure of either an afternoon visit to the house or a longer holiday in one of the Estates self-catering holiday cottages.

CONTACT

Miss Jean R Emary
The Estate Office
Mapledurham House
Mapledurham
Reading
RG4 7TR

Tel: (0734) 723350
Fax: (0734) 724016

LOCATION

Mapledurham is 4 miles north west of Reading on the north bank of the Thames. From London M4 45 minutes. Off A4074 Reading (Caversham) to Oxford/Woodcote Road

Rail: Reading Station plus boat from Caversham. 2.00pm on Open Days or by arrangement.

River: As above.

Taxi: From Reading Station.

SUITABILITY FOR OTHER EVENTS

Film locations, product launches, corporate entertaining, riverside setting for marquee receptions/dinners etc. Craft fairs, meetings.

EXTRA FACILITIES

Large riverside picnic/park area. 12 self-catering period holiday cottages on Estate, Golf course, Large covered river launch departs Caversham at 2pm on all open days and for pre-booked parties/events as required. River journey approx 40 minutes.

ADVICE TO COURIERS & DRIVERS

All parties must be pre-booked. Parking, entrance and refreshments free to driver.

FACILITIES FOR THE DISABLED

Disabled visitors can be driven to the entrance of Mill, Tea Rooms and House. Ground floors accessible to wheelchairs.

PARKING FOR COACHES & CARS

Large area for parking cars and ample room for coaches.

CATERING

Tea rooms in 14th century Old Manor and Stables on open days. each seating 50. Lunches/Dinners by prior arrangement. Marquee facilities available.

CONFERENCE AND FUNCTION FACILITIES

OLD MANOR AND STABLES ARE AVAILABLE. PLEASE APPLY TO ADMINISTRATOR FOR FULL DETAILS

GUIDED TOURS

All mid-week party visits are guided. At weekends guides are on duty in most rooms.

GIFT SHOP

1 Gift Shop adjoins Tea Rooms, the other is inside the Watermill.

GUIDE BOOKS

Available from Shop or Office, House £1.20. Watermill 70p and Bardolf Aisle 70p.

SCHOOL VISITS/CHILDREN

Visits to the Watermill fit particularly well in to the National Curriculum requirements and can be made throughout the year by prior arrangement. School packs for teachers are available.

OPENING TIMES

Summer
Easter Sat. - end Sept.

Saturdays, Sundays and Bank Holiday Mondays
Country Park
          12.30 - 7.0pm
Watermill   1.00-5.00pm
House   2.30-5.00pm

Pre-booked parties:
Tuesdays, Wednesdays, Thursdays only.

Winter

Closed to the general public.

ADMISSION

Summer
Combined House/Watermill
Adult   £4.00
Child*   £2.00

House only
Adult   £3.00
Child*   £1.50

Watermill only
Adult   £2.50
Child*   £1.30

* aged 5-14 years.

STONOR
Henley-on-Thames, Oxfordshire

Stonor, family home of Lord and Lady Camoys and the Stonor family for over 800 years, is set in a valley in the beautiful woods of the Chiltern Hills and surrounded by an extensive deer park.

The earliest part of the house dates from the 12th Century, whilst most of the house was built in the 14th Century. Early use of brick in Tudor times resulted in a more uniform facade concealing the earlier buildings, and changes to the windows and the roof in the 18th Century reflect the Georgian appearance still apparent today.

Inside, the house shows strong Gothic decoration, also from the 18th Century, and contains many items of rare furniture, sculptures, bronzes, tapestries, paintings and portraits of the family from Britain, Europe and America.

The Catholic Chapel used continuously through the reformation is sited close by a pagan stone circle. In 1581, Stonor served as a sanctuary for St Edmund Campion, and an exhibition at the house features his life and work.

GARDENS

Extensive gardens enclosed at the rear of the house face South and have fine views over the park. The springtime display of daffodils is particularly outstanding.

For 1994 the garden will feature a display of stone sculpture from Zimbabwe

CONTACT

D Boddy
Stonor Park
Henley-on-Thames
Oxfordshire
RG9 6HF

Tel: (0491) 638587

LOCATION

1 hour from London, M4 to Junct. 8/9. A4130 to Henley-on-Thames, then A4130/B480 to Stonor.

Bus: 3 miles along the Oxford - London route.

Rail: Henley-on-Thames Station 5 miles.

SUITABILITY FOR OTHER EVENTS

Grounds available for filming, craft fairs, car displays, product promotion, clay pigeon shooting.

EXTRA FACILITIES

Coffee for morning tours, by arrangement. There are also a limited number of evening tours and buffet suppers, also by prior arrangement. Lectures can be given on the property, its contents and history.

ADVICE TO COURIERS & DRIVERS

Admissions from groups must be by single payment on arrival unless prior arrangements are made for payment with vouchers. No dogs except on leads and not allowed within the House, tearoom or shop. No smoking in House, tearoom or shop. No photography in House.

FACILITIES FOR THE DISABLED

Disabled and elderly visitors may be left at the entrance to the house before parking. There are no toilets for the disabled, although access to the toilets is level. Ramp access to gardens, tearoom and shop.

PARKING FOR COACHES & CARS

Capacity of the Car Park: unlimited area for cars and space for 30 coaches, 100 yards from the House.

CATERING

Groups can book lunch or supper. Afternoon Teas are available during all open times without prior booking. Menus available upon request.

GUIDED TOURS

Guided tours are available outside normal public hours. From 20 to 60 people can be taken round at any one time. Tour takes $1\frac{1}{4}$-$1\frac{1}{2}$ hours.

GIFT SHOP

Open for same hours as the House. Selection of Stonor and general souvenirs.

GUIDE BOOKS

Colour guide book, with separate handlist of contents, price £1.50.

SCHOOL VISITS/CHILDREN

School groups are welcome, cost £2.00 per head. Lectures and guided tours by arrangement.

OPENING TIMES

Summer
April - September

Sun	2pm - 5.30pm
Mon	Bank Hols only 12.30pm - 5.30pm
Tues	By appointment only (groups).
Wed	April: only by appointment May - Sept 2pm - 5.30pm
Thurs	Jul & Aug 2pm - 5.30pm Other times by appointment
Fri	Closed
Sat	Aug: 2pm-5.30pm

Winter
October - March
Closed

ADMISSION

Summer

HOUSE & GARDEN
Adult	£3.50
Child*	Free
Concessions**	£3.20
Groups***	£3.00

GARDENS ONLY
Adult	£1.50

* Under 14 years.
** National Trust and English Heritage members,. HHA FREE.
*** Min 12 persons, in a single payment. Visits outside normal hours at full rate.

OXFORDSHIRE

- 🏛 **Ardington House**, Wantage.
  (0235) 833244 12 miles south of Oxford.

- ❦ **Ashdown House**, Lambourn.
  3¹/₂ miles north of Lambourn.

- **Botanic Gardens**, Oxford

- **Brook Cottage**, AlKerton.
  (029587) 303 6 miles north west of Banbury.

- ❦ **Buscot Old Parsonage**, Buscot, Faringdon.
  (0494) 528051   2 miles south east of Lechlade.

- ❦ **Buscot Park,** near Faringdon.
  (0367) 242094 3 miles north west of Faringdon on A417.

- **Ditchley Park,** Enstone.
  (0608) 677346 1¹/₂ miles west of A44 at Kiddington.

- 🏛 **Fawley Court - Marian Fathers Historic House & Museum,** Henley on Thames.
  (0491) 574917   1 mile north of Henley on Thames via A4155 to Marlow.

- ❦ **The Great Barn,** Great Coxwell.
  (0494) 528051   2 mile south west of Faringdon .

- ❦ **Greys Court,** Henley on Thames.
  (0491) 628529 At Rotherfield Greys, 3 miles west of Henley on Thames.

BROUGHTON CASTLE (SEE P. 128)

Milton Manor House, Abingdon.
(0235) 831287 9 miles south of Oxford.

- ✿ **Minster Lovell Hall and Dovecote,** Minster Lovell.
  (0993) 75315   2¹/₂ miles north west of Witney.

Nuffield Place, Nettlebed.
(0491) 641224 Approx. 7 miles from Henley on Thames just off A423.

Rousham House, Steeple Aston
(0869) 47110 12 miles north of Oxford, 1 mile Hopcrofts Holt Hotel.

KINGSTON BAGPUIZE HOUSE

OPEN
1 April-30 Sept.
Sun & Bank Hol.
Mons.
2.30-5.30pm

Groups by
written
appointment on
Weekdays only

KINGSTON BAGPUIZE HOUSE, ABINGDON TEL: 0865 820259
(The Lord and Lady Tweedsmuir)

This Charles II manor house was built before 1670 in the style of Inigo Jones. It has a fine cantilevered staircase, and panelled rooms with some good furniture and pictures. The large garden contains many unusual trees and shrubs. There are attractive 17th century stables and outbuildings. Visitors are shown round the House by the family and their friends.

Location: In Kingston Bagpuize village, off A415 Abingdon Road near A415/A420 bypass intersection. Abindon 5 miles, Oxford 9 miles.
Admission: House & Garden: Adults £2.50. OAP's £2.00. Children £1.50. Garden only: 50p (children under 5 years - Free to garden but not admitted to House).

KINGSTON LISLE PARK (SEE P 129)

STANTON HARCOURT MANOR

OPEN
Thurs., Sun and
Bank Hol Mon.
Stated dates only
2.00-6.00pm
April 3, 4, 14, 17,
28
May 1,2,12,15,
26,29,30
June 9,12,23,26
July 7,10,21,24
Aug.4,7,18,21,25,
28,29
Sept. 8,11,22,25.

STANTON HARCOURT MANOR HOUSE & GARDENS, WITNEY
TEL: 0865 881928
(Mr Crispin & The Hon Mrs Gascoigne)

12 acres of garden with Great Fish Pond and Stew Ponds provide tranquil surroundings for the unique mediaeval buildings - old Kitchen (Alexander) Pope's Tower and domestic Chapel. The House, a fine example of a very early unfortified house built to house the Harcourt family and its retainers, is still maintained as the family home.

Location: 9 miles west of Oxford, 5 miles south east of Witney on B449, between Eynsham and Standlake.
Admission: House & Gardens: £3, child (under 12) /OAP's £2. Garden only £1.50, child (under 12) /OAP's £1 Coaches by prior arrangement.

Wallingford Castle Gardens, Castle Street, Wallingford.

Waterperry Gardens, Wheatley.
(0844) 339226 2¹/₂ miles from A40 , turn off at Wheatley.

ATTINGHAM PARK
Shrewsbury, Shropshire

ATTINGHAM PARK, home of the Hill family and more recently their descendants, the Berwicks, dates from 1785 when the present house, designed by George Steuart, largely replaced the earlier Tern Hall. The Nash Picture Gallery and new staircase in the 1820s were the only major alterations to the house. After a period of inactivity in the 19th century the present house owes much to the late Lord and Lady Berwick who lived at Attingham from 1920. The house and 3,000-acre estate were given to the National Trust in 1953.

The elegant neo-classical house is a fine setting for French and Italian furniture, an extensive picture collection and the Ambassadorial silver used by members of the family serving in Italy. The delicate circular boudoir and the impressive red Dining Room are among the memorable rooms in this, the great country house of Shropshire.

GROUNDS

The house is set in a 250-acre deer park. landscaped by Repton; features include the Mile Walk along the River Tern, a circular park walk (2 miles) through mixed woodland, specimen trees and parkland which is home to a herd of Fallow Deer. The Park is open to the public at all times of the year (except 25 December).

CONTACT

The Administrator
Attingham Park
Shrewsbury
SY4 4TP

Tel: (0743) 709203
Fax: (0743) 709352

LOCATION

Attingham Park is 4 miles S.E. of Shrewsbury on B4380 (formerly A5): 7 miles west of end of M54 via B5061/B4380.

From London M40/M42/M6/M54, 3 hours/

Rail: Shrewsbury.

SUITABILITY FOR OTHER EVENTS

Meetings in Servants Hall or Upper Tea-room. Park and Exterior for film locations. Lectures on the property can be arranged by request for up to 80 people.

ADVICE TO COURIERS & DRIVERS

Parking free. No dogs in house and deer park. Refreshments: £5 voucher for drivers. Please advise clients there is no indoor photography.

FACILITIES FOR THE DISABLED

Disabled visitors may be driven to the rear of the house. 4 wheel electric vehicle for use in park. Braille and large print guide to house. Adapted lavatories. Access to tea garden but difficult access to tea-room.

PARKING FOR COACHES & CARS

Extensive free parking for coaches and cars 120 yards from house.

CATERING

Licensed tea-room seats 50. Upper tea-room seats 50. Group bookings welcomed for lunch and tea.

GUIDED TOURS

Visiting is normally free flow. Group tours can be arranged in advance, and morning and evening opening for pre-booked groups, minimum 20 (£5 per head).

GIFT SHOP

Open as house selling quality National Trust gifts.

GUIDE BOOK

Cost £1.80. Short guide also available. Family activity guide to Park £1.50. Children's house quiz 25p.

SCHOOL VISITS/CHILDREN

Environmental education facilities in park available all year, including exhibition and rooms for school use. Please contact Education Assistant Tel: (0743) 709483.

OPENING TIMES

Summer
26 March - 28 September
Sat
Sun
Mon*   1.30-5pm
Tues   Last Adm
Wed   4.30pm
*Bank Hol 11am - 5pm.
October
Sat.
Sun.   1.30 - 5pm

Winter
House closed

Grounds open dawn to dusk all year (except 25 December).

ADMISSION

Summer
National Trust members free.

House and Park
Adult   £3.30
Child*   £1.65
Family   £8.25
Groups**   £2.64

Grounds only
Adult   £1.30
Child*   £0.65

Evenings Tours+   £5.00

* Aged up to 17 (under 5 free)
** Minimum 20 people
+ (min. 20 or £100)

OAKLEY HALL
Market Drayton, Shropshire

OAKLEY HALL is situated in magnificent countryside on the boundary of Shropshire and Staffordshire. The present Hall is a fine example of a Queen Anne mansion house and was built on the site of an older dwelling mentioned in the Domesday Survey of 1085. Oakley Hall was the home of Chetwode family until it was finally sold in 1919.

GARDENS

Set in 100 acres of rolling parkland, the Hall commands superb views over the surrounding countryside and the gardens include wild areas in addition to the more formal parts.

The surrounding countryside is rich in historical associations. St Mary's Church at Mucklestone, in which parish the Hall stands, was erected in the 13th Century and it was from the tower of this Church that Queen Margaret of Anjou observed the Battle of Blore Heath in 1459. This was a brilliant victory for the Yorkist faction in the Wars of the Roses and the blacksmith at Mucklestone was reputed to have shod the Queen's horse back to front in order to disguise her escape.

CONTACT

Mrs Ann E Fisher
Oakley Hall
Market Drayton
Shropshire
TF9 4AG

Tel: (0630) 653472
Fax: (0630) 653282

LOCATION

From London 3hrs: M1, M6 to exit 14, then A5013 to Eccleshall, turn right at T-junction, 200 yards, then left onto B5026. Mucklestone is 1³/4 mls from Loggerheads on B5026. Turn left before Church, to end of lane then right. 200 yards turn left into small lane opposite telephone kiosk. Bear left between two lodges.

SUITABILITY FOR OTHER EVENTS

Concerts, conferences, wedding receptions, fashion shows, product launches, seminars, clay pigeon shooting, garden parties and filming.

EXTRA FACILITIES

Grand piano, hard tennis court, croquet lawn, horse riding.

CONFERENCE FACILITIES

See below for rooms available. Slide projector, word processor, fax and secretarial assistance are all available by prior arrangement.

ACCOMMODATION

Oakley Hall offers 3 double and one twin bedroom with baths.

ADVICE TO COURIERS & DRIVERS

No stiletto heels. No dogs.

FACILITIES FOR THE DISABLED

Disabled and elderly visitors may alight at the entrance to the Hall, before parking in the allocated areas. There are no toilets for the disabled.

PARKING FOR COACHES & CARS

Parking for 100 cars, 100/200 yds from the Hall.

CATERING

Buffets, lunches and dinners can all be arranged, Menus available on request.

GROUP VISITS

By prior arrangement groups will be met and entertained by members of the Fisher family.

OPENING TIMES

All Year

Open by pre-booked appointment only and for conferences and other functions.

ADMISSION

Please telephone for details.

CONFERENCE AND FUNCTION FACILITIES

ROOM	DIMENSIONS	CAPACITY	LAYOUT	POWER POINTS	SUITABLE FOR A/V
Hall	50'x30'	130	Theatre	10	✓
		130	Buffet		
		150	Lunch/Dinner		
Dining Room	40'x27'	80	Theatre	6	✓
		30	U-shape		
		20	Boardroom		
		60	Buffet		
		80	Lunch/Dinner		
Ballroom	40'x27'	80	Theatre	6	✓
		30	U-shape		
		20	Boardroom		
		60	Buffet		

WESTON PARK
Weston-under-Lizard, Shropshire

WESTON PARK has been the home of successive generations of the Earls of Bradford since the 12th Century and is today owned by a charity, 'The Weston Park Foundation'.

The present House was built on the site of the original medieval Manor House in 1671 and was designed by Lady Elizabeth Wilbraham. It boasts a fine collection of paintings with works by Stubbs, Van Dyck, Holbein, Gainsborough and Lely. The contents of the House, brought together by the family over the centuries, include some fine examples of 18th Century English and European furniture, rare Parisian tapestries from the Gobelin factory and porcelain collections.

The House stands in 1,000 acres of formal gardens, arboretum and parkland designed by the great 'Capability' Brown. Particular features are the Italian Broderie and the Rose Garden of the South Terrace.

The Park now houses numerous visitor attractions, including a Woodland Adventure Playground, Miniature Railway and Pets Corner.

An extensive programme of events is held each season, and includes Classical Concerts, Horse Trials and the Midland Game & Country Sports Fair. Further details available from Weston Park.

CONTACT

Park: Helen Howat
House: Vivien Williamson
Weston Park
Nr Shifnal
Shropshire
TF11 8LE

Tel: (095276) 201/207
Fax: (095276) 430

LOCATION

Birmingham 30 minutes. Manchester 1 hour. Motorway access - Junct. 12 M6 or Junct. 3 M54. House situated on A5.

Nearest Railway Stations - Wolverhampton or Stafford.

Nearest Airport - Birmingham

SUITABILITY FOR OTHER EVENTS

Residential parties, special dinners, wedding receptions, conferences, product launches, outdoor concerts and events, filming location.

Weston Park offers a full event organisation service.

EXTRA FACILITIES

Helipad and airstrip. Wide variety of sporting activities organised for private groups eg Clay Pigeon Shooting, Archery, Hovercrafts, Rally Driving, Treasure Hunts.

ACCOMMODATION

Weston Park offers 19 delightful bedrooms with bathrooms, 15 doubles/twins, 3 singles and 1 three-bedded suite.

ADVICE TO COURIERS & DRIVERS

Dogs must always be kept on leads. Interior photography by prior arrangement only.

PARKING FOR COACHES & CARS

There is unlimited parking at the front door for cars and coaches containing private parties. There is a public car and coach park 100 yards from the property.

FACILITIES FOR THE DISABLED

House and part of the grounds accessible by wheelchair. There are toilets for the disabled.

CATERING

The Old Stables Restaurant & Tea Room provides meals and snacks on public open days.

Dine and Stay arrangements in the House on selected dates.

GIFT EMPORIUM

Open at the same time as the Park.

GUIDE BOOKS

Colour guide book, £1.00.

SCHOOL VISITS/CHILDREN

Weston Park is open on Tuesdays, Wednesdays and Thursdays in the latter half of June and all July. Advance booking is essential. Cost per child £1.50. Teachers' guidance notes and National Curriculum related Workpacks available.

OPENING TIMES

Summer

Easter - mid June
Bank Hols & Weekends

Mid June - End July
Daily, except Mon & Fri.

August
Daily

September
Weekends only

House Open   1 - 5pm
Park open 11am - 7pm

Winter
October - Easter

Closed

NB Visitors are advised to telephone first to check this information.

ADMISSION

Summer

HOUSE & GARDEN
Adult   £4.50
Child*   £3.00
OAP   £3.75

GARDEN ONLY
Adult   £3.00
Child*   £2.00
OAP   £2.50

* Aged 3-16.

CONFERENCE AND FUNCTION FACILITIES

ROOM	DIMENSIONS	CAPACITY	LAYOUT	POWER POINTS	SUITABLE FOR A/V
Dining Room	52'x23'	40-150	Various	15	✓
Orangery	51'x20'	40-150	Various	12	
Music Room	50'x20'	30-100	Various	24	✓
The Old Stables	58'x20'	30-95	Various	4	✓
Conference Room	40'x7'6"	20-60	Various	14	✓

SHROPSHIRE

Acton Round Hall, Bridgenorth.
  6 miles west of Bridgenorth.

Adcote, Little Ness, Shrewsbury.
  (0939) 260202 7 miles north west of Shrewsbury.

✿ **Benthall Hall,** Broseley.
  (0952) 882159 1 mile north west of Broseley.

BOSCOBEL HOUSE

OPEN
Summer
1 April-31
October
Daily
10.00am-6.00pm

Winter
Wed.-Sun.
10.00am-4.00pm
(Closed Jan)

BOSCOBEL HOUSE & THE ROYAL OAK, BREWOOD TEL: 0962 850244
(English Heritage)

When John Giffard built his hunting lodge in the 17th century, he little knew that it would become a refuge for the future King Charles II after his defeat at the battle of Worcester in 1651. It is now fully re-furnished with historic tapestries, paintings and antique furniture as the Victorians thought it would have appeared when Charles II hid in the priest's hole and took refuge in the oak tree in the grounds. Exhibition and shop.

Location: On unclassified road between A41 and A5, 8 miles north west of Wolverhampton.
Admission: £3.15 adult, £2.35 concessions, £1.55 child.

⌗ **Buildwas Abbey,** Much Wenlock.
  (095245) 3274 3¼ miles north east of Much Wenlock.

✿ **Carding Mill Valley & Long Mynd,** Church Stretton.
  (0694) 722631 15 miles south of Shrewsbury.

✿ **Dudmaston,** Quatt, Bridgnorth.
  (0746) 780866 4 miles south east of Bridgenorth on A442.

⌗ **Haughmond Abbey,** Shrewsbury.
  (074377) 661 3½ miles miles north east of Shrewsbury.

ATTINGHAM PARK (SEE P. 133)

HODNET HALL GARDENS

OPEN
1 April-30
September
Mon-Sat.
2.00-5.00pm

Sundays & Bank
Holidays
12noon-5.30pm

HODNET HALL GARDENS, MARKET DRAYTON
TEL; 0630 685202
(Mr and the Hon Mrs A Heber-Percy)

Beautiful woodland walks through trees and shrubs in 60 acres of flowering lakeside gardens. Tea Rooms (with animal trophy display). Gift Shop. Kitchen Garden sales. Free car park. Dogs allowed (on leash). Parties catered for. Contact the Secretary.

Location: 12 miles north east of Shrewsbury on A53; M6 Junction 15; M54 junction 3.
Admission: Adults £2.60, Children £1.00, OAPs £2.10.

Ludford House Gardens, Ludlow.
  ½ mile south of Ludlow, B4361.

Ludlow Castle, Castle Square, Ludlow.
  (0584) 873947 Castle Square, Ludlow.

Mawley Hall, Cleobury Mortimer.
  1 mile south of Cleobury Mortimer (A4117).

Preen Manor Gardens, Church Preen, Church Stretton.
  (0694) 771207 5 miles west of Much Wenlock.

🏛 **Shipton Hall,** Much Wenlock.
  (074636) 225 In Shipton, 6 miles south west of Much Wenlock.

⌗ **Stokesay Castle,** Craven Arms.
  (0588) 672544 8 miles from Ludlow.

🏛 **Upton Cressett Hall,** Bridgenorth.
  (074631) 307 2 miles west of Bridgenorth.

⌗ **Wenlock Priory,** Much Wenlock
  (0952) 727466 In Much Wenlock.

✿ **Wilderhope Manor,** Wenlock Edge.
  (06943) 363 7 mile south west of Much Wenlock.

⌗ **Wroxeter (Viroconium) Roman City,** near Shrewsbury.
  (0743) 761330 5½ miles south east of Shrewsbury.

WALCOT HALL

OPEN
House & Garden
May-Sept.
Bank Holiday
Suns & Mons
(except Xmas &
New Year)
May: Sun., Wed.,
and Fri.
June: Wed. & Fri.
July & Aug.
Sundays
Sept:: Wed.
2.15-4.30pm.

WALCOT HALL, BISHOP'S CASTLE TEL: 071 581 2782
(C R W Parish Esq)

Georgian home of Lord Clive of India who commissioned Sir William Chambers to re-design it, and the Stable Block in 1763. His son added the free-standing Ballroom and developed 30 acres of Arboretum and Pools to the rear, with mile-long Lakes in the front. Suitable Film Locations; Balls, Corporate Events; Holiday Accommodation, Receptions, Parties and Shows.

Location: On the edge of the Clun Forest. 3 miles east of Bishop's Castle on B4385; ½ mile outside Lydbury North.
Admission: Adults £2.50, children under 15 free. Groups of 10+ by arrangement. Teas when available.

Barford Park, Enmore.
(0278) 671269 5 miles west of Bridgwater.

Barrington Court Gardens, Ilminster.
(0985) 847777 In Barrington village, 5 miles north west of Ilminster.

The Bishop's Palace, Wells.
(0749) 78691 In the city of Wells at end of Market Place.

Clapton Court Gardens and Plant Centre, Crewkerne.
(0460) 73220 3 miles south of Crewkerne on B3165 to Lyme Regis.

Cleeve Abbey, Washford.
(0984) 40377 In Washford.

Coleridge Cottage, Nether Stowey, Bridgwater.
(0278) 732662 At west end of village on south side of A39.

Combe Sydenham Country Park, Monksilver, Taunton.
(0984) 56284 5 miles north of Wiveliscombe.

Crowe Hall, Widcombe, Bath.
(0225) 310322   1/4 mile on right up Widcombe Hill.

Doddington Hall, Nether Stowey, Bridgwater.
(027874) 400   1/2 mile from A39.

Dunster Castle, Dunster Minehead.
(0643) 821314 In Dunster, 3 miles south east of Minehead on A396.

Farleigh Hungerford Castle, near Trowbridge.
(0225) 754026 In Farleigh Hungerford.

Gaulden Manor, Tolland, Taunton.
(09847) 213 9 miles north west of Taunton.

Hadspen Garden & Nursery, Castle Cary.
(0963) 50939 2 miles east of Castle Cary on A371.

Hatch Court, Hatch Beauchamp.
(0823) 480120 6 miles south east of Taunton.

Kelways Nurseries Ltd, Langport.
(0458) 250521 On Somerton Road from Langport 200 yards from A372.

Lytes Cary Manor, Ilchester.
(0985) 847777 On west side of Fosse Way (A37), 2 1/2 miles north east of Ilchester.

MAUNSEL HOUSE

OPEN
Weddings,
Private Parties,
Conferences,
Functions,
Filming, Fashion
Shows, Archery,
Clay Pigeon
Shooting,
Equestrian
Events, Garden
Parties, Coach &
Group Parties
welcome by
appointment.

MAUNSEL HOUSE, NORTH NEWTON TEL: 0278 663413
(Sir Benjamin Slade)

Imposing 13th century manor house, partly built before the Norman Conquest but mostly built around a Great Hall erected in 1420. Geoffrey Chaucer wrote part of "The Canterbury Tales" whilst staying at the house. Maunsel House is the ancestral seat of the Slade family and is now the home of the 7th baronet, Sir Benjamin Slade.

Location: Bridgwater 4 miles, Bristol 20 miles, Taunton 7 miles, junct. 24 M5, turn left North Petherton 1 1/2 miles North Newton, 1/2 mile south St. Michael Church.
Admission: For further information please telephone: 0895 272929 during office hours.

FORDE ABBEY

OPEN
Gardens:
Open daily All
Year
10.00am-4.30pm

House:
1 April-end Oct.
Sundays,
Wednesdays &
Bank Holidays
1.00-4.30pm
Last admission.

FORDE ABBEY, CHARD TEL: 0460 220231
(Mark Roper Esq)

"Winners of Christies/HHA Garden of Year Award 1993"
Founded by Cistercian monks almost 900 years ago. Today it remains a genuine family, home unchanged since the middle of the 17th century. Situated in some of the most beautiful countryside in west Dorset. 30 acres of gardens with herbaceous borders, arboretum, magnificent trees and shrubs, 5 lakes, Bog garden. Visit us and enjoy the peace and beauty of a past age. There are no ropes or barriers in the house and no sideshows in the gardens.
Location: Just off the B3167 4 miles south of Chard.
Admission: House & Gardens Adult £4.50, OAP £4.00, Groups £3.50, Child Free.
Gardens only Adult £3.50, OAP £2.75, Groups £2.75, child Free.

Midelney Manor, Drayton, Langport.
Signposted from A378 at Bell Hotel, Curry Rivel and also B3168.

Milton Lodge Gardens, Wells.
(0749) 672168   1/2 mile north of Wells.

Montacute House, Yeovil.
(0935) 823289 In Montacute village 4 miles west of Yeovil on east side of A3088.

Orchard Wyndham, Williton, Taunton.
(0984) 32309 1 mile from A39 at Williton.

Stoke-Sub-Hamdon Priory, Montacute.
(0985) 847777   Between A303 and A3088, 2 miles west of Montacute.

Tintinhull House Garden, Yeovil.
(0985) 847777 5 miles north west of Yeovil on outskirts Tintinhull village.

HATCH COURT

SANDON HALL
Stafford

SANDON HALL, the home of the Earl and Countess of Harrowby, is in the heart of Staffordshire. The Estate has been in the family since 1776 when an earlier house designed by Joseph Pickford of Derby was bought by Nathanial Ryder, 1st Baron Harrowby, son of Sir Dudley Ryder, Lord Chief Justice of England. After damage by fire in 1848 the house was re-built by William Burn, the most proven Country House architect of the day.

The family has been prominent in legal and parliamentary affairs for 250 years, with seven generations in parliament, three successive ones in the Cabinet.

The House and Grounds including the park, are impressive and much is available for specifically booked functions.

CONTACT

M J Bosson Esq MA
Sandon Hall
Stafford
ST18 OBZ

Tel: (0889) 508338/392
Fax: (0889) 508586

LOCATION

A51. 10 miles north of Rugeley and 4 miles south of Stone. Entrance through double lodges opposite Sandon village War Memorial. From south (incl. Birmingham Airport): M42, exit 9, Lichfield, Rugeley. London 2¾ hours, 151 miles From north (incl. Manchester Airport) 1 hour: M6, exit 14. Stafford ringroad B5066

Rail: Stafford station

Taxi: 5 miles..

SUITABILITY FOR EVENTS

STATE ROOMS: these can be booked for a variety of functions (see dimensions below), and a conservatory featured in the text books (ideal for light catering). The Saloon has excellent acoustics, a grand piano and an organ, suitable for musical events, dances, large cocktail parties etc. Trade exhibitions, fashion shows etc., can easily be accommodated. A large Dining Room provides an ideal setting for prestige dinner parties (16), as also for business meetings. Catering by outside contractors.

THE MUSEUM; comprises the State Drawing Room with 18th century hand-painted Chinese wallpaper, and upstairs many items of varying and unusual interest including early costumes, childhood toys and photographs of early 20th century house parties. Also manuscript letters, albums and prints. There are political objets d'art and a probably unique collection of First World War Recruiting Posters. One of the rooms has a very rare hand-painted Chinese wallpaper of 1840. Pre-booked guided tours only, max. 20, at £2.50 per head (discount for OAP's and children). Tea available in Conservatory.

THE GARDEN: (47 acres) is landscaped and especially beautiful at azalea/rhododendron time and the Autumn with many magnificent trees. It is suitable for most garden events, including just visiting (pre-booked groups only, £1.50 per head with similar discounts).

LARGE TOPOGRAPHICALLY BEAUTIFUL PARK: laid out in the mid-18th century, of nearly 400 acres, can be booked for many types of outdoor events.

Alongside is Sandon Wood listed in the Staffordshire inventory of Ancient Woodland and in its Environmental Record as a Grade 1A site of biological interest.

The Park or Hall provides a wonderful backdrop for marquees.

ADVICE TO COURIERS & DRIVERS

No smoking indoors. No unaccompanied children. Dogs only in park on lead.

FACILITIES FOR THE DISABLED

Generally not ideal, but possible except for Museum.

PARKING FOR COACHES & CARS

Ample in park on grass.

CATERING

By outside contractors with space available but see Museum tours. Alternatively booked meals can be arranged with Dog & Doublet Inn, opposite Lodge Gates. Tel: (0889) 508331

GUIDED TOURS

Museum only - see under suitability for events.

SCHOOL VISITS
CHILDREN

Internal and external welcome, but never unaccompanied. Especially suitable for agricultural, forestry and nature studies. Bookings only.

OPENING TIMES

Pre booked parties and available for a variety of functions and outdoor events.

CONFERENCE AND FUNCTION FACILITIES

ROOM	DIMENSIONS	CAPACITY	LAYOUT	POWER POINTS	SUITABLE FOR A/V
Conservatory	1,600 sq.ft.				Adequate
North Library	228 sq. ft.				
Main Library	820 sq.ft.				
Saloon	1,932 sq.ft.				
Dining Room	840 sq. ft.				

SHUGBOROUGH
Nr Stafford, Staffordshire

SHUGBOROUGH is the ancestral home of the fifth Earl of Lichfield, who as Patrick Lichfield is known worldwide as a leading photographer.

The 18th century Mansion House contains a fine collection of ceramics silver, paintings and french furniture. Part of the House continues to be lived in by the Earl and his family. Nothing could be more English!

Visitors can enjoy the 18 acre Grade I Historic Garden and a unique collection of neo-classical monuments by James Stuart.

Other attractions include the original servants quarters. The working laundry, kitchens, brewhouse and coach houses have all been lovingly restored. Costumed guides can show how the servants lived and worked over 100 years ago.

Shugborough Park Farm is a georgian farmstead that features an agricultural museum, working corn mill and rare breeds centre.The livestock are all historic breeds and in the farmhouse visitors can see brick bread ovens in operation and butter and cheese making in the dairy.

The Estate is set in 900 acres of park and woodland with many walks and trails

CONTACT
Jane Spier
Marketing Manager
Shugborough
Milford
Stafford
ST17 0XB

Tel: (0889) 881388
Fax: (0889 881323

LOCATION
From London M1, M6 from Junct.19, leave M6 Junct.13, follow signs.

Rail: British Rail Intercity trains at Stafford.

Air: Birmingham Int'l 30 miles

Taxi: Anthony's, Stafford 0785 52255

SUITABILITY FOR OTHER EVENTS
Private and corporate entertainment, Conferences, product launches and dinner parties. Catering can be arranged . Filming and event location.

EXTRA FACILITIES
Over 900 acres of parkland and gardens available for hire. Themed activities, tours and demonstrations.

FACILITIES FOR THE DISABLED
Disabled and elderly visitors may alight at the entrance to the property before parking in the allocated areas.. Toilets for the disabled. Stair climber to House. Batricars available. Disabled friendly picnic tables available. Taped tours..

ADVICE TO COURIERS & DRIVERS
Discounted vouchers for drivers meals available. Please advise clients that there is no photography allowed within the property.

PARKING FOR COACHES & CARS
Capacity of car park - 200 cars and 28 coaches, 150 yards from the House. Additional parking on the grass.

CATERING
Licensed Tea Room/Cafe seating 95 also tearoom at Farm seats 30. Prior notice for large groups. Catering for special functions/conferences.

GUIDED TOURS
Pre-booked tours of approx. 1 hour duration. Themed tours as required. Minimum size of each groups - 15 Please telephone for full adult group and educational package details.

GIFT SHOP/GUIDE BOOKS
National Trust Shop at main site open at the same time as the property. Selection of colour guide books available.

SCHOOL VISITS/CHILDREN
Variety of award winning educational packages and demonstrations available all year in all areas. Curriculum related. Pre-visits for teachers. Please contact education officer.

OPENING TIMES

Summer
26 March - 28 October

Mon	
Tues	
Wed	
Thur	11am - 5pm
Fri	
Sat	
Sun	

Booked parties from 10.30 am throughout the year.

Winter
BOOKED PARTIES ONLY
31 October - 23 Dec & 3 January - 25 March

Mon	
Tues	
Wed	
Thur	10.30am - 4pm
Fri	
Sat	
Sun	

ADMISSION

ALL ATTRACTIONS
Inclusive
| Adults | £7.50 |
| Concessions* | £5.00 |

Family
| 3 Sites | £15.00 |
| 2 sites | £10.00 |

GARDENS & PARK
| Cars | £1.50 |
| Coaches | Free |

SINGLE SITES
(House, Musuem or Farm)
Per site
| Adult | £3.50 |
| Concessions* | £2.00 |

* Concessions for children (under 5s FREE), OAPs, Students, unemployed & groups.
**Nat. Trust Members free to Mansion House, reduced rate to Museum and Farm..

CONFERENCE AND FUNCTION FACILITIES

ROOM	DIMENSIONS	CAPACITY	LAYOUT	POWER POINTS	SUITABLE FOR A/V
Saloon	60'x24'	80	Theatre	✓	✓
			Lunch/Dinner		
Conference	35'x24'	50	Theatre	✓	✓
Suite		50	U-shape		
		50	Boardroom		
		50	Buffet		

Ancient High House, Stafford.
(0785) 223181 ext. 353   In Stafford town.

Biddulph Grange Garden, Biddulph, Stoke on Trent.
(0782) 517999   ½ mile north of Biddulph.

Chillington Hall, Wolverhampton.
(0902) 850236   4 miles south west of A5 at Gailey.

Dorothy Clive Garden, Willoughbridge.
9 miles south west Newcastle under Lyme.

Hanch Hall, Lichfield.
(0543) 490308   4 miles north west of Lichfield on B5014.

Moseley Old Hall, Wolverhampton.
(0902) 782808   4 miles north of Wolverhampton.

Rode Hall, Scholar Green, Stoke on Trent.
(0270) 873237   5 miles south west of Congleton between A34 and A50.

Tamworth Castle, Tamworth.
(0827) 63563   In Tamworth.

Wall (Letotcetum) Roman Site, Lichfield.
(0543) 480768   2 miles south west of Lichfield.

Whitmore Hall, Whitmore, Newcastle-under-Lyme.
(0782) 680478   4 miles from Newcastle-under-Lyme on A53.

THE MAZE AT SOMERLEYTON HALL, SUFFOLK (P.142)

KENTWELL HALL
Long Melford, Suffolk

KENTWELL HALL is a beautiful redbrick Tudor Manor House surrounded by a broad moat.

Built by the Clopton Family, from wealth from the wool trade, Kentwell has an air of timeless tranquillity created by its moats and mellowed brick. The exterior is little altered in 400 years. The interior was re-modelled by Hopper in 1820 and his work has been embellished and enhanced in restoration by the present owners. Hopper's interiors, notably the Great Hall and Dining Room, emphasise their Tudor provenance, but the Drawing Room and Library are simply and restrainedly classical; all are eminently habitable.

Kentwell has been a frequent location for filming and videos since the BBC's acclaimed 'Woman in White' in 1981.

The gardens are part of Kentwell's delight. Intimate yet spacious, the visitor is never far from a Moat or mellow brick wall. There is a fine Walled Garden with original 17th Century layout and a well established large new Herb Garden. All set amidst parkland in open country. 'Tudor' Farm is based upon traditional timber-framed farm buildings and Rare Breed farm animals.

Kentwell is now best known for its Unique Award Winning Re-Creations of Tudor Domestic Life which take place on selected week-ends throughout the season.

CONTACT

Mrs J G Phillips
Kentwell Hall
Long Melford
Suffolk
CO10 9BA

Tel: (0787) 310207

LOCATION

Off the A134. 4 miles north of Sudbury, 14 miles South of Bury St Edmunds.

Rail: Sudbury Stn 4 miles, Colchester Stn 20 miles.

Air: Stanstead 30 miles.

Taxi: Felix (0787) 310574.

SUITABILITY FOR OTHER EVENTS

Kentwell specialises in: Genuine Tudor Style Banquets, Wedding Receptions, formal but friendly luncheons and dinners and particularly 'Company Days' when the whole company, or a division, come to Kentwell for a specially devised one-day programme of fun, stimulation and challenge.

EXTRA FACILITIES

A wide variety of 'Tudor-style' activities can be arranged for visitors, including longbow shooting, working bakery, dairy and stillroom, spinning etc. The 'Kentwell Olympics' might test the SAS!

ADVICE TO COURIERS & DRIVERS

No dogs or unaccompanied children. No photography in House.

FACILITIES FOR THE DISABLED

Disabled or elderly visitors may alight at house with prior notice. New disabled toilet.

PARKING FOR COACHES & CARS

There is parking for several hundred cars and coaches.

CATERING

Kentwell provides its own catering, often from produce home grown or raised from Kentwell's own organic farm. Home-made teas and lunches on open days up to full catering for grander functions. The undercroft can comfortably seat 120.

GIFT SHOP

Open at the same time as the House and selling a variety of local and 'Tudor-style' items. New range of colour guide books will be introduced.

SCHOOL VISITS/CHILDREN

School groups are encouraged: Kentwell has a highly developed schools' programme dealing with 700 parties per year. Schools can visit a Re-creation of Tudor Life, themselves re-create Tudor life in the Moat House or take one of our tours conducted by a qualified teacher on the House, Garden, Farm or aspects of each.

CONFERENCE AND FUNCTION FACILITIES

ROOM	DIMENSIONS	CAPACITY	LAYOUT	POWER POINTS	SUITABLE FOR A/V
Great Hall	40'x24'	100	Buffet	✓	✓
		120	Theatre		
		30	Boardroom		
		60	Lunch/Dinner		
Main Dining Room	24'x24'	75	Buffet	✓	
		40	Lunch/Dinner		
Drawing Room	35'x24'	75	Buffet	✓	
		50	Lunch/Dinner		
Library	36'x20'	20	Boardroom	✓	

THE 15TH CENTURY MOAT HOUSE

SOMERLEYTON HALL
Lowestoft, Suffolk

SOMERLEYTON HALL is a perfect example of a House built to show off the wealth of the new Victorian aristocracy. The house was remodelled from a modest 17th Century Manor House by the rich railwayman Sir Morton Peto. When he was declared bankrupt in 1863, his extravagant concoction of red brick, white stone and lavish interiors was sold to another hugely successful businessman, carpet manufacturer Sir Francis Crossley. The present owner, Lord Somerleyton, is his great-grandson.

The Oak Room retains its carved oak panelling and Stuart atmosphere: the rest is lavishly Victorian. Grandest of all is the Ballroom with its crimson damask walls reflected in rows of long white and gilt mirrors. The Dining Room boasts paintings by Wright of Derby, Clarkson Stanfield and Guido Reni.

GARDENS

Somerleyton's 12 acre gardens are justly renowned. The 1846 yew hedge maze is one of the few surviving Victorian mazes in Britain. Colour is added to the gardens by rhododendrons, azaleas and a long pergola trailing mauve, pink and white wisteria. Special features include: a sunken garden; the Loggia Tea Room; glasshouses by Sir Joseph Paxton; an aviary; fine statuary. The chiming clock in the stables was built as a prototype for Big Ben by Vuilliamy.

SUITABILITY FOR OTHER EVENTS

Somerleyton Hall is suitable for conferences, receptions, fashion shows, archery, clay pigeon shooting, equestrian events, garden parties, shows, rallies, filming, wedding receptions.

EXTRA FACILITIES

The Winter Gardens, Loggia, Conference Rooms and Ballroom can be hired throughout the year.

ADVICE TO COURIERS & DRIVERS

No dogs or photography in the House.

FACILITIES FOR THE DISABLED

If visitors are badly disabled they may alight at the entrance to the house, before parking in the allocated areas. Wheelchair and ramps are available. There are toilets for the disabled.

PARKING FOR COACHES & CARS

Capacity of the Car Park: 100 cars and 10 coaches, 20 yards from Garden entrance.

CATERING

Loggia Tea Room, fresh home baked cooking light lunches and the ever popular cream teas.

GUIDED TOURS

By prior arrangement. If requested, the owner may meet groups. Average time for tour 3/4 hour.

GIFT SHOP

Open at same time as the Hall and Gardens.

GUIDE BOOKS

Colour guide book, £1.50.

SCHOOL VISITS/CHILDREN

Groups of children welcome during the season every morning, by prior arrangement, from 9.30am-2.30pm. A guide is provided. Areas of particular interest include: Maze and garden trail, aviary, dolls house.

CONTACT

Lord Somerleyton
Estate Office
Somerleyton Hall
Nr Lowestoft
Suffolk
NR32 5QQ

Tel: (0502) 730224
Fax: (0502) 732143

LOCATION

From London, A12 to Lowestoft.
From Bury St Edmunds, A143.

Rail: Somerleyton Station 1 mile.

Taxi: St Olaves' Service Station, Great Yarmouth 488278.

OPENING TIMES

Summer

Bank Hols 2.00 - 5.00pm

Easter Sunday - Last Sunday in September

Mon	
Tues	Closed
Wed	
Thurs	2.00 - 5.00pm
Fri	Closed
Sat	
Sun	2.00 - 5.00pm

July & August

Mon	Closed
Tues	
Wed	2.00 - 5.00pm
Thur	
Fri	Closed
Sat	
Sun	2.00 - 5.0 0pm

Gardens open and light luncheons available from 12.30pm

Miniature Railway open Sun, Thurs and, when possible, on other days.

Winter
October - Easter

Closed except by appointment.

ADMISSION

Summer

Adult	£3.50
OAP	£3.00
Child*	£1.60

GROUP**	
Adult	£2.70
OAP	£2.70
Child*	£1.40

* Under 15 Years.
** Min 15 people.

CONFERENCE AND FUNCTION FACILITIES

ROOM	DIMENSIONS	CAPACITY	LAYOUT	POWER POINTS	SUITABLE FOR A/V
Conference Suite	34'3"x22'	75	Theatre	4	✓
The Loggia	47'4"x10'2"	80	Various	3	✓
Winter Garden	99'x16'	80	Various	3	✓

Belchamp Hall, Belchamp Walter, Sudbury.
(0787) 72744 5 miles south west of Sudbury.

Blakenham Woodland Garden, Little Blakeham, Ipswich.
4 miles north west of Ipswich.

Christchurch Mansion, Christchurch Park, Ipswich.
(0473) 253246 In Christchurch Park near centre of Ipswich.

Euston Hall, Thetford.
(0842) 766366 A1088 3 miles south Thetford.

Framlingham Castle, Framlingham.
(0728) 723330 North side of Framlingham

Gainsborough's House, Sudbury.
(0787) 372958 46 Gainsborough Street, Sudbury.

Guildhall of Corpus Christi, Lavenham.
(0787) 247646 Market Place, Lavenham.

Haughley Park, Stowmarket.
4 miles west of Stowmarket.

Ickworth, Bury St Edmunds.
(0284) 735270 3 miles south west of Bury St Edmunds on A143.

Ipswich Museum, High Street Ipswich.
(0473) 213761 In town centre.

Little Hall, Lavenham.
(0787) 247179 In Market Place, Lavenham.

Melford Hall, Sudbury.
(0787) 880286 In Long Melford.

Nether Hall, Cavendish, Sudbury.
12 miles south of Bury St Edmunds.

Orford Castle, Orford.
(03944) 50472 In Orford.

Otley Hall, Otley, Ipswich.
(0473) 890264

HELMINGHAM HALL

OPEN

Gardens only

May 1-Sept. 11
Sundays only
2.00-6.00pm

Wednesdays
between the
above dates for
prior arranged
groups for 30+.

HELMINGHAM HALL GARDENS, IPSWICH TEL: 0473 890363
(The Lord and Lady Tollemache)

The Tudor Hall surrounded by its wide moat is set in a 400 acre deer park. Two superb gardens, one surrounded by its own moat and walls extends to several acres. One has wide herbaceous borders and an immaculate kitchen garden. The second enclosed within yew hedges has a special rose garden with a Herb and Knot garden containing plants grown in England before 1750.

Location: B1077 9 miles north of Ipswich.
Admission: Adult £2.50, concessions £2.30, child (5-15) £1.50. Groups (over 30) £2.10.

THE PRIORY, LAVENHAM

OPEN

12 March-31 Oct.

Daily

10.30am-5.30pm

THE PRIORY, LAVENHAM TEL: 0787 247003
(Mr and Mrs Alan Casey)

Beautiful medieval timber-frame house in the heart of Lavenham, yet backing onto rolling countryside. Once the home of Benedictine monks, rich cloth merchants and an Elizabethan Rector. Superbly restored and furnished with a blend of antique and modern furniture, paintings and stained glass by Ervin Bossanyi (1891-1975); aromatic herb garden with culinary, medicinal and dyers herbs; kitchen garden, orchard and pond.

Location: The Priory is in the centre of Lavenham in Water Street.
Admission: Adult £2.50, child £1.00

Saxtead Green Post Mill, Framlingham.
(0728) 82789 2 miles west of Framlingham.

Wingfield Collge, Eye.
(0379) 384505 Signposted off B1118, 7 miles south east of Diss.

EUSTON HALL

LOSELEY PARK
Guildford, Surrey

LOSELEY PARK, built in 1562 by Sir William More, is a fine example of Elizabethan architecture, its mellow stone brought from the ruins of Waverley Abbey now over 850 years old. The House is set amid magnificent parkland grazed by the Loseley Jersey herd. Many visitors comment on the very friendly atmosphere of the House - it is a country house, the family home of descendants of the builder.

Furniture has been acquired by the family and includes an early 16th Century Wrangelschrank beautifully inlaid with many different woods, a Queen Anne cabinet, Georgian arm chairs and settee, a Hepplewhite four-poster bed, King George IV's coronation chair. The King's bedroom has Oudenarde tapestry and a carpet commemorating James I's visit.

The Christian pictures include the Henri Met de Bles triptych of the Nativity and modern mystical pictures of the living Christ, St Francis and St Bernadette. The Christian Trust Centre is in the Oak Room and a small Chapel is available for use by visitors. A Christian Cancer Help Centre meets twice monthly

GARDEN

A magnificent Cedar of Lebanon presides over the front lawn. Parkland adjoins the lawn and a small lake adds to the beauty of Front Park.

In the Walled Garden are Mulberry Trees, Yew hedges, a grass terrace and the Moat Walk with herbaceous borders including a newly planted rose garden.

CONTACT

Jane Trueblood
Loseley Park
Guildford
Surrey
GU3 1HS

Tel: (0483) 304440
Telex: 859972 LOSELG
Fax: (0483) 302036

LOCATION

From London (30 miles) A3, leave at Compton, South of Guildford, on B3000 for 2 miles, signposted.

Bus: 1 1/4 miles from House.

Rail: Guildford Stn 2 miles, Godalming 3 miles.

Air: Heathrow 30 miles, Gatwick 30 miles.

SUITABILITY FOR OTHER EVENTS

Ideal for wedding receptions. Business launches and promotions. A 12 acre field adjoining can also be hired for events in addition to the lawns. Fashion shows, air displays, archery, garden parties, shows, rallies, filming.

EXTRA FACILITIES

These include: Parkland, moat walk and terrace. Lectures can be arranged on the property, its contents, gardens and history. Loseley Christian Trust Exhibition.

ADVICE TO COURIERS & DRIVERS

Coaches approach Loseley from B3000 only, as other roads too narrow. No dogs, except on leads in the car park, no unaccompanied children, no photography in the House, no videos on Estate. All party visits to the House and Farm must be booked in advance. Children's play area. Picnic area.

FACILITIES FOR THE DISABLED

Disabled and elderly visitors may alight at the entrance to the property. Vehicles can then be parked in the allocated area. There are toilet facilities for the disabled. Wheelchair access to ground floor of the House.

PARKING FOR COACHES & CARS

Capacity of the car park - 150 cars, 100 yards from the House and 6 coaches. Summer overflow car park.

CATERING

Health, and wholeness are in the forefront at Loseley. The Barn Restaurant has a capacity of up to 150 people. For special functions, banquets and conferences held in the Barn, catering can be arranged. Permanent marquee (70'x40') capable of seating 250 people. Additional marquees can also be hired. Sunday lunches available from May.

GUIDE BOOKS

Colour guide book, £1.50.

GUIDED TOURS

Average time for a tour of the House 3/4 hour. Guided group farm tours take up to 2 hours and must be booked in advance.

SCHOOL VISITS/CHILDREN

School Groups are welcome and by prior arrangement a guide can be provided. Prices: House £2.00, Farm Trailer Ride £2.00 and Farm Walk £2.00. Special rates for school groups. Of particular interest is the farm, where milking can be seen at the appropriate time. Also introducing this year a 30 minute Nature Trail..

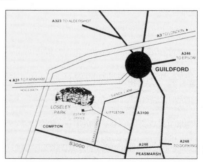

OPENING TIMES

Summer
2 May - 2 October

Mon	Bank Hols 2pm - 5pm
Tues	Pre-booked parties only.
Wed ⎫ Thurs ⎪ Fri ⎬ Sat ⎭	2pm - 5pm Last entry 4.30pm
Sun	Grounds & facilities open. House closed

House closed Friday 27th May

Tithe Barn, restaurant open as above   11am - 5pm. Closed on Saturdays. All catering will take place in our marquee.

NB Group Farm tours, May - October must be pre-booked.

Winter

Tithe Barn available for weddings and private/business functions all year.

ADMISSION

HOUSE & GARDEN
Adult	£3.50
Child*	£2.00
Group**	£2.75

GARDEN ONLY
Adult	£1.50
Child*	£0.50
Group**	£1.20

FARM TOUR & GROUNDS
Adult	£4.00
Child*	£2.00
Group**	£2.50

Under 3's Free
* Aged 3-16.
**Min. payment 20 people.

ABOVE: THE GREAT HALL

THE TITHE BARN AT LOSELEY PARK

The Tithe Barn (originally 1635) is situated on the sweeping lawns of Loseley House and offers unrivalled views of the surrounding parkland and magnificent Cedar of Lebanon.

It is adaptable for a wide range of functions and will comfortably accommodate 50-150 people for a full sit-down meal, or up to 200 for a cocktail reception. Should a larger group be envisaged, our permanent marquee may be used and further marquees erected. The South Room of the Tithe Barn is ideal for small meetings and private lunches.

The location is ideal for business and corporate hospitality events and is in easy reach of the A3 and M25, an hour from London and some 40 minutes from Heathrow and Gatwick Airports. Ample car parking is available.

CONFERENCE AND FUNCTION FACILITIES

ROOM	DIMENSIONS	CAPACITY	LAYOUT	POWER POINTS	SUITABLE FOR A/V
C17th Tithe Barn	100'x18'	200	Reception Theatre Schoolroom U-shape Boardroom Buffet Lunch/Dinner	3	3
South Room	30'x15'	40	Private Parties Syndicate Room		
Marquee	70'x40'	250	Various		

BELOW: THE TITHE BARN

BELOW: THE TITHE BARN

Albury Park, Albury, Guildford.
1¹/₂ miles east of Albury off A25.

Asgill House, Richmond.

Chilworth Manor, Guildford.
3³/₄ miles south east of Guildford in Chilworth village.

*Clandon Park, West Clandon, Guildford.
(0483) 222482 At West Clandon 3 miles east of Guildford.

Claremont, Esher.
(0372) 467841 ¹/₂ mile south west from Esher on A307.

Claremont Landscape Garden, Esher.
(0372) 469421 ¹/₂ mile south east of Esher on east side of A307.

Coverwood Lakes, Peaslake Road, Ewhurst.
(0306) 731103 ¹/₂ mile from Peaslake village, 8 miles from Guildford.

Crosswater Farm, Churt.
(0252) 792698 6 miles Farnham/Haslemere.

Farnham Castle, Farnham.
¹/₂ mile north of Town centre on A287.

Farnham Castle Keep, Farnham.
(0252) 713393 ¹/₂ mile north of Town centre on A287.

Goddards, Abinger Common, Dorking.
(0306) 730487 4¹/₂ miles south west of Dorking in Abinger Common.

Greathed Manor, Lingfield.
2¹/₂ miles south east of Lingfield on B2028.

Hatchlands Park, East Clandon.
(0483) 222482 East of East Clandon on north side of A246.

Painshill Park, Portsmouth Road, Cobham.
(0932) 868113 West of Cobham on A245 200 yards east of A3/A245 roundabout.

Polesden Lacey, Dorking.
(0372) 458203 5 miles north west of Dorking

Pyrford Court, Pyrford Common Road, near Woking.
(0483) 765880 2 miles east of Woking.

Ramster, Chiddingfold.
(0428) 644422 On A283 1¹/₂ miles south of Chiddingfold.

The RHS Garden Wisley, Wisley.
(0483) 224232 In Wisley just off M25 junction. 10 on A3.

Vann, Hambledon.
(0428) 683413 6 miles south of Godalming.

Winkworth Arboretum, near Godalming.
(048632) 265 2 miles south east of Godalming.

R.H.S. Garden, Wisley

ARUNDEL CASTLE
Arundel, West Sussex

This great castle, home of the Dukes of Norfolk, dates from the Norman Conquest, containing a very fine collection of furniture and paintings, Arundel Castle is still a family home, reflecting the changes of nearly a thousand years.

In 1643, during the Civil War, the original castle was very badly damaged and it was later restored by the 8th, 11th and 15th Dukes in the 18th and 19th Centuries. It has amongst its treasures personal possessions of Mary Queen of Scots and a selection of historical, religious and heraldic items from the Duke of Norfolk's collection.

The Duke of Norfolk is the Premier Duke, the title having been conferred on Sir John Howard in 1483 by his friend King Richard III. The Dukedom also carries with its the hereditary office of Earl Marshal of England. Among the historically famous members of the Howard family are Lord Howard of Effingham who, with Drake, repelled the Spanish Armada; the Earl of Surrey, the Tudor poet and courtier and the 3rd Duke of Norfolk, uncle of Anne Boleyn and Catherine Howard, both of whom became wives of King Henry VIII.

CONTACT

The Administrator
Arundel Castle
Arundel
West Sussex
BN18 9AB

Tel: (0903) 883136/
882173
Fax: (0903) 884581

LOCATION

Brighton 40 minutes,
Worthing 15 minutes,
Chichester 15 minutes.
From London A3 or A24,
1½ hours.

Bus: Bus stop 100 yards.

Rail: Station ½ mile.

Air: Gatwick 25 miles.

Motorway: M25, 30 miles.

SUITABILITY FOR OTHER EVENTS

Fashion shows and filming.

ADVICE TO COURIERS & DRIVERS

No unaccompanied children, dogs or photography inside the Castle.

FACILITIES FOR THE DISABLED

Disabled and elderly visitors may alight at the entrance to the property, before parking in the allocated areas. There are toilets for the disabled.

PARKING FOR COACHES & CARS

Capacity of the car park: 200 cars within the grounds, 200 yards from the Castle with further space for cars elsewhere. Coaches can park opposite the Castle entrance.

CATERING

Groups need to book in advance for afternoon tea, lunch or dinner. The Restaurant seats 140 people and prices range from £1.95 for tea and £3.75 for lunch. Special rates are offered to pre-booked groups only. Self Service Restaurant within the Castle serves home-made food for lunch and afternoon tea.

GUIDED TOURS

These are available for pre-booked parties only at £6.00 per head. Tours are also available in French, Japanese and German. Average time taken for a tour 1½ hours.

GIFT SHOP

The shop sells many items chosen by the Countess of Arundel and is always open at the same time as the Castle.

GUIDE BOOKS

Colour guide book, published in English, French, and German, £1.80.

SCHOOL VISITS/CHILDREN

A special guide book can be purchased for children. Items of particular interest include a Norman Keep and Armoury. Special rates for schoolchildren (aged 5-15) and teachers.

CHARLESTON FARMHOUSE
Lewes, East Sussex

A mile or so from Firle village, near the end of a track leading to the foot of the Downs, lies Charleston Farmhouse. It was discovered in 1916 by Virginia and Leonard Woolf when Virginia's sister, the painter Vanessa Bell, was looking for a place in the country. Here Vanessa moved with fellow artist Duncan Grant, the writer David Garnett, her two young sons, and an assortment of animals. It was an unconventional and creative household which became the focal point for artists and intellectuals later to be known as Bloomsbury - among them Roger Fry, Lytton Strachey and Maynard Keynes.

Over the years the artists decorated the walls, furniture and ceramics with their own designs, influenced by Italian fresco painting and post-impressionist art. Creativity extended to the garden too. Mosaics were made in the piazza, sculpture was cleverly positioned to intrigue, and subtle masses of colour were used in the planting.

After Duncan Grant's death in 1978, the Charleston Trust was formed to save and restore the house to its former glory. The task has been described as "one of the most difficult and imaginative feats of restoration current in Britain".

CONTACT

Mrs Christina Jeffrey
Charleston Farmhouse
Firle
Lewes
East Sussex
BN8 6LL

Tel: (0323) 811265
(Visitor information)
(0323) 811626 (Admin.)

LOCATION

6mls east of Lewes on A27 between Firle and Selmeston. The lane to Charleston leads off the A27, 2 miles beyond the Firle turning.
London 60 miles, Brighton 15 miles, Monk's House, Rodmell (Leonard and Virginia Woolf's house) 11 miles.
Air: Gatwick 20 miles.
Rail: London (Victoria) hourly to Lewes (65 minutes). Occasional train to Berwick.

Bus: Route on A27.

Taxi: George and Graham, Lewes 473692.

SUITABILITY FOR OTHER EVENTS
Filming.

EXTRA FACILITIES
Small lecture room available by special arrangement.

ADVICE TO COURIERS & DRIVERS
No dogs, no photography. It is essential to arrange visits in advance and out of public hours. Please telephone the office. Details on restriction of coach size shown under 'parking'.

FACILITIES FOR THE DISABLED
Disabled and elderly visitors may alight at the entrance. Wheelchair visitors by prior arrangement, outside public hours. There is no access beyond the ground floor for wheelchairs. Special toilets are available.

PARKING FOR COACHES & CARS
There is car parking for 30 cars, 50 yards from the property. Mini coaches only (up to 26 seats) may use the lane to the property. Large coaches may set down at the end of the lane - 10 minutes walk - or effect a Mini-Bus transfer. Details from office.

FUNCTION FACILITIES
The New Studio is available for hire by small groups. Full details available from the administrator.

CATERING
There is no restaurant at Charleston but refreshments are made available to groups by prior booking.

GUIDED TOURS
Tours are available on Wednesdays, Thursdays, Fridays and Saturdays. The maximum size of each group is 12. Groups of up to 50 can be arranged with prior notification, out of public hours. Tours available in French if booked in advance. There is no charge for the tour and the average time taken is 1 hour.

GIFT SHOP
The Gift Shop is open whilst the house is open.

GUIDE BOOKS
'Charleston Past and Present' contains photographs and reminiscences of family members and friends together with full details of the house and gardens, price £8.99. Guide notes are available at £2.00.

SCHOOL VISITS/CHILDREN
Charleston is particularly suitable for 6th Form and art groups. A guide is provided and at times a schoolroom is available for hire.

ADDITIONAL INFORMATION
Changing series of Exhibitions in Shop Gallery. The Charleston Festival is held in May every year. For Summer School details contact office. Special openings for Friends of Charleston.

GOODWOOD HOUSE
Chichester, West Sussex

GOODWOOD has been the country home of the Dukes of Richmond and Gordon for more than three centuries. The first Duke was the son of King Charles II and his French mistress, Louise de Keroualle. He was famous for his love of life and his brilliance at entertaining, a tradition which has continued at Goodwood to this day.

The third Duke not only built the great house but also collected many of its magnificent treasures. Paintings by Stubbs, Canaletto and Van Dyck, and a porcelain collection of exceptional excellence make this one of England's most important historic houses.

No other estate can offer the unique attraction of 19 days' racing on its own racecourse from May to October. Glorious Goodwood week in July is a renowned sporting and social event of international stature. Goodwood also offers the famous motor racing circuit founded by the ninth Duke in 1948, which became the very centre of all that was best about British motor racing.

Whether it is to reward the achievements of your sales team or to launch a new product, choosing Goodwood as the place to celebrate reflects the stature and style of your company. The estate is the essence of English life at its best with the famous racecourse, the historic motor circuit, the aerodrome and the secluded hotel, all within a mile of the house itself.

Simply, there is no better place to celebrate your success.

CONTACT

James Parker or
Julie Evans
Goodwood House
Goodwood
Chichester
West Sussex
PO18 0PX

Tel: (0243) 774107
Fax: (0243) 774313

LOCATION

Goodwood House is 4 miles north east of Chichester. M27/A27 from Southampton, Portsmouth, Worthing and Brighton. A3 from London, then A286 or A285 then signposted.

Rail: Chichester 5 miles
Arundel 9 Miles.

Taxi: Central (0243) 789432

Goodwood House is used throughout the year for all kinds of corporate and social events. The State Apartments can be used for Product Promotions, Company Entertaining, One-Day Seminars, Conference Dinners, Luncheon and Dinner Parties including a private tour of the art collections, Wedding Receptions, Fashion Shows and as a location for filming.

All catering is planned and prepared by Goodwood chefs. Buffets, lunches, dinners and receptions can be arranged all year round.

PUBLIC OPENING TIMES

Summer
Commencing Easter Sunday and Monday, 3 and 4 April, the House will be open on Sundays and Mondays until Monday 26 September PLUS Tuesdays, Wednesdays and Thursdays in August only 2 - 5pm each day.

The House will be CLOSED on the following Event days:
April
Sunday 17th
Monday 18th
May
Sunday 1st
Sunday 15th
Sunday 22nd
June
Sunday 19th
Monday 20th
Sunday 26th
Monday 27th
September
Sunday 25th

No Guided Tours

ADVICE TO COURIERS & DRIVERS

Free coach park; free tea for drivers.

PARKING FOR COACHES & CARS

Free car park with capacity for 300 cars and 20 coaches, 75 yards from the House.

FACILITIES FOR THE DISABLED

Disabled and elderly visitors may be dropped at door; State Apartments all on ground floor; 1 lavatory with wheelchair access.

PUBLIC OPEN DAY TEAS

Afternoon teas served most days: choice from buffet for individuals, pre-booked set menus for parties (min.15).

For more information contact The Visitors Secretary (0243) 774107

CONFERENCE AND FUNCTION FACILITIES

ROOM	DIMENSIONS	CAPACITY	LAYOUT	POWER POINTS	SUITABLE FOR A/V
Ballroom	79'x23'	74-350	Various	✓	✓
Drawing Room	50'x20'	40-90	Various	✓	✓
Front Hall	38'x35'	40-90	Various	✓	✓

NINE OTHER ROOMS ALSO AVAILABLE.

LEONARDSLEE GARDENS
Horsham, West Sussex

LEONARDSLEE GARDENS represent one of the largest and most spectacular woodland gardens in England with one of the finest collections of mature rhododendrons, azaleas, choice trees and shrubs to be seen anywhere. It is doubly fortunate in having one of the most magnificent settings, within easy reach of London, only a few miles from the M23. Laid out by Sir Edmund Loder since 1889 the gardens are still maintained by the Loder family today. The 240 acre (100 hectare) valley is world-famous for its spring display of azaleas and rhododendrons around the 6 lakes, giving superb views and reflections.

The delightful Rock Garden - a photographers paradise - is a kaleidoscope of colour in May. The superb exhibition of Bonsai in a walled courtyard shows the fascinating living art-form of Bonsai to perfection. The Alpine House has 400 different alpine plants growing in a natural rocky setting. Wallabies (used as mowing machines!)have lived wild in part of the garden for over 100 years, and deer (Sika, Fallow and Axis) may be seen in the parklands.

Many superb rhododendrons have been raised as Leonardslee. The most famous is Rhododendron loderi raised by Sir Edmund Loder in 1901. The original plants are still to be seen in the garden. In May the fragrance of their huge blooms pervades the air throughout the valley.

With many miles of paths to enjoy, visitors return frequently to savour a paradise in spring, serene in summer and mellow in autumn.

CONTACT

R Loder
Leonardslee Gardens
Lower Beeding
Horsham
West Sussex
RH13 6PP

Tel: (0403) 891212

LOCATION

M23 to Handcross then A279 (signposted Cowfold) for 4 miles.
From London: 1 hour 15 mins.

Rail: Horsham Station 4½ miles.

Bus: No. 107 from Horsham and Brighton

OPENING TIMES

Summer
1 April-31 October

Daily 10am-6pm
MAY 10am-8pm

Winter
1 Nov.-31 March

Closed to the general public

Available for functions.

ADMISSION

MAY
Adults £4.00
Child £2.00
APRIL, JUNE-OCTOBER
Adult £3.00
Child £2.00

Season Tickets £10.00

GROUP
Adult
MAY
Mon-Fri £3.50
Sat, Sun B.Hol
Mons. £4.00
APRIL, JUNE-OCT. £2.50

Child (any time) £2.00

SUITABILITY FOR OTHER EVENTS
Photography - Landscape and fashion, film location.

EXTRA FACILITIES
Clock Tower Restaurant available for private or corporate function in the evenings and out of season

ADVICE TO COURIERS & DRIVERS
Parking and refreshments free to drivers. Average length of visit 2- 4 hours.

FACILITIES FOR THE DISABLED
Not suitable for the disabled.

PARKING FOR COACHES & CARS
Ample free parking.

CATERING
Clock Tower Restaurant and Garden Cafe. Morning coffee, lunches, teas.

GIFT SHOP
Large range of quality goods.

PLANTS FOR SALE
Good selection, especially Rhododendrons and Azaleas,

GUIDE BOOKS
Colour guide book £1.50.

SCHOOL VISITS/CHILDREN
So as to maintain the peace and tranquillity of the gardens, school visits are not encouraged.

CONFERENCE AND FUNCTION FACILITIES

ROOM	DIMENSIONS	CAPACITY	LAYOUT	POWER POINTS	SUITABLE FOR A/V
Clock Tower		80	Dinner	4	
		100	Buffet		

THE ROYAL PAVILION
Brighton, Sussex

OPENING TIMES

Summer
June-Sept. inclusive

Daily   10am - 6pm
Last entry at 6pm

Winter
Oct. - May inclusive
Daily   10am-5pm
Last entry at 5pm

Closed 25th and 26th
December only.

ADMISSION

All Year

Adult	£3.60
Child	£1.90
OAP	£2.70
Student	£2.70
GROUPS (20+)	
Adult	£3.20

Prices valid until 31.3.94.

Justifiably termed "the most extraordinary palace in Europe," The Royal Pavilion, the famous seaside palace of King George IV, is one of the most exotically beautiful buildings in the British Isles.

First built as a simple, classical villa by Henry Holland in 1787, it was transformed into its current Indian style by John Nash between 1815-1822. The interiors are decorated in the Chinese taste, here carried to unique heights of splendour.

Extensive restoration has revealed the magnificent decorations and fantastic furnishings, from the opulence of the State rooms to the beauty of the recently restored apartments of Queen Victoria.

In the Banqueting Room, with its spectacular central lamp, is exhibited one of the most important collections of Regency silver gilt on public view. In the Great Kitchen with its cast-iron palm trees is displayed a superb collection of copper containing over 500 pieces

Experience the fantasy of the Music Room, a sight which moved George to tears when he first saw it, wander through the King's private apartments, promenade along the corridor with its real and imitation bamboo furniture, including the famous cast-iron staircases ... and much much more. Furniture and works of art include many original pieces on loan from H M the Queen .

A recent restoration programme has transformed the surrounding gardens to their original Regency design and due to open mid-1994 are the Royal Bedrooms of the Dukes of York and Clarence.

As a tourist attraction or a venue for corporate hospitality this Regency Palace is breathtaking.

CONTACT

Anne Burrill
Head of Public Services
The Royal Pavilion
Brighton
East Sussex
BN1 1UE

Tel: (0273) 603005
Fax: (0273) 779108

LOCATION

The Royal Pavilion is in the centre of Brighton easily reached by car and road.

From London M25, M23, A23 - 1 hr. 30 mins.

Rail: From Victoria to Brighton station 55 mins.

Air: From Gatwick 20 mins.

15 mins. walk from Brighton station
.

SUITABILITY FOR OTHER EVENTS

Ideal for prestigious entertaining: Dinners, buffets, drinks receptions, concerts, presentations and Weddings. Also available for filming and photography.

EXTRA FACILITIES

Surrounding gardens relaid to the original regency designs. Special events programme. Slide lecture presentations can be arranged in house and out.

ADVICE TO COURIERS & DRIVERS

Free entry and refreshments for drivers. Please advise clients that there is no photography inside.

FACILITIES FOR THE DISABLED

Disabled toilet. Wheelchair access ground floor. Admission free. Tactile tours offered, hearing sets available for specialist tours. Tours available for all those with special needs.

PARKING FOR COACHES & CARS

Close to NCP car parks, town centre voucher parking. Coach drop-off point in New Road, parking in Madeira Drive.

CATERING

Superb Queen Adelaide tearooms - from coffees to light lunches. Balcony terrace with sweeping views across the Pavilion lawns.

GUIDED TOURS

By arrangement with public services section (0273-713232) available also in French and German, General Interest to specialist Art Tours. Special Needs also.

GIFT SHOP

'The most unusual shop in Brighton'. Everything from reproduction Pavilion furniture to Regency jams and teas.

GUIDE BOOK

Colour Guide £1.70. Furniture catalogue 75p. Spanish, German and French translations.

SCHOOL VISITS/CHILDREN

Specialist tours relating to all levels of national curriculum. Must be booked in advance.

CONFERENCE AND FUNCTION FACILITIES

ROOM	DIMENSIONS	CAPACITY	LAYOUT	POWER POINTS	SUITABLE FOR A/V
Banqueting Room		90-200	Various	✓	
Great Kitchen		40-90	Various	✓	
Music Room		180	Various	✓	
Queen Adelaide Suite		60-100	Various	✓	
Small Adelaide		35-40	Various	✓	
William IV		70-80	Various	✓	✓

ST MARYS
Bramber, West Sussex

FAMOUS historic house in the downland village of Bramber. Built in 1470 by William Waynflete, Bishop of Winchester, founder of Magdalen College, Oxford. Classified (Grade I) as "the best example of late 15th Century timber-framing in Sussex." Fine panelled rooms, including the unique trompe l'oeil 'Painted Room', decorated for the visit of Elizabeth I. The 'Kings Room' has connections with Charles II's escape to France in 1651. Rare 16th Century painted wall leather. English furniture, ceramics, manuscripts and fine English costume-doll collection.. The Library houses important private collection of works by Victorian poet and artist Thomas Hood. Still a lived in family home, St Mary's was awarded the 'Warmest Welcome' Commendation by the S.E. Tourist Board.

GARDENS

Charming gardens with amusing Topiary as seen on BBC TV. Features include an exceptional example of the Living Fossil Tree, Ginkgo Biloba, a magnificently tall Magnolia Grandiflora, and the mysterious ivy-clad Monk's Walk.

SUITABILITY FOR OTHER EVENTS

Exclusive corporate or private functions, promotional product launches, wedding receptions Atmospheric film-location..

EXTRA FACILITIES

Lecture/demonstration facilities for up to 70 people. Projector/screen available .Grand piano

ADVICE TO COURIERS & DRIVERS

Parties must be booked in advance. Please allow 2¹/₂ hours for your visit. Free tour and tea for coach driver. Dogs on leads in car park only. No photography in House.

PARKING FOR COACHES & CARS

Pull-in gravel car park - 30 cars or 2 coaches, 20 yards from House. Also a village car park 50 yds.

CATERING

Superb Victorian Music Room seats up to 70.. Groups can book in advance for morning coffee or afternoon teas. Quality catering for functions by in-house and top London caterers..

GIFT SHOP

Souvenirs of the House.

GUIDED TOURS

The owner and/or family usually meet groups visiting the House. Larger parties, maximum 60, divided into smaller groups. Average time taken for tour 1 hour. Allow extra time for refreshments.

SCHOOL VISIT/CHILDREN

Groups welcome by prior arrangement.

CONTACT

Peter Thorogood or Roeger Linton (Curator)
St Mary's House
Bramber
West Sussex
BN44 3WE

Tel: (0903) 816205

LOCATION

In Bramber village off A283.

From London 56 miles., via M23/A23, A24.

Bus: From Shoreham to Steyning, alight Bramber.

Taxi: Southern Taxis (0273) 461655, Access Cars (0273) 452424.

Train: To Shoreham-by-Sea with connecting bus 20 (4 miles).

OPENING TIMES

Summer
PUBLIC:
Easter-End September

Sun and Thurs. 2pm-6pm.
Bank Hol Mons and Mons in July, Aug. and Sept. 2pm-6pm.

GROUPS:
Easter - End October Daily, by appointment, avoiding public opening times.

Winter

November-March

Open by appointment only.

ADMISSION

Summer

House & Garden	
Adult	£3.50
Child	£2.00
OAP	£3.20
Student	£2.50

Group	
Adult/OAP	
25 or more	£3.00
Less than 25	£3.20
Child*	£2.00
Student	£2.50

Winter

Group only	£5.50

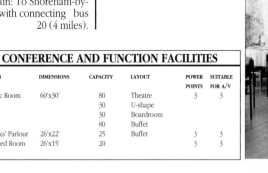

CONFERENCE AND FUNCTION FACILITIES

ROOM	DIMENSIONS	CAPACITY	LAYOUT	POWER POINTS	SUITABLE FOR A/V
Music Room	60'x30'	80	Theatre	3	3
		30	U-shape		
		30	Boardroom		
		80	Buffet		
Monks' Parlour	26'x22'	25	Buffet	3	3
Painted Room	26'x15'	20		3	3

Alfriston Clergy House, Alfriston, Seaford.
(0323) 870001 4 miles north east of Seaford just east of B2108

Bateman's, Burwash.
(0435) 882302 ½ mile south of Burwash on the A265.

Battle Abbey, Battle.
(04246) 773792 In Battle.

Bayham Abbey, Lamberhurst.
(0892) 890381 1¾ miles west of Lamberhurst.

Bentley House and Gardens, Halland.
(0825) 840573 7 miles north east of Lewes.

Berri Court, Yapton.
(0243) 551663

Bodiam Castle, near Robertsbridge.
(0580) 830436 3 miles south of Hawkhurst.

Borde Hill Garden, Haywards Heath.
(0444) 450326 1½ miles north of Haywards Heath on Balcombe Road.

Brickwall House, Northiam, Rye.
(0797) 252494 7 miles north west of Rye on B2088.

Chichester Cathedral, West Street, Chichester.
(0243) 782595 In the centre of the city.

Denmans, Denmans Lane, Fontwell.
(0243) 542808 Between Arundel and Chichester.

FIRLE PLACE

OPEN
May-Sept.
Tours Wed.,
Thurs., Suns.
also B.Hol.Mons.
2-5 pm(Last tkts)
Connoisseurs
unguided tours
with additional
rooms shown,
1st Wed. in each
month.
Exclusive Private
Viewing 25+ by
arrangement

FIRLE PLACE, NR. LEWES TEL: 0272 858335
(The Viscount Gage)

Home of the Gage family since the 15th century, the original Tudor house was largely altered c1730. House contains important collection of European and British Old Masters. Also fine French and English furniture together with notable Sévre porcelain. A House for connoisseurs. American connections.

Location: On A27 equidistant Brighton/Eastbourne, Lewes 5 miles.
Admission: Adults £3.50, pre-booked groups 25+ £3.00. Connoisseurs Day £4.50.
Private Viewing 25+ £5.50 by arrangement.

Glynde Place, Lewes.
(0273) 858337 In Glynde village 4 miles south east of Lewes on A27.

Great Dixter, Northiam.
(0797) 253160 ½ mile north of Northiam.

Hammerwood Park, East Grinstead.
(0342) 850594 3½ miles east of East Grinstead on A264.

Hastings Castle and 1066 Story, Hastings.
(0424) 717963 On West Hill Cliff adjacent to town centre.

High Beeches Gardens, Handcross.
(0444) 400589 1 mile east of A23 at Handcross on B2110.

Lamb House, Rye.
(0892) 890651 In West Street facing west end of Church.

Michelham Priory, Hailsham.
(0323) 844224 ½ mile east of Upper Dicker just off A22.

Monks House, Rodmell.
3 miles south east of Lewes in Rodmell village.

Newtimber Place, Newtimber.
(0273) 833104 Off A281 between Poynings and Pyecombe

Nymans Garden, Handcross.
(0444) 400321 At Handcross just off M23/A23.

PARHAM

OPEN
East. Sun-1st
Sun. in October
Wed., Thur.,
Suns., &
B.H.Mons.

Garden/Picnic
Area
1.00-6.00pm

House/Shop
2.00-6.00pm
last entry 5.00pm

Guided tours:
Wed, & Thu.
mornings.

PARHAM HOUSE & GARDENS, PULBOROUGH,
TEL: 0903 744888/742021

This beautiful Elizabethan house contains an important collection of portraits, furniture, embroidery and carpets. The flowers for the arrangements in the House are all home-grown in the 4 acre walled garden, with its orchard, herb garden and herbaceous borders. A brick and turf maze, lake and fine statuary are the main features of the 18th century Pleasure Grounds. Plants for sale in garden shop . Self-service teas in the Big Kitchen.

Location: Main gate on A283 road mid-way between Pulborough and Storrington.
Admission: House & Gardens Adult £4, OAP £3.50, child £2 Family (2+2) £10. Gardens only:
Adult/OAP £2.50, child £1.

Pashley Manor, Ticehurst, Wadhurst.
(0580) 200692 Between Ticehurst and A21 on B2099.

Petworth House, Petworth.
(0798) 42207 In centre of Petworth.

Pevensey Castle, Pevensey.
(0323) 762604 In Pevensey.

PRESTON MANOR

OPEN
Mon 1-5pm
(open 10am-
5pmB.Hols).
Tues.-Sat.
10.00am-5.00pm
Sunday
2.00-5.00pm

Closed:
Good Friday,
25/26 Dec.

PRESTON MANOR, BRIGHTON TEL: 0273 603005
(Brighton Borough Council)

The beautifully preserved historic home of the Stanford family. Notable collections of fine furniture, portraits and antiquities show life upstairs and down, including the superbly renovated servants' quarters, day nursery and toy collection & Butlers Pantry. The beautiful lawns surrounding the manor also contain a walled and scented garden, Pets Cemetery and the 13th century Parish Church of St. Peter. The manor is also available for hire - the perfect setting for select entertaining, combining elegance and tradition. Also used for filming and photographic work.

Location: Within easy reach of Brighton town centre in Preston Park.
Admission Adults £2.60. Student/OAP £2.10. Groups of 20 adults £2.25. Children £1.50.

Sackville College, East Grinstead.
(0342) 323279 In High Street, East Grinstead.

Sheffield Park Garden, Uckfield.
(0825) 790655 Midway between East Grinstead and Lewes on A275.

Standen, East Grinstead.
(0342) 323029 2 miles south of East Grinstead.

Wakehurst Place Garden, Ardingly
(0444) 892701 1½ miles north west of Ardingly on B2028.

The Weald and Downland Open Air Museum, Singleton, Chichester.
(024363)348 6 miles north of Chichester on A286.

West Dean Gardens, Chichester.
(024363) 301 6 miles north of Chichester on A286 near Weald and Downland Open Air Museum.

GIBSIDE

OPEN

1 April-30 Oct.

11.00am-5.00pm

Closed Monday
(open Bank Hol.
Mondays).

GIBSIDE, BURNOPFIELD, TEL: 0207 542255
(The National Trust)

Gibside Chapel, an outstanding example of Palladian architecture, was designed by James Paine as the mausoleum for the Bowes family. It stands at one end of The Great Walk of Turkey Oaks, looking towards the Column of Liberty. Estate walks are reopened with views to the ruined Hall, Orangery and other features which enliven this 18th century landscape park.

Location: 6 miles south west of Gateshead A694 to Rowland Gill then B6314.
Admission: £2.50.

Souter Lighthouse, Whitburn.
(091) 529 3161 2½ miles south South Shields on A183.

Tynemouth Castle and Priory, Tynemouth.
(091) 257 1090 In Tynemouth.

WASHINGTON OLD HALL

OPEN

1 April-30 Oct.

11.00am-5.00pm

Closed Friday
and Saturday
(open Good
Friday).

Last admission
4.30pm.

WASHINGTON OLD HALL, WASHINGTON TEL: 091 416 6879
(The National Trust)

Hall built mainly about 1613 but incorporating parts of an earlier medieval manor house. Jacobean furniture. From 1183 to 1288 the seat of the Washington family and their lineal descendants. Small formal garden.

Location: 5 miles west of Sunderland (A19), 2 miles from A1. Follow signs for Washington New Town (District 4) then Washington village.
Admission: £2.20.

GIBSIDE

ARBURY HALL
Nuneaton, Warwickshire

Built on the site of the Augustinian Priory of Erdbury, Arbury Hall has been the seat of the Newdegate family for over 400 years. The Tudor/Elizabethan house was 'gothicised' by Sir Roger Newdigate, the 5th Baronet in the 18th Century to become "The Gothick Gem of the Midlands".

The Saloon and Dining Room ceilings are especially spectacular, the former modelled on the Henry VII Chapel in Westminster Abbey. Portraits include works by Lely, Romney, Reynolds and Devis, and furniture includes Hepplewhite and Gothick Chippendale. The collection of porcelain consists of oriental and Chelsea pieces amongst others and there is a particularly splendid display of Jacobite Toasting Glasses.

The Hall stands in secluded parkland and the delightful landscaped garden of rolling lawns, winding paths and beautiful trees and lakes are mainly the result of the 2nd Baronet's influence. Spring flowers, especially daffodils are profuse, and seen at their glorious best in June is the vista of rhododendrons and the giant wisteria. North of the house lies the haven of the Rose Garden.

The Stables portico was designed by Wren.

The novelist George Eliot was born on the estate and Arbury and Sir Roger were immortalised by her in her book, 'Scenes of Clerical Life'.

CONTACT

Maj. W D Morris-Barker
Arbury Hall
Nuneaton
Warwickshire
CV10 7PT

Tel: (0203) 382804

LOCATION

London, M1, M6 exit 3
(A444-Nuneaton), 1³/4
hours.
Chester A51, A34, M6
(from exit 14 to exit 3),
2¹/2 hours.
Nuneaton 10mins.

Bus: Nuneaton 3 miles.

Rail: Nuneaton Station
3 miles.

Air: Birmingham Int'l
17 miles.

SUITABILITY FOR OTHER EVENTS

Corporate Hospitality, Buffets, Luncheons, Dinners, small conferences, product launches, promotions, film location etc. Incentive groups. Marquee functions.

EXTRA FACILITIES

Clay pigeon shooting, archery and other sporting activities. Grand piano in Saloon. Helicopter Landing Site.

ADVICE TO COURIERS & DRIVERS

Follow local road signs. Approach map available for coach drivers. Dogs on leads only allowed in Gardens. No cameras or videos allowed. Parking for 1,000 cars and 6 coaches, 250 yards from the Hall.

FACILITIES FOR THE DISABLED

Ramp access to main hall. Disabled visitors may alight at the Hall main entrance before parking in allocated areas.

GIFT SHOP

Open during opening hours and for private parties.

CATERING

Stables Tearooms for teas and light meals. Menus available for pre-booked parties. Exclusive lunches and dinners for corporate parties in Dining Room, max. 50, buffets 120.

GUIDE BOOKS

Colour guide, £1.50.

GUIDED TOURS

All tours are guided. Duration of tours, 1¹/2 hour.s

SCHOOL VISITS

Pre-arranged school parties are welcome, school room available. Children's guide book 25p.

OPENING TIMES

Summer
Easter - End September

Sun   2pm - 5.30pm
Mon   2pm - 5.30pm
       Hall: Bank Hol Mons
       only.
       Gardens: every Mon.

Last admission   5pm.

Open for pre-booked parties on most days. Minimum 25 persons.

Winter
October - Easter

Corporate Functions only.

ADMISSION

Summer

Hall, Park & Gardens
Adult   £3.00
Child*   £1.60

Garden Only
Adult   £1.60
Child*   £0.80

GROUPS
Special rates for pre-booked parties of 25 or more persons.

* Aged up to 14.

CONFERENCE AND FUNCTION FACILITIES

ROOM	DIMENSIONS	CAPACITY	LAYOUT	POWER POINTS	SUITABLE FOR A/V
Dining Room	35'x28'	50	Lunch/Dinner		
		120	Buffet		
Saloon	35'x30'	70	Theatre	4	
		18	Schoolroom		
Drawing Room	38'x21'	40	Theatre	3	✓
		24	Schoolroom		
Long Gallery	48'x11'	40	Theatre	4	✓
Stables Tea					
Rooms	31'x18'	60	Cafeteria	3	✓
		80	Theatre		

COUGHTON COURT
Alcester, Warwickshire

COUGHTON COURT has been the home of the Thockmortons since the fifteenth century and the family still live there today. The magnificent Tudor gatehouse was built around 1530 with the north and south wings completed ten or twenty years later. The gables and the first storey of these wings are of typical mid-sixteenth century half-timber work.

Of particular interest to visitors is the Thockmorton family history from Tudor times to the present generation. On view are family portraits through the centuries, together with other family memorabilia and recent photographs. Also furniture, tapestries and porcelain

A long-standing Roman Catholic theme runs through the family history as the Thockmortons have maintained their Catholic religion until the present day. The house has a strong connection with the Gunpowder Plot and also suffered damage during the Civil War.

GARDENS

The house stands in 25 acres of gardens and grounds which also contain two churches and a lake. A new formal garden was constructed in 1992 with designs based on an Elizabethan knot garden in the courtyard. Visitors can also enjoy a specially created walk beside the River Arrow, returning to the house alongside the lake.

CONTACT

Mr A McLaren
Coughton Court
Alcester
Warwickshire
B49 5JA

Tel: (0789) 400777
Fax: (0789) 765544

LOCATION

Located on A435, 2 miles north of Alcester, 10 miles N-W of Stratford-on-Avon. 16 miles from Birmingham City Centre.

SUITABILITY FOR OTHER EVENTS

Coughton is suitable for receptions, special dinners in the panelled dining room, filming, buffets, business meetings, fairs and garden parties. The excellent acoustics of the Saloon make it ideal for concerts, especially chamber music concerts.

EXTRA FACILITIES

Marquees can be erected on the large lawn area and there is a Grand Piano in the Saloon.

ADVICE TO COURIERS & DRIVERS

Coughton Court is located on the A435, 2 miles north of Alcester. Dogs allowed in car park only. No photography or stiletto heels in house. Unlimited parking for coaches and cars.

FACILITIES FOR THE DISABLED

Only the ground floor of the house is suitable for disabled visitors. Toilet partially adapted for the disabled.

CATERING

There is a licensed restaurant open 12.30 - 5.45pm on days when the house is open. Capacity: 65 inside and 60 outside. Buffet or sit down meals can be provided, by arrangement, in the Dining Room and Saloon. Also in-house catering can be arranged for other events.

GUIDED TOURS

By arrangement.

GIFT SHOP

Open when house is open.

GUIDE BOOKS

Guide book, £2.50.

OPENING TIMES

Summer

April
Sat-Sun 1.30 - 5.30pm

Easter Sat - Wed
Daily   1.30 - 5.30pm*
* Open 12.30 on Easter Mon

May - September
Mon ⎫
Tues ⎬   1.30 - 5.30pm*
Wed ⎭
Thur ⎫ Closed
Fri ⎭
Sat ⎫   1.30 - 5.30pm*
Sun ⎭
* Grounds open 12 - 6pm
House open 12.30 on Bank Hol. Mons

October
Sat-Sun   1.30 - 5pm
Grounds open 12noon-5pm

Winter
Closed

ADMISSION

Summer

HOUSE & GROUNDS
Adult   £4.50
Child   £2.25
Family*   £12.00
* 2 adults and up to 4 children.

GROUNDS ONLY
Adult   £2.50
Child   £1.25

Winter
Closed

CONFERENCE AND FUNCTION FACILITIES

ROOM	DIMENSIONS	CAPACITY	LAYOUT	POWER POINTS	SUITABLE FOR A/V
Dining Room	45'x27'	40	Schoolroom	4	✓
		25	U-shape		
		20	Boardroom		
		55	Buffet		
		60	Theatre		
		46	Lunch/Dinner		
Saloon	60'x36'	60	Schoolroom	6	✓
		35	U-shape		
		30	Boardroom		
		90	Buffet		
		90	Theatre		
		60	Lunch/Dinner		

THE SALOON, WHICH HAS PARTICULARLY GOOD ACOUSTICS, IS OFTEN USED FOR MUSIC RECORDING.

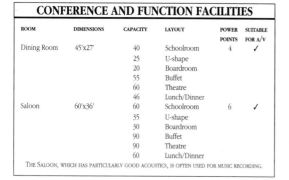

RAGLEY HALL
Alcester, Warwickshire

RAGLEY HALL, home of the Earl & Countess of Yarmouth was designed by Robert Hooke in 1680 and is one of the earliest and loveliest of England's great Palladian country houses. The perfect symmetry of its architecture remains unchanged except for the massive portico added by Wyatt in 1780.

The present interior is almost entirely due to two widely separated generations: in 1750, when Francis Seymour owned Ragley, James Gibbs designed the magnificent baroque plasterwork of the Great Hall. On completion, Francis filled the Hall with French and English furniture and porcelain and had portraits of himself and his sons painted by Sir Joshua Reynolds.

The present owners are the Earl and Countess of Yarmouth who are continuing the ongoing task of restoration and renovation to maintain Ragley in its present glory. Notable also is the mural, by Graham Rust, in the South Staircase Hall which was completed in 1983.

GARDENS

The main formal garden descends in a series of wide rose covered terraces. The rest of the 24 acre garden consists of shrubs and trees interspersed with spacious lawns providing vistas across the 400 acre park.

Other features are the lake created in 1625, the cricket pitch, still in regular use and the Adventure Playground and Maze.

CONTACT

Michael Barbour
Ragley Hall
Alcester
Warwickshire
B49 5NJ

Tel: (0789) 762090
Fax: (0789) 764791

LOCATION

From London 100 miles, M40 via Oxford and Stratford-on-Avon.

Bus: Birmingham - Evesham, from Lodge gates.

Rail: Evesham Station 9 miles.

Air: Birmingham Int'l 20 miles.

Taxi: Conway Taxi (0789) 762828

SUITABILITY FOR OTHER EVENTS

Private and corporate entertainment. Conferences and seminars, product launches, dinner parties and activity days can all be arranged. A comprehensive service is provided Film and photographic location..

EXTRA FACILITIES

The park, lake and picnic area are also available for use.

ADVICE TO COURIERS & DRIVERS

Please advise in advance, especially if catering is required. Coach drivers admitted free and receive information pack and luncheon voucher. No dogs; no photography in house please. Guide book in in French and German.

FACILITIES FOR THE DISABLED

Disabled and elderly visitors may alight at the entrance to the property, before parking in the allocated areas. Toilets for the disabled and lifts to the first and main floor for wheelchairs at the north side of the house.

CATERING

The licensed Terrace Tea Rooms are open 12 - 5pm for light lunches, snacks, afternoon teas and cakes. Groups must book.

Supper and private tours can be arranged, as can Private Luncheons and Dinners in the State Dining Room or Great Hall for 2-150 people. Please contact the Business Manager for full details.

GIFT SHOP

Open same time as the Hall, with an excellent selection of unusual and traditional gifts.

SCHOOL VISITS/CHILDREN

School groups are welcome, £2.50 per head, children's guide is available on request. Children can enjoy the Adventure Wood and Farm and Woodland Walk. Childrens Guide Book.

GUIDED TOURS

Private tours are given by Lord Yarmouth outside opening hours. The maximum size for the party is 100. For a guided tour there is a cost of £9.00 per head, plus VAT. Duration of the tour is approximately 1 hour.

OPENING TIMES

Summer
2 April -2 October

House   12 noon - 5 pm
Garden & Park
        10am - 6pm

Mon   Bank Hols Only
       (July & Aug: Park
       & Gardens open.)
Tues
Wed } Open
Thurs
Fri   Closed, except
       July & Aug, when
       Park & Gardens
       open.
Sat }
Sun } Open

Winter
3 October - Easter

Open any time by prior arrangement.

ADMISSION

HOUSE & GARDEN

Adult	£5.00
Child*	£3.50
OAP	£4.00
Group**	
Adult	£4.00
Schoolchild*	£2.50
OAP	£4.00

GARDEN ONLY

Adult	£4.00
Child*	£2.50
OAP	£4.00

* Aged 5-16.
** Minimum payment £70.00 for parties of 20 or more.

Winter

HOUSE & GARDEN
Private conducted tour
£9.00 + VAT per person.
Min. £95.00 + VAT.

CONFERENCE AND FUNCTION FACILITIES

ROOM	DIMENSIONS	CAPACITY	LAYOUT	POWER POINTS	SUITABLE FOR A/V
Great Hall	70'x40'	up to 150	Various	✓	✓
Red Saloon	30'x40'	150	Reception	✓	
Green Drawing Room	20'x30'	150	Reception	✓	
Supper Room	45'x22'	up to 100	Various	✓	✓

WARWICK CASTLE
Warwickshire

Warwick Castle, the finest medieval castle in England, and set on the picturesque banks of the River Avon. There are few buildings as steeped in history and as marvellously preserved as Warwick Castle.

William the Conqueror ordered the first castle to be built in 1068AD shortly after the Norman Conquest. The succeeding Norman Earls of Warwick rebuilt the Castle in stone, so that by the 14th century it had become the principal stronghold of the mighty Beauchamp warlords. As the military importance of the Castle declined, the main living quarters were converted and refurbished into a residence in the grandest style. The magnificent interiors date from the late 17th to the late 19th centuries and today most of the main fortifications have altered little from the 14th century.

NEW MEDIAEVAL ATTRACTION FOR 1994 "Kingmaker - A preparation for battle" - depicts the life of the Castle on the eve of battle in 1471

"A Royal Weekend Party, 1898" by Madame Tussaud's recreates a Victorian house party.

The State Rooms and Great Hall typifies the baronial splendour of the Castle. The gloomy Dungeon and Torture Chamber are both reminders of the Castle's mediaeval past.

GARDENS

Landscaped by 'Capability' Brown, the 60 acres of Grounds and Gardens are a delight in all seasons and where peacocks roam freely.

CONTACT

Warwick Castle
Warwick
Warwickshire
CV34 4QU

Info. Tel: (0926) 408000
Fax: (0926) 401692
Admin. Tel: (0926) 495421

LOCATION

Warwick Castle is part of Warwick town, 8 miles north east of Stratford. From London M40, Junc.15, well signposted 1½ hours drive.

Rail: Warwick Station - 5 mins walk to Castle, London to Warwick rail connections tel. 071 387 7070

Air: Birmingham Int'l then 25 minutes drive to Warwick.

OPENING TIMES

Summer
1st April - 22nd October

Mon	
Tues	
Wed	
Thurs	10am - 6pm
Fri	
Sat	
Sun	

August weekend 7pm

Winter
23rd October - 31st March

Mon	
Tues	
Wed	
Thurs	10am - 5pm
Fri	
Sat	
Sun	

ADMISSION

All Year
From 3rd April 1994

Adult	£7.75
Child	£4.75
Sen. Citizen	£5.50
Students	£5.95
Family (2+2)	£19.95

GROUPS*

Adult	£6.25
Child	£3.95
Sen. Citizen	£4.95
Students	£5.25

* Min 20 people.

ADVICE TO COURIERS & DRIVERS

Recommended duration of visit is 4 hours to see all the attractions. Couriers and coach drivers admitted free of charge. Please book groups in advance.

FACILITIES FOR THE DISABLED

Allocated parking areas and toilet facilities. Please telephone for details.

PARKING FOR COACHES & CARS

Free car parking for over 200 cars and 25 coaches.

CATERING

The Castle offers a wide range of refreshment facilities throughout the year.

GUIDED TOURS

Available for pre-booked groups of 20-50 people at an additional cost.

GIFT SHOP

Two main gift shops offering a wide variety of souvenirs and gift items.

GUIDE BOOK

A full colour guide book, available in English, French and German.

SCHOOL VISITS/CHILDREN

Groups of 20 or more with an all inclusive rate. A new school/education pack will be available from February 1994. Please book groups in advance.

CONFERENCE AND FUNCTION FACILITIES

Warwick Castle offers a range of conference and evening corporate entertainment. Stables Conference facilities available during the day, off-season to seat 70 people theatre style. Evening reception and formal dinners can be held in the Great Hall, State Dining Room and Evening Dinners and Medieval Banquets also available in the Undercroft.

ROOM	DIMENSIONS	CAPACITY	LAYOUT	POWER POINTS	SUITABLE FOR A/V
Great Hall		140	Formal Dinner		
		200	Drinks Reception		
State Dining Room		25	Formal Dinner		
Stables Conf. Facilities		70	Theatre	6	Hired

BADDESLEY CLINTON

OPEN
2 March-30 Sept.
Wed to Sun. &
B.H. Mon.
Closed Good Fri.
2.00-6.00pm
Grounds from
12.30pm
October:
Wed-Sun 12.30-
4.30pm
March 1995
Wed-Sun 2-6pm
Last Adm. to
House, Shop &
Restaurant 30
mins before
closing.

BADDESLEY CLINTON, SOLIHULL TEL: 0564 783294
(The National Trust)

A romantically sited medieval moated manor house, dating from 14th century; little changed since 1634; family portraits; priest holes; garden; ponds and lake walk.

Location: ³/4 mile west of A4141 Warwick/Birmingham road at Chadwick End, 7¹/2 miles north west of Warwick, 15 miles south east of central Birmingham.
Admission: Adult £4.00, Fam. Ticket £11.00 (2 + up to 4 childlren). Grounds only £2.00, children half price.

CHARLECOTE PARK

OPEN
April-Oct 30
Daily Fri. to Tue.
closed Good Fri.
11.00am-6.00pm
House closed
1.00-2.00pm
Last.Adm.5pm
Eve. guided
tours for pre-
booked parties
May-Sept. Mons.
7.30-9.30
£4.00 (Inc. N.T.
members min
charge £80 per
party.)

CHARLECOTE PARK, STRATFORD UPON AVON
TEL: 0789 470277
(The National Trust)

Home of the Lucy family since 1247; present house built in 1550's and later visited by Queen Elizabeth I; part landscape by 'Capability' Brown, supports herd of red and fallow deer, reputedly poached by Shakespeare, and a flock of Jacob sheep, first introduced in 1756; principal rooms altered 1830's in Elizabethan Revival style.

Location: 1 mile west of Wellesbourne, 5 miles east of Stratford upon Avon, 6 miles south of Warwick on north side of B4086.
Admission : Adult £4.00, Family Ticket £11.00 (2 + up to 4 children), children half price.

FARNBOROUGH HALL

National Trust/Nick Meers

OPEN
House Grounds
& Terrace Walk
April-30 Sept.
Wed. & Sat
2.00-6.00pm
also 1 & 2 May
2.00-6.00pm
Terrace Walk
only
Thu. & Fri.
2.00-6.00pm
Last Adm.
5.30pm.

FARNBOROUGH HALL, BANBURY TEL: 0295 89202
(The National Trust)

A classical mid 18th century stone house, home of the Bolbech family for 300 years; notable plasterwork, the entrance hall, staircase and 2 principal rooms are shown; the grounds contain charming 18th century temples, a ²/3 mile terrace walk and an obelisk.

Location: 6 miles north of Banbury, ¹/2 mile west of A423.
Admission: House, grounds & terrace walk, Adult £2.60, Garden & Terrace walk, Adult £1.50,Terrace walk only (Thu. & Fri.) Adult £1.00, children half price.

Hall's Croft, Stratford upon Avon.
  In the Old Town.

Anne Hathaway's Cottage, Stratford upon Avon.
  In Shottery.

HATTON HOUSE

OPEN
Hatton House is
open only
through prior
appointment for
corporate
groups.
Hatton Country
World is open
from 10,00am-
5.00pm seven
days week
throughout the
year.

HATTON HOUSE, HATTON TEL: 0926 842044/843411
(J Arkwright)

CORPORATE EVENTS can be staged at either Hatton Action Park for outdoor pursuits, or at Hatton House and the adjacent parkland.

Tour groups are catered for at Hatton Country World which houses the largest craft centre in the UK, a Rare Breeds Farm, the famous Hatton Locks on the Grand Union Canal and an adventure playground.

Location: Just off A41/A4177 Solihull to Warwick road, 5 minutes from Junction 15, M40.
Admission: Dependent on requirements. Full details upon application.

HONINGTON HALL

OPEN
1 June-31 Aug.
Wednesdays
only
Bank Holiday
Mondays
2.30-5.00pm

Parties at other
times by
appointment.

HONINGTON HALL, SHIPSTON-ON-STOUR TEL: 0608 661434
(Benjamin Wiggin Esq)

This fine Caroline manor house was built in the early 1680's for Henry Parker in mellow brickwork and stone quoins and window dressings. Modified in 1751 when an octagonal saloon was inserted. The interior was also lavishly restored around this time and contains exceptional mid-Georgian plasterwork. Set in 15 acres of grounds.

Location: 10 miles south of Stratford-upon-Avon. 1¹/2 miles north of Shipston-on-Stour. Take A3400 towards Stratford, then signed right to Honington.
Admission: Adults £2.00, children 50p.

KEY TO SYMBOLS

 Historic Houses Association Member

National Trust Property

Property in care of English Heritage

National Trust for Scotland Property

WARWICKSHIRE

✠ **Kenilworth Castle,** Kenilworth.
　(0926) 52078　West side of Kenilworth.

Lord Leycester Hospital, Warwick.
　(0926) 492797　West gate of Warwick.

New Place/Nash's House, Stratford upon Avon.
　In Chapel Street, Stratford upon Avon .

The Shakespeare Countryside Musuem at Mary Arden's House, Stratford upon Avon.
　At Wilmcote.

Shakespeare's Birthplace, Stratford upon Avon.
　In Henley Street, Stratford upon Avon.

PACKWOOD HOUSE

OPEN
April-30 Sept.
Wed.-Sun &
Bank Hol. Mons.
2.00-6.00pm
Closed Good Fri.

October
Wed. to Sun.
12.30-4.30pm
Last adm. to
house 30 mins
before closing.

PACKWOOD HOUSE, SOLIHULL TEL: 0564 782024
(The National Trust)

A fascinating timber framed Tudor house containing a wealth of fine tapestries and furniture; superb gardens, noted mainly for their yew topiary and Carolean Garden.

Location:　2 miles east of Hockley Heath (on A3400), 11 miles south east of central Birmingham.
Admission:　Adult £3.20. Family ticket £8.80 (2 + up to 4 children). Garden only £2.00, children half price.

UPTON HOUSE

OPEN
House,
Tearoom, Shop
11 June-31 Oct.
Sat. to Wed.
incl. B.H. Mons.
2.00-6.00pm
Last adm.
5.30pm
Garden only as
house also April:
Sat, Sun & B.H.
Mons
2.00-6.00pm and
1 May-8 June
Daily Sat to
Wed. 2.00-
6.00pm

UPTON HOUSE, BANBURY TEL: 0295 670266
(The National Trust)

The house contains an outstanding collection of paintings by English and Continental Old Masters, Brussels tapestries, Sévres porcelain, Chelsea figures and 18th century furniture,. The famous garden has terraces descending into a deep valley; herbaceous borders, the national collection of Asters, over an acre of kitchen garden laid out in the 1930's and pools with ornamental fish.

Location:　On A422, 7 miles north west of Banbury, 12 miles south east of Stratford-upon-Avon.
Admission:　Adult £4.30. Fam tkt £11.80 (2+ 4 children). Garden only £2.15, children half price.

HONINGTON HALL: THE SALOON

HAGLEY HALL
Stourbridge, West Midlands

HAGLEY HALL, set in 350 acres of landscaped park, is the premier location in the West Midlands for a wide variety of corporate entertaining, with superb catering for 20-300 guests in the House and virtually unlimited capacity with the help of marquees.

The Hall is let on a truly exclusive basis. There is no access for the general public while corporate hospitality events are held and, as guests have exclusive use, the rooms may be used in any combination, giving great flexibility. It is open all year for functions, which include conferences, seminars, product launches, lunches, country pursuits, dinners and wedding receptions.

The elegant Palladian House, completed in 1760, contains some of the finest surviving examples of Italian plasterwork. Hagley's rich Rococo decoration is a remarkable tribute to the artistic achievement of the great 18th Century amateurs, and it still remains the much loved home of Viscount and Viscountess Cobham.

Our resident chef and his team offer an extremely high standard of classic English country cuisine. Menus to help you make your selection are available but we are happy to help you create the menu and dishes of your choice.

OPENING TIMES

Summer
3-5 April, 29-31 May,
28-30 Aug.

Open   2pm - 5pm

Winter
3 January - 3 March

Mon	
Tues	
Wed	} 2pm -5pm
Thurs	
Fri	
Sat	Closed
Sun	2pm - 5pm

ADMISSION

Adult	£3.00
Child*	£1.50
OAP	£2.50
Student	£2.50

GROUPS
By arrangement.

* Under 16 years.

CONTACT

Simon Insull
Hagley Hall
Stourbridge
West Midlands
DY9 9LG

Tel: (0562) 882408
Fax: (0562) 882632

LOCATION

The Hall is easily accessible from all parts of the country close to M40, M42, M6,and only 5 miles from M5 Juncts 3 and 4.
It is 25 minutes from Birmingham Int'l Airport, the NEC and Int'l Railway Station, and is 12 miles west of Birmingham City Centre.

SUITABILITY FOR OTHER EVENTS

Hagley Hall is also available for filming.

New for 1994, an evening of wine. Information on request.

ACCOMMODATION

Accommodation is not available at the Hall, but can be arranged with a luxurious local hotel, offering a comprehensive range of amenities for Hagley Hall guests.

EXTRA FACILITIES

These include parkland, unlimited car parking and a Helicopter landing pad.

We can also offer the services of a Film and Video production company, Triton Television, which is based at Hagley Hall.

ADVICE TO COURIERS & DRIVERS

Please treat the Hall and contents with care.

FACILITIES FOR THE DISABLED

Disabled and elderly visitors may alight at the entrance to the Hall. There are no toilets for the disabled.

GUIDE BOOKS

Colour guide book, £1.20.

PARKING FOR COACHES & CARS

There is unlimited parking for coaches and cars, 20 yards from the Hall.

CATERING

As well as our in house catering, we offer a unique outside catering service. We bring professional advice, imagination, contacts, resources, fine furniture and tableware, to the venue of your choice.

CONFERENCE AND FUNCTION FACILITIES

ROOM	DIMENSIONS	CAPACITY	LAYOUT	POWER POINTS	SUITABLE FOR A/V
			U-shape		
Gallery	85'x17'	50-140	Schoolroom	8	✓
Crimson Room	23'x31'	30-80	Theatre	6	✓
State Dining Room	34'x27'	40-120	Boardroom	10	✓
Westcote	31'x20'	30-60	Buffet	6	✓
Lyttleton	31'x20'	30-60	Lunch	6	✓
			Dinner		

Aston Hall, Birmingham.
(021) 327 0062   2½ miles from city centre.

Blakesley Hall, Blakesley Road, Birmingham.
(021) 783 2193   3 miles from city centre.

Castle Bromwich Hall Gardens, Birmingham.
(021) 749 4100   4 miles east of Birmingham.

Perrott's Folly, Edgbaston.
Waterworks Road, Edgbaston, 2 miles west of city centre.

Wightwick Manor, Wolverhampton.
(0902) 761108   3 miles west of Wolverhampton.

HANBURY HALL, NR DROITWICH, WORCESTERSHIRE (SEE P.169)

WILTON HOUSE, WILTSHIRE: THE DOUBLE CUBE ROOM (SEE P. 167)

BOWOOD HOUSE
Calne, Wiltshire

BOWOOD is the family home of the Earl and Countess of Shelburne, the Earl being the eldest son of the Marquess of Lansdowne. Begun c.1720 for the Bridgeman family, the House was purchased by the 2nd Earl of Shelburne in 1754 and completed soon afterwards. Part of the House was demolished in 1955, leaving a perfectly proportioned Georgian home, over half of which is open to visitors. Robert Adam's magnificent Diocletian wing contains a splendid library, the Laboratory where Joseph Priestly discovered oxygen gas in 1774, the Orangery - now a Picture Gallery, the Chapel and a Sculpture Gallery in which some of the famous Lansdowne Marbles are displayed. Among the family treasures shown in the numerous Exhibition Rooms are Georgian costumes, including Lord Byron's Albanian dress; Victoriana; Indiana (the 5th Marquess was Viceroy 1888-94); and superb collections of watercolours, miniatures and jewellery. The House is set in one of the most beautiful parks in England. Over 2,000 acres of gardens and grounds were landscaped by Capability Brown between 1762 and 1768, and are embellished with a Doric Temple, a cascade, a pinetum and an arboretum. The Rhododendron Gardens are open for six weeks during May and June. All the walks have seats.

CONTACT

The Administrator
Bowood House and
Gardens
Calne
Wiltshire
SN11 0LZ

Tel: (0249) 812102

LOCATION

From London M4, Junct. 17, 2 hours.

Bus: to the gate, 1½ miles through park to House.

Rail: Chippenham Stn 5 miles, Swindon 17 miles, Bristol 26 miles and Bath 16miles.

Taxi: AA Taxis, Chippenham 657777.

SUITABILITY FOR OTHER EVENTS

Receptions, film location.

EXTRA FACILITIES

Internationally renowned Garden Centre, 2,000 acre park, 40 acre lake, massive adventure playground, golf course and Country Club.

ADVICE TO COURIERS & DRIVERS

2-3 hours should be allowed to visit the house, gardens and grounds. We recommend parties who require lunch or tea to book in advance. No dogs allowed. Parking for over 1,000 cars and unlimited parking for coaches, 400 yards from the House.

FACILITIES FOR THE DISABLED

Disabled and elderly visitors may alight at the House before parking in the allocated area. There are toilet facilities for the disabled in the House and in the Garden Centre.

CATERING

Both The Bothy (self-service light snacks, capacity 50) and the Restaurant (waitress-service, capacity 85) are available. Pre-booked prices range from £5.95 to £7.25 for a two course lunch and coffee; £6.65 to £10.30 for the daily buffet, dessert and coffee; £2.80 for a cream tea. Catering facilities can be provided for functions, for 45 to 85 persons.

GUIDED TOURS

Groups can be met and given an introductory talk, and if requested can be given a guided tour, for which there is an additional charge. Average time for tour of House 1¼ hours.

GIFT SHOP

Garden centre open throughout the year, selling Bowood souvenirs, china, toiletries etc. as well as a wide range of plants. Kitchen Shop open in the House.

GUIDE BOOKS

Colour guide book, £2.00. Translation sheets available in French, German, Japanese and Dutch. Comprehensive guide to Bowood's trees and shrubs £1.50, Catalogue of the Collection of paintings £1.50.

SCHOOL VISITS/CHILDREN

School parties are welcome. Special guide books for children. Educational visit with teacher's notes for pre-, during and post-school visit, for both primary and secondary schools. Many picnic areas. Exciting and unique Adventure Playground.

GOLF COURSE & COUNTRY CLUB

In May 1992, the Bowood Golf and Country Club opened. The 18 hole course and practice area covers two hundred acres in the western corner of Capability Brown's park. Access to the course and club house is through Sir Charles Barry's famous 'golden gates' in Derry Hill. The course is open to all players holding a current handicap.

OPENING TIMES

Summer
26 March-30 Oct.

Mon	
Tues	
Wed	
Thurs	11am - 6pm
Fri	
Sat	
Sun	

NB Open Bank Hols

Winter
31 October-25 March

House closed.
Garden Centre Open.

ADMISSION

Summer

Adult	£4.50
Child*	£2.30
OAP	£4.00

GROUPS**	
Adult	£4.15
Child*	£2.05
OAP	£3.50

RHODODENDRON GARDENS
Open for six weeks in May and June.

Adult	£2.50
Child*	£2.50
OAP	£2.50

* Aged 5-15.
** Min. 20 people.

CORSHAM COURT
Corsham, Wiltshire

CONTACT

Lord Methuen
Corsham Court
Corsham
Wiltshire
SN13 0BZ

Tel: (0249) 712214

LOCATION

Corsham is signposted from the M4. From Edinburgh, A1, M62, M6, M5, M4, 8 hours. From London, M4, 2$\frac{1}{4}$ hours. From Chester, M6, M5, M4, 4 hours.

Rail: Chippenham Stn 6 miles.

Motorway: M4 Junct. 17, 9 miles.

Taxi: (0249) 715959.

CORSHAM COURT, currently the home of Lord Methuen, is an Elizabethan house of 1582 that was bought by Paul Methuen in the mid-18th Century, to house a collection of 16th and 17th Century Italian and Flemish master paintings and statuary. In the middle of the 19th Century, the House was enlarged to receive a second collection, purchased in Florence, principally of fashionable Italian masters, rare Italian primitives and stone inlaid furniture.

Paul Methuen (1723-95) was a great-grandson of Paul Methuen of Bradford-on-Avon and cousin of John Methuen, ambassador and negotiator of the Methuen Treaty of 1703 with Portugal which permitted export of British woollens to Portugal and allowed a preferential 33$\frac{1}{3}$% duty discount on Portuguese wines - bringing about a major change in British drinking habits.

The architects involved in the alterations to the House and Park were Lancelot Capability Brown in the 1760s, John Nash in 1800 and Thomas Bellamy in 1845-9. Brown set the style by retaining the Elizabethan Stables and Riding School, but rebuilding the Gateway, retaining the gabled Elizabethan stone front and doubling the gabled wings at either end and, inside, by designing the East Wing as Stateroom-Picture Galleries. Nash's work has now largely disappeared, but Bellamy's stands fast, notably in the Hall and Staircase.

The State Rooms, including the Music Room and Dining Room, provide the setting for the outstanding collection of over 150 paintings, statuary, bronzes and furniture. The collection includes work by such names as Chippendale, the Adams brothers, Carvaggio, Reni, Rosa, Rubens, Lippi, Reynolds, Romney and a pianoforte by Clementi.

GARDENS

Capability Brown planned to include a lake, avenues and specimen trees such as the Oriental Plane now with a 200 yard perimeter. The Gardens, designed not only by Brown but also by Repton, contain a Ha-ha, herbaceous borders, secluded gardens, lawns, rose gardens, a lily pool, a stone bath house and the Bradford Porch.

SUITABILITY FOR OTHER EVENTS

Corsham is suitable for filming.

ADVICE TO COURIERS & DRIVERS

Bring coach parties up to the front door. PLEASE BOOK coach parties in advance. No photography, no umbrellas, dogs must be kept on leads in the garden.

FACILITIES FOR THE DISABLED

Disabled and elderly visitors may alight at the entrance to the property, before parking in the allocated areas.

PARKING FOR COACHES & CARS

Capacity of the Car Park: 400 cars, 120 yards from the House and coaches may park at the door to the House.

CATERING

No catering is provided. Audrey's Tea Rooms are recommended. Tel: Corsham 714931.

GUIDED TOURS

These are offered for up to 50-55 people on any one tour. If requested the owner may meet the group visiting the House. Approximate duration of the tour is 1$\frac{1}{2}$ hours.

GIFT SHOP

There is a sales area, stocking postcards, slides and books.

GUIDE BOOKS

Colour guide book, for sale or hire.

SCHOOL VISITS/CHILDREN

School visits can be arranged: rate negotiable. A guide will be provided.

OPENING TIMES

Summer
Good Friday - 30 Sept

Mon	Bank Hols Only
Tues	
Wed	
Thurs	2pm - 6pm
Fri	
Sat	
Sun	

Last Admission 5.30pm

Winter
1 Oct - Good Friday

Mon	Closed
Tues	
Wed	2pm - 4.30pm
Thurs	
Fri	Closed
Sat	2pm - 4.30pm
Sun	

Last admission 4pm.

NB Closed December

ADMISSION

All Year

HOUSE & GARDEN
Adult	£3.50
Child*	£2.00
OAP(U.K)	£3.00
Student	£3.50
Group**	
Adult	£3.00
Child*	£1.50
OAP(U.K)	£2.50
Student	£3.00

GARDEN ONLY
Adult	£2.00
Child*	£1.00
OAP	£1.50
Student	£2.00
Group**	£1.50

* Aged 5-16.
** Min payment £40.00

LONGLEAT HOUSE
Warminster, Wiltshire

LONGLEAT HOUSE lies in a sheltered valley amidst rolling parkland, landscaped by Capability Brown in the late 18th Century. The magnificent Elizabethan property, built by Sir John Thynne with the help of the celebrated mason-architect Robert Smythson was completed in 1580 and has been the home of a member of the same family ever since.

The House contains many treasures, including paintings by Titian, Tintoretto, Wootton, a fine Louis XVI desk, and a fabulous silver table centre - piece weighing 1000 ounces.

Between 1801 and 1811 the architect Jeffrey Wyatville designed the magnificent stable block and also carried out many alterations to the House. However, the Great Hall was not altered and remains the same fine Elizabethan room as Sir John left it in 1580. The formal gardens contain a beautiful Orangery and a delightful boathouse.

In 1949 Longleat became the first Stately Home to open to the public thus starting a new industry in Britain. Equally pioneering, Longleat developed the first Safari Park outside Africa in 1966.

The latest attraction at Longleat is The Life and Times of Henry Lord Bath - A Memorial Exhibition. The long and active life of the 6th Marquess is told through this personal collection from early childhood memories on the Estate, through World War Two, to his twilight years. Following his fascination for Churchill, he amassed one of the finest collections of Churchill memorabilia, which is housed in this moving and nostalgic exhibition.

Lord Bath's Murals are a recent addition to the House continuing the tradition of each generation adding to and embellishing their family home.

CONTACT

Mrs C Everard
The Estate Office
Longleat
Warminster
Wiltshire
BA12 7NW

Tel: (0985) 844400
Fax: (0985) 844885

LOCATION

London 2 hours.
M3, A303, A36, A362
Midway between Warminster and Frome or from North West M4 exit 18.

Rail: mainline Paddington to Westbury 12 miles.

Bristol Airport 30 miles.

Taxi: Beeline Taxis (0985) 212215

SUITABILITY FOR OTHER EVENTS

Fashion shows, concerts, archery, equestrian events, garden parties, shows, rallies, filming, promotions, product launches.

EXTRA FACILITIES

Also available for use: Grand Piano, Parkland, Helicopter Pad. Lectures can be arranged by prior appointment on the property and its history for up to 50 people. A room can be hired.

ADVICE TO COURIERS & DRIVERS

Facilities available for coach drivers. Parking for up to 650 cars and 100 coaches, 300 yards from the House; and nearby grass parking for thousands.

FACILITIES FOR THE DISABLED

Disabled and elderly visitors may alight at the entrance to the House. There are toilets for the disabled.

GUIDED TOURS

These are available for groups of up to 20 people, at no additional cost. Tours in French, Spanish and German are available by appointment. Average time taken 1 hour.

CATERING

There is a Cellar Café (capacity 80). Parties can be booked in advance for tea and other meals. Menus are available on request. Cream Teas available, lunch from £5, sandwiches and snacks from £1.20.

GIFT SHOP

The Gift Shop is open daily except 25th December. 10am-6pm in Summer; 10am-4pm in Winter. Range of souvenirs available.

GUIDE BOOKS

Guide book with colour photographs available. French and German translations available on request.

SCHOOL VISITS/CHILDREN

Groups are welcome with 1 teacher given free entry per 10 children. There is also a special animal safari plan with teachers notes and questionnaires included.

CONFERENCE AND FUNCTION FACILITIES

ROOM	DIMENSIONS	CAPACITY	LAYOUT	POWER POINTS	SUITABLE FOR A/V
Green Library	44'6"x21'6"	150	Various	✓	✓
		100	Dinner/Dance (with Great Hall)		
Great Hall	48'9"x30'6"	200	Various	✓	✓

SHELDON MANOR
Chippenham, Wiltshire

THE surviving manorhouse of a long-gone medieval village has a great Porch described by Pevsner as 'astounding' . The parvise is late 13th Century, the east wing dates from 1431 and the west wing was rebuilt in 1659. The oak staircase with carved open finials and dog-gate is contemporary with this. The Hall and Dining Room are oak-panelled and the main bedroom has William and Mary panelling.

The stone cistern in the thickness of the Plantagenet wall, fed by a wooden pipe from the roof, is unique. The Priest's Room has its original oak waggon roof and carved wallplates. The Chapel was built c.1450, and has three original windows and windbraces in the roof. The apple-house of half-timbered brick and thatch stands on staddle-stones.

Inside are collections of early oak furniture, Nailsea glass, Persian rugs and saddle bags, porcelain and American Revolutionary War Memorabilia; a warm welcome, and no "ropes".

GARDENS

The forecourt probably comprises the medieval garden, with two exceptional yew trees. The terraces descending southwards to a long swimming pool in natural stone contain many old fashioned roses. -- a connoisseur collection - trees, and flowering shrubs, some planted in old Dutch cheese vats. Newly-established, a maze of edible plants.

CONTACT

Major & Mrs M Gibbs
Sheldon Manor
Chippenham
Wiltshire
SN14 ORG

Tel: (0249) 653120

LOCATION

From London: M4 to Exit 17, 4 miles. A429 towards Chippenham, A420 towards Bristol. Follow sign posts.

Chippenham Railway Station 3 miles.

Chippenham Bus Station 3 miles.

Taxi: Webbs, Chippenham 660022.

SUITABILITY FOR OTHER EVENTS

Wedding receptions, birthday celebrations, garden parties, clay-pigeon shooting, archery, shows, rallies, filming are a speciality

EXTRA FACILITIES

Video, upright piano. Talks on the property, contents, garden and history can be arranged for up to 100 people. No extra charge for this Projector and screen can be hired.

ADVICE TO COURIERS & DRIVERS

No dogs or photography indoors. Facilities tailored to suit any function, always with a personal touch. Pre-booked coaches welcome. Parking for 200 cars, 100 yards from Manor. Area for coaches nearer house.

FACILITIES FOR THE DISABLED

Disabled and elderly visitors may alight at the entrance to the property, before parking in the allocated areas. Toilet facilities for the disabled on request.

CATERING

The Restaurant/Tea Room, which has won much praise from visitors, seats up to 84. The adjoining Cockloft (3 rooms) may be hired for private functions. Buffet lunches/dinners, cream teas, medieval/17th century meals, garden barbecues are all bookable for groups. Menus/prices on request.

GUIDED TOURS

Leisurely t ours of the house can be arranged, usually with the owners (in French/Italian also). Average time for tour 1 hour.

SCHOOL VISITS/CHILDREN

School groups are welcome out of normal opening hours. Cost dependent on age and length of visit, guide and schoolroom available. Teachers welcome on familiarisation visit. Items of interest: dolls' house, Jacob sheep, parrot. Swimming is available for school visits provided there is a life saver in the party.

OPENING TIMES

Summer
Public Days, Sundays, Thursdays and Bank Holidays from Easter Day to 2nd October.
12.30-6.00pm

House opens 2pm.

Private parties at anytime by prior arrangement

Winter
Closed.
Private parties anytime by arrangement.

ADMISSION

Summer
HOUSE & GARDEN
Adult	£3.00
Child*	£1.00
OAP	£2.75
Student	£2.75

GARDEN ONLY
Adult	£1.75
Child*	£0.35
OAP	£1.50
Student	£1.50

GROUPS**
Adult	£3.50 private days, £2.75 open days.
Child*	Dependent on age/length of visit.
OAP	No private day concessions.

*Free under 11, £1 11-16 House & Garden. Free Garden only.
**Min. Payment 20 people. If no catering required, extra charge made.

Winter
Same as Summer.
Groups only.

CONFERENCE AND FUNCTION FACILITIES

ROOM	DIMENSIONS	CAPACITY	LAYOUT	POWER POINTS	SUITABLE FOR A/V
Great Hall	21'x30'	100	Various	1	✓
Stables	21'x38'	150	Various	6	✓
	21'x24'	50			
Cockloft	3 rooms	50	Various	4	✓
Reception Room	21'x21'		Various		
Library	18'x15'		Various		

WILTON HOUSE
Salisbury, Wiltshire

The 17th Earl of Pembroke and his family live in Wilton House which has been the ancestral home for 450 years. In 1544 Henry VIII gave the Abbey and lands of Wilton to Sir William Herbert who had married Anne Parr, sister of Catherine, sixth wife of King Henry.

The Tudor Tower, in the centre of the east front, is the only part of the original building to survive a fire in 1647. Inigo Jones and John Webb were responsible for the rebuilding of the House in the Palladian style, whilst further alterations were made by James Wyatt from 1801. The chief architectural features are the magnificent 17th century state apartments (including the famous Single and Double Cube rooms) and the 19th century cloisters.

The House contains one of the finest art collections in Europe, with over 230 original paintings on display, including works by Van Dyck, Rubens, Joshua Reynolds and Breughel. Also on show - Greek and Italian statuary, a lock of Queen Elizabeth's I hair, Napoleon's despatch case, and Florence Nightingale's sash.

The exhibition centre houses a dynamic introductory film (narrated by Anna Massey), the reconstructed Tudor kitchen and Victorian Laundry, with a special 50th anniversary display commemorating the D-Day Landings, when Wilton House was the H.Q. for Southern Command

CONTACT

Mr Alun Williams
Wilton House
Wilton
Salisbury
SP2 OBJ

Tel: (0722) 734115
Fax: (0722) 744447

LOCATION

2¹/₂ miles west of Salisbury on the A30.

Rail: Salisbury Station (2¹/₂ miles)

Bus: Every 10 minutes from Salisbury.

Taxi: Sarum Taxi (0722) 334477

SUITABILITY FOR OTHER EVENTS

Film location, Fashion Shows, Product Launches, Equestrian Events, Garden Parties, Antiques Fairs, Concerts, Vehicle Rallies, Exclusive Banquets.

ADVICE TO COURIERS & DRIVERS

Free coach parking. Group rates (Min 15 pax), meal vouchers, drivers lounge. No photography /dogs in House.

FACILITIES FOR THE DISABLED

Toilets for the disabled. Excellent wheelchair access. Visitors may alight at the Entrance Guide dogs admitted..

PARKING FOR COACHES & CARS

Car (200+) and coach (12) park 100 yards from visitor entrance.

CATERING

Self-service restaurant open 11am-1730. Advance booking required for groups (waitress service available for coffee, lunch and tea).

GIFT SHOP

Open as House. Stocks a wide variety of quality souvenirs.

GUIDE BOOKS

24 page full colour guide book £2. French, German, Spanish, Italian, Japanese and Dutch information sheets.

GUIDED TOURS

Pre-booking a necessity

SCHOOL VISITS/CHILDREN

Teachers handbook for National Curriculum and worksheets. EFL students welcome. Free preparatory visit for group leaders.

OPENING TIMES

Summer

29 March - 30 October

Mon Tues Wed Thurs Fri Sat Sun	11am-6pm

NB. Last admission 5pm

Winter

Closed, except for private parties.

ADMISSION

Summer
HOUSE, GROUNDS & EXHIBITION.

Adults	£5.50
Child	£3.50
OAP	£4.50
Family (2+2)	£14.50

GROUP*
Adult	£4.50
OAP	£4.50
Child	£3.00

* Minimum number 15 people.

Winter

Prices on application

CONFERENCE AND FUNCTION FACILITIES

ROOM	DIMENSIONS	CAPACITY	LAYOUT	POWER POINTS	SUITABLE FOR A/V
Double Cube	60'x30'	120	Dinner	12	
		150	U-Shape		
Exhibition Centre	50'x40'	140	Dinner	6	
Film Theatre	34'x20'	67	Theatre	2	✓

Avebury Manor and Garden, Avebury.
(06723) 388

Avebury Museum, Avebury.
(06723) 250 In Avebury, 7 miles west of Marlborough.

Broadleas Gardens, Devizes.
(0380) 722035 1½ miles south west of Devizes on A360.

Charlton Park House, Malmesbury.
1½ miles north east of Malmesbury.

The Courts Garden, Holt.
(0225) 782340 2½ miles east of Bradford on Avon on B3107.

Fitz House Garden, Teffont Magna, Salisbury.
(0722) 716257 In village, 10 miles west of Salisbury.

Great Chalfield Manor, Melksham.
(0985) 847777 2½ miles north east of Bradford on Avon via B3109.

Hampworth Lodge, Landford, Salisbury.
(0794) 390215 10 miles south east of Salisbury on the C44 link road.

Hazelbury Manor Gardens, Box.
(0225) 812113 5 miles south west of Chippenham.

IFORD MANOR GARDENS

OPEN
April & Oct.
Suns. only +
Easter Mon.
2.00-5.00pm
May-Sept.
Tue., Wed.,
Thurs., Sat., Suns
& B.H. Mons.
2.00-5.00pm
Coaches by
appointment at
other times.

IFORD MANOR GARDENS, BRADFORD-ON-AVON
TEL: 0225 863146 & 862364
(Mrs E Cartwright-Hignett)

An enchanted garden. Iford Manor, a tudor house with a classical facade, was once a busy centre of the woollen industry. Set in a romantic river valley it is now surrounded by a peaceful terraced garden of unique character. Designed by the Edwardian architect Harold Peto, it has pools, statuary, a colonnade, terraces and a cloister. Featured in Gardeners World in 1993.

Location: 7 miles S.E.. from Bath via A36, signposted Iford.
Admission: £2.00 adult, £1.50 OAP/Student/Child 10+ Free car parking. Picnic area by river.

HEALE GARDEN

OPEN
Garden, Plant
Centre & Shop
throughout the
year
10.00-5.00pm.

Tours of the
house,
lunches/teas for
parties of over
20 by
arrangement.

HEALE GARDEN & PLANT CENTRE, WOODFORD
TEL: 072273 504
(Mr Guy & Lady Anne Rasch)

Winner of Christie's/HHA Garden of the Year award 1984. Early Carolean manor house where King Charles II hid during his escape. The garden provides a wonderfully varied collection of plants, shrub, musk and other roses, growing in the formal setting of clipped hedges and mellow stonework. Particularly lovely in Spring and Autumn is the water garden surrounding an authentic Japanese Tea House and Nikko Bridge which create an exciting focus in this part of the garden.

Location: 4 miles north of Salisbury on the Woodford Valley road between A345 and A360.
Admission: £2.50 per person, accompanied children under 14 Free.

Newhouse, Redlynch.
(0725) 20055 9 miles south of Salisbury.

Old Sarum, Salisbury.
(0722) 335398 2 miles north of Salisbury.

Old Wardour Castle, Tisbury.
(0747) 870487 2 miles south of Tisbury.

Philipps House, Dinton.
(072276) 208 9 miles west of Salisbury on B3089.

Pythouse, Tisbury.
2½ mile west of Tisbury.

Stonehenge, Amesbury.
2 miles west of Amesbury.

Lacock Abbey, Chippenham.
(0249) 730227 In the village of Lacock, 3 miles north of Melksham.

Luckington Court, Luckington.
(0666) 840205 6 miles west of Malmesbury on B4040.

Lydiard House, Lydiard Park, Lydiard Tregoze, Swindon.
5 miles west of Swindon.

Mompesson House, Salisbury.
(0722) 335659 In Cathedral Close on north side of Choristers' Green.

STOURHEAD

OPEN
Garden:
All year daily
8.00am-7.00pm
or sunset if
earlier (except
20-23 July closes
5.00pm for
Fête Champêtre
House:
26 March-30 Oct.
daily except
Thurs. & Fri.
12noon-5.30pm
or dusk if earlier.
Last Adm.5pm
Other times by
appointment.

STOURHEAD GARDEN & HOUSE, STOURTON
TEL: (0747) 840348
(The National Trust)

Britain's foremost landscaped garden with enchanting lakes and temples, rare trees and plants. One of the most famous examples of early 18th century English landscape movement. Fine Palladian mansion, designed in 1721 for Henry Hoare by Colen Campbell. Many fine works of art; furniture designed by the younger Chippendale; fine paintings, and ceramics. Lunches and teas in Spread Eagle Inn and Village Hall in Stourton village.

Location: 3 miles north west of Mere off A303, 9 miles south of Frome, off B30092.
Admission Garden: March-Oct. £4.10. Child £2.10, Parties £3.50. Nov-Feb £3.10, child £1.50 no reduction for parties. House: £4.10, children £2.10. Parties £3.50.

Tottenham House, Savernake Forest, Marlborough.
(0672) 870331 3 miles from A4, 6 miles Marlborough.

Westwood Manor, Bradford on Avon.
(0225) 863374

KEY TO SYMBOLS

 Historic Houses Association Member

National Trust Property

 Property in care of English Heritage

National Trust for Scotland Property

HANBURY HALL
Droitwich, Worcestershire

HANBURY HALL is every Englishman's idea of a substantial squire's house, tucked away in a large park free from reminders of the modern world. The home of the Vernon family for more than three centuries, it was entirely remodelled in 1701.

The magnificent staircase paintings were an afterthought (about 1710) painted by Sir James Thornhill, famous for the Painted Hall at Greenwich. The Dining Room has a most spectacular ceiling incorporating more Thornhill.

Emma Vernon created two further imposing rooms in the 1770's - the Library and the Drawing Room - this time in a light neo-classical style. She had married a selfish and extravagant man (who later became the Marquess of Exeter), who drove her to "Norris's drops and Madeira" and divorce in 1791. Luckily the splendid collection of family portraits survived these difficult times.

As well as the two family armorial dinner services, (c.1725 & c.1850), the house is now the permanent home of the Watney collection of porcelain and Dutch flower paintings. In the Blue bedroom can be found the Angel bed c.1725 with its original hangings in fine condition .

GARDENS AND PARKLAND

With changing fashion a fairly elaborate formal layout was swept away in the mid 18th century. However, 1993 has seen the start of the re-creation of principal elements of the original scheme by reintroducing the sunken parterre, topiary/fruit garden and formal wilderness. In addition the handsome Orangery (c.1740), an excellent example of the 18th century ice house and the orchard remain with gentle walks acrosss 400 acres of parkland.

CONTACT

The Administrator
Hanbury Hall
Droitwich
Worcestershire
WR9 7EA

Tel: (0527) 821214
Fax: (0527) 821251

LOCATION

Hanbury's central location gives easy access form all parts of the country.

10 minutes from the M5 at junction 5 - follow Droitwich/Hanbury Hall signs.

Birmingham: City Centre, Airport, N.E.C., I.C.C. all within 30 minutes.

OPENING TIMES

Summer
26th March-31st October
Sat. Sun & Mon.
2pm-5.30pm

In addition:
Tues. & Wed. afternoons during August

Winter
Available throughout the year for private use.

Closed to the general public.

ADMISSION

Summer

Adult	£3.50
Child	£1.70
Family	£9.60

GARDEN ONLY
Adult	£1.00
Child	50p.

GUIDED TOURS

Private guided tours by prior arrangement with Administrator. Maximum 60 people, minimum charge £70.

GIFT SHOP

National Trust gift shop when house open to the general public

SUITABILITY FOR OTHER EVENTS

To use Hanbury Hall is no skirmish with illusion, it is genuine elegant country living. The house garden and parkland may be hired exclusively. Everything can be organised in distinctive style. Help given with:

- Activity days and other such country pursuits.
- Location filming.
- Hotel accommodation..
- Various meeting facilities for up to 50 people
- Lunch and/or dinner for up to 68 people.
- Receptions for up to 100 people.
- Marquee events linked to the house for larger numbers.

ADVICE TO COURIERS & DRIVERS

Coach parties welcome by prior arrangement only. Driver admitted free. No dogs, photography, limited space in tea room.

FACILITIES FOR THE DISABLED

Disabled may alight at the entrance before parking in the allocated area. Ramp to ground floor with level access to principal rooms & tea room. Toilets for the disabled, wheelchairs available.

PARKING FOR COACHES & CARS

General public car park: 120 cars, 2 coaches 300 yds (disabled 30 yds) from Hall. Unlimited private use extending onto grass.

CATERING

Waitress service tea room within the house seating up to 60 people. Full in-house catering can be arranged for private use and other events.

GUIDE BOOKS

Short guide, full guide book and colour souvenir leaflet.

CONFERENCE AND FUNCTION FACILITIES

ROOM	DIMENSIONS	CAPACITY	LAYOUT	POWER POINTS	SUITABLE FOR A/V
Dining Room	11m x 5.5m	28	Dinner	2	✓
Drawing Room	7.4m x 8.3m	50	Various	4	✓
Hall	6.7m x 13.5m	70	Various	6	✓
Library	8.1m x 5.8m	40	Reception	2	
Meetings	7.6m x 5.6m	1-24	Boardroom/	12	✓
Suite	3.4m x 5.6m	12-25	Theatre	6	

WORCESTERSHIRE

Avoncroft Museum of Buildings, Stoke Heath, Bromsgrove.
(0527) 31886 At Stoke Heath, 2 miles south of Bromsgrove off A38.

Burford House Gardens, Tenbury Wells,
(0584) 810777 1 mile west of Tenbury Wells on the A456.

Eastgrove Cottage Garden Nursery, Sankyns Green, Shrawley, Little Witley.
(0299) 896389 Near Shrawley, 4 miles south west of Stourport.

Spetchley Park, Worcester.
(0905) 65213   3 miles east of Worcester on A422.

Stone House Cottage Gardens, Kidderminster.
(0562) 69902 2 miles south east of Kidderminster on A448.

THE GREYFRIARS

"National Trust/V Heminway"

OPEN
April-31 Oct.
Wed. Thu. & Bank Hol Mons.
2.00-5.30pm
Last admissions 30 mins before closing.
Other times by prior written
appointment only.

THE GREYFRIARS, WORCESTER TEL: 0905 23571
(The National Trust)

Built in 1480, with early 17th and late 18th century additions, this timber-framed house was rescued from demolition at the time of the Second World War and has been restored and refurbished; interesting textiles and furnishings add character to the panelled rooms; an archway leads through to a delightful garden.

Location: Centre of Worcester.
Admission: £2.00 adult, £1.00 child,
£5.50 Family ticket (2 + up to 4 children).

WITLEY COURT

OPEN
Summer
1 April-31 Oct.
Daily
10.00am-6.00pm

Winter
1 Nov.-31 March
Wed.-Sun.
10.00am-4.00pm

WITLEY COURT, WORCESTER TEL: 0299 89636
(English Heritage)

This is one of the most spectacular country house ruins. Cast in the Victorian Italian style of the 1860's, it is on a huge scale, with a glorious facade. Looking from the house to the gardens, a view enjoyed by Edward VII, who as Prince of Wales often stayed at the house, the scene is dominated by the immense Perseus Fountain.

Location: 10 miles north west of Worcester on the A443.
Admission: Adult £1.25, concessions 95p, child 60p.

Hartlebury Castle, near Kidderminster.
(0299) 250410 In village of Hartlebury. 5 miles south of Kidderminster.

Harvington Hall, near Kidderminster.
(0562777) 267 3 miles south east of Kidderminster 1 1/2 miles from junction of A448 and A50 at Mustow Green.

Little Malvern Court and Gardens, near Great Malvern.
(0684) 892988 3 miles south of Great Malvern on A4104.

BROUGHTON HALL
Skipton, North Yorkshire

BROUGHTON HALL was built in 1597 by Henry Tempest and continues to be the home of the Tempest family, whose ancestry can be traced back 29 generations to Roger Tempest who was established in the area by 1120. This Grade I listed historic building has Elizabethan origins but was extensively added to during the 18th and 19th Centuries, hence its Palladian appearance.

Set in 3,000 acres of beautiful Yorkshire parkland and countryside, the Broughton Hall family home and Estate, is open to the public by prior arrangement and is also available as an exclusive venue for both business and pleasure.

The present design of the grounds owes much to the landscape architecture of Nesfield around 1855. To the east of the Hall is a fine Italianate garden with balustrades and a gazebo. To the rear there are sweeping lawns (ideal for marquee events) enhanced by extensive wooded views and fountains.

The owner likes to make every event unique and highly successful so he is always ready to discuss with clients how he can help them to achieve their objectives by placing his facilities and experience at their disposal. To arrange such a consultation it is only necessary to telephone the Estate Office on 0756 799608.

SUITABILITY FOR EVENTS

Broughton Hall and its grounds are ideal for a wide range of activities dinners, seminars, corporate entertainment, product launches, clay shoots, archery, fashion shows, equestrian events, firework and laser shows etc. The diversity of the Estate is ideal for filming and still photography. Being a private house your event will have exclusive use of the Hall and Grounds.

EXTRA FACILITIES

Ample parking and an area for light aircraft/helicopters. Lectures on property, contents, garden and history can be held in a lecture room seating 80. Musical evenings are very successful and a grand piano is available. Full size billiard table.

ADVICE TO COURIERS & DRIVERS

When travelling from Skipton on the A59 towards Clitheroe watch for the Bull Inn on left hand side 3 miles from Skipton. Take turning to left approx. 200 yards past Bull Inn. The Hall and entrance gates can then be seen.

FACILITIES FOR THE DISABLED

Disabled and elderly visitors may alight at the front door. The vehicle should then be parked in the allocated area.

PARKING FOR COACHES & CARS

Capacity of the car park - unlimited.

CATERING

This can be provided by prior arrangement. Wide range of options. Buffets and full sit down meals with accent on quality and value. Up to 150 people can be catered for.

GUIDED TOURS

At no additional cost guided tours are conducted for up to 200 people at any one time. Large groups are split up into smaller parties. If requested the owner will meet the group. Average time taken for a tour 1 hour 30 minutes.

LOCAL PLACES OF INTEREST

Broughton is only three miles from the historic market town of Skipton with its roofed castle. The Yorkshire Dales National Park with some of the finest countryside in England is on the doorstep. There are excellent local hotels for overnight accommodation.

CONTACT

H R Tempest
Broughton Hall
Skipton
North Yorkshire
BD23 3AE

Tel: (0756) 792267
Fax: (0756)792362

LOCATION

Skipton A59, 3 miles.
From London M1 to Leeds and Skipton, A59 to Broughton.

Bradford/Leeds Airport 40 minutes, Manchester 1 hour.

Rail: Skipton Station 3 miles.

Bus: Regular service.

OPENING TIMES

Summer & Winter

Bank Holiday Mondays 11am - 4pm

Guided Tours can be arranged by prior appointment. The duration of a tour is approx. $1^1/_2$ hours.

ADMISSION

Summer & Winter

HOUSE & GARDEN
£4.00

GUIDED TOURS
Group*   £4.00

* Minimum payment if by prior appointment £60.

CONFERENCE AND FUNCTION FACILITIES

SUBJECT TO PRIOR ARRANGEMENT ALL ROOMS CAN BE MADE AVAILABLE FOR FUNCTIONS.

BURTON AGNES HALL
Driffield, East Yorkshire

BURTON AGNES HALL, is an outstanding example of late Elizabethan architecture built of the characteristic richly mellowed red brick. Building was begun in the year 1598 when Elizabeth I was Queen and her Royal Arms are carved over the front entrance. Finished in 1610, the Hall has been little altered and is still the home of descendants of the family who built it.

The ceilings and overmantels, wonderfully carved in oak, plaster, stone and alabaster, are unique and world famous.

There are notable paintings by Gainsborough, Reinagle, Cotes, Marlow and others; also a fine collection of modern French paintings by Gaugin, Pissaro, Utrillo, Manet, Lorjou, Courbet, Renoir, Minous, Maufra, Montane, Segonzac, Vlaminck and others of the Impressionist schools which merge remarkably well into this ancient setting.

GARDENS AND GROUNDS

The Hall is surrounded by lawns with clipped yews, ponds and fountains. The walled garden contains a pôtager of herbs and vegetables, shrub roses, herbaceous borders, a maze with a garden on thymes and a riddle to solve, a jungle garden, campanula, clematis and hardy geranium collections, green houses and coloured 'games' gardens. There are also woodland gardens and a woodland walk.

CONTACT

M E Wilson
The Estate Office
Burton Agnes
Driffield
East Yorkshire
YO25 OND

Tel: (0262) 490324
Fax: (0262) 490513

LOCATION

From London A1, M18, M62, A166, 4 hours.

Bus: Stop 300 yards from Hall. Regular services from Bridlington, Driffield, Hull, Scarborough, York and Leeds

Bridlington 6 miles
Hull 25 miles
York 35 miles.

SUITABILITY FOR OTHER EVENTS

Fashion shows, garden parties, rallies and filming can all be arranged.

ADVICE TO COURIERS & DRIVERS

Cafe open to visitors not wishing to visit the Hall.

FACILITIES FOR THE DISABLED

Cars and Coaches containing disabled or elderly people may leave them at the entrance to the Hall. The vehicles can then be parked in the allocated areas. Toilets are available. Special entrance for wheelchairs giving access to the ground floor rooms. Tea room accessible. The gardens are especially suitable for wheelchairs with ramps and flag paths.

CATERING

A Restaurant/Tea Room with Table Licence is available for approx 80 people. Groups can book in advance for afternoon tea, buffets and lunches. Menus are available on request. Café open to visitors not wishing to visits the Hall. Available for party bookings outside normal opening hours.

GIFT SHOP

Open at the same time and dates as the Hall. Items include home grown produce and plants.

GUIDE BOOKS

A full colour guide book is available price £1.75. Translation available in French and German. Children's guide available.

GUIDED TOURS

Guided tours, at no additional cost, are available for booked parties. Large parties split into smaller groups of 20/30. Average time taken 1^{1}/4 hours.

OPENING TIMES

Summer
1 April - 31 October 94

Mon	
Tues	
Wed	
Thurs	11am-5pm daily
Fri	
Sat	
Sun	

Parties welcome, by appointment outside these times.

Winter
1 Nov '94 - 31 Mar '95

Open for pre-booked parties of guaranteed minimum numbers.

ADMISSION

All Year

HOUSE & GARDEN
Adult	£3.00
Child	£2.00
OAP	£2.50
Group*	
Adult	£2.70
Child	£1.80
OAP	£2.25

*Minimum Number 30 people.

GARDEN ONLY
Adult	£1.50
OAP	£1.25
Child	£0.50

No Group Concessions

Group visits, by appointment outside public opening hours are charged at £3.00 per person. Minimum charge £90.00.

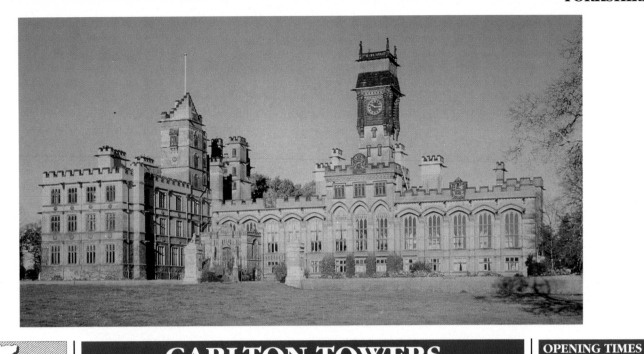

CARLTON TOWERS
Goole, East Yorkshire

THIS magnificent Victorian Gothic house has belonged to the ancestors of the Duke of Norfolk since the Norman Conquest and is the most complete house of its type which is still a family home. The present mansion was begun in 1614, extended in the 18th Century and completely remodelled between 1871 and 1877.

As a Conference and Banqueting Centre etc., Carlton Towers offers a unique opportunity for professional, commercial, business and private organisations, to hold events in the true atmosphere of a stately home. Because all the staterooms are interconnecting, we are able to

seat from 25 to 225. The Venetian Drawing Room is used for lecture purposes, the Card Room as an extension for either the Venetian Drawing Room or the Picture Gallery, the latter making an excellent dining room capable of seating 150. The Inner Hall and Armoury immediately adjacent the three main staterooms can be used for bar facilities and promotional displays.

Outside there is a large lawn in front of the South Wing and also a large gravel area suitable for static displays. There are 20 to 100 acres of parkland, depending on availability and also a Rose garden on the West front of the house.

CONTACT

Mrs P Meanwell
Carlton Towers
Carlton
Nr Goole
Yorkshire
DN14 9LZ

Tel: (0405) 861662
Fax: (0405) 861917

LOCATION

Situated 6 miles south of Selby and 1 mile north of Snaith on A1041, 6 miles from M62, exit 34. From London M1, M18, A614, A1041. Approx. 2 hours.

Train: Snaith 1 mile.

Bus: Selby and York buses stop at gates.

Taxi: Barbara's (0405) 861284.

OPENING TIMES

By appointment only for parties of 20 or more. House and garden closed to the casual visitor. However, it is planned to stage some Special Events throughout the year - please telephone for further details.

ADMISSION

Winter & Summer

GUIDED TOURS
Adults   £3.00
Children   £1.50

SUITABILITY FOR OTHER EVENTS

Conferences, Seminars, Receptions, VIP and Informal Lunches and Dinners, Wedding Receptions, Product Launches, Fashion Shows, Corporate Hospitality Days, Clay Pigeon Shoots, Archery, Equestrian Events, Filming etc.

EXTRA FACILITIES

Slide projector, overhead projector, screen, audio visual and secretarial assistance can be hired. Helicopters can land on the South Lawn.

ADVICE TO COURIERS & DRIVERS

No dogs, other than guide dogs.

FACILITIES FOR THE DISABLED

There are toilet facilities for the disabled, but unfortunately whichever entrance is used, means climbing several steps into the house.

PARKING FOR COACHES & CARS

There is parking for up to 200 cars and coaches 100 yards from the house.

CATERING

Can be made to suit the client and the function or to end a guided tour.

GUIDED TOURS

A guided tour takes approximately $1^1/4$ hours and is available to groups of 20 or more.

GUIDE BOOKS

Colour guide book, £1.00. Special Childrens Guide Book 50p.

SCHOOL VISITS/CHILDREN

Groups are welcome, charge £1.50 per child. A guide is provided. There is a special guide book available.

CONFERENCE AND FUNCTION FACILITIES

ROOM	DIMENSIONS	CAPACITY	LAYOUT	POWER POINTS	SUITABLE FOR A/V
Venetian Drawing Room	55'x23'	150	Theatre	2	
		50	U-shape		
		70	Buffet/Dinner		
Card Room	22'x24'	40	Theatre	8	
		25	Buffet/Dinner		
Picture Gallery	70'x25'	200	Theatre	2	
		80	U-shape		
		150	Buffet/Dinner		
Armoury	45'x23'	75	Theatre	3	
		40	U-shape		
		50	Buffet/Dinner		

CASTLE HOWARD
York

IN a dramatic setting between two lakes with extensive gardens and impressive fountains, this 18th Century Palace was designed by Sir John Vanbrugh in 1699. Undoubtedly the finest private residence in Yorkshire it was built for Charles Howard, 3rd Earl of Carlisle, whose descendants still live here.

With its painted and gilded dome reaching 80ft into the Yorkshire sky, this impressive house has collections of antique furniture, porcelain and sculpture, while its fabulous collection of paintings is dominated by the famous Holbein portraits of Henry VIII and the Duke of Norfolk.

GARDENS

Designed on a heroic scale covering 1,000 acres. The gardens include memorable sights like The Temple of the Four Winds and the Mausoleum, New River Bridge and the recently restored waterworks of the South Lake, Cascade, Waterfall and Prince of Wales Fountain.

The walled garden has collections of old and modern roses.

Ray Wood has a unique collection of rare trees, shrubs, rhododendrons, magnolias and azaleas.

CONTACT

The Hon Simon Howard
Castle Howard
York
North Yorkshire
YO6 7BZ

Tel: (0653) 648444

LOCATION

York 15 miles (20 minutes), A64. From London M1 exit 32, M18 to A1(M) to A64, York/Malton Road, 3$^{1}/_{2}$ hours.

Train: York to Malton Station 5$^{1}/_{4}$ miles.

Bus: W Yorkshire bus from York to Castle Howard.

Taxi: (0653) 600030

SUITABILITY FOR OTHER EVENTS

Concerts, craft fairs, fashion shows, clay pigeon shooting, equestrian events, garden parties, filming, product launches.

EXTRA FACILITIES

Helicopter Landing, Rose Garden Receptions, Firework Displays. Lectures (by arrangement) covering the House, History, Contents and Gardens.

ADVICE TO COURIERS & DRIVERS

Approaching on A64 from south, access is through the Carmire gate 9' wide by 10' high. Alternative route: follow the A64 to Malton, follow signs via Coneysthorpe Village to Castle Howard.

FACILITIES FOR THE DISABLED

Disabled toilets. Transport equipped for wheelchairs. Chairlift in House to main floor.

PARKING FOR COACHES & CARS

Car park capacity - 400 cars and 20 coaches.

CATERING

Cafeteria seats 180 people. The Grecian Hall available for pre-booked private parties of 25 minimum, must be pre-booked. Menus and prices on request. Private dinners, lunches, buffets and functions by arrangement.

GIFT SHOP

Open 10.30am-5pm when House open and sells a large selection of gifts and souvenirs.

GUIDE BOOKS

Full colour guide book.

GUIDED TOURS

Guides are available throughout the House, no charge. Private tours by arrangement.

SCHOOL VISITS/CHILDREN

School parties are welcome, information leaflet available. Teacher/pupil ratio required is 1/20. Items of special interest, 18th Century history, gardens, architecture.

OPENING TIMES

Summer
18 March-31 October

Mon	
Tues	
Wed	
Thur	11am-4.30pm
Fri	(last admission)
Sat	
Sun	

NB Grounds, Rose Gardens, and Plant Centre open 10am.

Winter
1 November-Mid March

Open by pre-booked appointment and availability. Grounds open some weekends, telephone for confirmation

ADMISSION

Summer

HOUSE, GARDEN
Adult	£6.00
Child**	£3.00
OAP	£5.00
Group*	
Adult	£5.00
Child**	£2.50
OAP	£4.50

GARDEN ONLY
Adult	£4.00
Child**	£2.00

* Minimum number 12 persons
**Age 4-16

Winter

By arrangement

CONFERENCE AND FUNCTION FACILITIES

ROOM	DIMENSIONS	CAPACITY	LAYOUT	POWER POINTS	SUITABLE FOR A/V
Long Gallery	197'x24'	280	Theatre	20	✓
		280	Buffet/Lunch/Dinner		
Grecian Hall	40'x40'	160	Various	20	✓
Chinese Room		60	Various	1	✓

PHOTOGRAPH: PETER HEATON

DUNCOMBE PARK
Helmsley, North Yorkshire

The house dates from 1713 and was built for Thomas Duncombe by William Wakefield, a friend of Vanbrugh. A fine forecourt and two pavilions were added by Sir Charles Barry in 1843. Its interiors were remodelled by the First Earl of Feversham after a fire in 1879. The main showrooms are now a fine example of the type of grand interior popular at the turn of the century.

Following the death of the second Earl of Feversham at the Battle of the Somme in 1916, Duncombe Park was leased as a girls school;. In 1985 the present Lord and Lady Feversham decided to restore the house to a family home. After the departure of the school, there was little more than an empty, echoing shell. Today the visitor will see a superb example of the best of British craftsmanship. The restoration is very much a family project and the interior finishes have been deliberately chosen to show visitors a selection of the styles of decoration typical in the 18th and 19th Centuries. There are fine family pictures and Lord Feversham's collection of English and Continental furniture.

The unique 30 acre early 18th Century landscape garden, set in 300 acres of dramatic parkland, has been described as "the supreme masterpiece of the art of the landscape gardener". Its vast expanses of lawn, terraces, temples, woodland walks and fine views across the surrounding North York Moors are something to be explored at leisure.

Visitor Centre, Restaurant, Gift Shop, Picnic Area, Playground. Waymarked Country Walks.

Winner British Tourist Authority Come to Britain Special Award and Yorkshire & Humberside White Rose Awards. Duncombe Park is now a National Nature Reserve.

CONTACT

Helen Cameron
Administrator
Duncombe Park
Helmsley
York
YO6 5EB

Tel: (0439) 770213
Fax: (0439) 771114

LOCATION

Entrance just off Helmsley Market Square, signed off A170 Thirsk-Scarborough road.

Taxi: (0439) 770817/771384/770512

SUITABILITY FOR OTHER EVENTS

Dinners, receptions, concerts, weddings, conferences, fashion shows, product launches, filming. Also suitable for wide range of outdoor events. Grand piano, tennis court, croquet lawn available.

EVENTS

Year round programme of events in house and park. Details from the Administrator.

PARKING FOR COACHES & CARS

Free parking. Main car park at Visitor Centre 400 yards from house. Coach park (passengers may disembark at front gates).

ADVICE TO COURIERS & DRIVERS

No flash photography in house. Video permits available. Allow 3 hours for group visits.

FACILITIES FOR DISABLED

Disabled toilet. Portable ramps. Parking usually allowed in main forecourt. The House is not particularly suited to those with walking difficulties.

GUIDE BOOK

Full colour guidebook available £2.00

GUIDED TOURS

Every day except Sundays and Bank Holiday Mondays. Garden tour also available.

CATERING

Home made lunches and teas. Maximum 60. Pre-booking recommended for groups.

NOTE

Joint visiting arrangement for groups, in conjunction with Hovingham Hall (£5.75pp)

OPENING TIMES

Summer

HOUSE AND GARDEN
  11am - 5pm

Easter Weekend(1-5 April)
April-October
  Wed & Sun
May, June & Sept
  Daily
  (not Fri & Sat)
2 July-31 August
  Daily
NB: House closed 15/16 June

PARKLAND,
RESTAURANT & SHOP
April - end October
Daily   10.30am - 5pm

ADMISSION

Summer

HOUSE, GARDEN & PARK	
Adult	£4.50
Child (10-16)	£2.00
O.A.P.	£3.75
Student	£3.75
Family (2+2)	£10.00
Group	£3.75

GARDEN & PARK	
Adult	£2.75
Child	£1.50

PARK ONLY	£1.00

FAIRFAX HOUSE
York

FAIRFAX HOUSE was acquired and fully restored by the York Civic Trust in 1983/84. The House, described as a classic architectural masterpiece of its age and certainly one of the finest townhouses in England was saved from near collapse after considerable abuse and misuse this century, being converted into a Cinema and Dance Hall.

The richly decorated interior with its plasterwork, wood and wrought iron, is now the home for a unique collection of Georgian furniture, clocks, paintings and porcelain.

The Noel Terry Collection, gift of a former treasurer of the York Civic Trust, has been described by Christie's as one of the finest private collections formed this century. It enhances and complements the House and helps to create that special 'lived-in' feeling, providing the basis for what can be considered a fully furnished Georgian Townhouse.

LOCATION

London 4 hours by car, 2 hours by train.
Fairfax House situated in the centre of York between the Castle Museum and the Jorvik Centre.

York Railway Station 10 minutes walk.

Station Taxis (0904) 623332

SUITABILITY FOR OTHER EVENTS

Fairfax House is suitable for filming.

EXTRA FACILITIES

By prior arrangement the group on a Connoisseur's Tour can be met by one of the trustees. Lectures can be given on the House, its contents and history. The lectures can be given in the hotel in which the group is staying. A screen and projector for such a lecture can be provided by Fairfax House.

For groups of up to 50 people a buffet can be arranged. The Dining Room may be used on certain evenings for special formal dinners. Limited to groups of up to 25 people.

ADVICE TO COURIERS & DRIVERS

Please telephone to arrange for map showing the nearest coach park and approach to the House. No photography inside the House.

FACILITIES FOR THE DISABLED

Disabled and elderly visitors may alight at the door of the property prior to parking in adjacent public car park. No toilet facilities at the House.

PARKING FOR COACHES & CARS

Capacity of the public car park - 300 cars, 50 yards from House. Coach park is $^1/_2$ mile away, parties are dropped off.

GIFT SHOP

Open every day except Friday from 1 March -1 January, 11am-5pm. Items include catalogues, tapes, gifts and antiques.

GUIDE BOOKS

Colour guide book, £3.50. Translations are available in French. A 150 page catalogue on the furniture collection is also available £19.95, softback £14.95.

SCHOOL VISITS/CHILDREN

A guided tour for school children can be arranged at a cost of £1.00 per head.

GUIDED TOURS

Connoisseur Tour - Guided tour showing secret drawers etc. Wine/sherry to follow tour. Parties split into groups of approx 12 persons, £10.00 per person (Min charge £100).

Evening Guided Tour - Guided tour plus wine/sherry to follow (Secret drawers not included). Parties split into groups of approx 20 persons £5.00 per person (Min. charge £75).

Evening Guided Tour - Guided Tour only (Does not include secret drawers, wine or sherry). Parties split into groups of approx 20/25 £4.00 per person (Min charge £60).

Daytime Parties - Guided - Accepted only within limits of staff availability/ number involved/other bookings etc. Children admitted only at a ratio of 8 to 1 adult. Adult parties split into groups of 20/25. £4 per person (Min charge £60).

Daytime Parties - Without Guide - To be arranged according to number involved and other bookings. Parties split into smaller groups, special party rate for pre-booked tour of 15 or more persons.

Tours available in French and German. The duration of the tour is approx $1^1/_2$ hours.

HAREWOOD HOUSE
Leeds, West Yorkshire

HAREWOOD is much more than a historic house, it is also the home of one of England's most distinguished families. Built for them in 1759, by John Carr, Harewood has been continually lived in by the Lascelles family ever since. The House is particularly noted for its superb Robert Adam interiors and ceilings. The amazing plasterwork continues to impress thousands of visitors each year.

There are a particularly noteworthy collection of paintings by Turner, El Greco, Girtin, Reynolds and many other names of international renown. The furniture through all the rooms reflects what many experts have described as "the richest collection of Chippendale in the world".

Much of the furniture was made especially for Harewood by Thomas Chippendale.

GARDENS

The grounds and gardens at Harewood were landscaped by another genius of his time Lancelot 'Capability' Brown. There are over 30 acres of woodland and gardens to be enjoyed.

BIRD GARDEN & TROPICAL HOUSE

Harewood Bird Garden has one of the most comprehensive collections in the north of England and includes exotic species from Africa, America and Australia. The Terrace Gallery was established in 1989 as a venue for exhibitions showing the best of contemporary art.

CONTACT

Gerald Long
The Estate Office
Harewood
Leeds
West Yorkshire
LS17 9LQ

Tel: (0532) 886331
Fax: (0532) 886467

LOCATION

A1 N or S to Wetherby, A659 via Collingham, Harewood is on the A61 between Harrogate and Leeds. It is easily reached from A1, M1m, M62 and M18 motorways. Leeds Station 7 miles.

Harewood House is 15 mins from the centre of Leeds or Harrogate.

CATERING & CORPORATE HOSPITALITY

Harewood House is available for quality corporate entertaining and offers: State Dining Room dinners (50 persons maximum), Drinks reception/buffets, Concerts (175 persons maximum), Wedding receptions, Marquee events, Product launches.

The Courtyard catering complex has recently been completely refurbished, introducing an exciting new theme able to cater for all conferences, exhibitions, product launches and functions held within the Courtyard or the magnificent grounds.

An ideal venue for any gathering, the Courtyard Suite will seat a maximum of 120 theatre style or, conference organisers may wish to also use the Study Centre directly overhead for a meeting then retire to the Courtyard Suite for a meal. The Drawing Room can be incorporated to provide a Reception area, additional dining area or exhibition space. The latest conference equipment is available to suit individual requirements.

Large launches etc. can be accommodated by using the full extent of the Courtyard area which can be covered by a 20'x24' marquee. This flexible approach has proven highly successful giving a maximum seating for dinner of 400. Marquees of any size can be completely accommodated within the grounds.

CORPORATE HOSPITALITY

The beautiful grounds of Harewood also provide the ideal setting to incorporate outside activities in your programme, a wide range of options are open from clay shoots to ballooning, jousting to a cricket match on Harewood's private ground - the management team will help make your conference a success.

EXTRA FACILITIES

Also available for use: grand piano, cricket and football pitch. Subject to availability lectures on the property, its gardens and history for up to 70. Projector and screen can be provided.

ADVICE TO COURIERS & DRIVERS

No unaccompanied children in the Bird Garden. Dogs on leads in grounds but not House (except Guide Dogs) or Bird Garden. Unlimited parking 400 yards from House and an area for 50+ coaches 500 yards from House.

FACILITIES FOR THE DISABLED

Disabled and elderly visitors may alight at entrance to House, before parking in the allocated areas. Guide Dogs allowed in the House. Most facilities are accessible and a wheelchair is available at House and Bird Garden. The toilet is near the car park shop. Special concessions apply to disabled groups.

GIFT SHOP

Gift Shops and Plant Centre are open same time as Park. Items include Leeds pottery, flower pictures, glass, perfume and toys. Full colour guide book price £2.50.

AUDIO TOUR OF HOUSE

Hire charge £1.00.

OPENING TIMES

Summer
13 March - 31 October

Mon }	
Tues }	Bird Garden
Wed }	and Grounds
Thurs }	open 10am.
Fri }	House at 11am.
Sat }	
Sun }	

Winter
November-March

House closed all Winter

ADMISSION

Summer

ALL ATTRACTIONS
Adult	£5.75
Child*	£3.00
Family	£16.00
Group**	
Adult	£4.75
Child*	Free if accomp.

BIRD GARDEN & OTHER ATTRACTIONS
Adult	£4.50
Child*	£2.50
Family	£12.00

GROUNDS ONLY
| Adult | £2.75 |
| Child* | £1.00 |

* Age 4-15
** Minimum 20 persons

Winter

House closed all Winter.

NEWBY HALL
Ripon, North Yorkshire

NEWBY HALL, the Yorkshire home of Mr and Mrs Robin Compton, is a late 17th Century house built in the style of Sir Christopher Wren. William Weddell, an ancestor of Mr Compton, made the Grand Tour in the 1760's and amongst the treasures he acquired were magnificent classical statuary and a superb set of Gobelins Tapestries. To house these treasures, Weddell commissioned Robert Adam to create the splendid domed Sculpture Gallery and Tapestry Room that we see today. The Regency Dining Room and Billiards Room were added later. There is much fine Chippendale furniture and in recent years Mrs Compton has restored the decoration of the house, painstakingly researching colour and decor of the Adam period.

GARDENS

25 acres of glorious gardens contain rare and beautiful shrubs and plants. Newby's famous double herbaceous borders, flanked by great bastions of yew hedges, sweep down to the River Ure. Formal gardens such as the Autumn and Rose Gardens - each with splashing fountains - a Victorian Rock Garden, the tranquillity of Sylvia's Garden, Pergolas and even a Tropical Garden, make Newby a 'Garden for all Seasons'. Newby holds the National Collection of the Genus Cornus and in 1987 won the Christies'/HHA Garden of the Year Award. The Gardens also incorporate an exciting children's Adventure Garden and Miniature Railway.

CONTACT

The Opening Administrator
Newby Hall
Ripon
North Yorkshire
HG4 5AE

Tel: (0423) 322583
Fax: (0423) 324452

LOCATION

Midway between London and Edinburgh, 4 miles west of A1, towards Ripon.

Taxi: Ripon Taxi Rank (0765) 601283.

Bus: On Ripon-York route.

SUITABILITY FOR OTHER EVENTS

Individual requests are considered. Newby Hall offers possibilities for filming. The Grantham Room is available for wedding receptions, promotions and lectures. Newby Park is suitable for special events such as Craft & Country Fairs, Vehicle Rallies etc.

ADVICE TO COURIERS & DRIVERS

Allow a full day for viewing House and Gardens. Dogs in picnic area only, no photography inside House.

FACILITIES FOR THE DISABLED

5 Wheelchairs available on request. Access around ground floor of House and key areas in Gardens. Disabled toilet at Restaurant.

PARKING FOR COACHES & CARS

Unlimited parking near House and Gardens.

CATERING

In Garden Restaurant, teas, hot and cold meals. Pre-booked parties in Grantham Room. Menus/rates on request.

THE NEWBY SHOP

Excellent, open from 11am - 5.30pm.

GUIDE BOOKS

Colour guide books of the House and Gardens. Illustrated leaflets for the Gardens and Woodland Discovery Walk can be bought at the shop and plant stall.

SCHOOL VISITS/CHILDREN

School groups welcome. Rates on request. Grantham Room for use as wet weather base subject to availability. Of special interest: Woodland Discovery Walk, Adventure Gardens and train rides on $10^{1}/4$" gauge railway.

CONFERENCE AND FUNCTION FACILITIES

ROOM	DIMENSIONS	CAPACITY	LAYOUT	POWER POINTS	SUITABLE FOR A/V
Grantham Room		200	Theatre	✓	✓
		200	Reception		
		100	Lunch/Dinner		

OPENING TIMES

Summer
April-September

Mon	Bank Hols only
Tues	
Wed	Gardens
Thur	11am-5.30pm
Fri	House
Sat	12noon-5pm
Sun	

NB Last admissions:-
House   4.30pm
Gardens   5.00pm

Winter
October-Easter
Closed.

ADMISSION

Summer
On application to Administrator

HOUSE & GARDEN
Adult	£5.20
Child*	£3.00
OAP	£4.00
Disabled	£3.00
Group**	
Adult	£4.00
Child***	£2.50

GARDEN ONLY
Adult	£3.30
Child*	£2.20
OAP	£2.60
Disabled	£2.20
Group**	
Adult	£2.60
Child***	£2.00

Additional charges made for train.

* Age 4-16
** Minimum Number 20 people
***Details from Administrator

Winter
October-Easter
Closed.

The Library in Newby Hall, Yorkshire.

RIPLEY CASTLE
Nr Harrogate, North Yorkshire

RIPLEY CASTLE has for twenty eight generations been the home of the Ingilby family and it retains that 'much loved and very much alive' feeling of a family home. The guides whilst being very knowledgeable, all have an excellent sense of humour, and the tours which take approximately one hour, are not only informative but great fun. The Castle contains fine portraits, paintings, furnishing and chandeliers and in the old (1555) tower, some splendid armour, books, panelling and a secret hiding place.

The extensive walled gardens have recently been transformed and now house The National Hyacinth Collection and fabulous Ripley tropical plant collection, which includes many rare and exotic species, 85,000 spring flowering bulbs create a blaze of colour in April/May, and are followed by the Bluebells and Rhododendrons, Delphiniums, Roses and Herbaceous Borders.

Ripley village, on the Castle's doorstep is also very beautiful, with many interesting shops, an Art Gallery and Farm Museum.

CONTACT

Tours: Chloe Evans
Meetings/Dinners: Sheila
Furness
Ripley Castle
Ripley
Harrogate
North Yorkshire
HG3 3AY

Tel: (0423) 770152
Fax: (0423) 771745

LOCATION

Just off A61, 3½ miles north of Harrogate, 8 miles south of Ripon. M1 18 mls South, M62 20 miles south.

Taxi: Blueline taxis
Harrogate 503037

SUITABILITY FOR OTHER EVENTS

Wedding Receptions, Dinners, Dances, Banquets, Outdoor Concerts, Meetings, Activity Days, Medieval Banquets, Management Training Courses.

EXTRA FACILITIES

Conference, Training and Syndicate Rooms, Clay Pigeon Shooting, Archery, Buggies and Hovercraft, Fishing, Cricket, Tennis, Croquet, Infra-Red Combat. Marquee events any size.

ADVICE TO COURIERS & DRIVERS

Dogs prohibited (except Guide Dogs). No photography inside Castle unless prior written consent.

FACILITIES FOR THE DISABLED

5 - 7 rooms available for disabled. Gardens easily accessible (except Tropical Collection). Disabled toilets at Hotel (100 yards) and in village car park (150 yards). Disabled parking 50 yards from Castle front door.

PARKING FOR COACHES & CARS

Free parking for 290 cars within 300 yards of the Castle entrance. Coach parking 50 yards from Castle entrance.

CATERING

Morning and Afternoon Tea and refreshments at Tearoom (seats 53) outside Castle walls. Pub lunches or Dinner at Hotel (100 yards). VIP lunches and dinners (maximum 66) inside Castle, unlimited in Marquees. Parties of 15+ must book in advance in Tearooms and Hotel.

ACCOMMODATION

At the Boars Head Hotel (RAC****) 100 yards from Castle. Owned and managed by the Estate.

GIFT SHOP

Open daily April to October , weekends only November-March - 10.30am-5.00pm.

GUIDE BOOKS

Colour guide book, £1.50. Special children's guide book is available price 99p.

GUIDED TOURS

Guided tours standard, and included in price.

SCHOOL VISITS/CHILDREN

Groups are welcome all year round, by prior arrangement, between 10.30am-7.30pm.

OPENING TIMES

Summer
CASTLE & GARDENS
April, May and October
Sat &
Sun } 11.30 - 4.30pm
Good Fri. & Bank Hols.
  11am - 4.30pm

June and September
Thurs -
Fri } 11.30-4.30pm
Sat
Sun

July and August
Daily   11.30 - 4.30pm

GARDENS ONLY

March
Thurs -
Fri } 11.00-4.00pm
Sat
Sun
April to October
Daily   11am-5pm
Nov.-Dec.23rd
Daily   11am-3.30pm

Winter

Open (except 25 December) to pre-booked parties of 15+.
  10.30 - 7.30pm

ADMISSION

All Year

CASTLE & GARDENS
Adult   £3.75
Child*   £2.00
OAP   £3.00
Groups**
 Adult   £3.00
 Child*   £1.75

GARDENS ONLY
Adult   £2.25
Child*   £1.75
OAP   £1.75
Groups**
 Adult   £1.75
 Child*   £1.00

*Under 16.
** Min. 25 people.

CONFERENCES AND FUNCTION FACILITIES

RIPLEY CASTLE is well located for Dinners, Banquets, Meetings and Presentations; it enjoys excellent access via road rail and air and is centrally placed for Northern and North Eastern England. Its setting is stunningly beautiful, and the organisation that runs it is efficient, friendly and cheerful. Activity Days can be incorporated into residential meetings or used to entertain clients and staff, and tours can be organised throughout the North of England to incorporate The Yorkshire Dales, The Northumbrian Coast and the Lake District.

Overnight accommodation can be booked at the 25 bedroom (Four Star) Boar's Head Hotel; the Estate owned and managed Hotel in the Market Square of Ripley Village, 100 yards from the Castle. The standard of cuisine at both the Castle and Hotel is legendary. A top class team of chefs being employed to work at both establishments.

For charm, character, quality, history, setting and value for money, Ripley is one of the U.K's outstanding Stately Home venues.

CONTACT SHEILA FURNESS ON 0423 770152 FOR FURTHER DETAILS.

ROOM	DIMENSIONS	CAPACITY	LAYOUT	POWER POINTS	SUITABLE FOR A/V
Morning Room	27'x22'	35	Schoolroom	6	✓
		32	U-Shape		
		42	Boardroom		
		50	Buffet		
		70	Theatre		
		66	Lunch/Dinner		
Large Drawing Room	30'x22'	27	Schoolroom	4	✓
		29	U-Shape		
		36	Boardroom		
		60	Buffet		
		80	Theatre		
		60	Lunch/Dinner		
Library	31'x19'	27	Schoolroom	3	✓
		26	U-Shape		
		36	Boardroom		
		48	Buffet		
		75	Theatre		
		48	Lunch/Dinner		
Tower Room	33'x21'	27	Schoolroom	3	✓
		26	U-Shape		
		36	Boardroom		
		48	Buffet		
		75	Theatre		
		48	Lunch/Dinner		
Map Room	19'x14'	18	Schoolroom	6	✓
		10	U-Shape		
		16	Boardroom		
		15	Buffet		
		24	Theatre		
		16	Lunch/Dinner		
Dining Room	23'3"x19'6"	16	Boardroom	2	✓
		25	Buffet		
		16	Lunch/Dinner		

YORKSHIRE

Aldborough Roman Town, Boroughbridge.
(0423) 322768 ¾ mile east of Boroughbridge.

Allerton Park, Knaresborough.
(0423) 330927 14½ miles west of York, ¼ mile east of A1 on A59.

Bagshaw Museum, Wilton Park, Batley.
(0924) 472514

The Bar Convent, York.
(0904) 643238 At Micklegate Bar on A1036.

Beningbrough Hall, York.
(0904) 470666 8 miles north west of York.

Beverley Guildhall, Beverley.
(0482) 867430 In Town centre.

Blaydes House, 6 High Street, Hull.
(0482) 26406

Bramham Park, Wetherby.
(0937) 844265 5 miles south of Wetherby on A1.

Burnby Hall Gardens, Pocklington.
(075930) 2068 13 miles east of York on A1079.

BURTON CONSTABLE HALL

OPEN
Easter Sun
to 30 Sept.
Suns-Thur. incl.
Also
Sats. in July &
August

Grounds &
Coffee Shop
open 12 noon.
Hall 1.00-4.15pm
(Last admission)

BURTON CONSTABLE HALL, NR. HULL TEL: 0964 562400
(Burton Constable Foundation)

Burton Constable, a magnificent 16th century house with 18th century additions by Adam, Lightoler and others. The collections include pictures, English furniture and scientific instruments collected in the 18th century by William Constable. With nearly 30 rooms open, a unique insight is possible into the patronage of the Constable family who have lived here since it was built.

Location: 14 miles from Beverley via A163 Bridlington Road, then follow Historic House signs. 7 miles from Hull via A1238 to Sproatley then follow Historic House signs.

Admission: Adults £3.00, Sen Citizens £2.25, child £1.50 Group rates available.

Byland Abbey, Coxwold.
(03476) 614 1 mile north east of Coxwold.

Cannon Hall, Cawthorne.
(0226) 790270 5 miles west of Barnsley on A635.

The Charterhouse, Charterhouse Lane, Hull.
(0482) 20026

Clifford's Tower, York.
(0904) 646940 Near The Castle Museum, York.

Conisbrough Castle, Doncaster.
(0709) 863329 4½ miles south west of Doncaster.

Constable Burton Hall, Leyburn.
(0677) 50428 On A684 between Leyburn, 3 miles.

East Riddlesden Hall, Keighley.
(0535) 607075 1 mile north east of Keighley

Ebberston Hall, Scarborough.
11 miles west of Scarborough on A170.

Fountains Abbey & Studley Royal, Ripon.
(0765) 608888 2 miles west of Ripon.

Georgian Theatre Royal, Richmond.
(0748) 823710 In Richmond centre.

Gisborough Priory
(0287) 38301 In Gisborough next to the parish church.

Harlow Carr Botanical Gardens, Harrogate.

Helmsley Castle, Helmsley.
(0439) 70442 In Helmsley.

Hovingham Hall, Hovingham, York.
((0653) 628206 20 miles north of York on B1257.

Kirkham Priory, Malton.
(065381) 768 5 miles south west of Malton.

Ledston Hall, Castleford.
2 miles north of Castleford off A656.

Lotherton Hall, Aberford.
(0532) 813259 1 mile east of A1 at Aberford on B1217.

Maister House, 160 High Street, Hull.
(0482) 24114

Markenfield Hall, Ripon.
3 miles south of R ipon off A61.

Middleham Castle, Leyburn.
(0969) 23899 2 mile south of Leyburn.

Monk Bretton Priory, Barnsley.
(0226) 204089 2 miles north east of Barnsley.

Mount Grace Priory, Northallerton.
(0609) 83249 7 miles north east of Northallerton.

Newburgh Priory, Coxwold.
(03476) 435 5 miles from Easingwold off A19.

Norton Conyers, Ripon.
(0765) 640333 3½ miles north west of Ripon near Wath.

FAIRFAX HOUSE

Nostell Priory, Wakefield.
(0924) 863892 6 miles south east of Wakefield on A638.

Nunnington Hall, Helmsley.
(04395) 283 In Ryedale, 4½ miles south east of Helmsley.

Oakwell Hall, Birstall.

Ormesby Hall, near Middlesbrough
(0642) 324188 3 miles south east of Middlesbrough.

Pickering Castle, Pickering.
(0751) 74989 In Pickering.

Red House, Gomersal, Cleckheaton.
(0274) 872165

Richmond Castle, Richmond.
(0748) 822493 In R ichmond.

Rievaulx Abbey, Helmsley.
(04396) 228 3 miles north west of Helmsley.

Rievaulx Terrace, Helmsley.
(04396) 340 2½ miles north west of Helmsley on B1257.

Roche Abbey, Maltby.
(0709) 812739 1½ miles south of Maltby.

Scarborough Castle, Scarborough.
(0723) 372451 East of town centre.

Sewerby Hall, Bridlington.
In Bridlington, on the cliff, 2 miles north east of town centre.

Shandy Hall, Coxwold.
(03476) 465 20 miles from York via A19.

Sheffield Botanic Gardens, Clarkehouse Road, Sheffield.

Shibden Hall, Halifax.
(0422) 352246 ¼ mile south east of Halifax on A58.

Sion Hill Hall, Kirby Wiske, Thirsk.
(0845) 587206 6 miles south of Northallerton.

Skipton Castle, Skipton.
(0756) 792442 At the head of the High Street in Skipton.

Sledmere House, Driffield.
(0377) 86028 24 miles east of York.

STOCKELD PARK

OPEN
Thursdays only

April 7-Oct.13

2.00pm-5.00pm

STOCKELD   PARK, WETHERBY TEL: 0937 586101
(Mr and Mrs P G F Grant)

Stockeld is a small and beautifully proportioned Palladian Villa designed for Middletons by James Paine in 1763. The present family have lived at Stockeld for over a century and it is still very much a home, housing a good collection of 18th and 19th century furniture and paintings. Stockeld is set in beautiful parkland and has well established gardens and woodland.

Location: York 12 miles, Haarrogate 5 miles, Leeds 12 miles.
Admission: Adults £1.50, Child 75p, OAP £1.00.

Temple Newsam, Leeds.
(0532) 647321 5 miles east of Leeds.

Tolson Memorial Museum, Ravensknowle Park, Huddersfield.
(0484) 530591

Treasurer's House, York.
(0904) 624247 Behind York Minster, York.

THORP PERROW ARBORETUM

OPEN
All year round from
Dawn to Dusk

THORP PERROW
ARBORETUM, BEDALE TEL:
0677 425323
(Sir John Ropner)

The Arboretum comprises over 1,000 trees and shrubs, set in 85 acres. Spectacular sights in Spring and Autumn. Woodland walks, Nature Trails, Lake, Islands, Water Steps. Tearoom. Plant Centre and Information Centre. Tours must be pre-booked.

Location: South of Bedale, N. Yorkshire on Well-Ripon road, 4 miles from Leeming Bar on A1.
Admission: Adults £2.20, children/OAP's £1.10.

Whitby Abbey, Whitby.
(0947) 603568 In Whitby.

Wilberforce House, 25 High Street, Hull.
(0482) 593902

CASTLE HOWARD

AYTON CASTLE
Ayton, Berwickshire

AYTON CASTLE was built in 1846 by the Mitchell-Dunes family and the architect was James Gillespie Graham. Within the last ten years it has been fully restored and is now lived in as a family home. It is a unique restoration project and the quality of the original and restored workmanship is outstanding.

The Castle stands on an escarpment surrounded by mature woodlands containing many interesting trees and has been a film-making venue on account of this magnificent setting.

To visit Ayton Castle is an experience. Visitors see an historic house lived in, and cared for, as a family home.

CONTACT

The Curator
Ayton Castle
Berwickshire
TD 14 5RD

Tel: 08907 81212

LOCATION

On A1, 7 miles North of Berwick-on-Tweed, 50 miles from Edinburgh, 70 miles from Newcastle.

4 hours, by train, from London.

ACCOMMODATION

Accommodation for up to 12 persons in single rooms and up to 22 in doubles.

SUITABILITY FOR OTHER EVENTS

Suitable for all outdoor usage: films, shooting, fishing, helicopters, equestrian events, car launches etc.

EXTRA FACILITIES

Anything can be arranged: contact the Curator.

ADVICE TO COURIERS AND DRIVERS

Because of a low arch, bus drivers should avoid the main entrance, and should approach the house via the entrance by the lodge on the Ayton-Eyenmouth road.

FACILITIES FOR THE DISABLED

There are toilets for the disabled and easy access to all rooms.

PARKING FOR COACHES AND CARS

There is ample parking.

CATERING

Can be arranged by request for any number.

GUIDED TOURS

All visitors are accompanied by a guide.

SCHOOL VISITS/CHILDREN

Welcome at any time.

OPENING TIMES

Summer
May - September

Sun   2pm - 5pm

Open at other times by appointment. Contact the Curator on 08907 81212 (24 hours)

ADMISSION

Adult	£2.00
Child	
under 15	FREE
15+	£2.00
OAP	£2.00

CONFERENCE AND FUNCTION FACILITIES

Room	Dimensions	Capacity	Layout	Power Points	Suitable for A/V
Gallery	10'x70'	60	Theatre		
		120	Reception		
		54	Small Tables		
Inner Hall	21'x18'	30	Theatre		
		120	Reception		
		24	Small Tables		
Main Hall	21'x24'	30	Theatre		
		120	Reception		
		30	Small Tables		
Dining Room	33'x30'	50	Theatre		
		80	Reception		
		60	Small Tables		
Small Dining Room	16'x16'	8	Small Tables		
Drawing Room	33'x24'	50	Theatre		

BLAIR CASTLE
Pitlochry, Perthshire

BLAIR CASTLE has been the ancient home and fortress of the Earls and Dukes of Atholl for over 725 years. Its central location makes it easily accessible from all major Scottish centres in less than two hours.

The Castle has known the splendour of Royal visitations, submitted to occupation by opposing forces on no less than four occasions, suffered siege and changed its architectural appearance to suit the taste of successive generations.

Today 32 rooms of infinite variety display beautiful furniture, fine collections of paintings, arms, armour, china, costumes, lace and embroidery, masonic regalia, Jacobite relics and other unique treasures giving a stirring picture of Scottish life from the 16th to 20th Centuries.

The 10th Duke of Atholl, who still lives at Blair Castle, has the unique distinction of having the only remaining Private Army in Europe - The Atholl Highlanders.

GARDENS

Blair Castle is set in extensive parklands. Near the free car and coach parks, there is a picnic area, a Deer Park and a unique two acre plantation of large trees known as 'Diana's Grove.' It has been said that "it is unlikely that any other two acres in the world contain such a number of different conifers of such heights and of such small age."

CONTACT

Brian H Nodes
Administrator
Blair Castle
Blair Atholl
Pitlochry
Perthshire
PH18 5TL

Tel: (0796) 481207
Fax: (0796) 481487

LOCATION

From Edinburgh (80 miles),M90 to Perth, A9, follow signs for Blair Castle. 1¹/₂ hours. Trunk Road A9 2 miles

Bus: Bus stop 1 mile in Blair Atholl.

Train: 1mile, Blair Atholl Euston-Inverness line. FREE Castle minibus from Station to Castle.

Taxi: Carry Cabs, (0796) 473333, Elizabeth Yule, (0796) 472290

SUITABILITY FOR OTHER EVENTS

Fashion shows, archery, clay pigeon shooting, equestrian events, garden parties, shows, rallies, filming, wedding receptions, Highland Balls, Charity Balls, Piping Championships, plus full range of concerts and banquets.

EXTRA FACILITIES

Grand Piano, helicopter pad, cannon firing by Atholl Highlanders, resident piper, parkland, picnic areas. Special arrangements for groups touring House and gardens can include lunches, dinners and entertainment, highland balls, piper, cannon, needlework displays.

ADVICE TO COURIERS & DRIVERS

Coach drivers and couriers free, plus free meal and weekly free prize draw for bottle of whisky. On first visit drivers/couriers receive free information pack. No dogs or smoking. Parking for 200 cars and 20 coaches 100 yards from Castle.

FACILITIES FOR THE DISABLED

Disabled and elderly visitors may alight at the entrance of the Castle, before parking in the allocated areas. Disabled toilets Wheelchair available.

CATERING

Two restaurants. Self-service area seats 112, 'The Old Gun Room' (waitress service) seats 48. Prices from £1.00-£3.50 for tea, snacks from £3.00, lunches from £6.00. Buffets, Dinners and Banquets for 70-200 can be provided. Details on application.

GIFT SHOP

Open as for Castle. Over 1,000 items sold, 72% are Scottish made.

GUIDE BOOKS

Colour guide book in English, German, French, Dutch, Italian, Spanish and Japanese, £1.50. Special guide book for children.

GUIDED TOURS

Tours available in English, German and French at no extra cost. Maximum size 25. Average time for tour of house 1¹/₂ hours.

SCHOOL VISITS/CHILDREN

School parties welcome £3.10 each, Primary Schools £2.50 each. Of particular interest: nature walks, deer park, collection of children's games, pony trekking. Special guide book .

OPENING TIMES

Summer
31 March - 28 October

Mon
Tues
Wed
Thur } 10am-6pm
Fri
Sat
Sun

NB Last entry
5pm.

Winter
29 October - 31 March

Closed

ADMISSION

Summer

HOUSE & GARDEN
Adult	£4.50
Child/Student**	£3.50
OAP	£3.50
Family	£13.50

GROUP*
Adult	£4.10
Child**	£3.10
OAP	£3.10
Disabled	£2.00

* Minimum payment £200 out of season.
**Age 5-16

Winter

Closed

FUNCTION FACILITIES

ROOM	DIMENSIONS	CAPACITY	LAYOUT	POWER POINTS	SUITABLE FOR A/V
Ballroom	88'x36'	400	Theatre	14	✓
		200	Schoolroom		
		200	Buffet		
		300	Dinner/Dance		
		200	Lunch/Dinner		
State Dining Room (Evenings only)	36'x25'	200	Receptions only	4	
Library	27'x15'	40	Theatre	6	

BLAIRQUHAN CASTLE
Straiton, Ayrshire

BLAIRQUHAN is the home of James Hunter Blair, the great great grandson of Sir David Hunter Blair, 3rd Baronet for whom it was designed by William Burn and built in 1821-1824.

All the Regency furniture bought for the house remains and the house has not been altered except discreetly to bring it up to date. There are 10 double bedrooms, including 4-posters, with bathrooms en suite, five singles and many public rooms which can be used for conferences and every sort of occasion.

The Castle is approached by a 3 mile private drive along the River Girvan and it is situated in one of the most charming parts of South West Scotland. There is a well-known collection of pictures. The River Girvan runs through the Estate and five miles of it is available for fishing for salmon and sea trout.

Blairquhan is only 50 miles from Glasgow and Glasgow Airport. It is within about half an hour's driving distance of the famous golf courses of Prestwick, Troon and Turnberry - the last two of which are venues for the British Open Golf Championships.

CONTACT

James Hunter Blair
Blairquhan Castle
Straiton
Maybole
Ayrshire
KA19 7LZ

Tel: (06557) 239
Fax: (06557) 278

LOCATION

From London, M6 to Carlisle, A76 to Dumfries, A75 to Crocketford, A712 to A713 near New Galloway, B741 to Straiton on B7045 to Ayr. Turn left.

Rail: Maybole 7 miles.

Taxi: Watson (06557) 208

SUITABILITY FOR OTHER EVENTS

Fashion shows, air displays, archery, clay pigeon shooting, equestrian events, garden parties, shows, rallies, filming, wedding receptions.

EXTRA FACILITIES

Grand piano, snooker, tennis, fishing, shooting. Slide projector, overhead projector, screen, and secretarial assistance available for meetings.

ACCOMMODATION

Blairquhan offers. 10 Doubles (4 4-posters) with bathrooms en suite, 6 Singles. The Dower House at Milton has 8 Doubles, 2 singles, 5 bathrooms. 6 holidays cottages on the Estate.

ADVICE TO COURIERS & DRIVERS

No photography within the Castle. Unlimited parking.

FACILITIES FOR THE DISABLED

Disabled and elderly visitors may alight at the entrance to the Castle. Toilets for the disabled.

CATERING

Restaurant: Afternoon teas, lunches, buffets and dinners. Groups can book in advance for tea and other meals. Special rates for groups. Prices start at £1.50 per person.

GIFT SHOP

The small shop is open when required.

GUIDED TOURS

Can be arranged at no extra charge for up to 100 people – duration 1 hour. Also available in French.

SCHOOL VISITS/CHILDREN

School visits are welcome. A guide and schoolroom can be provided. Cost negotiable.

OPENING TIMES

Summer
19 July -14 August
(except Mondays)

Mon	Closed
Tues	
Wed	
Thur	Open
Fri	
Sat	
Sun	

NB Open at all other times by appointment.

Winter

Open by pre-booked appointment.

ADMISSION

Summer & Winter

HOUSE & GARDEN
Adult	£3.00
Child**	£2.00
OAP	£2.50

GROUP*
Negotiable

* Minimum payment £20.
** Age 5-14

CONFERENCE AND FUNCTION FACILITIES

ROOM	DIMENSIONS	CAPACITY	LAYOUT	POWER POINTS	SUITABLE FOR A/V
Drawing Rooms (2 rooms)	1200 sq ft	100	Theatre	4	3
		50	Schoolroom		
		30	U-Shape		
		20	Boardroom		
		100	Dinner/Dance		
		100	Buffet/Lunch/Dinner		
		50	Seated Lunch/Dinner		
Dining Room	750 sq ft	100	Dinner/Dance	4	3
		100	Buffet/Lunch/Dinner		
		50	Seated Lunch/Dinner		
Library	400 sq ft	25 (Using other rooms 100)			
Saloon	600 sq ft	100	Dinner Dance		
		100	Buffet/Lunch/Dinner		
		50	Seated Lunch/Dinner		
Meeting Room	255 sq ft	50	Buffet/Lunch/Dinner		

BOWHILL
Selkirk

SCOTTISH Borders home of the Duke and Duchess of Buccleuch, dating mainly from 1812 and christened 'Sweet Bowhill' by Sir Walter Scott in his 'Lay of the Last Minstrel'.

Many of the works of art were collected by earlier Montagus, Douglases and Scotts or given by Charles II to his natural son James Duke of Monmouth and Buccleuch. Paintings include Canaletto's "Whitehall", works by Guardi, Claude, Ruysdael, Gainsborough, Raeburn, Reynolds, Van Dyck, Wilkie and a selection from the renowned Buccleuch collection of portrait miniatures. Superb French furniture, Meissen and Sevres porcelain, silver and tapestries.

Historical relics include Monmouth's saddle and execution shirt, Sir Walter Scott's plaid and some proof editions, Queen Victoria's letters and gifts to successive Duchesses of Buccleuch, her Mistresses of the Robes.

Completely restored Victorian Kitchen, 19th Century horse-drawn fire engine, 'Bowhill Little Theatre', a lively centre for the performing arts and where, prior to touring the house, visitors can see 'The Quest for Bowhill', a twenty minute audio-visual by Dr Colin Thompson.

Conference Centre, Arts Courses, Education Service, Riding Centre, Mountain Bike hire, Visitor Centre. Shop, Tearoom, Adventure Playground, Woodland Walks, Nature Trails, Picnic Areas. Garden and landscape designed by John Gilpin.

CONTACT

Mrs M Carter
Buccleuch Heritage Trust
Bowhill House &
Country Park
Bowhill
Selkirk
Scotland
TD7 5ET

Tel: (0750) 20732

LOCATION

3 mls W of Selkirk off A708 Moffat Road, A68 from Newcastle, A7 from Carlisle or Edinburgh.

Bus: 3 miles Selkirk.

Taxi: (0750) 20354

SUITABILITY FOR OTHER EVENTS

Fashion shows, air displays, archery, clay pigeon shooting, equestrian events, charity garden parties, shows, rallies, filming, all requests considered. By prior arrangement.

EXTRA FACILITIES

As "education" is the prime function of the Buccleuch Heritage Trust, with emphasis on outstanding works of art and their relationship to their historic associations, the House is opened specially by appointment, outside the scheduled public hours to groups of any age led by officials of a recognised museum, gallery or educational establishment. Lecture theatre and equipment available on request.

ADVICE TO COURIERS & DRIVERS

Photography prohibited inside the House. Free parking for 60 cars and 6 coaches within 50yds of House.

FACILITIES FOR THE DISABLED

Disabled and elderly visitors may alight at the House entrance. Special toilet facilities in the Stables Courtyard. Wheelchair visitors admitted Free of Charge.

CATERING

Restaurant (seating 72). Parties can be booked in advance for tea and other meals. Inside caterers normally used but outside caterers considered. Special rates for groups, menus on request.

GUIDED TOURS

Available for groups. There is no additional charge for this, average time taken to see the House 1 hour 15 minutes.

GIFT SHOP

Open at the same time as the House, or by appointment. Mini shop open when grounds only open.

SCHOOL VISITS/CHILDREN

Groups are welcome, £1.00 per child. The services of Education Officers are provided free and a schoolroom is available. Areas of interest include: projects in Bowhill House and Victorian Kitchen, Ranger-led Nature Walks. Adventure Playground, Pony trekking/riding. Please telephone to discuss requirements.

OPENING TIMES

Summer
1st May to late Summer Bank Hol (UK)

COUNTRY PARK
Sat ⎫
Sun ⎪
Mon ⎪
Tues ⎬ 12noon-5pm
Wed ⎪
Thur ⎭
Fri   Closed

HOUSE
Sat ⎫
Sun ⎪
Mon ⎪ July
Tue ⎬ 1pm-4.30pm
Wed ⎪
Thur ⎪
Fri ⎭

Winter
By appointment only, for educational groups.

ADMISSION

Summer
HOUSE & COUNTRY PARK
Adult	£3.50
Child*	£1.00
OAP/Student	£2.00
Group**	£2.50

COUNTRY PARK ONLY
All groups	£1.00

*Age 5-16
** Minimum number 20 persons

Winter
HOUSE &COUNTRY PARK
Adult	£4.00
Child	£1.00

For pre-booked educational groups over 20 persons

CONFERENCE AND FUNCTION FACILITIES

ROOM	DIMENSIONS	CAPACITY	LAYOUT	POWER POINTS	SUITABLE FOR A/V
Bowhill Little Theatre		72	Theatre	✓	✓
		72	Buffet		
		72	Lunch/Dinner		

CAWDOR CASTLE
Nairn, Scotland

This splendid romantic castle dating from the late 14th Century was built as a private fortress by the Thanes of Cawdor, and remains the home of the Cawdor family to this day. The ancient medieval tower was built around the legendary holly-tree.

Although the house has evolved over 600 years, later additions mainly of the 17th Century were all built in the Scottish vernacular style with slated roofs over walls and crow-stepped gables of mellow local stone. This style gives Cawdor a strong sense of unity, and the massive, severe exterior belies an intimate interior that gives the place a surprisingly personal friendly atmosphere.

Good furniture, fine portraits and pictures, interesting objects and outstanding tapestries are arranged to please the family rather than to echo fashion or impress. Memories of Shakespeare's 'Macbeth' give Cawdor an elusive, evocative quality that delights visitors.

The Flower Garden has again a family feel to it, where plants are chosen out of affection rather than affectation. This is a lovely spot between spring and late summer. The Wild Garden beside its stream leads into beautiful trails through a spectacular mature mixed woodland, through which paths are helpfully marked and colour-coded.

CONTACT

The Secretary
Cawdor Castle
Nairn
Scotland
IV12 5RD

Tel: (0667) 404615
Fax: (0667) 404674

LOCATION

From Edinburgh A9
3¹/₂ hours,
Inverness 20 minutes,
Nairn 10 minutes.

Rail: Nairn Station
5 miles.

Bus: Inverness to Nairn
bus route 200 yards.

Main road: A9 14 miles.

Taxi: Piperhill Taxis
(0667) 404680.

Air: Inverness Airport 5
miles.

SUITABILITY FOR OTHER EVENTS

Conferences and day functions

EXTRA FACILITIES

9 hole golf course, putting green, golf clubs for hire. Special arrangements can be made for groups to include lunches, sherry or champagne receptions, whisky tasting, musical entertainments. Specialised garden visits.

ADVICE TO COURIERS & DRIVERS

Two weeks advance notice for group catering. Coach drivers/couriers free. Refreshments or lunch in restaurant. Drivers entered in monthly prize draw. No photography, video photography or tripods inside. No dogs. Parking for 250 cars and 25 coaches.

FACILITIES FOR THE DISABLED

Disabled and elderly visitors may alight at the entrance to the Castle, before parking in the allocated areas. Disabled toilets.

CATERING

The licensed Castle Buttery provides hot meals, snacks and home baking from May to October, capacity 50. Groups should book in advance, Tel: 0667 404615. Menus on request.

GIFT SHOP

There are three shops open at the same time as Castle. The Gift Shop items include: cashmere, china, leather goods, children's toys, sweets and a wide selection of products made in Scotland, many exclusively for Cawdor Castle. The Book Shop sells a

wide and unusual selection of books, prints, stationery and cards. The Wool Shop: the best of Scottish cashmere, capes, ponchos and a large collection of sweaters and children's clothes including tartans.

GUIDE BOOKS

Colour guide book and room notes. French, German and Japanese translations available,

SCHOOL VISITS/CHILDREN

School groups are welcome £1.90 per child. Room notes, quiz and answer sheet can be provided. Of particular interest: Ranger service and nature trails.

OPENING TIMES

Summer
1 May - 2 October

Daily 10am-5.30pm
Last admission
5pm.

Winter
3 October-30 April

Closed

ADMISSION

Summer

HOUSE & GARDEN
Adult	£4.00
Child**	£2.20
OAP	£3.10
Family (2+5)	£12.00
Group*	
Adult	£3.70
Child**	£1.90

GARDEN ONLY
Adult	£2.00
Child**	£2.00
OAP	£2.00

* Minimum number 20 people
**Age 5-15

CONFERENCE AND FUNCTION FACILITIES

ROOM	DIMENSIONS	CAPACITY	LAYOUT	POWER POINTS	SUITABLE FOR A/V
Cawdor Hall		40	Boardroom Lunch/Dinner	✓	✓

CULZEAN CASTLE
Maybole, Ayrshire

Culzean Castle stands on a cliff top, looking over the Firth of Clyde towards the mountains of Arran, surrounded by 563 acres of gardens and parklands. This was the home of the Kennedy family for over 500 years and since 1945 has been in the care of the National Trust for Scotland.

In 1969 the grounds were declared Scotland's first Country Park which now attracts over 300,000 visitors annually.

Robert Adam designed the magnificent Castle for Thomas, 10th Earl of Cassillis and completed his work in 1790. Visitors to Culzean take away memories of the beauty of the oval staircase and the breathtaking splendour of the Round Drawing

Room which Adam designed to contrast the natural glories without against the comfort and grandeur within.

So much is there to see and enjoy that visitors to Culzean should preferably allow themselves at least four hours. The gardens benefit from the effects of the Gulf Stream, reflected in the wide variety of plants with an Australasian flavour. The Fountain Court and terraced gardens are immediately beside the Castle, only ten minutes walk away from the wonders of the walled garden. Visitors return frequently to Culzean to enjoy the beauties of the Swan Pond, its many varieties of wildfowl and the migratory patterns.

CONTACT

Michael L Tebbutt
Administrator Culzean
Culzean Castle
Maybole
Ayrshire
KA19 8LE

Tel: (06556) 274
Fax: (06556) 615

Party Bookings:
(06556) 269

LOCATION

Culzean is off A719, 4 miles west of Maybole and 12 miles south of Ayr.

SUITABILITY FOR OTHER EVENTS

Concerts, craft fairs, equestrian events, rallies, filming, garden parties, wedding facilities, banquets. product launches, activity days and a wide variety of prestige occasions. Traditional Scottish Banquet in Castle principal Dining Room from £100.00 per head including entertainment.

EXTRA FACILITIES

Licensed restaurant, Ranger-led activities, Culzean Exhibition, audio visual shows, adventure playground, sandy safe beaches, helicopter pad, grand piano, Pipers, a/v equipment etc. Excellent film location. Culzean's nearest neighbour is the world famous Turnbury Hotel, with its championship Golf Courses. There are nearly twenty good courses near Culzean.

ADVICE TO COURIERS & DRIVERS

Coach drivers and couriers are offered a meal voucher. Smoking, dogs and photography not allowed in the Castle. Dogs are not allowed in the walled garden, welcome elsewhere but always under control.

FACILITIES FOR THE DISABLED

2 wheelchairs and an electric car available for visitors. Lift provided in the Castle. Many pathways designed with convenience of the disabled in mind. Audio loop system. Special provision for those with learning difficulties. Staff are always glad to help in whatever way then can.

PARKING FOR COACHES & CARS

Visitors are required to park about 200 yards away from the Castle, with easy access over the Viaduct. Those with disabled passengers (not coaches) may drive to the door before parking.

GIFT SHOP

Two shops, one in the Castle, one at the Visitor Centre.

GUIDED TOURS OF CASTLE AND/OR GARDENS & COUNTRY PARK

Tours must be booked in advance, duration 1 hour in Castle, variable according to demand in Country Park.

GUIDE BOOKS

Full colour guide book and other publications.

SCHOOL VISITS/CHILDREN

Groups are welcome and 30 different programmes covering a wide range of subject matter are offered. The services of an Education officer and Guides in the Castle and Rangers in the Park are available. Other interests include a mystery map and trail, a Young Naturalists' Club and an adventure playground.

CULZEAN CASTLE APARTMENTS

These are the rooms given to General Eisenhower in 1945 on behalf of a grateful Scottish people, which he used as his home in Scotland. Now available to a wider clientele they offer exclusive accommodation in a unique setting for up to 12.

Guests are cared for by the Cordon-bleu cook/housekeeper and her staff.

OPENING TIMES

CASTLE
1 April-23 October
10.30am-5.30pm Daily
(Last admission 5pm).

VISITOR CENTRE, SHOP, RESTAURANT
1 April-23 October
10.30am-5.30pm Daily

COUNTRY PARK
Open all year daily.
9.00am-Sunset

ADMISSION

COUNTRY PARK
Adults   £3.00
Concessions   £1.50
Parties of 20 or more
Adults   £2.50
Concessions   £1.25
School Coaches   £20.00

CASTLE
Adults   £3.50
Concession incl.
  School Pupils   £1.80

COMBINED TICKET
Castle/Country Park
Adults   £5.50
Concessions   £3.00

All NTS/NT Members Free

Parties of 20 or more
Adults   £4.50
Concessions   £2.50

Party: 20 or more persons (nonNTS/NT Members).

Concessions:
OAP's of retired status over 60.
Children of 17 and under.

DALMENY HOUSE
South Queensferry, West Lothian

DALMENY HOUSE rejoices in one of the most beautiful and unspoilt settings in Great Britain, yet it is only seven miles from Scotland's capital, Edinburgh, fifteen minutes from Edinburgh Airport and less than an hour's drive from Glasgow. It is an eminently suitable venue for group visits, business functions, meetings and special events, including product launches and outdoor activities such as off-road driving.

Dalmeny Estate, the family home of the Earls of Rosebery for over three hundred years, boasts superb collections of porcelain and tapestries, fine paintings by Gainsborough, Raeburn, Reynolds and Lawrence, together with the exquisite Mentmore Rothschild collection of 18th Century French furniture. There is also the Napoleonic collection, assembled by the Fifth Earl of Rosebery, Prime Minister, historian and owner of three Derby Winners.

The Hall, Library and Dining Room will lend a memorable sense of occasion to corporate receptions, luncheons and dinners. Alternatively, there are the recently-renovated areas of the former kitchen and servants' hall (now named the Rosebery Rooms) and the new Courtyard Restaurant, with facilities specifically designed for business meetings, small conferences, promotions, exhibitions and product launches. A wide range of entertainment can also be provided, from piano recitals to a floodlit pipe band Beating the Retreat.

CONTACT

Mrs Lindsay Morison
Dalmeny House
South Queensferry
West Lothian
EH30 9TQ

Tel:031 331 1888
Fax: 031 331 1788

LOCATION

From Edinburgh A90, B924, 7 mls west. A90 1/2 mile.

Bus: From St Andrews Square to Chapel Gate 1 mile from House.

Rail: Dalmeny Railway Station 3 miles.

Taxi: Hawes Landing 031 331 1077, Ken Taylor 031 331 1402.

OPENING TIMES

Summer
May-September inclusive.

Sun	1pm-5.30pm last admission 4.45pm.
Mon Tues }	12noon-5.30pm last admission 4.45pm.

Open at other times by appointment only.

ADMISSION

Summer

Adults	£3.40
Students	£2.70
Children*	£1.80
Groups (Min. 20)	£2.70

* 10-16 years

SUITABILITY FOR OTHER EVENTS

Fashion shows, product launches, archery, clay pigeon shooting, equestrian events, shows, filming, background photography, small meetings and special events.

EXTRA FACILITIES

Lectures can be arranged on House, contents and family history. Screen and projector can be provided. Helicopter landing area. House is in the centre of a 41/2 mile shore walk from Forth Rail Bridge at South Queensferry to small foot passenger ferry at Cramond. Walk open throughout the year, ferry 9am-1pm. 2pm-7pm summer, 4pm winter and closed Fridays.

ADVICE TO COURIERS & DRIVERS

Fires, picnics, dogs and cameras not permitted.

FACILITIES FOR THE DISABLED

Disabled and elderly visitors may alight at the entrance, before parking in the allocated areas. Disabled toilets available.

PARKING FOR COACHES & CARS

Capacity of the car park: 60 cars, 150 yards from the House and 3 coaches, 250 yards from the House. Parking for functions and special groups visits in front of the House.

CATERING

Afternoon tea and light lunches - self service. Cost for catering for functions on application. Groups can book in advance for tea and other meals. Buffets, lunches, dinners can be arranged for conferences and special functions.

GUIDED TOURS

Please apply for details. Guided tours for special interest groups can be arranged outside normal opening hours.

CONFERENCE AND FUNCTION FACILITIES

ROOM	DIMENSIONS	CAPACITY	LAYOUT	POWER POINTS	SUITABLE FOR A/V
Library	10.4 x 7m	20	Informal Meeting		
Dining Room	11.2 x 7.4m	25	Boardroom	4	✓
		30-50	Lunch/Dinner		
		80-100	Buffet		
Garden Restaurant	12.7 x 9m	120	Theatre	3	✓
		96	Round Tables		
		200	Buffet Receptions		
Rosebery Rooms					
I	9 x 6m	64	Theatre	8	✓
II	6.4 x 6m &	18	Boardroom	8	✓
	4.6 x 3.3m	45	Theatre style or back-projection		
I and II		150	Reception		

DUNROBIN CASTLE
Golspie, Sutherland

DUNROBIN is the most northerly of Scotland's great castles, the ancient Earldom of Sutherland being created about 1235. In 1845 Sir Charles Barry re-modelled the early castle into a massive baronial residence, and after a fire in 1915 the main rooms were re-designed by Sir Robert Lorimer.

The principal rooms include the Drawing Room, where hang a fine set of Mortlake tapestries and a series of Canaletto's Views of Venice, the Green and Gold Room, Queen Victoria's bedroom, containing the exquisite gilt fourposter bed in which she slept on a visit in 1872. Lorimer's sycamore Library containing over 10,000 volumes and a gorgeous portrait of Duchess Eileen by Philip de Lazlo.

The castle is notable for the collection of portraits by leading painters of the day. A study, bedrooms, nurseries, displays of ceremonial robes, medals and memorabilia, china and kitchen equipment can all be seen, and the rooms are decorated with flowers from the gardens.

The Victorian Museum in the grounds, formerly a summerhouse, contains a collection of big game trophies, a unique collection of pictish stones, items of local history, ornithology, geology and ethnography.

GARDENS

The castle is set in fine woodlands with magnificent formal gardens overlooking the sea.

CONTACT

Keith Jones
Curator
Golspie
Sutherland
Scotland
KW10 6RR

Tel: (0408) 633177
Office: (0408) 633268
Fax: (0408) 633800

LOCATION

From Edinburgh A9, north for 4 hours.

Rail: Castle has own Railway Station. Details of trains stopping at Castle and special excursions from B. Rail.

Bus: Stop at main gate 300 yards from Castle.

SUITABILITY FOR OTHER EVENTS

Fashion shows, air displays, archery, clay pigeon shooting, garden parties, rallies, filming, and concerts.

EXTRA FACILITIES

Grand piano. Lectures can be arranged on the property, contents, gardens and history.

ADVICE TO COURIERS & DRIVERS

Go north of Inverness, the wild scenery is the best in Scotland. No smoking, dogs, or photography in the Castle. Parking for 300 cars and 10 coaches.

FACILITIES FOR THE DISABLED

Disabled and elderly visitors may be left at the entrance to the Castle, before parking in the allocated areas. No toilets for the disabled and access to the main rooms difficult. Access to gardens is possible by prior arrangement.

GIFT SHOP

Open at same time as Castle. Items include: knitwear, pottery, various crafts, cosmetics, jewellery, honey and souvenirs.

GUIDE BOOKS

Full colour guide book. Translations in French and German.

CATERING

The Tea Room can cater for 50. Prices from £1.00-£2.50 for afternoon tea and light refreshments. For special functions/ conferences, buffets, lunches and dinners can be arranged.

GUIDED TOURS

Tours are normally self guided but guided tours can be organised for groups by prior arrangement. If requested the owner may meet visitors. Average time for tour 1 hour. Tours available in French and German by prior arrangement. Personally guided tours by Lord Strathnaver accompanied by a piper, can be arranged. Shortbread, whisky or sherry included £15 per head.

SCHOOL VISITS/CHILDREN

Tours for local groups are free, otherwise group rates apply. Guide at no additional cost with advance notification. Areas of interest: nursery exhibition, dolls house and toys. Croquet in the garden and sometimes a children's quiz.

OPENING TIMES

Summer
Easter & Summer
April 1-4 and
1 May - 15 October
April, May & October
Monday to Saturday
    10.30am-4.30pm
Sun   1pm-4.30pm
Last entry   4pm

1 June - 30 September
Monday to Saturday
    10.30am-5.30pm
Sun   1pm-5.30pm
Last admission 5pm

Winter

Open at all times for pre-booked parties.

ADMISSION

Summer

HOUSE & GARDEN
Adult	£3.50
Child*	£1.80
OAP	£2.20
Family (2+4)	£9.00

GROUPS**
Adult	£3.30
Child*	£1.70
OAP	£2.20

*Age 5-14
** Minimum payment £33

Winter

Same as Summer rates. When the Castle is closed the gardens are open free of charge.

CONFERENCE AND FUNCTION FACILITIES

ROOM	DIMENSIONS	CAPACITY	LAYOUT	POWER POINTS	SUITABLE FOR A/V
Drawing Room	100'x30'	200	Theatre	✓	✓
		50	Lunch/Dinner		
Dining Room	70'x30'	20	Boardroom	✓	✓
		20	Lunch/Dinner		

DUNS CASTLE
Duns, Berwickshire

CONTACT

Mrs A D Hay
Duns Castle
Duns
Berwickshire
TD11 3NW

Tel: (0361) 83211
Fax: (0361) 82015

LOCATION

10 miles off the A1.

Rail: Berwick Station
16 miles.

Bus: Edinburgh to
Berwick Route.

DUNS CASTLE is a private family home not open to the public. The owners, Alexander Hay and his family, offer it as an occasional and unique venue for businesses, private guests or parties to share with them either for individual lunches, dinners, meetings or for residential stays. The essence of the arrangement is that those visiting are in every respect as guests in a private home,

The Castle built around a 1320 Pele Tower given by Robert the Bruce to the Earl of Moray, was built by the Earl of Tweedale in 1696 for his son William Hay and has been lived in by the family in unbroken succession ever since.

Over the years, the Castle has been enlarged and embellished. The interior with intricately carved wood and plater work and well furnished from the 17th Century onwards, now has all the comforts of modern heating and plumbing. The whole aspect of the house is sunny and the large dining room in particular is a dramatic warmly panelled room with its richly carved fireplace and original 14th Century walls.

GARDENS

The beautiful landscaped park surrounding the Castle incorporating a nature reserve and lake, leads into the Lammermuir Hills.

Nearby are the ancient Abbey towns of Kelso, Melrose and Jedburgh, as are the woollen mills of the Tweed Valley. The area has much of interest several well-known golf courses, the fortified town of Berwick-upon-Tweed and four large houses open to the public.

OPENING TIMES

Not generally open to the public, except to groups by prior arrangement. Facilities for meetings, corporate hospitality and accommodation throughout the year (individual couples welcome).

ADMISSION

Not open to the public, but only for groups, meals, accommodation etc. Rates upon application, eg group tour with tea, £3.50 per person + VAT.

SUITABILITY FOR OTHER EVENTS

Fashion shows, air displays, archery, clay pigeon shooting, equestrian events, garden parties, shows, filming.

EXTRA FACILITIES

Also available for use: Grand Piano, Organ, Croquet Lawn, Table Tennis, Billiards Room, 9 hole golf course nearby. Lectures on the Castle and its history can be arranged for up to 60. Projector and screen can be provided. Details on shooting and country sports on request.

ADVICE TO COURIERS & DRIVERS

No dogs, photography or unaccompanied children. Dogs in grounds and in nature reserve on leads. Parking for up to 50-60 cars and coaches adjacent to the Castle.

CATERING

There are two Dining Rooms, the main seating 46 (75 for a buffet) and the small seating up to 10. Special rates are given to groups. Menus available upon request.

ACCOMMODATION

Duns Castle offers: 3 singles, 6 twin/doubles with bathrooms and 4 four poster rooms with bathroom. These are available when staying at the house for dinner and breakfast. 3 houses are also available.

FACILITIES FOR THE DISABLED

Disabled and elderly visitors may alight at the Castle entrance.

GUIDED TOURS

These are available for up to 60. The owner will meet groups visiting the house. Tours in Italian upon request. Average for tour is 45 minutes.

SCHOOL VISITS/CHILDREN

Groups are welcome £2.00 + VAT per child. A guide is provided and there is a schoolroom for their use. Areas of interest include: nature reserve, games room, swings.

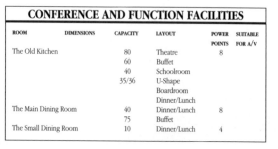

CONFERENCE AND FUNCTION FACILITIES

ROOM	DIMENSIONS	CAPACITY	LAYOUT	POWER POINTS	SUITABLE FOR A/V
The Old Kitchen		80	Theatre	8	
		60	Buffet		
		40	Schoolroom		
		35/36	U-Shape		
			Boardroom		
			Dinner/Lunch		
The Main Dining Room		40	Dinner/Lunch	8	
		75	Buffet		
The Small Dining Room		10	Dinner/Lunch	4	

DUNVEGAN CASTLE
Isle of Skye

LOCATION

1 mile north of village.

From Inverness A82 to Invermoriston, A887 to Kyle of Lochalsh 82 miles. From Fort William A82 to Invergarry, A87 to Kyle of Lochalsh 76 miles. Ferry to the Isle of Skye, 'roll-on, roll-off'; 4 minute crossing. Kyle of Lochalsh to Dunvegan 45 miles.

Rail: Inverness to Kyle of Lochalsh 3/4 trains per day - 45 miles.

Bus: Portree 25 miles, Kyle of Lochalsh 45 miles.

DUNVEGAN is unique. It is the only Great House in the Western Isles of Scotland to have retained its family and its roof. It is the oldest home in the whole of Scotland continuously inhabited by the same family - the Chiefs of the Clan Macleod. A Castle placed on a rock by the sea - the curtain wall is dated before 1200 A.D. - its superb location recalls the Norse Empire of the Vikings, the ancestors of the Chiefs.

Dunvegan's continuing importance as a custodian of the Clan spirit is epitomised by the famous Fairy Flag, whose origins are shrouded in mystery but whose ability to protect both Chief and Clan is unquestioned. To enter Dunvegan is to arrive at a place whose history combines with legend to make a living reality.

GARDENS

The gardens and grounds extend over some ten acres of woodland walks, peaceful formal lawns and a water garden dominated by two spectacular natural waterfalls. The temperate climate aids in producing a fine show of rhododendrons and azaleas, the chief glory of the garden in spring. Always one is aware of the proximity of the sea and many garden walks finish at the Castle Jetty, from where traditional boats make regular trips to view the delightful Seal Colony.

EXTRA FACILITIES

SEAL COLONY. 1/2 mile from Castle. Boat trips to see seals at frequent intervals from the Castle Jetty. The Seals are generally undisturbed by people in our small boats and are a joy to study and photograph at close quarters. Loch Cruises on 35 seater motor vessel 1 1/2 hours. cruises throughout the day. Also available for charter and fishing trips. Herd of pedigree Highland Cattle.

ADVICE TO COURIERS & DRIVERS

Please park in Coach Park, 150 metres walk from Castle. DO NOT attempt to take passengers to Castle Jetty, it is a further 50 metres walk. Allow at least 1 hour preferably 2. If possible please book in advance, particularly if it is intended to include the Seal Boat Trip. However, this facility is dependant upon the weather and can not be pre-booked. Dogs allowed in grounds only and must be kept on a leash. No photography within Castle. Parking for 120 cars and 10 coaches 150 yards from the Castle.

FACILITIES FOR THE DISABLED

Disabled and elderly visitors may be left at the entrance to the Castle before parking in the allocated areas. Toilets for the disabled.

CATERING

Licensed restaurant. The Castle Restaurant provides snacks and hot meals throughout the season. Seating 70, special rates are offered to groups, menus upon request. Tel: (0470 22) 310. Open late at height of season for evening meals.

GUIDED TOURS

Tours available by appointment in English or Gaelic at no extra charge. If requested the owner may meet groups. Average time for tour is 45 minutes.

GIFT SHOPS

2 Gift and Craft Shops, one in car park, the other in the Castle. Shops open 10am-5.30pm seven days a week.

GUIDE BOOKS

Full colour guide book £1.70. Translations in French, German, Spanish, Italian and Japanese.

SCHOOL VISITS/CHILDREN

Groups of children are welcome by arrangement. If requested a guide can be available.

ACCOMMODATION

Dunvegan offers 4 self-catering units, 3 of which sleep 6 and 1 of which sleeps 7.

Paul Tomkins

OPENING TIMES

Summer
21 March-29 October

Mon	
Tues	
Wed	10am-5.30pm
Thur	Last entry 5pm
Fri	
Sat	

Sun:-
Gardens, Craft Shop and Restaurant
      10am - 5.30pm
Castle 1.00pm-5.30pm
     Last entry 5pm

Winter
November-March

By appointment.
No boat trips.

ADMISSION

Summer
CASTLE & GARDENS
Adult	£4.00
Child*	£2.20
OAP/Student	£3.60
Group	£3.60

GARDEN ONLY
Adult	£2.40
Child*	£1.50

SEAL BOAT TRIP
Adult	£3.40
Child*	£2.40

LOCH CRUISES
Adult	£6.50
Concessions	£4.50

*Under 16

Winter
By appointment.
No Boat Trips.

FLOORS CASTLE
Kelso, Roxburghshire

FlOORS CASTLE, home of the Roxburghe family is situated in the heart of the Scottish Border Country. It is the largest inhabited Castle in Scotland. Designed by William Adam, who was both masterbuilder and architect, for the first Duke of Roxburghe, building started in 1721.

It was the present Duke's great, great grandfather, James the 6th Duke, who embellished the plain Adam features of the building. In about 1849 Playfair, letting his imagination and talent run riot, transformed the Castle creating a multitude of spires and domes.

Externally the Castle has not been altered since the 6th Duke's time, but internally, several of the rooms, including the Dining Room and Ballroom were remodelled at the turn of the century. These apartments now display the outstanding collection of French 17th and 18th Century furniture,

magnificent tapestries, Chinese and European porcelain and the many other fine works of art. Many of the treasures in the Castle today were collected by Duchess May, American wife of the 8th Duke.

The Castle has been seen on cinema screens worldwide in the film 'Greystoke', as the home of Tarzan, the Earl of Greystoke.

GARDENS

The extensive parkland and gardens overlooking the Tweed provides a variety of wooded walks. The Walled Garden contains splendid herbaceous borders and in the outer walled garden a summerhouse built for Queen Victoria's visit in 1867 can still be seen. An excellent children's playground and picnic area is very close to the Castle.

CONTACT

Frances Brown
Roxburghe Estates Office
Kelso
Scotland
TD5 7SF

Tel: (0573) 223333
Fax: (0573) 226056

LOCATION

From South A68, A698.
From North A68, A697/9.
In Kelso follow signs.

Bus: Kelso Bus Stn 1 mile

Rail: Berwick 20 miles.

OPENING TIMES

Summer

Easter Weekend 1-4 April,
24-28 April, May, June and
September
      Sunday to Thurs.
July & August
      Open Daily
Open   10.30-5.30pm
Last admission
      4.45pm

October
      Sun & Wed.
      10.30am-4.30pm

Winter

November to March
Closed to the general
public.

ADMISSION

Summer

Adults	£3.40
OAPs	£2.60
Children*	£1.70
Family	£8.50
GROUPS**	
Adults	£2.60
OAPs	£2.40
Child*	£1.40

* Aged 8 and over.
** Must be pre-booked.

SUITABILITY FOR OTHER EVENTS

Gala dinners, conferences, product launches, incentive groups, 4x4 driving, highland games and other promotional events.

EXTRA FACILITIES

Include: extensive park, helicopter pad, fishing, clay pigeon shooting and pheasant shooting.

ADVICE TO COURIERS & DRIVERS

Coaches can be driven to the front door of the Castle, there is a waiting area close to the Restaurant exit. Coach drivers are offered a choice of lunch or tea. No photography inside the Castle. No dogs. Unlimited parking for cars, 100 yards away from the Castle, coach park situated 50 yards from the Castle. Guide book in French, German and Italian £1.50.

FACILITIES FOR THE DISABLED

Disabled and elderly visitors may alight at the entrance to the

property, before parking in the allocated areas. Toilets for the disabled.

CATERING

There is a self-service, licensed restaurant seating 125 open from 10.30am, where coffee, lunch and tea are served. Groups can book in advance.

GIFT SHOP

Open same hours as the Castle, Wide range of quality goods.

GUIDED TOURS

Tours lasting $1^1/4$ hours are available on request for up to 100.

SCHOOL VISITS/CHILDREN

School visits are welcome and a guide will be provided. Cost per child £1.40. Playground facilities.

CONFERENCE AND FUNCTION FACILITIES

ROOM	DIMENSIONS	CAPACITY	LAYOUT	POWER POINTS	SUITABLE FOR A/V
Dining Room	18.3mx7.3m	150	Theatre	✓	✓
		90	Lunch/Dinner		
		50	Boardroom		
Ballroom	21.1mx7.9m	150	Theatre	✓	✓
		50	Boardroom		
Roxburghe Room		25	Boardroom	✓	✓
(In Sunlaws House Hotel)					

GLAMIS CASTLE
Glamis, Angus

GLAMIS CASTLE is the family home of the Earls of Strathmore and Kinghorne and has been a royal residence since 1372. It is the childhood home of Her Majesty Queen Elizabeth The Queen Mother, the birthplace of Her Royal Highness The Princess Margaret and the legendary setting of Shakespeare's play 'Macbeth'. Though the Castle is open to visitors it remains a family home lived in and loved by the Strathmore family.

The Castle, a five-storey 'L' shaped tower block, was originally a royal hunting lodge. It was remodelled in the 17th Century and is built of pink sandstone. It contains the Great Hall, with its magnificent plasterwork ceiling dated 1621, a beautiful family Chapel constructed inside the Castle in 1688, an 18th Century Billiard Room housing what is left of the extensive library once at Glamis, a 19th century Dining Room containing family portraits and the Royal Apartments which have been used by Her Majesty Queen Elizabeth The Queen Mother. The Castle stands in an extensive park, landscaped towards the end of the 18th Century, and contains the beautiful Italian Garden which reflects the peace and serenity of the Castle and grounds.

CONTACT

Lt Col. P J Cardwell Moore
Estates Office
Glamis Castle
Glamis
By Forfar
Angus
DD8 1RJ

Tel: (0307) 840242
Fax: (0307) 840257

LOCATION

From Edinburgh M90, A94, 81 miles. From Forfar A94, 6 miles. From Glasgow 101 miles.

Motorway: M90.

Rail: Dundee Station 12 miles.

Air: Dundee Airport 12 miles.

Taxi: C M Walker, Glamis 270.

SUITABILITY FOR OTHER EVENTS

Grand dinners, receptions, fashion shows, archery, clay pigeon shooting, equestrian events, garden parties, shows, rallies, filming, product launches, highland games and wedding receptions.

EXTRA FACILITIES

Grand piano in the Great Drawing Room.

ADVICE TO COURIERS & DRIVERS

Coach drivers and couriers are admitted free of charge. No photography within the Castle. Beware the narrow gates, they are wide enough to take buses.

FACILITIES FOR THE DISABLED

Disabled toilet available. Disabled visitors may alight at the Castle entrance. Those in wheelchairs will be unable to tour the Castle but may visit the Coach House Exhibition.

PARKING FOR COACHES & CARS

Capacity of the car park - 500 cars, 30 yards from Castle, 20 coaches 50 yards from Castle.

CATERING

Self-service, licensed restaurant serving morning coffees, light lunches and afternoon teas. Seating for 100 in old Castle Kitchen. The State Rooms are also available for Grand Dinners.

GIFT SHOP

Open when Castle is open to visitors. Items include: glass, china, clothing, pictures and tea towels. The Garden Shop is open at the same time.

GUIDE BOOKS

Full colour guide book in English, French, German, Italian, Spanish and Japanese £2.20.

GUIDED TOURS

All visits are guided - average time 50/60 minutes. Tours can be conducted by prior arrangement in French, German, Italian and Spanish.

SCHOOL VISITS/CHILDREN

School groups are welcome with one teacher admitted free for every 10 children. Facilities include a nature trail, family exhibition room, Estate exhibition in Coach House, dolls house and play area.

OPENING TIMES

Summer
1 April - 30 October

Daily 10.30 - 5.30pm
Last Admission 4.45pm.

Winter

By appointment,
Visits are welcome.

ADMISSION

Summer

HOUSE & GARDEN
Adult	£4.20
Child*	£2.30
OAP/Student	£3.30
Family	£12.50
Group**	
Adult	£3.80
Child*	£2.00
OAP	£2.90

GARDEN ONLY
Adult	£2.00
Child*	£1.00
OAP	£1.00
Disabled	FREE
Group**	
Adult	£2.00
Child*	£1.00
OAP	£1.00

*Under 16.
** Minimum payment 20 people.

Winter

By arrangement.

CONFERENCE AND FUNCTION FACILITIES

ROOM	DIMENSIONS	CAPACITY	LAYOUT	POWER POINTS	SUITABLE FOR A/V
Dining Room	84 sq.m.	120	Buffet	✓	✓
		120	Theatre		
Restaurant	140 sq.m.	100	Buffet	✓	✓
		100	Theatre		

HARBURN HOUSE
West Lothian

HARBURN HOUSE is a magnificent Georgian mansion built in 1807 after the original mansion was blown up by Oliver Cromwell. The stables belonging to the old house still remain and are in use. The estate and immediate locality provide riding, tennis, fishing and for the golf enthusiast there is a local course adjoining the estate and Gleneagles, St Andrews, Muirfield and Dalmahoy courses are all an easy drive. Harburn House can be rented for any period whether it be a few hours or weeks at a time, EXCLUSIVELY FOR YOUR USE. It is an ideal place for executives seeking a business meeting retreat for client contact and entertainment or for parties wanting the 'away from it all' luxury of a country residence.

GARDENS

Harburn House is completely secluded within its own 3,000 acres of farmland and forest. The house is set in 100 acres of Parkland overlooking lakes with commanding view of the Pentland Hills.

CONTACT

Rozi Spurway
Harburn House
Harburn
West Calder
West Lothian
EH55 8RN

Tel: (0506) 461818
Fax: (0506) 416591

LOCATION

Almost equidistant between Glasgow and Edinburgh and within one hour of The Borders, Perth, Stirling or Dundee.

SUITABILITY FOR OTHER EVENTS

Weddings, Activity Days. Conferences. Incentives, Product Launches, Shooting Parties, Filming, Concerts.

EXTRA FACILITIES

Any form of facilities available; i.e. Golf, Riding, Shooting, Falconry, Archery and most other sports. Also members of nearby Golf and Country Club for guest use.

ACCOMMODATION

Harburn House offers: 12 Double/Twin rooms with bathrooms, 2 Four poster suites and two self-catering units (1 for 8, 1 for 4/6).

The House is always exclusive to one party. The grounds are available for almost any leisure pursuit. The bedrooms are available for single or double occupancy. All catering is done by our own staff.

ADVICE TO COURIERS & DRIVERS

Dogs on leads. All traffic to follow one way system. Vehicles should not park on grass verges. Parking for up to 300 cars/coaches 100 yards from house summer, 50 cars/coaches winter.

FACILITIES FOR THE DISABLED.

Disabled and elderly visitors may alight at the house entrance.

CATERING

High quality in-house catering available for all functions. Menus, prices available upon request.

ADMISSION

The exclusive use of House and Grounds for activity days with no accommodation
Per day   £575

Accommodation Rates:
Single with Bath   £78.50
Double with Bath   £105

Dinner, Bed & Breakfast
Single   £94.50
Double per person
                    £78.50
Day Delegate Rate
                     £27

VAT is not included in the above rates.

CONFERENCE AND FUNCTION FACILITIES

ROOM	DIMENSIONS	CAPACITY	LAYOUT	POWER POINTS	SUITABLE FOR A/V
Conference Room	30'x18'	20	Boardroom	6	✓
		20	Lunch/Dinner		
Drawing Room	30'x18'	30	Schoolroom	10	✓
		20	Boardroom		
		40	Theatre		
Dining Room	30'x18'	30	Schoolroom	6	✓
		20	Boardroom		
		40	Theatre		
		40	Lunch/Dinner		
Library	14'x12'	10	Schoolroom	4	✓
		8	Boardroom		
		15	Theatre		
Morning Room	16'x15'	12	Schoolroom		✓
		12	Boardroom		
		20	Theatre		
WHOLE HOUSE	All above rooms	80	Buffet		
		60	Lunch/Dinner		✓
Marquee	120'x40' MAX	400	Schoolroom	As required	✓
		500	Buffet		
		500	Theatre		
		400	Lunch/Dinner		

HOPETOUN HOUSE
South Queensferry, Near Edinburgh

HOPETOUN HOUSE, 'Scotland's Finest Stately Home', is a gem of Europe's architectural heritage. Set in a hundred acres of parkland on the shores of the Forth with fine views of the famous Forth bridges to the east.

Hopetoun has been the home of the Hope family since it was built. The head of the family, formerly known as the Earl of Hopetoun was created Marquess of Linlithgow in 1901 after serving as the first Governor General of Australia. The 2nd Marquess served as Viceroy of India from 1936-1943. The present head of the family, Adrian, the 4th Marquess of Linlithgow lives in a private wing of the House.

The original House was designed by Sir William Bruce and built between 1699 and 1702. Enlargements were made by William Adam and his 3 sons John, Robert and James from 1721. Much of the original furniture made for the rooms in the 1760's survives today. Paintings by many famous artists adorn the State Apartments and there is a fine collection of 17th century tapestries and Meissen ornaments.

Separate exhibitions include 'The Building of Hopetoun', 'Horse and Man in Scotland' and 'Wildlife' a seasonal display of particular interest to children. To the west of the House there are magnificent woodland walks, a Red Deer Park, nature trails and a profusion of wild flowers. A Countryside Ranger is in attendance.

CONTACT

Capt R H Fox RN
Hopetoun House
South Queensferry
Edinburgh
EH30 9SL

Tel: (031) 331 2451
Fax: (031) 319 1885

LOCATION

2¹/2 miles west of Forth Road Bridge.

12 miles west of Edinburgh (25 mins. drive).

34 miles east of Glasgow (50 mins. drive).

SUITABILITY FOR OTHER EVENTS

A major venue in Scotland for private functions and special events throughout the year; Receptions, Gala Dinners, Antique Fairs, Concerts, Scottish Gala Evenings, Conferences.

EXTRA FACILITIES

Grand piano in Library. Boules (Petanque), Piste and Croquet Lawn. Helicopter landing.

ADVICE TO COURIERS & DRIVERS

Pre-book if possible. No smoking or flash photography in House. No dogs in house but welcome (on leads) in Grounds. Free parking close to the house.

CATERING

The Tapestry Room licensed Restaurant caters for 50-60 people. Groups (up to 250) can book in advance for lunch, afternoon tea and other meals in the Ballroom. Menus available on request (Tel: Banqueting Dept. 031 331 4305)

FACILITIES FOR THE DISABLED

Restaurant, toilet facilities and exhibitions all on ground floor and easily accessible.

GIFT SHOP

Daily 10.30am-5.30pm. Wide range of quality Scottish goods.

GUIDED TOURS

Normally visitors tour at leisure but special guided tours can be arranged in advance. Foreign language guides usually available.

SCHOOL VISITS/CHILDREN

Holders of 2 Sandford Awards for Heritage Education. Special tours in House and/or Grounds for different age/interest groups. Of particular interest; Family life in Georgian and Victorian times, Nature trails with Countryside Ranger, Red Deer park. Teachers information pack available. Childrens Guide Book.

OPENING TIMES

Summer

1 April - 2 October

Mon	
Tues	
Wed	
Thur	10am-5.30pm
Fri	Last entry 4.45pm
Sat	
Sun	

Earlier admission for parties by prior arrangement. Booking for large groups advisable.

Winter

3 October - Easter

Closed except for group visits by prior arrangement.
Open throughout the year for booked functions.

ADMISSION

Summer

HOUSE & GROUNDS
Adult	£3.80
Child**	£1.90
OAP	£3.10
Student	£3.10

GROUP*
Adult	£3.10
Child**	£1.70
OAP	£3.10
Student	£3.10

* 20 or more people
**Age 5-16
   Under 5's Free

Guided Tours (Max 20 per guide) £10.00.

Winter

Out of season rates

CONFERENCE AND FUNCTION FACILITIES

ROOM	DIMENSIONS	CAPACITY	LAYOUT	POWER POINTS	SUITABLE FOR A/V
Ballroom	92'x35'	350	Theatre/Buffet	✓	✓
	Height 28'	250	Dinner/Dance		
		370	Lunch/Dinner		
Tapestry Room	37'x24'	100	Theatre	✓	✓
(adjacent to	Height 28'	50	U-Shape/Boardroom/Dinner/Dance		
Ballroom)		70	Lunch/Buffet		
*Red Drawing Room	44'x24'	100	Theatre	✓	
	Height 22'	40	U-Shape/Boardroom		
		60	Lunch/Dinner		
*State Dining Room	39'x23'16'	20	Lunch/Dinner	✓	
* (In Main House)					

Ballroom

INVERARAY CASTLE
Argyll

The Duke of Argyll's family have lived in Inveraray since the early 15th Century. The present Castle was built between 1740 and 1790.

The ancient Royal Burgh of Inveraray lies about 60 miles north west of Glasgow by Loch Fyne in an area of spectacular natural beauty combining the ruggedness of highland scenery with the sheltered tidal loch 90 miles from the open sea.

The Castle, is the home of the Duke and Duchess of Argyll. Its fairy tale exterior belies the grandeur of its gracious interior. The building was designed by Roger Morris and decorated by Robert Mylne, the clerk of works being William Adam, father of Robert and John, who did much of the laying out of the present Royal Burgh, an unrivalled example of an early planned town.

Visitors to the Castle may see the famous Armoury Hall containing some 1300 pieces, French tapestries made especially for the Castle, fine examples of Scottish, English and French furniture together with a wealth of other works of art including China, Silver and family artifacts, all of which form a unique collection spanning the generations which are identified by a magnificent genealogical display in the Clan Room.

CONTACT

The Factor
Dept HHD
Argyll Estates Office
Cherry Park
Inveraray
Argyll
PA32 8XE

Tel: (0499) 2203
Fax: (0499) 2421

LOCATION

From Edinburgh 2¹/₂-3 hours via Glasgow.

Bus: Bus route stopping point within ¹/₂ mile.

ADVICE TO COURIERS & DRIVERS

It is preferable that party bookings are made in advance. No dogs and no photography.

FACILITIES FOR THE DISABLED

Disabled and elderly visitors may alight at the entrance to the castle before parking in the car park close by. There is a wheelchair ramp to the Castle plus two steps. All main public rooms may be visited by the infirm and those in wheelchairs, but there are two long flights of stairs to the smaller rooms upstairs. Toilet facilities are suitable for disabled visitors although not specially adapted.

PARKING FOR COACHES & CARS

Parking for approximately 100 cars. Separate coach park close to Castle.

CATERING

The Tea Room seats up to 50 people for afternoon tea and other meals. Menus are available on request and groups can book in advance. Telephone 0499 2112.

GIFT SHOP

Open at the same time as the Castle.

GUIDE BOOKS

Colour guide book, £1.50. French, Italian, Japanese and German translations available.

GUIDED TOURS

Tours can be arranged for up to 100 people at no additional cost. Average time taken 1 hour.

SCHOOL VISITS/CHILDREN

School parties are welcome. £1.25 per child in organised party. If requested a guide can be provided. Areas of interest include a nature walk, special school project, wild life park (nearby) and War Museum.

OPENING TIMES

Summer
2 April-9 October

Mon	
Tues	10am-1pm &
Wed	2pm-5.30pm
Thur	
Fri	Closed
Sat	10am-1pm &
	2pm-5.30pm
Sun	1pm-5.30pm

July - August
Open 10am-5.30pm
(inc. Fridays)

Last admissions
12.30pm & 5..00pm

ADMISSION

Summer

HOUSE ONLY
Adult	£3.50
Child*	£1.75
OAP	£2.50
Family (2+2)	£9.00
Group**	
20% Discount	

*Under 16
** Minimum number 20 people

Winter

Closed

CONFERENCE AND FUNCTION FACILITIES

THE PUBLIC ROOMS ARE AVAILABLE DURING THE WINTER PERIOD IN CONJUNCTION WITH THE GREAT INN, INVERARAY AS REQUIRED FOR ACCOMMODATION

ROOM	DIMENSIONS	CAPACITY	LAYOUT	POWER POINTS	SUITABLE FOR A/V
State Dining Room	30'x22'	50	Lunch/Dinner	3	
Tapestry Drawing	45'x21'	200	Lecture Room	4	✓
Room		90	Lunch/Dinner		
Armoury Hall	23'x31'	120	Assembly	2	✓
Saloon	24'x44'	200	Lecture	2	✓

KELBURN CASTLE
Fairlie, Ayrshire

The historic home of the Boyle family, later Earls of Glasgow, Kelburn is situated on the picturesque north Ayrshire coast. Kelburn Castle dates from the 13th Century and is thought to be the oldest Castle in Scotland to be inhabited by the same family throughout its history. The original 1200 Norman Keep was extended in 1580 by a Tower House, and an elegant William and Mary Mansion House was added in 1700 by David Boyle, who was created 1st Earl of Glasgow by Queen Anne in 1703 for his role in persuading reluctant Jacobite nobles to sign the Act of Union. A Victorian wing was built in 1879. Kelburn's essential charm is its informal family atmosphere, varied interior decor, and stunning location.

The grounds at Kelburn are quite lovely. Romantic Kelburn Glen with winding woodland trails, waterfalls and deep gorges. Featured gardens are the Plaisance, a formal walled garden dominated by two magnificent 1000 year old Yew trees, and the Children's Garden which is planted in the shape and colours of the Saltire. An extraordinary mutant Weeping Larch, Scotland's oldest and tallest Monterey Pine, a Robert Adam Monument, 18th Century Sundial and Ice House are among Kelburn's featured natural and historical attractions.

The Country Centre includes a Riding Centre, Commando Assault Course, Adventure Course, Children's Stockade, Soft Play Room, Pets Corner, Ranger Centre, The Kelburn Story, Museum, Craft Workshop, Information Office and Picnic Areas.

A new attraction in 1994 will be the "Discovery Wood".

CONTACT

Earl of Glasgow
Kelburn Castle & Country
Centre
South Offices
Fairlie
Ayrshire
KA29 0BE

Tel: (0475) 568685
Fax: 0475 568328

LOCATION

M8 Edinburgh to Glasgow, M8 Glasgow to Greenock, A78 to Largs, A78 main coastal trunk road.

Rail: Largs station 2 miles.

Bus: A78 main bus route to Ayr, stop adjacent to property.

Taxis: A2B taxis (0475) 673976.

SUITABILITY FOR OTHER EVENTS

The property is suitable for a variety of indoor and outdoor events. Consideration given to all enquiries, rates negotiable.

EXTRA FACILITIES

Gardens, Grounds. Golf Club adjacent. The pavilion is available for buffets, exhibitions, nature activities and barbecues.

ADVICE TO COURIERS & DRIVERS

Visitors to Kelburn Castle arriving by coach can alight at the Castle forecourt. The coach must then leave and return via the estate exit and use Country Centre car park. This is approx 5/10 mins walk from the Castle, next to the Country Centre buildings.

PARKING FOR COACHES & CARS

Space for 60 or more cars and 20 coaches, see advice above

CATERING

There is a licensed restaurant and a cafe at the country centre. Groups can book in advance. Special rates offered to groups. Full catering facilities available for special functions/conferences in the Castle, outside caterers may also be used.

FACILITIES FOR THE DISABLED

Elderly and disabled visitors may alight at the entrance to the Castle before vehicles are parked. Toilets for the disabled.

GIFT SHOP

The gift shop in the country centre carries souvenirs, craft items etc. Open throughout the summer season.

GUIDED TOURS

Tours available with maximum party size of 25 at no additional cost. Average time for a tour is 45 minutes. With prior notice lectures can be provided on the Castle, grounds, history etc.

SCHOOL VISITS/CHILDREN

Groups welcome £1.25 per child. Guide provided on request, schoolroom available at Ranger Centre. Nature activities, pets corner, assault course, soft play room, mini Quad Bikes (high season), pony trekking, riding lessons, Adventure Course. Opening in 1994 "Discovery Wood".

OPENING TIMES

Summer

KELBURN CASTLE
July and August
(Except when there are afternoon functions)

Tours hourly
          2pm and 5pm.
Tours can be arranged at other times of the year.

COUNTRY CENTRE & GARDENS
Easter-mid October
Daily   10am-6pm.

Winter

CASTLE
By special arrangement only.

COUNTRY CENTRE
Mid October-Easter
          11am-5pm
Grounds only.

ADMISSION

Summer
HOUSE ONLY
		Group*
Adult	£1.50	£1.20
Child**	£1.50	£1.20
OAP	£1.50	£1.20
Student	£1.50	£120

(These prices are Exclusive of entry fee to Centre)
COUNTRY CENTRE
		Group*
Adult	£3.50	£2.00
Child**	£2.00	£1.50
OAP	£2.00	£1.30
Student	£1.50	£1.25

Winter
HOUSE ONLY
As Summer rates

COUNTRY CENTRE
Adult	£1.50
Child**	£1.00

*Minimum number 12
**Accompanied children 2-school age.

CONFERENCE AND FUNCTION FACILITIES

ROOM	DIMENSIONS	CAPACITY	LAYOUT	POWER POINTS	SUITABLE FOR A/V
Drawing Room	33'x24'	60	Lunch/Dinner		
Dining Room		53	Seated Dinner		
		120	Buffet		

PRESENTLY THERE ARE NO FORMAL CONFERENCE FACILITIES.

MANDERSTON
Berwickshire, Scotland

MANDERSTON, together with its magnificent stables, stunning marble dairy and 56 acres of immaculate garden, forms an ensemble which must be unique in Britain today.

The House was completely rebuilt between 1903 and 1905, with no expense spared.

Visitors are able to see not only the sumptuous State Rooms and bedrooms, decorated in the Adam manner, but also all the original domestic offices, in a truly 'Upstairs Downstairs' atmosphere. Manderston boasts a unique and recently restored silver staircase.

There is a special museum with a nostalgic display of valuable tins made by Huntley and Palmers from 1868 to the present day.

GARDENS

Outside, the magnificence continues and the combination of formal gardens and picturesque landscapes is a major attraction: unique amongst Scottish houses.

The stables, still in use, have been described by 'Horse and Hound' as "probably the finest in all the wide world."

CONTACT

The Lord or Lady Palmer
Manderston
Duns
Berwickshire
Scotland
TD11 3PP

Tel: (0361) 83450
Fax: (0361) 82010

LOCATION

From Edinburgh 47 miles, 1 hour.

Bus: 400 yards.

Rail: Berwick Station 12 miles, 3½ hours, from London.

Taxi: Chirnside 818216.

Air: Edinburgh or Newcastle Airport, both 60 miles.

SUITABILITY FOR OTHER EVENTS

Fashion shows, air displays, archery, clay pigeon shooting, equestrian events, garden parties, shows, rallies, filming, wedding receptions, product launches and marathons. Almost anything is possible by arrangement.

EXTRA FACILITIES

Two airstrips for light aircraft, approx 5 mls. Grand Piano, Full-size Billiard Table. Fox hunting, pheasant shoots (up to 600 birds per day). Sea Angling on coast, salmon on River Tweed. Stabling for 20 horses, cricket pitch, tennis court, lake. Nearby: 9 hole golf course, indoor swimming pool, squash court.

ACCOMMODATION

Manderston offers : 5 twin and 4 doubles.

ADVICE TO COURIERS& DRIVERS

It is appreciated and helpful if party fees can be paid by one person on arrival. Dogs (grounds only) on leads. No photography inside House. Please allow plenty of time as there is so much to see. Parking for 400 cars, 125 yds from House, 30 coaches 5 yds from the House.

FACILITIES FOR THE DISABLED

Cars containing disabled visitors can park outside the House. No special toilet facilities.

CATERING

Tea Room (capacity 80) open during day, waitress service. Afternoon Tea from £1.60, £10-£35 other meals. Meals can be booked in advance. menus upon request. Menu can include local smoked trout pate, pheasant in mushroom and red wine sauce and strawberry mousse, prices include pre-meal cocktails and wines. For special functions/conferences, buffets, lunches and dinners can be arranged.

GIFT SHOP

Open same time as House, other times by arrangement. Colour guide book, £2.00.

GUIDED TOURS

At no additional cost tours available in French and English. When House open, guides posted in most rooms. If requested the owner may meet groups. Average time for tour 1¼ hours.

SCHOOL VISITS/CHILDREN

Groups welcome, £1.50 per child, min. £45. A guide can be provided. The Biscuit Tin Museum is of particular interest.

OPENING TIMES

Summer
5 May - 29 September

Mon	Bank Holidays 30 May, 29 Aug 2pm-5.30pm
Tue Wed	By arrangement
Thurs	2pm-5.30pm
Fri Sat	By arrangement
Sun	2pm-5.30pm

NB Any other date/time by arrangement.

Winter
September-May

Any date by arrangement.

ADMISSION

Summer and Winter

HOUSE & GARDEN

		Group*
Adult	£5.00	£3.00
Child**	£1.00	£1.50

GARDEN ONLY

		Group*
Adult	£2.50	£2.00
Child**	£0.50	£0.50

*Minimum payment - Open Days £60.00, Non-Open Days £100.00.
**Up to 16 years

CONFERENCE AND FUNCTION FACILITIES

ROOM	DIMENSIONS	CAPACITY	LAYOUT	POWER POINTS	SUITABLE FOR A/V
Dining Room	22'x35'	22	Boardroom	✓	✓
		100	Buffet		
		40	Lunch/Dinner		
Ballroom	34'x21'	150	Theatre	✓	✓
Hall	22'x38'	130	Theatre	✓	✓
Drawing Room	35'x21'	150	Theatre	✓	✓

SCONE PALACE
Perth

SCONE PALACE, just outside Perth is the home of the Earls of Mansfield. Here Kenneth MacAlpine united Scotland and in 838AD, placed the stone of Scone upon the Moot Hill which became the Crowning Place of Scottish kings, including Macbeth and Robert the Bruce. Edward I moved the Coronation Stone to Westminster in 1296.

The Abbey of Scone and the Bishops' Palace were ransacked and burned in 1559. The Gowries built a new Palace in 1580, which was enlarged and embellished around 1804 by the Third Earl and houses a fabulous collection of French furniture, clocks, 16th Century needlework (including bed hangings, worked by Mary Queen of Scots), ivories, objets d'art and Vernis Martin and one of the finest collections of Porcelain in the country.

GARDENS

Scone's famous Pinetum is a unique collection of rare pines, some of which are over 150 feet high and still growing. There are pleasant walks through 100 acres of Wild Garden which offer the visitor magnificent displays of daffodils, rhododendrons and azaleas.

There is a fine picnic area, an adventure playground and a collection of veteran machinery. A cricket pitch and pavilion in an attractive setting is ideal for a variety of outdoor functions.

SUITABILITY FOR OTHER EVENTS

Grand dinners, receptions, fashion shows, war games, archery, clay pigeon shooting, equestrian events, garden parties, shows, rallies, filming, shooting and fishing, floodlit tattoos, weddings, product launches, highland games.

EXTRA FACILITIES

Including organ, parkland, cricket pitch, airfield, helicopter landing and croquet. Speciality lectures can be arranged. Race course, polo field, firework displays, adventure playground.

ADVICE TO COURIERS & DRIVERS

Please advise in advance, especially if catering required. Couriers and drivers admitted free to all facilities, free meal available. Advisable to pre-book especially groups over 60. Advise ticket seller at coach park if handicapped visitors require transport to Palace. Couriers of booked parties receive token on last visit of season, value dependent on visits.

FACILITIES FOR THE DISABLED

Ideal as all the State Rooms on one level. Special wheelchair access to Restaurants. Disabled and elderly visitors may alight at entrance. Toilet facilities for the disabled.

PARKING FOR COACHES & CARS

500 cars and 15 coaches 100 yards from the Palace.

CATERING

Two Restaurants/Tea Rooms capacity 54 and 66. Teas from £1.75, lunches from £5, dinners from £18. All meals can be booked in advance, menus upon request, special rates for groups. Large numbers can be accepted for buffets and grand dinners in State Rooms a speciality. Receptions, weddings, cocktail parties etc., all prepared by the Palace's own chef.

GIFT SHOP

Produce Shop and Gift Shop open as Palace. Guide book, £2.20, in seven languages. 1 page introduction available in 10 languages.

GUIDED TOURS

Free. English speaking guides in all rooms. Out of hours parties have 1 guide per tour. Average time for tour 45 minutes. Personal French and German guides usually available by appointment for which there is a charge.

CONTACT

Lt Cdr. A R Robinson
Scone Palace
Perth
PH2 6BD

Tel: (0738) 52300
Fax: (0738) 52588

LOCATION

From Edinburgh Forth Bridge M90, M85, A85, A93 1 hour.

Bus: 2 buses a day from Perth.

Rail: Perth Station 3 miles.

Motorway: M90 from Edinburgh.

Taxi: Perth Radio Cabs (0738) 28171.

OPENING TIMES

Summer
1 April-10 October

Mon	
Tues	
Wed	
Thur	9.30am-5pm
Fri	
Sat	
Sun	1.30pm-5pm
	July & Aug
	10am-5pm

Evening tours by appointment.

Winter
11 October-13 April

By appointment only.

ADMISSION

Summer
HOUSE & GARDEN

		Group*
Adult	£4.20	£3.70
Child**	£2.30	£2.10
OAP	£3.40	£3.10
Family	£12.50	

GARDEN ONLY

		Group*
Adult	£2.10	£2.10
Child**	£1.15	£1.15
OAP	£2.10	£2.10

*Minimum 20 people
**Age 5-16

Winter

Per person	£8.00

(£160 minimum payment)

CONFERENCE AND FUNCTION FACILITIES

ROOM	DIMENSIONS	CAPACITY	LAYOUT	POWER POINTS	SUITABLE FOR A/V
State Dining Room	50'x24'	20/50	Lunch/Dinner	16	✓
Long Gallery	140'x20'	250	Theatre/Buffet	8	✓
		90	Lunch/Dinner		
Queen Victoria's Room	20'x20'	35	Theatre\Buffet	4	✓
		20	Schoolroom		
		24	U-Shape		
		18	Boardroom		
		16	Lunch/Dinner		
Drawing Room	50'x24'	90	Theatre	20	✓

TRAQUAIR
Innerleithen, Peeblesshire

TRAQUAIR, situated amidst beautiful scenery and close by the River Tweed, is the oldest inhabited house in Scotland - visited by twenty-seven kings. Originally a Royal Hunting Lodge it was owned by the Scottish Crown until 1478 when it passed to a branch of the Royal Stuart family whose descendants still live in the house today.

From a single tower block the building grew reflecting the growth and importance of the Stuarts of Traquair and no exterior alterations were made after the end of the 17th Century. At the end of the tree lined avenue leading to the House are the famous Bear Gates, still closed since 1745 when the last person to pass through them was Bonnie Prince Charlie (not to be opened again until the restoration of the Stuarts).

Nearly ten centuries of Scottish political and domestic life can be traced from the collection of treasurers in the House. It is particularly rich in associations with the Catholic Church in Scotland, Mary Queen of Scots and the Jacobite Risings.

GARDEN

70 acres of grounds with peacocks, ducks and other wild life. In spring there is a profusion of daffodils followed by rhododendrons, wild flowers and herbaceous plants. A maze in Beech/Leylandi Cyprus is behind the House.

CONTACT

Ms C Maxwell Stuart
Traquair House
Innerleithen
Peeblesshire
EH44 6PW

Tel: (0896)830323

LOCATION

From Edinburgh 1 hour, Glasgow 1 1/2 hours, Carlisle 1 1/2 hours, Newcastle 2 1/2 hours. On B709 near Junction with A72.

Rail: Edinburgh Waverley 30 miles.

Bus: Hourly bus service from Edinburgh to Innerleithen. Enquiries Eastern Scottish (031) 558 1616.

Taxi: Leithen Valley Taxis. Innerleithen 830486.

SUITABILITY FOR OTHER EVENTS

Garden parties, Weddings receptions, product launches, filming, archery clay pigeon shooting, theatre, son et lumiere.

EXTRA FACILITIES

18th Century fully operational Brewhouse, ale tasting every Friday between 3pm-4pm. 17th Century harpsichord in Drawing Room, croquet (mallets can be hired) Lectures provided on the property, contents , history and grounds.

ADVICE TO COURIERS & DRIVERS

Coaches preferably booked in advance. Drivers please apply for vouchers on arrival. Dogs on leads in grounds. No photography in House. Introductory talks can be given to groups. Out of hours visits with meals and refreshments by prior arrangement.

GIFT SHOP

Open as House, selling Traquair House Ale, wine and crafts.

CATERING

Licensed self-service 1745 Cottage Tearoom. One fine days lunches and teas can be taken outdoors. Marquee (lined and floored) available for receptions, weddings, etc., in the gardens or the courtyard. Parties up to 45 can be served in the Bear Cottage. Lunches and dinners in the house dining room from £25 by special arrangement

ACCOMMODATION

Traquair offers 2 fourposter suites with bathroom. 1 self-catering flat with double bedroom.

FACILITIES FOR THE DISABLED

Disabled and elderly visitors may alight at the entrance to the property, before parking in the allocated area. Toilets for the disabled.

PARKING FOR COACHES & CARS

Capacity of car park: 200 cars and 5 coaches 85 yards from the House. (Advance booking requested for coaches).

GUIDE BOOKS

Colour guide book, £1.50. Translations in French, Spanish, German, Dutch, Swedish, Japanese and Italian. Childrens guide books and quiz sheets.

GUIDED TOURS

Tours only outside opening hours £3.75 per person (£75 min).

CONFERENCE AND FUNCTION FACILITIES

ROOM	DIMENSIONS	CAPACITY	LAYOUT	POWER POINTS	SUITABLE FOR A/V
Dining Room	33'x18'	22	Lunches	3	✓
		16	Schoolroom		
		30	Buffet		
			Lunch/Dinner		
Drawing Room	27'x24'	50/60	Drinks	3	✓

BORDERS

Abbortsford House, Melrose.
(0896) 2043   3 miles west of Melrose just south of A72.

The Hirsel Grounds, .& Dundock Wood, Coldstream.
(0890) 882834

MELLERSTAIN HOUSE

OPEN
Easter
Weekedend
Friday-Monday

1 May-30 Sept.
Daily except
Saturdays

12.30pm-5.00pm

MELLERSTAIN, KELSO TEL: 0573 410225
(The Earl of Haddington)

One of Scotland's great Georgian houses and a unique example of the work of the Adam family; the two wings built in 1725 by William Adam, the large central block by his son, Robert 1770-78. Rooms contain fine plasterwork, colourful ceilings and marble fireplaces. The Library is considered as Robert Adam's finest creation. Many fine paintings and period furniture.

Location: From Edinburgh A68 to Earlston, turn left 5 miles, signposted.
Admission: Adults £3.50, OAP £3.00. Children £1.50. Groups (Min. 20) £3.00.

Mertoun Gardens, St. Boswells, Roxburghshire.
(0835) 23236. 2 miles north east of St Boswells on the B6404.

Neidpath Castle, Peebles.
(0721) 720333 1 mile west of Peebles on A72.

PAXTON HOUSE

OPEN
Good Friday - 31
October

Daily

Noon- 5.00pm

Last tour of
House
4.15pm.

PAXTON HOUSE, BERWICK UPON TWEED TEL: 0289 386291
(Paxton Trust)

Built in 1756 by John and James Adam for Patrick Home of Billie, Paxton House is a fine example of an 18th century Neo-Palladian mansion. A later picture gallery has been completely restored and is now exhibiting pictures on loan from the National Galleries of Scotland. The House and Picture Gallery were furnished respectively by Chippendale and Trotter and many examples of their furniture are on display.

Location: 5 miles west of Berwick upon Tweed on B6461, on north bank of River Tweed.
Admission: Adults £3.50, Children £1.75.

Priorwood Garden, Melrose.
(089682) 2965 In Melrose.

Robert Smail's Printing Works, Tweeddale.
(0896) 830206   In Innerleithen High Street, 30 miles south of Edinburgh.

THIRLESTANE CASTLE

OPEN
Easter 1-8 April
1 May-30 Sept.
Sun, Mon, Wed,
Thurs afternoons
from 2pm (Last
adm. 4.30pm)
July & Aug.
Every afternoon
except Sat.

Party tours at
other times by
arrangement.

THIRLESTANE CASTLE, LAUDER TEL: 0578 722430
(Thirlestane Castle Trust)

One of Scotland's oldest and finest castles standing in lovely Border countryside. Thirlestane was the seat of the Earls and Dukes of Lauderdale and is still home to the Maitland family. Unsurpassed 17th century ceilings, fine portrait.collection, large collection of historic toys, country life exhiibitions. Tearoom, gift shop, woodland walks. ASVA commended. MGC Registered. State rooms available for functions.

Location: Off A68 at Lauder, 28 miles south of Edinburgh.
Admission: Adults £3.50, Family £9.00. Party £3.00. Grounds only £1.00

CENTRAL

Stirling Castle, Stirling.
(031 244) 3101 In Stirling.

DUMFRIES & GALLOWAY

ARBIGLAND GARDENS

OPEN
1 May-30 Sept.

Tues - Sun
Plus Bank Hol.
Mons.

2.00-6.00pm

House Open
21-30 May

ARBIGLAND GARDENS, KIRKBEAN TEL: 038788 283
(Capt. and Mrs Beauchamp Blackett)

Formal, woodland and water gardens which have evolved through three centuries. The ideal family outing garden as the gardens run down to a sheltered sandy bay where the younger members (and dogs!) can let off steam. 400 yards from John Paul Jones Birthplace Museum, whose father created the gardens circa 1750.

Location: 15 miles from Dumfries off A710 'Solway Coast Road'.
Admission: Adults £2.00, OAP £1.50, Youngsters 50p, toddlers Free.

Caerlaverock Castle, near Dumfries.
8 miles south south east of Dumfries on B725.

Carlyle's Birthplace, Ecclefechan.
(05763) 666   5 miles south east of Lockerbie on A74.

Drumlanrig Castle & Country Park, Thornhill.
(0848) 31682   18 miles north of Dumfries, 3 miles north of Thornhill off A76.

Logan Botanic Garden, Port Logan.

Rammerscales, Lockerbie.
(038781) 0229   5 miles west of Lockerbie.

Sweetheart Abbey, New Abbey.
7 miles south of Dumfries on A710.

Threave Garden, near Castle Douglas.
(0556) 2575   1 mile west of Castle Douglas off A75.

CASTLE KENNEDY GARDENS

OPEN

1 April-30 Sept.
Daily

10.00am-5.00pm

Gardens Only

CASTLE KENNEDY GARDENS, STRANRAER, TEL: 0776 702024
(The Earl of Stair)

Outstanding garden in south west Scotland. Set between two lochs in beautiful countryside. These extensively landscaped gardens extend over 70 acres between the ruined Castle Kennedy and Lochinch Castle, the home of the Earl of Stair. Famous for Rhododendrons, Embothriums and Azaleas, many of original stock. Terraces and mounds built by man and horse provide spectacular views above gardens and water.

Location: 5 miles east of Stranraer on A75 Dumfries-Stranraer road.
Admission: Adults £2.00. OAP £1.50 children £1.00. 20% reduction for groups 30+.

BALLINDALLOCH CASTLE

OPEN

1 April-30 Sept.

Daily

10.00am-5.00pm

BALLINDALLOCH CASTLE, GRANTOWN-ON-SPEY
TEL: 0807 500206
(Mr and Mrs Oliver Russell)

Ballindalloch is one of the most beautiful and romantic castles in Scotland. It is first and foremost a much loved family home and lived in continuously, by its original family the Macpherson-Grants, since 1546. Filled with family memorabilia, fine 17th century Spanish paintings and home of the famous Aberdeen Angus cattle. Delightful rock garden, audio visual, shop and tearoom.

Location: 13 miles north east of Grantown on Spey on A95,
Admission: Adults £3.75, children under 5 free, 5-16 £2.00. Groups £3.50.

MAXWELTON HOUSE

OPEN

Easter-end Sept.

Daily

10.30am-5.30pm

Group Bookings
Welcome

MAXWELTON HOUSE, MONIAIVE TEL: 08482 384/385
(Maxwelton House Trust)

The birthplace of Annie Laurie made famous by the well loved ballad. Glencairn Castle now Maxwelton House dates back to 1370, the home of the Earls of Glencairn. Stephen Laurie bought Glencairn Castle in 1611 and changed the name to Maxwelton. Annie Laurie was born here in 1682. The Laurie family remained in possession until 1968 when Mr and Mrs Hugh Stenhouse bought it and carried out one of the largest restorations to a private house within Scotland. The restoration took three years and the continuing labour of no less than 65 men. It was completed in 1972.

House, Museum, Chapel, Garden Tearoom, Gift Shop. Free parking.

Location: Entrances on B729 near Wallaceton or A702 near Penpont.

FIFE

Balcarres, Colinsburgh.
(033334) 206 ¹/₂ mile north of Colinsburgh.

Balcaskie, Pittenweem.
(0333) 311202 1 mile north north west of Pittenweem.

Falkland Palace & Garden, Fife.
(0337) 57397 In Falkland, 11 miles north of Kirkcaldy on A912.

Hill of Tarvit, Cupar.
(0334) 53127 2¹/₂ miles south west of Cupar on A916.

Kellie Castle and Garden, Fife.
(03338) 271 3 miles north north west of Pittenweem on B9171.

The Townhouse & The Study, Culross.
(0383) 880359 12 miles west of Forth Road Bridge, off A985.

GRAMPIAN

Braemar Castle, Braemar.
(03397) 41219 ¹/₂ mile north east of Braemar on A93.

Brodie Castle, Nairn, Moray.
(03094) 371 Off A96 between Nairn and Forres.

CASTLE FRASER

OPEN

Easter 1-4 April
1 May-30 June &
September
1.30-5.30pm

July & August
11.00am-5.30pm

Plus 1st two
weekends in
Oct. (Sat/Sun)
1.30-5.30pm.

CASTLE FRASER, KEMNAY TEL: 0330 833463
(National Trust for Scotland)

This magnificent Castle, one of the "Castles of Mar" dates from 1575 and incorporates earlier building. The Castle comprises a wealth of historic furnishings, paintings and fine embroidery.

The Great Hall is regularly used for concerts and other events. The Castle is surrounded by extensive Parkland and has adequate parking. Castle and Grounds available for corporate and private functions.

Location: Off B993 3 miles south of Kemnay and 16 miles west of Aberdeen.
Admission: Adults £3.50, children £1.80. Booked party: adult £2.80, child £1.40.

CRATHES CASTLE

OPEN

1 April-23 Oct.

Daily

11.00am-5.30pm

CRATHES CASTLE, BANCHORY TEL: 0330 844525
(National Trust for Scotland)

Crathes is one of the best preserved 16th century Castles in Scotland with charming furnishing and period painted ceilings. The extensive gardens which cover 3³/₄ acres are noted for unusual plants and are considered amongst the finest in Britain. 600 acres of grounds, with Adventure Playground and trails, are available with the Castle, for corporate and private functions. Adequate parking. Tea Room Gift Shop.

Location: On A93, 3 miles east of Banchory and 15 miles west of Aberdeen.
Admission: House, Gardens, Grounds Adults £4.00. children £2.00. Adult party £3.20, children party £1.60, Grounds only adults £1.80, children 90p.

DRUM CASTLE

OPEN

Easter 1-4 April
1 May-30 June &
September
1.30-5.30pm

July & August
11.00am-5.30pm

Plus 1st two
weekends in
Oct. (Sat/Sun)
1.30-5.30pm.

DRUM CASTLE, ABERDEEN TEL: 0330 811204
(National Trust for Scotland)

Drum Castle is one of the most beautiful Castles of Royal Deeside combining a medieval keep, a Jacobean mansion house and a Victorian extension; with a fine collection of paintings and furniture The grounds contain the walled Garden of Historic Roses and adequate parking. Situated close to Aberdeen the Castle and Grounds are available for corporate and private functions. Tea room, Gift shop.

Location: Off A93 10 miles west of Aberdeen.
Admission: Adults £3.50. child £1.80. Grounds only Adults £1.50, child 80p.
Booked party: Adult £2.80, child £1.40.

FYVIE CASTLE

OPEN

Easter 1-4 April
1 May-30 June &
September
1.30-5.30pm

July & August
11.00am-5.30pm

Plus 1st two
weekends in
Oct. (Sat/Sun)
1.30-5.30pm.

FYVIE CASTLE, TURRIFF TEL: 0651 891266
(National Trust for Scotland)

The five towers of Fyvie Castle enshrine five centuries of Scottish history. The magnificent interior reflects the opulence of the Edwardian era; there is a very important collection of portraits. Two unusual features are a restored American Racquets Court and Bowling Alley; the Court, Castle and Grounds are available for private and corporate functions. Fully equipped catering kitichen and adequate parking. Tea room, gift shop.

Location: Off A947, 8 miles south east of Turriff and 25 miles north west of Aberdeen.
Admission: Adults £3.50, child £1.80. Booked party: Adult £2.80, child £1.40.

HADDO HOUSE

OPEN

Easter 1-4 April
1 May-30 June &
September
1.30-5.30pm

July & August
11.00am-5.30pm

Plus 1st two
weekends in
Oct. (Sat/Sun)
1.30-5.30pm.

HADDO HOUSE, ELLON TEL: 0651 851440
(National Trust for Scotland)

Designed by William Adam in 1731, Haddo House combines Victorian comfort with Georgian elegance. Much of the interior is 'Adam Revival' with fine furniture and ornate plasterwork. The House is bordered by Rose Gardens, a Country Park and has adequate parking. The House and Haddo Hall are available for private and corporate functions; fully equipped catering kitchen.

Location: Off B999, 19 miles north of Aberdeen
Admission: Adult £3.50, child £1.80. Booked party: Adult £2.80, child £1.40.

Fasque, Fettercairn.
(05614) 569 1 mile north of Fettercairn.

Kildrummy Castle Garden, Donside.
(09755) 71277 On A97 off A944 10 miles west of Alford.

LEITH HALL

OPEN

Easter 1-4 April
1 May-30 June &
September

1.30-5.30pm

LEITH HALL, HUNTLY TEL: 04643 216
(National Trust for Scotland)

The mansion house of Leith Hall is at the centre of a 286 acre estate which was the home of the Leith family from 1650, most of whom followed a tradition of military service. There is an outstanding Military Exhibition. With charming Walled Gardens, two lochs and extensive parkland, the Hall and Grounds are available for corporate and private functions. Adequate parking.

Location: Off B9002 1 mile west of Kennethmont and 34 miles north west of Aberdeen.
Admission: Adults £3.50, child £1.80. Booked party: Adult £2.80, child £1.40.

Pitmedden Garden
(06513) 2352 14 miles north of Aberdeen on A920.

Provost Ross's House, Aberdeen.
(0224) 572215 In Aberdeen city centre.

HIGHLANDS

Dochfour Gardens, Inverness.
(046386) 218 6 miles south west of Inverness on A82.

DUART CASTLE

OPEN
1 May-14 Oct.

10.30am-6.00pm

DUART CASTLE. ISLE OF MULL TEL: 06802 309
(Sir Lachlan Maclean Bt.)

Duart Castle has been a Maclean stronghold since the 12th century. The keep was built by a Lachlan Lubanach, 5th Chief, in 1360. Burnt by the English in 1758, the castle was restored in 1912 and today is still the home of the Chief of the Clan Maclean. It has a spectacular position overlooking the Sound of Mull.

Location: Off A849 on the east point of the Isle of Mull.
Admission: Adult £3.00. OAP £2.00. Children £1.50. Family Ticket £7.50.

Eilean Donan Castle, Wester Ross.
(059985) 202 In Dornie, Kyle of Lochalsh. 8 miles east of Kyle on A87.

Fort George, Ardersier.
At Ardersier, 11 miles north east of Inverness.

Inverewe Garden, Poolewe, Wester Ross.
(044586) 229 7 miles from Gairloch.

Hugh Miller's Cottage, Cromarty.
(03817) 2245 In Cromarty 22 miles from Inverness A832.

Urquhart Castle, Loch Ness.
On west shore of Loch Ness 1½ miles south east of Drumnadrochit.

LOTHIAN

Amisfield Mains, Haddington.
(08757) 201 Between Haddington & East Linton and A1.

Beanston, Haddington.
(08757) 201 Between Haddington & East Linton on A1.

Dirleton Castle & Garden, Dirleton.
In the village of Dirleton on A198.

THE DRUM

OPEN

Not open to the general public. By appointment only.

THE DRUM, GILMERTON, EDINBURGH
TEL: 031 664 7215   FAX: 031 658 1944
(G A More Nisbett Esq)

William Adam's most sumptous villa, superb high relief plasterwork by Thomas Clayton & Samuel Calderwood, attached to 15th century Tower House set in magnificent 18th century landscape. Available exclusively for commercial activities, conferences, promotion, film, location, incentive etc. Sleeps 20+.

Location: Edinburgh centre (Waverley Station) 4 miles, Edinburgh airport 10 miles, Edinburgh Bypass A720 0.5 mile. Drum lies between A7 and A772.
Admission: By arrangement

Edinburgh Castle, Edinburgh.
Castlehill, Edinburgh.

The Georgian House, 7 Charlotte Square, Edinburgh.
031 225 2160 In city centre.

Gladstone's Land, Edinburgh.
031 226 5856 477B Lawnmarket, Edinburgh.

Gosford House, East Lothian.
(08757) 201 On A198 between Aberlady and Longniddry.

The House of the Binns, Linlithgow.
(050683) 4255 3½ miles east of Linlithgow off A904.

Inveresk Lodge Garden, Inveresk.
In Inveresk village 6 miles east of Edinburgh off A1.

Lamb's House, Leith.
031 554 3131 In Leith.

Lauriston Castle, Edinburgh.
Crammond Road South, Davidsons Mains.

Lennoxlove, Haddington.
(0620082) 3720 1½ miles south of Haddington on B6369.

Luffness, Aberlady.
18 miles east of Edinburgh.

Malleny Garden, Balerno.
In Balerno, off A70.

Palace of Holyroodhouse, Edinburgh.
031 556 7371 In Central Edinburgh.

Preston Mill, East Linton.
(0620) 860426 5½ miles west of Dunbar off A1.

Stevenson House, Haddington.
(062082) 3376 20 miles approx from Edinburgh, 1½ miles approx. from A1.

Winton House, Pencaitland.
(0875) 340222 In Pencaitland, 6 miles from Haddington.

STRATHCLYDE

Arduaine Garden, Argyll.
(08522) 287 A816, 20 miles south of Oban and 17 north of Lochgilphead.

Bachelors' Club, Tarbolton.
(0292) 541940 In Tarbolton village, 7½ miles north east of Ayr off A758.

Balloch Castle Country Park, Balloch
(0389) 58216

Bothwell Castle, Bothwell.
(031 244) 3101 At Bothwell but approached from Uddingston.

Brodick Castle, Garden and Country Park, Isle of Arran.
(0770) 2202 1½ miles north of Brodick pierhead on the Isle of Arran.

Finlaystone House and Gardens, Langbank.
(047554) 285 On A8 between Langbank and Port Glasgow.

Greenbank Garden, Glasgow.
041 639 3281 Flenders Road near Clarkston Toll.

The Hill House, Helensburgh.
(0436) 73900 In Upper Colquhoun Street, Helensburgh, north west of Glasgow via A814.

Hutcheson's Hall, Glasgow.
041 552 8391 158 Ingram Street near south east corner of George Square.

Pollok House and Park, Glasgow.
041 632 0274 3½ miles from city centre.

Sorn Castle, Sorn.
(0292) 268181 4 miles east of Mauchline on B743.

Souter Johnnie's Cottage, Kirkoswald.
(06556) 603 In Kirkoswald village 4 miles west of Maybole on A77.

The Tenement House, Glasgow.
041 333 0183 145 Buccleuch Street, Garnethill.

Torosay Castle and Gardens, Craignure, Isle of Mull.
(06802) 421 1½ miles south east of Craignure by A849.

Weaver's Cottage, Kilbarchan.
In Kilbarchan village, 12 miles south west of Glasgow off A737.

TAYSIDE

Angus Folk Museum, Glamis.
(030784) 288 In Glamis Village, 12 miles north of Dundee A94.

Barrie's Birthplace, Kirriemuir.
(0575) 72646 No 9 Brechin Road, Kirriemuir.

Barry Mill, Carnoustie.
(0241) 56761 2 miles north west of Carnoustie.

Branklyn Garden, Perth.
(0738) 25535 On Dundee Road, Perth (A85).

Castle Menzies, Weem.
1½ miles from Aberfeldy on B846.

Edzell Castle & Gardens.
1 mile west of Edzell, 6 miles north of Breechin off B996.

House of Dun, Montrose.
(067481) 264 4 miles west of Montrose.

CARDIFF CASTLE
Cardiff, South Glamorgan

CONTACT

Mrs J Brown
Cardiff Castle
Castle Street
Cardiff
South Glamorgan
CF1 2RB

Tel: (0222) 822083
Fax: (0222) 231417

LOCATION

The Castle is situated in central Cardiff. Signposted from the M4 Motorway 'To City Centre'. From London M4 direct 2 hours

Rail: Cardiff Central

Air: Cardiff Airport

CARDIFF CASTLE, situated at the centre of the capital city of Wales, occupies a large and historic site that provides many levels of interest to the visitor.

Reconstructed Roman Walls enclose the area, which contains the spectacular remains of mediaeval defences, including the 12th Century shell keep which overlooks the grounds.

The Castle Lodgings, which partly date from the mid-15th Century, were rebuilt during the 19th Century and form perhaps the greatest creation of Art-Architect William Burges (1827-81), who transformed the Castle into a mediaevalist fantasy for his patron, the wealthy and cultured Third Marquess of Bute.

Access to the Lodgings is by public or pre-arranged specialist tours, and includes visits to some of Burges' magnificent and imaginative interiors which blend the mediaeval and the exotic to create some of the most extraordinary rooms in the country. These include an Arab Room - a Burges vision of the Middle East which has sumptuous carved and gilded decoration, plus the three fantastic rooms of the Clock Tower, which celebrate themes of astrology and alchemy in a blaze of decorated tiles, marquetry and painting.

The superb Banqueting Hall recreated a uniquely Victorian vision of the mediaeval, and is available for functions.

SUITABILITY FOR OTHER EVENTS

The Castle is suitable for a number of events and functions. Please apply to the Administrator for further details.

ADVICE TO COURIERS & DRIVERS

No photography of the interiors, except by special prior permission. The Lodgings are unsuitable for disaabled/wheelchair visitors.

FACILITIES FOR THE DISABLED

Disabled or elderly visitors may alight at the entrance to the Castle. Toilet facilities for the disabled are available in the grounds.

The Lodgings are unsuitable for disaabled/wheelchair visitors.

PARKING FOR COACHES & CARS

The Castle does not have parking facilities but there are Public Car Parks nearby. Please contact the Administrator for advice on parking coaches.

CATERING

A Tea Room, seating 46, is available. Please note, groups CAN NOT book in advance.

NATIONAL TRUST SHOP

Shop open at same hours as the Castle. Items include souvenirs, gifts, postcards etc..

GUIDE BOOKS

Availablle from National Trust Shop

SPECIALIST TOURS

Tours of the Burges Interiors, or the De Morgan Collection of Ceramics available by the Keeper of Collections. Strictly by advance appointment and only for specialist groups. Tours of the interior by public guides. Maximum size for tour is 40.

OPENING TIMES

Summer
1 May - 30 September

Mon	
Tues	
Wed	
Thurs	10am - 6pm
Fri	
Sat	
Sun	

Winter

March, April & October
10am - 5pm

November to February
10am - 4.30pm

ADMISSION

All Year

HOUSE & GROUNDS
Adult	£3.30
Child*	£1.70
OAP	£1.70

GROUNDS ONLY
Adult	£2.20
Child*	£1.10
OAP	£1.10

GROUP
10% reduction on parties of 20+. Tour operators & travel agents discount on request.
* Under 16

The Banqueting Hall

CONFERENCE AND FUNCTION FACILITIES

ROOM	DIMENSIONS	CAPACITY	LAYOUT	POWER POINTS	SUITABLE FOR A/V
Banqueting Hall		110-150	Various	✓	
Drawing Room		50-60	Various	✓	
Small Dining Room		20	Various		
George Thomas Suite		18-30	Various	✓	

A
SELECTION OF
THE IMPRESSIVE
FUNCTION FACILITIES
AT CARDIFF CASTLE

The Dining Room

The Library

The Roof Garden in Summer

The Drawing Room

LLANCAIACH FAWR MANOR
Nelson, Mid-Glamorgan

CONTACT

Val Williams
Llancaiach Fawr
Nelson
Treharris
Mid Glamorgan
CF46 6ER

Tel: (0443) 412248
Fax: (0443) 412688

LOCATION

30 minutes north of Cardiff (junc. 32, M4): just off the A470 at Nelson, on the B4254 Nelson to Gelligaer road.

Rail: Ystrad Mynach 3 miles.

Bus: Local (Cardiff-Bargoed) services run past Llancaiach Fawr.

LLANCAIACH FAWR MANOR, one of the best surviving examples of the late Tudor semi-fortified manor house in Wales is now a superb award-winning living history museum of the Civil War period.

Llancaiach Fawr was built in 1530 by the Prichard family of Glamorgan. Over 100 years later, during the Civil War, King Charles I visited the house in 1645. Intrigue surrounds the visit, for shortly afterwards Colonel Prichard, Master of Llancaiach, dramatically switched his loyalty from the Royalist to the Parliamentarian cause.

Llancaiach Fawr has now been restored to its 1645 glory and furnished with beautiful reproduction pieces. The gardens have been laid out as a simple period garden of box and lavender beds. Today the house is alive again, as costumed stewards guide visitors around with fascinating tales of 17th Century life. Visitors can try out the furniture, dress in period costumes, try on armour and weaponry and even take a turn in the stocks!

Candlelit ghost tours of the house during winter months retell many of the mysterious events the house has witnessed during its 400 year history. 17th Century evening banquets are a speciality.

'Best New Welsh Tourist Attraction 1992'

'BTA Come to Britain Special Award Winner 1991'

SUITABILITY FOR OTHER EVENTS

Ideal for small wedding receptions. Popular film/TV location; also radio. Meadow for outdoor concerts.

EXTRA FACILITIES

Seminar/teaching room available. Please contact the manager to discuss requirements.

ADVICE TO COURIERS & DRIVERS

Allow 1¹/2 - 2 hours for tour of house and shop/restaurant.

FACILITIES FOR THE DISABLED

All visitor centre facilities, garden and ground floor of the house are wheelchair accessible.

PARKING FOR COACHES & CARS

Parking for 70 cars and 2 coaches within 20 yards of the house.

CATERING

All-day menu ranging from 17th Century Dish of the Day for lunch, to cream teas and light snacks.

GUIDED TOURS

Guided tours are available for maximum of 50 people at no extra cost. Average time taken is 1³/4 hours.

GIFT SHOP

Open when house is open, selling a good selection of local crafts, pottery, books etc.

GUIDE BOOKS

Full colour guide book £1.95.

SCHOOL VISITS/CHILDREN

Groups are welcome. School room available. Special Activities include pomander and candle-making. Contact Educational Manager.

OPENING TIMES

All Year

Mon Tues Wed Thur Fri	10am - 5pm
Sat Sun	10am - 6pm

Last admission 1¹/2 hours before closing.

Closed Christmas Day, Boxing Day and New Years Day.

ADMISSION

All Year

Proposed Rates:
Adult   £3.50
Child   £2.00
OAP   £2.00
Family   £9.50

CONFERENCE AND FUNCTION FACILITIES

ROOM	DIMENSIONS	CAPACITY	LAYOUT	POWER POINTS	SUITABLE FOR A/V
Conference Room		60	U-shape Boardroom Buffet Lunch/Dinner Theatre	6	✓

TREDEGAR HOUSE
Newport, Gwent

SOUTH WALES' finest country house, ancestral home of the Morgan dynasty for over 500 years.

Parts of a mediaeval house in stone remain, but Tredegar owes its reputation to lavish rebuilding in brick at the end of the 17th Century. The new house was built on an exceptionally grand scale and included a glittering series of State Rooms complemented by a more intimate family wing, although the mediaeval courtyard plan was retained. The service wing was built in the 19th Century.

The house and contents were sold in 1951 and for 23 years served as a school. Purchased by Newport Borough Council in 1974, it has been carefully restored and refurnished, often with original pieces. Visitors have a lively and entertaining tour through 40 rooms in a variety of historical decorative styles. Exquisite carving, plasterwork and decorations, fine painting and tapestries, and special attention to the accurate use of recreated fabrics, textiles and floor coverings are features of rooms above stairs, while a host of domestic bygones capture the visitor's imagination in the Great Kitchen, Housekeeper's Room, Servants' Hall and other rooms 'below stairs'.

GARDENS

The basic mediaeval garden plan survives on two sides of the house in a series of Walled Gardens currently undergoing restoration. Late 18th Century landscaping by Mickle swept away all but one of the avenues of oak and chestnut radiating from the house. Ninety acres of parkland. The Sunken Garden has now been restored with an early 20th Century planting scheme.

CONTACT

The Curator
Tredegar House and Park
Newport
Gwent
NP1 9YW

Tel: (0633) 815880

LOCATION

From London M4,
signposted Junction 28
2½ hours.
Newport 2 miles

Rail: London to Newport station.

Bus: Bus within 300 yards of entrance.

Taxi: Dragon (0633) 216216.

SUITABILITY FOR OTHER EVENTS

Press launches, concerts, lectures, filming and wedding receptions.

EXTRA FACILITIES

Park and gardens.

ADVICE FOR COURIERS & DRIVERS

Please book in advance and allow at least three hours at the house for tours and refreshments. No dogs, unaccompanied children, photography, stilettos or smoking allowed in house.

FACILITIES FOR THE DISABLED

Disabled access to ground floor. Please give advance warning.

PARKING FOR COACHES & CARS

Parking for 1800 cars and 10 coaches 150 yards from the house.

CATERING

The Restaurant/Tea Room can cater for up to 80 people. Prices from £1.80 (tea), £5 (2 course lunch), £16 (3 course dinner). Groups can book in advance; menus available. Catering facilities available for special functions/conferences.

GIFT SHOP

Country Park Shop open daily 10.30am - 6pm. Housekeeper's Shop open as house. Items include: souvenirs, Welsh crafts, books, spices, toiletries and souvenirs.

GUIDED TOURS

Parties of 40 people can be taken round the house at no additional cost. Average time for tour 1¼ hours.

SCHOOL VISITS/CHILDREN

Groups welcome and guide available. £1 per child (house only). Areas of interest include: 'Below Stairs', boating, carriage rides, woodland walk, craft workshops and adventure play farm.

OPENING TIMES

Summer
Good Friday -30 Sept.
Mon   Bank Hol. Mons 11am-5pm
Tues   School summer Hols
11.30am-4.00pm
Wed
Thur   Tours
Fri   11.30am-4.00pm
Sat
Sun

NB Country Park open.
Daily   8am-Dusk

Evening Tours by appointment only.

Winter
October only - weekend opening as Summer.

Day & Evening tours by appointment only.

Christmas opening: Details from September

ADMISSION

Summer

HOUSE & GARDEN
Adult	£3.80
Child	£2.60
OAP	£2.60
Student	£2.60
Family	£9.00

Prices correct at time of going to press.

Winter

As Summer.

CONFERENCE AND FUNCTION FACILITIES

ROOM	DIMENSIONS	CAPACITY	LAYOUT	POWER POINTS	SUITABLE FOR A/V
Morgan Room	58'x20'x8'	40-120	Various	4	✓
Tea Room & Bar	50'x20'x8'	30-80	Various	4	✓

CLWYD

BODELWYDDAN CASTLE

OPEN
ALL YEAR
26 Mar - 30 June
& 1 Sept - 30 Oct
Daily except Fri.
10am*-5.00pm
1 July-31 Aug.
Daily
10am*-5.00pm
31 Oct-7 April 95
Daily except
Mons. & Fri.
11.00am-4.0pm
Last adm. 1 hour
before closing
*Castle galleries
open at 10.30am.

BODELWYDDAN CASTLE, ST ASAPH TEL: 0745 584060
(Clwyd County Council)

This magnificently restored Victorian mansion set in rolling parkland displays extensive collections from the National Portrait Gallery, furniture from the Victoria and Albert Museum, and John Gibson sculpture from the Royal Academy. Exhibitions of Victorian amusements and inventions and a programme of large and small indoor and outdoor events throughout the year.

Winner of the Museum of the Year Award

Location: Follow signs off A55 Expressway near St Asaph, opposite the Marble Church.
Admission: Castle & Grounds: Adult £4.00, Child/OAP £2.50, Family (2+3) £10. Grounds only: £1.50, Family £5.00. Group rates available

Chirk Castle, Chirk, Wrexham.
(0691) 777701 ½ mile from Chirk.

Erddig, Wrexham.
(0978) 355314   2 miles south of Wrexham off A525.

Ewloe Castle, Hawarden.
1 mile north west of Ewloe on A55.

Gyrn Castle, Llanasa, Holywell.
(0745) 853500 26 miles west of Chester, 4 miles south east of Prestatyn.

Valle Crucis Abbey, Llangollen.
B5103 from the A5 west of Llangollen.

DYFED

Carreg Cennen Castle, Trapp.
Minor roads from A483 to Trapp village near Llandeilo.

Cilgerran Castle, Cilgerran.
3 miles soutoh of Cilgerran off A478.

Colby Woodland Garden, Amroth.
(0558) 822800   North east of Tenby off A477.

Kidwellly Castle, Kidwelly.
Kidwelly via A484.

Lamphey Bishop's Palace, Lamphey.
2½ miles east of Pembroke on A4139.

Llawhaden Castle, Llawhadden.
Llawhadden off A40(T).

Picton Castle, Haverfordwest.
(0437) 751296   4 miles south east of Haverfordwest.

St Davids Bishop's Palace, St Davids.
A487 to St Davids, minor road past Cathedral.

Strata Florida Abbey, Strata Florida.
1½ miles south east of Pontrhydfendigaid reached from B4340 or B4343.

Talley Abbey, Talley.
Talley on B4302 6 miles north of Llandeilo.

Tudor Merchant's House, Tenby.
(0834) 2279   On Quay Hill, Tenby.

MID GLAMORGAN

Caerphilly Castle, Caerphilly.
A468 from Newport or A470/A469 from Cardiff.

Coity Castle, Coity.
In Coity village, 2 miles north east of Bridgend.

SOUTH GLAMORGAN

Castell Coch, Tongwynlais, Cardiff.
A470 and signposted.

WEST GLAMORGAN

Margam Park, Port Talbot.
(0639) 881635   Easy access on A48. Near Port Talbot.

Neath Abbey, Neath.
In Neath.

Weobley Castle, Weobley.
Minor road from Llanrhidian village.

GWENT

Caerleon Roman Fortress, Caerleon.
B4236 to Caerleon.

Chepstow Castle, Chepstow.
In Chepstow.

Penhow Castle, Newport.
(0633) 400800   On A48 midway between Chepstow/Newport.

Raglan Castle, Raglan.
Via the A40.

Tintern Abbey, Tintern.
In Tintern.

White Castle, Llantilio Crossenny.
6 miles east of Abergavenny off B4233.

GWYNEDD

Aberconwy House, Conwy.
(0492) 592246   In the town at junction of Castle Street and High Street.

Beaumaris Castle (World Heritage Site), Beaumaris, Anglesey.
In Beaumaris.

Bodnant Garden, Tal-y-Cafn.
(0492) 650460 8 miles south of Llandudno and Colwyn Bay on A470.

Caernarfon Castle (World Heritage Site), Caernarfon.
A4085, A487(T), A4086 and B4366.

Cochwillan Old Hall, Talybont, Bangor.
(0248) 364608   3¹/₂ miles Bangor, 1 mile Talybont village off A55.

Conwy Castle (World Heritage Site), Conwy.
Conwy via A55 or B5106.

BRYN BRAS CASTLE

OPEN

Not finalised at time of going to press.

BRYN BRAS CASTLE, CAERNARFON TEL: 0286 870210
(Neville E & Marita Gray-Parry)

Built in 1830, on an earlier structure and thought to have been designed by Thomas Hopper. Fine stained glass, panelling, interesting ceilings, richly carved furniiture. Gardens include herbaceous borders, walled Knot Garden, stream and pools, woodland walks and ¹/₄ mile mountain walk with views of Snowdon, Anglesey and sea. Home made Welsh Teas in Tea Room and Tea Gardens.   Picnic Area.

Location: 4¹/₂ miles east of Caernarfon, 3¹/₂ miles north west of Llanberis, ¹/₂ mile off A4086
Admission: Castle & Grounds £3.50 (Children between 5 and under 15 half price). Free parking. Reduction for parties.

Criccieth Castle, Cricceth.
A497 to Criccieth from Porthmadog or from Pwllheli.

Cymer Abbey, Cymer.
2 miles north of Dolgellau A494

Gwydir Uchaf Chapel, Llanrwst.
On Foresstry Commission land ¹/₂ mile south west of Llanrwst.

Harlech Castle (World Heritage Site), Harlech.
A496 from Blaenau Ffestiniog.

Penrhyn Castle, Bangor.
(0248) 353084   1 mile east of Bangor on A5122.

Plas Brondanw Gardens, Penrhyndeudraeth.
(0766) 771136   2 miles north of Penrhyndeudraeth.

Plas Mawr, Conwy.

Plas Newydd, Isle of Anglesey.
(0248) 714795   1 mile south west of Llanfairpwll on A4080.

Ty Mawr Wybrnant, Penmachno.
(06903) 213   At the head of the little valley of Wybrant, 3¹/₂ miles south west of Betws-y-Coed.

POWYS

Gregynog, Newtown.
(0686) 650224   Near village of Tregynon, 5 miles north of Newtown off B4289.

Powis Castle, Welshpool.
(0938) 554336   1 mile south of Welshpool on A483.

Tretower Court & Castle, Crickhowell.
3 miles north west of Crickhowell off A479 and A470.

BODELWYDDAN CASTLE

MALAHIDE CASTLE
Malahide, Co. Dublin

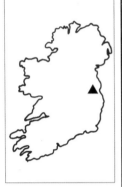

MALAHIDE CASTLE was founded in 1175 by Sir Richard Talbot de Malahide. The Talbot family took up residence in 1185, the year Richard Talbot received the Lordship of Malahide from Prince John of England. Except for a short period during the Cromwellian era, when the family were dispossessed because of their royalist sympathies, the Talbots lived in Malahide until 1976 - 791 years. Upon the death of the last Lord Talbot de Malahide in 1973 the castle, together with its 250 acres of woods, parkland and exotic shrubs was sold and a family connection which stretched back to the Norman invasion was broken.

Immeasurable interest is added to the house by virtue of the National Gallery's decision to house a large part of the National Portrait Collection at the Castle where it is on permanent display.

THE TALBOT BOTANIC GARDENS

The ornamental gardens adjoining the castle cover an area of about 20 acres and were largely created by Milo Talbot. In all, there are in excess of 5,000 different species and varieties of plants present. The gardens can be described as small Botanic gardens.

CYRIL FRY MODEL RAILWAY EXHIBITION

This is adjacent to the Castle and is a rare collection of O Gauge Trains and Trams. It is a history of Irish Rail transport of both broad and narrow gauge starting from the first train that ran in Ireland on the Dublin-Kingstown (now Dun Loaghaire) Railway in 1834. The O Gauge operational layout is a Grand Transport Complex which includes stations, bridges, trams, buses, barges, boats, the Liffey and the Hill of Howth.

CONTACT

Ms Ann Chambers
Ms Maria Morgan
Malahide Castle
Malahide
Co Dublin
Ireland

Tel: Dublin 8452655/
8452371/8452758
Fax: Dublin 8452528

FROM APRIL 1st:
Tel: Dublin 8462184
Fax: Dublin 8462537

LOCATION

Road - 30 mins from
Dublin City

Bus: Stop 1/2 mile from
Castle entrance

Rail: Station 1/2 mile from
Castle.

Airport: Dublin airport
4 miles

Taxi - Airport Taxi 360111

SUITABILITY FOR OTHER EVENTS

Receptions, filming. Private Banquets held in the Great Hall all year round.

EXTRA FACILITIES

Parkland and Golf Course.

ADVICE TO COURIERS & DRIVERS

No photography or video filming is allowed in the house. Dogs are not allowed. Parking for 500 cars within 250 yards. Parking for 15 coaches within 300 yards

FACILITIES FOR THE DISABLED

Disabled and elderly visitors may alight at the entrance to the Castle, before parking in the allocated area. There are no special toilets for the disabled.

CATERING

The Restaurant seats up to 80. Prices from £4.50 for Afternoon Tea to £12.50 for Lunch. Groups can book in advance and special prices can be arranged. Catering facilities available for special functions, conferences, buffets, lunches, dinners etc. Banquets in the Great Hall are a speciality.

GIFT SHOP

Open as the House. It stocks a selection of Irish made gifts.

GUIDE BOOK

Two colour guide books available, £1.00 and £2.50. Translations available in French, Spanish, German, Japanese and Italian.

GUIDED TOURS

Tours are self-guided by means of an automatic speaking system. This is available in French, Italian, Spanish, German, Dutch and Japanese.

SCHOOL VISITS/CHILDREN

Visits are welcome to the Fry Railway Collection which is of particular interest to children. Playground beside the castle. Combined children's rate for Castle and Model Railway £1.85.

OPENING TIMES

All Year
January - December
Mon ⎫
Tues ⎪
Wed ⎬ 10am-5pm
Thur ⎪
Fri ⎭

November - March
Sat, Sun & Public Hols
2pm-5pm

April - October
Sat   11am - 6pm
Sun & Public Holidays
11.30am - 6pm.

House closes for Tours
12.45-2pm.
Restaurant remains open.

ADMISSION

All Year

HOUSE

	Single	Group*
Adult	£2.65	£2.25
Child		
3-11	£1.30	£1.20
12-17	£2.00	£1.80
OAP	£2.00	£1.80
Family	£7.25	

RAILWAY

	Single	Group*
Adult	£2.25	£1.90
Child		
3-11	£1.20	£1.00
12-17	£1.60	£1.40
OAP	£1.60	£1.40
Family	£6.50	

*Minimum number 20 (Family is 2 adults and 3/4 children)

Combined Castle & Model Railway tickets available.

CONFERENCE AND FUNCTION FACILITIES

ROOM	DIMENSIONS	CAPACITY	LAYOUT	POWER POINTS	SUITABLE FOR A/V
Blue Room Apartment	19'x34'		Theatre Schoolroom U-Shape/Boardroom		
Great Hall		76	Banquets		

Annes Grove Gardens, Castletownroche.
(022) 26145

Ayesha Castle, Killiney, Co. Dublin.

Bantry House, Bantry, Co. Cork.
(027) 50047   On outskirts of Bantry, 56 miles south west of Cork.

Birr Castle Demesne, Co. Offaly.
(509) 20056

Blarney Castle and Blarney House, Blarney, Co. Cork.
7 miles from Cork City.

Bunratty Castle & Folk Park, Bunratty, Co. Clare.

Castletown House, Celbridge, Co. Kildare.
(01) 628 8252   12 miles west of Dublin.

Cloghan Castle, Banagher, Co. Offaly.
(0509) 51650   8 miles west of Birr Castle, 3 miles south of Banagher.

Clonalis House, Castlerea, Co. Roscommon.
(0907) 20014

Craggaunowen - The Living Past, Kilmurry, Sixmilebridge, Co. Clare.
6 miles east of Quin.

Cratloe Woods House, Cratloe, Co. Clare.
(061) 327028

Dunguaire Castle, Kinvara, Co.Galway.

Dunkathel, Dunkathel, Glanmire.
(021) 821014   3 miles east of Cork.

Dunloe Castle Hotel Gardens, Beaufort, Killarney, Co. Kerry.
(064) 44111/31900   Situated adjacent to Hotel Dunloe Castle approx. 8 miles from Killarney.

Emo Court, Portlaoise, Co. Leix.
(0502) 26110

Fernhill Garden, Sandyford.
(01) 956000

Fota, Fota Island, Carrigtwohill, Co. Cork.

GPA-Bolton Library, John Street, Cashel, Co. Tipperary
(062) 61944   In John Street, immediate opposite Cashel Palace Hotel.

CARRIGGLAS

OPEN
4 June-4 Sept.
Thu.-Mon. incl.
(closed Tue. &
Wed.)
1.00-5.30pm
weekdays.
2.00-6.00pm
Sundays & Aug.
Guided Tours of
House
2pm,3pm,4pm,5
pm Sundays &
August.

CARRIGGLAS MANOR, LONGFORD   TEL: 043 45165
(Jeffry & Tessa Lefroy)

Combining the best of both worlds, a Gothic Revival house of great style built by Thomas Lefroy (youthful inamorato of Jane Austen) ancestor of the present owner, and the magnificent classical double farmyards designed by renowned 18th century architect James Gandon. A charming woodland/water garden connects the two and the stableyard houses a costume museum, Tea Room and Gift Shop.

Location: 3 miles from Longford on T15 Granard road, 2 miles off main N4 route
signposted 4 miles east of Longford at Cathedral in Longford
Admission: Garden/Stableyard Adults IR£1.00, Children/OAP 50p House Adults IR£1.50,
Children/OAP 50p, Costume Museum 50p.

IRISH HERITAGE PROPERTIES

Historic Irish Tourist Houses & Gardens Association Ltd
(H.I.T.H.A.)
represents more than 50 properties in Ireland, many of which are included
in these pages. Further details can be obtained from:

Fred Martin
Irish Heritage Properties
3a Castle Street
Dalkey
Co. Dublin   Tel: 2859343

(From the UK - 010 353 - 1 2859343)

GLIN CASTLE

OPEN
1-31 May
10.00am-12noon
2.00-4.00pm

Other times by
arrangement

GLIN CASTLE, GLIN TEL: 068 34173/34112
(The Knight of Glin & Madam Fitzgerald)

Near Ballybunion Golf Course and 1 hour's drive from Shannon Airport 18th century Glin Castle has magnificent plaster ceilings and fine collections of Irish paintings and furniture. Fully staffed and very comfortable it welcomes no more than 8 guests for dinner and overnight stays. Well kept gardens surround the Castle which has wonderul views over the River Shannon. The Castle can be rented.

Location: Situated on the Foynes Tarbert Road N69, 9 km. west of Foynes and 5 km. east of Tarbert and the car ferry.

Admission: Adults £2.00, students/children £1.00. Group rate £1.50.

Japanese Gardens, Tully, Co. Kildare.
(045) 21617 1 miles from Kildare Town, 5 miles from Newbridge.

Johnstown Castle Demesne, Wexford.
5 miles south west of Wexford.

The James Joyce Tower, Sandycove.
02809265/02808571

Knappogue Castle, Quin, Co. Clare.
(061) 71103

Kylemore Abbey, Kylemore, Connemara.
(095) 41146.

Lismore Castle, Lismore, Co. Waterford.
(058) 54424. In Lismore Town, 45 miles west of Waterford.

&Lissadell, Sligo.
8 miles north west of Sligo overlooking Sligo Bay.

Lough Gur Visitor Centre, Lough Gur.

Lough Rynn Estate & Gardens.
Mohill, Co. Leitrim

Mount Usher Gardens, Ashford.
(0404) 40205/40116 In Ashford, 1 mile from Wicklow.

Muckross House and Gardens, Killarney, Co. Kerry.
(064) 31440 6 miles from Killarney on Kenmare road.

National Botanic Gardens, Glasnevin, Dublin.
2 miles from city centre,

Newbridge House, Donabate, Co. Dublin.
0436534/5 12 miles from centre of Dublin.

Powerscourt Gardens and Waterfall, Enniskerry, Co. Wicklow.
(1) 2867676/7/8 12 miles south of Dublin.

Powerscourt Townhouse Centre, Dublin 2.
(1) 687477 59 South William Street. Dublin 2.

The Royal Hospital Kilmainham/The Irish Museum of Modern Art.
(01) 718666 In Kilmainham.

Russborough, Blessington, Co. Wicklow.
(045) 65239

Slane Castle, Slane
(041) 24207

Stokestown Park House, Stokestown, Co. Roscommon.
(078) 33013

Thoor Ballylee, Gort.
(091) 31436 4 miles from Gort Town.

Timoleague Castle Gardens, Bandon.
(023) 46116 Adjoining Timoleague village, 8 miles from Brandon.

Tullynally Castle, Castlepollard, Co. Westmeath.
(044) 61159

NORTHERN IRELAND

Ardress House, Co. Armagh.
(0762) 851236 7 miles west of Portadown on B28.

The Argory, Co. Armagh.
(08687) 84753 4 miles from Moy on Derrycaw Road.

Castle Coole, Co. Fermanagh.
(0365) 322690 1¹/2 miles south east of Enniskillen on A4.

Castle Ward, Co. Down.
(039686) 204 7 miles north east of Downpatrick.

Downhill, Londonderry.
(0238) 510721 5 miles west of Coleraine on A2.

Florence Court, Co. Fermanagh.
(0365) 249 8 miles soutoh west of Enniskillen via A4 and A32.

Gray's Printing Press, Strabane, Co. Tyrone.
(0504) 884094 In Main Street, Strabane.

Hezlett House, Co. Londonderry.
(0265) 848567 4 miles west of Coleraine on A2.

Mount Stewart House, Garden and Temple, Co. Down.
(024774) 387 On east shore of Strangford Lough. 15 miles east of Belfast A20.

Rowallane Garden, Saintfield, Co. Down.
(0238) 510131 11 miles south east of Belfast.

Springhill, Moneymore, Co. Londonderry.
(06487) 48210 1 mile from Moneymore on Moneymore/Coagh Road.

Wellbrook Beetling Mill, Cookstown, Co. Tyrone.
(06487) 51735 3 miles from Cookstown on Cookstown/Omagh Road.

Accommodation

in

Privately Owned Historic Houses

The houses in this section are NOT hotels. Included are those houses where accommodation is provided as an ancillary to the house's function as a family home.

Staying at one of these houses provides visitors with the opportunity to be private guests in comfortable, historic, listed country houses. You will be made to feel at home as personal guests of your host and hostess.

Bedroom and bathroom arrangements are as you would find when staying in any private country residence. Often en-suite bathrooms are available otherwise your bathroom will be close by, probably exclusive to you.

Because these houses are not hotels, visitors should observe usual courtesies as when staying with friends. The visits must be arranged in advance and hostesses will want to know the time of your arrival, which because they may be out and about during the day should not normally be much before 5pm. Meals will be served at normal times rather than on demand and on occasion it may not be possible for the hostess to provide dinner but visitors would be informed beforehand and recommended to a local restaurant if they so wish.

Accommodation is also available in some houses listed in the previous (blue banded) section but usually on either a totally exclusive basis or in conjunction with conferences and functions *(see the accommodation index)*.

LOCATION MAP

The numbers on the map refer to the houses listed below, details of which are given in the following three pages. Irish houses offering accommodation are located on a seperate map on page 222.

1. Ballaachulish House
2. Bardrochat
3. Castle Forbes
4. Cross Tree House
5. Delbury Hall
6. Drakestone House
7. Drummond House
8. Glenfeochan House
9. Halewell Close
10. Moat House
11. Montys Court
12. 28 Northumberland Street
13. Penyclawdd Court
14. Rossie Priory
15. Silkhouse
16. Trotton Old Rectory
17. Upton House
18. Winstone Glebe

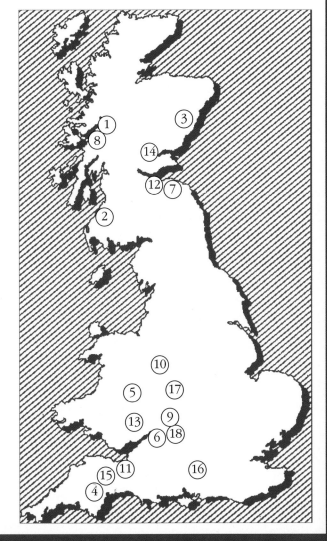

BALLACHULISH HOUSE

PRICES
B & B £25-£37.50
Dinner   £19.50

OPEN
All Year
Closed Christmas
& New Year

HOST
Liz & John Grey

(08552) 266

BALLACHULISH HOUSE, BALLACHULISH, ARGYLL.

For centuries a Stewart House, Ballachulish dates back to the 17th century, The final order for the Massacre of Glencoe was signed here. The plot of R.L.S.Stevenson's "Kidnapped" centred on the area around Ballachulish. It is an ideal base for hill walking or touring the West Highlands,

Antique furniture, log fires and spectacular views combined with food which consists of much local game and shellfish create an atmosphere to which many guests return every year.

Location: The driveway is ½ mile south of the Ballachulish Bridge on A828.

CROSS TREE HOUSE

PRICES
B & B   £18-£22
Dinner   £14

OPEN
March-October

HOST
Phyllis &
Stephen Landor

(0647) 40726

CROSS TREE HOUSE, MORETONHAMPSTEAD, DEVON

Grade II listed Tudor Rectory with Georgian update, historic features and antique furniture, by the Dancing Tree round which the villagers danced to the tunes of the band up in the tree and still do sometimes. An ancient stone cross below the tree used to guide the monks across the wild moor. Pretty courtyard where stables used to be with well, pump and hayloft. Beautiful, peaceful Walled Garden. Spacious bedrooms all with en-suite or private bathrooms. Imaginative Cordon Bleu and English cooking.

Location: Dartmoor National Park, 12 miles from Exeter along B3212.

BARDROCHAT

PRICES
B & B   £55 p.p.
Dinner £45 incl.
all drinks.

OPEN
April - October

HOST
Mr & Mrs A
McEwan

(0465) 88242

BARDROCHAT, GIRVAN, AYRSHIRE.

Built by Robert Lorimer in 1893 for the present owner's grandfather, Bardrochat stands high on the south side of the Stinchar Valley. The house sleeps six couples in great comfort with their own bathrooms. The maximum is eighteen. Centrally situated for the great golf courses and gardens with its own tennis court, croquet and salmon fishing. The Walled Garden provides all the vegetables for the house and memorable food. All drinks are included in the price.

Location: Nr Colmonell, 10 miles south of Girvan.

DELBURY HALL

PRICES
B & B   £30-£45
per person
Dinner   £20.00
excl. alcohol., by
arrangement.

OPEN
All Year
Closed Christmas
& New Year

HOST
Mr & Mrs Patrick
Wrigley
Tel (0584) 76267
Fax (0584) 76441

DELBURY HALL, LUDLOW, SHROPSHIRE

Delbury is in a tranquil setting, with flower filled gardens, two trout lakes for fly fishing and a hard tennis court. A home farm provides Jersey milk and hand churned butter and a walled garden produces vegetables. Patrick and Lucinda Wrigley have 2 small children, Jack and Kate and Patrick is an experienced cook (Leith's). Extremely comfortable bedrooms, with private bathroom, colour TV and telephone, guests sitting room, dining room and snooker room with full size table.

Location: In Shropshire's Corvedale, between Ludlow and Much Wenlock.

CASTLE FORBES

PRICES
B & B   £75.00
Dinner   £45.00

OPEN
All Year

HOST
The Hon. Mrs
Malcolm Forbes

(09755) 62574/
62524

CASTLE FORBES, ALFORD, ABERDEENSHIRE.

Built in 1815 by the 17th Lord Forbes, Castle Forbes occupies a magnificent site in parkland overlooking the Don. It is now owned and occupied by his Great-Great-Great-Grandson Malcolm, The Master of Forbes, and his wife Jinny. Flowers from the delightful courtyard garden that Jinny created, wonderful dinners based on fresh Estate produce and fine wine complement the warm friendly and relaxed atmosphere. Outdoor activities including fishing, Roe stalking, tennis and walks, are available on Forbes Estate.

Location: Four miles north east of Alford on River Don. Aberdeen 25 miles.

DRAKESTONE HOUSE

PRICES
B & B   £22 p.p.
Dinner   £15.00

OPEN
April-October
inclusive

HOST
Hugh & Crystal
St. John-Mildmay

(0453) 542140

DRAKESTONE HOUSE, DURSLEY, GLOUCESTERSHIRE

A fine listed Edwardian country house with links with the Arts and Craft Movement. Hugh's grandparents laid out the formal gardens with terraces and yew hedges before the First World War, and Hugh and Crystal since taking over the family home have been engaged in a steady process of restoration.

Guests are offered a warm welcome and a relaxing atmosterre at Drakestone. It is an ideal centre for touring the Cotswolds and within easy reach of Bath and Bristol.

Location: Midway between Dursley and Wotton-under-Edge on B4060.

DRUMMOND HOUSE

PRICES
B & B   £35.00
Dinner   £25.00

OPEN
All Year

HOST
Alan and
Josephine
Dougall

Tel/Fax
031 557 9189

DRUMMOND HOUSE, 17 DRUMMOND PLACE, EDINBURGH

Drummond House, set in the heart of Edinburgh's historic 'New Town' is one of the few remaining complete and original Town Houses. Its handsome rooms and high ceilings exemplify the grace and style of Georgian architecture. Elegant decoration, antiques and sumptous furnishings blend to create a warm and welcoming atmosphere.

Josephine and Alan, who enjoy speaking French and Spanish, host excellent dinners in the fine bow-ended dining room. A no-smoking house.

Location: 1/4 mile north of St Andrew Sq. at the east end of Great King Street.

MOAT HOUSE

PRICES
B & B   £32p.p.
Dinner from £20.

OPEN
1st March to
30th November

HOST
Peter & Margaret
Richards

Tel/Fax
(0743) 718434

MOAT HOUSE, SHREWSBURY, SHROPSHRE

A 15th Century timber framed manor house, set within its 700 year old water filled moat. Dine in the open hall beneath the unique carved timbers with its massive stone fireplace. Enjoy the medieval hospitality, and ambience of this peaceful, friendly home. Capture a sense of timelessness in a changing world, En suite facilities and central heating ensure 20th Century comforts.

The natural grounds harbour many wild herbs, flowers, birds and animals.

Location: 8 miles south of Shrewsbury A49, turn east to Longnor, through village, left into lane signed 'No Through Road', lane turns sharp left, Moat House straight ahead.

GLENFEOCHAN HOUSE

PRICES
B & B Double
Room price £124
incl. VAT
Dinner £30 p.p.

OPEN
March to
31 October

HOST
David & Patricia
Baber
(0631) 77273

GLENFEOCHAN HOUSE, KILMORE, OBAN, ARGYLLSHIRE

Glenfeochan House is a turreted Victorian Country Mansion built in 1875 and set amidst a 350 acre Estate of Hills, Lochs, Rivers and Pasture. The House is surrounded by one of the Great Gardens of the Highlands. Rare trees, magnificent Rhododendrons, Azaleas, carpets of spring bulbs and a spectacular Walled Garden. There, the vegetables, herbs and flowers that decorate the house grow. With three beautifully appointed rooms and the excellent cuisine, this house is an exceptional place to stay.

Location: 5 mile south of Oban on the A816

MONTYS COURT

PRICES
B & B   £30-£25
Dinner   £15.00
(optional)

OPEN
All Year

HOST
Major & Mrs A C
W Mitford-Slade

(0823) 432255

MONTYS COURT, TAUNTON, SOMERSET

Described by one visitor as a house that opens its arms to welcome you. Built in 1838 for the Slade family the house is set in parkland with views to the Quantock and Blackdown Hills. At the end of a large well maintained garden are hard tennis courts and a heated swimming pool (May-Sept.). Exmoor, the North Devon coast and numerous National Trust properties are within easy reach. A new 18 hole golf course at Oake (2 miles) opened Aug.93.

Location: South side of B3227, 1 mile west of Norton Fitzwarren (home of Taunton Cider), 4 miles west of Taunton.

HALEWELL CLOSE

PRICES
B & B Double   £37.50-£38.50
B & B Single   £47.50-£49.50
Dinner   £18.50
OPEN
All Year
HOST
Mrs E J Carey-Wilson
(0242) 890 238

HALEWELL CLOSE, WITHINGTON, GLOUCESTERSHIRE

Halewell is in the heart of the Cotswolds, on the edge of a quiet and pretty village off the main tourist routes.

The main reception rooms were a fifteenth century Monastery. The six double or twin rooms are all ensuite and include two family suites and one especially built for disabled Guests. The fifty acre grounds include formal and informal gardens, a secluded childrens play area, a newly landscaped pool and a five acre lake.

Location: 8 miles east of Cheltenham, south of A40. London 90 miles, Oxford 35 miles.

28 NORTHUMBERLAND STREET

PRICES
B & B   £30
Dinner   £20
By arrangement

OPEN
All Year

HOST
Mrs Eirlys Smith

031 557 8036

28 NORTHUMBERLAND STREET, EDINBURGH

An elegant Georgian house of architectural interest, Grade A listed, situated amidst Edinburgh's famous 18th century "New Town" with its terraces and gardens, it is furnished with antiques and offers a friendly, relaxing and comfortable location in the heart of Edinburgh. The bedrooms are luxurious and beautifully appointed, all with private bath, or shower rooms. Within 5 minutes walk of Princes Street, its central position enables guests to take advantage of Edinburgh's many attractions.

Location: Head for city centre, drive along Princes St. About midway (Opp. The Mound) turn up Frederick St., Northumberland St., parallel to Princes St. 5 main streets north. Turn right into Northumberland St.

PENYCLAWDD COURT

PRICES
B & B   £30 p.p.
Dinner   £16.50

OPEN
All Year

HOST
Julia Horton
Evans
(0873) 890719

PENYCLAWDD COURT, ABERGAVENNY, GWENT

Set in the Brecon Beacons National Park this Tudor Manor House is a perfect setting for exploration. Julia, an archaeological restorer is reviving the mediaeval ambience of the house but its interior authenticity and eccentricity means it is not best suited to all! A Norman Motte and Bailey abuts the traditional Herb Garden and recently planted Knot Garden. Free range hens and a flock of pedigree Jacob Sheep complete the charm of this rural retreat.

Location: Four miles north east of Abergavenny 1/3 mile west of A465

TROTTON OLD RECTORY

PRICES
B & B   £30-£35
Dinner   £20

OPEN
All Year but
closed
Chistmas & New
Year

HOST
Capt. & Mrs John
Pilley
(0730) 813612

TROTTON OLD RECTORY, NR. PETERSFIELD, HAMPSHIRE

Grade II 18th Century former Rectory with attractive French inspired slate roof and shutters set in typical large English garden with formal beds of old fashioned roses framed in yew and box, mature trees and herbaceous borders. River frontage with views of ancient bridge and Church as well as a lake with a small island. Back of house has an untouched very old cobbled yard surrounded by stone and tiled coach house and stables. Croquet lawn, Tennis Court, Pool, Vegetable Garden.

Location: Trotton is on the A272 between Midhurst and Petersfield.

ROSSIE PRIORY

PRICES
B & B   £30-£40
Dinner   £30

OPEN
April to October

HOST
G R Spencer
(0828) 86028

ROSSIE PRIORY, INCHTURE, PERTHSHIRE

This classic gothic mansion faces South over the river Tay to Fife. The glorious view is shared by the magnificent reception rooms and the large comfortable bedrooms with private bathrooms. Pathways wander among fine trees, with rhododendrons bursting into colour during May and June. Near the herbaceous borders are the heated swimming pool and asphalt tennis court. Rossie is an hour from Edinburgh Airport. Carnoustie, Gleneagles and St. Andrews are about half an hour.

Location: On the A85, 1 mile east of Inchture, turn north at the signpost for Knapp.   Drive immediately left through lodge gate for 1 mile to the house.

UPTON HOUSE

PRICES
B & B   £32.50p.p
Dinner   £23.50
Supper   £13.50

OPEN
All year except
Christmas &
New Year

HOST
Angela & Hugh
Jefferson
(0905) 381226

UPTON HOUSE, UPTON SNODSBURY, WORCESTER

A 12th century village manor house, offers guests a winning combination of a lovely house with country cottage cosiness, outstanding decor, treasured antiques and carefully tended flower filled gardens. Attention has been paid to the smallest details, tea caddies are packed with every imaginable type of tea, bathrooms are supplied with every extra. Spend a day at Cheltenham races, visit the Royal Porcelain Factory with its second shop in Worcester, see a play at Stratford or tour the lesser known Cotswold villages. A No Smoking house.

Location: Upton Snodsbury is 6 miles east of Worcester on the A422, to Stratford. M5 Junction 6 or 7, 5 miles away.

SILKHOUSE

PRICES
B & B   £25
Dinner   £15

OPEN
All Year

HOST
James Clifton
064 723 1267

SILKHOUSE, DREWSTEIGNTON, EXETER, DEVON

Picturesque 16th century south facing Devon Longhouse, set in a beautiful wooded valley, surrounded by a cottage garden and boarded by streams. This cottage allows total peace and seclusion. Beamed ceilings, granite fireplaces, combined with antique furnishings make for a relaxed atmosphere with 20th century comfort. The cooking is mainly English taking advantage of local and own produce.

Location: Within the Dartmoor National Park, 15 miles west of Exeter, 3 miles from Chagford.

WINSTONE GLEBE

PRICES
B & B   £25-£30
Dinner   £15
Single Sup.   £5

OPEN
All Year

HOST
Mrs Susanna
Parsons
(0285) 821451

WINSTONE GLEBE, CIRENCESTER, GLOUCESTERSHIRE

Winstone Glebe is a Georgian Rectory set in 5 acres of gardens and paddocks. Overlooks a Saxon church in a Domesday listed village. The house is traditionally furnished, has spectacular views and is very quiet.

Being an area of "Outstanding Natural Beauty" there are numerous sign-posted walks. Those less energetic can enjoy the warm hospitality, country house weekend party atmosphere and the good food prepared by Susanna who trained as a professional cook and ran the Cordon Bleu Restaurant.

Location: 20 mins. from M5 junction 11; 30 mins. from M4 junction 15. Winstone is 6 miles north west of Cirencester off the A417.

OTHER PRIVATE HOUSES OFFERING ACCOMMODATION

ENGLAND

The Old Rectory, Wath, Nr Ripon, North Yorkshire, HG4 5ET.
Mrs Tulip Bemrose. Tel: 0765 640311.

Mardon House, Cornhill-on-Tweed, Northumberland, TD12 4SJ.
Alyson & Michael Bowman-Vaughan. Tel: 0890 820510.

Hornby Castle, Bedale, North Yorkshire, DL8 1NQ.
Julia & Roger Clutterbuck. Tel: 0748 811579.

The Citadel, Weston-under-Redcastle, Nr Shrewsbury, Shropshire, SY4 5JY.
Mrs Sylvia Griffiths. Tel: 0630 685204.

Tickencote Hall, Nr Stamford, Lincolnshire, PE9 4AE.
Mr & Mrs Peter Dearden. Tel: 0780 65155.

Golden Grove, Llanasa, Holywell, Clwyd, CH8 9NE.
The Steele-Mortimer Family. Tel: 0745 854452.

Upper Court, Kemerton, Nr Tewkesbury, Gloucestershire, GL20 7HY.
Bill & Diana Herford. Tel: 0386 725351.

Rushmere Manor, Nr Leighton Buzzard, Bedfordshire, LU7 0ED.
Mr & Mrs Paul Goudime. Tel: 0525 237336.

Sedgeford Hall, Sedgeford, Nr Hunstanton, Norfolk, PE36 5LT.
Professor & Mrs Bernard Campbell. Tel: 0485 70902/70941.

Crugsillick Manor, Ruan High Lanes, Nr St. Mawes, Truro, Cornwall, TR2 5LJ.
Jeremy & Diana Lloyd. Tel: 0872 501214.

Erth Barton, Saltash, Cornwall, PL12 4QY.
Guy Bentinck & Clio Smeeton. Tel: 0752 842127.

SCOTLAND

Forbes Lodge, Gifford, Haddington, East Lothian, EH41 4JE.
Lady Marioth Hay. Tel: 062 081 221.

Blervie, Forres, Moray, IV36 0RH.
Lt Cdr & Mrs I P F Meiklejohn. Tel: 0309 672358.

Eden House, by Banff, AB45 3NT.
Diana & Anthony Sharp. Tel: 02616 282.

Prestonhall, Pathhead, Midlothian, EH37 5UG.
Henry & Jackie Callander. Tel: 0875 320949.

Dinnet House, Aboyne, Aberdeenshire, AB34 5LN.
Marcus & Sabrina Humphrey. Tel: 03398 85332.

Dupplin Castle, by Perth, Perthshire, PH2 0PY.
Derek & Angela Straker. Tel: 0738 23224.

CASTLE FORBES, ABERDEENSHIRE

CARRIGGLAS

PRICES
B & B   £40-£50
Dinner   £20

OPEN
May-October

HOST
Jeffry & Tessa
Lefroy

Tel (043) 45165
Fax (043) 45875

CARRIGGLAS MANOR, LONGFORD, CO. LONGFORD

You will be received as private guests of the Lefroy family in their magnificent ancestral home, featured in the recent publication "Great Irish Houses & Castles". Situated in the heart of Ireland's lakeland region and half way to everywhere it is the perfect base for exploring, stately home and garden visiting, golf, riding and fishing. Evenings are spent dining with your hosts with emphasis on elegance, superb food and sparkling conversation.

ADVANCE BOOKING ESSENTIAL

Location: 3 miles from Longford on T15 Granard road, 2 miles off main N4.

GLIN CASTLE

OPEN
April - October

HOST
The Knight of
Glin & Madam
Fitzgerald
(068)
34173/34112

GLIN CASTLE, GLIN CO. LIMERICK

Near Ballybunion Golf Course and 1 hour's drive from Shannon Airport 18th century Glin Castle has magnificent plaster ceilings and fine collections of Irish paintings and furniture. Fully staffed and very comfortable it welcomes no more than 8 guests for dinner and overnight stays. Well kept gardens surround the Castle which has wonderul views over the River Shannon. The Castle can be rented.

Location: Situated on the Foynes Tarbert Road N69, 9 km. west of Foynes and 5 km. east of Tarbert and the car ferry.

Carrigglas

Glin Castle

OTHER PRIVATE HOUSES OFFERING ACCOMMODATION

IRELAND

Drenagh, Limarvady, Co. Londonderry, BT49 0HP.
Peter & June Welsh. Tel: 05047 22649.

Carnelly House, Clarecastle, Co. Clare.
Rosemarie Gleeson. Tel: 353 65 28442.

Bantry House, Bantry, Co. Cork.
Egerton Shelswell White. Tel: 027 50047.

Glendalough House, Caragh Lake, Co. Kerry.
Josephine Roder. Tel: 066 69156.

Hilton Park, Clones, Co. Monaghan.
Johnny & Lucy Madden. Tel: 047 56007

Temple House, Ballymote, Co. Sligo.
Sandy & Deb Perceval. Tel: 071 83329.

Ballinkeele House, Ballymurn, Enniscorthy, Co. Wexford.
John & Margaret Maher. Tel: 053 38105.

HILTON PARK, CO. MONAGHAN, IRELAND

HOTELS
IN
HISTORIC
HOUSES

AMBERLEY CASTLE
Nr. Arundel, West Sussex

CONTACT

Tim Morton
Amberley Castle
Amberley
Arundel
West Sussex
BN18 9ND

Tel: (0798) 831992
Fax: (0798) 831998

LOCATION

Amberley Castle is situated on the B2139 between A29 at Bury Hill, and Storrington

Rail: Located 1/2 mile from Amberley station (Direct line service to London Victoria).

Begun in the early 1100's by Bishop Luffa of Chichester as a country manor house, Amberley Castle's raison d'etre was to provide a peaceful retreat and a setting for lavish entertainment. For half a millenium Amberley Castle fulfilled this role for a succession of episcopal chatelains.

Its subsequent secular tenants continued the tradition to the highest level in the land, extending hospitality to King Charles II and his Queen, Catherine of Braganza. The 17th century mural in the Queen's Room, Amberley Castle's handsome barrel-vaulted restaurant, commemorates the occasion.

Marauding pirates may have threatened the peace within the mighty 14th century walls which Oliver Cromwell's soldiers tried to reduce to rubble. But Amberley Castle has endured, bringing with it to the present day its tranquillity, its security and the wonderful sense of history that envelopes all who enter beneath the great oaken portcullis.

Since 1989, Amberley Castle's owners, Joy and Martin Cummings, have wrought a miracle in the ancient building, transforming it into a peaceful, luxurious hotel, its 14 superbly appointed rooms, each named after a Sussex castle and boasting an en suite Jacuzzi bath.

The three lovely lounges, each with its own individual character offer space and comfort conducive to conversations and relaxation. There are two private dining rooms for parties or small business meetings, and the magnificent Great Room for banquets and receptions of every kind.

The magic of Amberley Castle has inspired another unique innovation: Castle Cuisine, the exciting creation of Award-winning Head Chef, Nigel Boschetti. English culinary tradition - the ingredients and cooking methods of our forebears - together with the castle's own history have inspired Nigel to create dishes which draw their origins from the past while pleasing the palates of today.

Just an hour from the clamour of the city, yet steeped in the peace of beautiful Sussex Downland, there is a treat in store for Amberley Castle's guests - friendly service, splendid food, serenity.

The warmth of Amberley Castle's welcome has resulted in an array of prestigious awards including an RAC Blue Ribbon, 2 AA Rosettes and "Best Family Run Hotel in the World Award 1993" (Gallivanter's Guide).

OPENING TIMES

Open all year round

PRICE GUIDE

Day Delegate Rate :
£35.00.
24 Hour Delegate Rate::
£135.00.

Single Rooms:
£95.00-£225.00
Double Rooms:
£95.00-£225.00
(incl. breakfast,
newspaper and VAT).

All rooms have En-Suite
Bathrooms.

FACILITIES

- 14 Luxury Rooms all with en suite Jacuzzi
- Peace and Tranquility
- Award winning Restaurant
- Full conference and Private Dining Facilities
- All major Credit Cards accepted
- Children welcome
- Colour T.V. Video and Video Library
- Direct dial telephones
- Helicopter landing facilities
- Croquet and Horse Riding
- Clay Shooting and Archery by prior arrangement
- Ornamental Gardens

ATTRACTIONS

The Castle is surrounded by a wealth of attractions for the discerning traveller including Parham and Petworth House, Goodwood House and Racecourse and only 40 minutes drive from Historic Portsmouth and Brighton.

CONFERENCE AND FUNCTION FACILITIES

ROOM	DIMENSIONS	CAPACITY	LAYOUT	POWER POINTS	SUITABLE FOR A/V
Great Room	35'11" x 14'10"	48	Banquet		✓
		30	Boardroom		
King Charles 1st Room	17' x 13'	12	Boardroom		✓

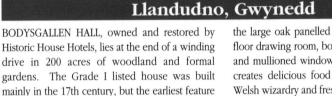

BODYSGALLEN HALL
Llandudno, Gwynedd

BODYSGALLEN HALL, owned and restored by Historic House Hotels, lies at the end of a winding drive in 200 acres of woodland and formal gardens. The Grade I listed house was built mainly in the 17th century, but the earliest feature is a 13th century tower reached by a spiral stone steps, once used as a lookout for soldiers serving the English kings at Conwy, now a wonderful place to enjoy magnificent views of the medieval castle and the mountains of Snowdonia.

The hotel is situated on the side of a hill not far from the Victorian resort of Llandudno. Bodysgallen Hall has 19 large, comfortable bedrooms in the house and 9 delightful cottage suites in the grounds, many with their own gardens. Two of the finest rooms in the house are the large oak panelled entrance hall and the first floor drawing room, both with splendid fireplaces and mullioned windows. Head Chef Mair Lewis creates delicious food using her own brand of Welsh wizardry and fresh local ingredients.

Bodysgallen Hall has been open since 1982 and has created a loyal following of regular clients who visit for a variety of reasons - the wonderful scenery which includes mountains, lakes, seaside and local beauty spots like the Swallow Falls at Betws-y-coed, well appointed bedrooms and a choice of inviting sitting rooms, award winning gardens and woodland walks. Above all, what most people value at Bodysgallen is the warmth of the hospitality and the atmosphere of peace and tranquility.

CONTACT

Andrew Bridgford
Bodysgallen Hall
Llandudno
Gwynedd
Ll30 1RS

Tel: (0492) 584466
Fax: (0492) 582519

LOCATION

1 mile from intersection of the A40 to Llandudno with the A55 North Wales Expressway.

Rail: Llandudno Junction 2 miles - direct line to London (Euston).

Air: Manchester Airport 1 1/2 hours. Helicopters may land in grounds.

ATTRACTIONS

The gardens at Bodysgallen are a great attractions and include a rose garden, a walled garden and a 17th century knot garden as well as a tennis court and croquet lawn. The hotel is well placed for visiting Welsh castles such as Caernarfon, Conwy and Harlech, stately homes like Plas Newydd and Penrhyn, the Victorian seaside town of Llandudno and the magnificent gardens at Bodnant. There are four golf courses within ten minutes drive and guests can go on fishing trips, horse-riding, pony trekking, rock climbing and hill walking as well as sailing in Conwy Bay and a variety of other water sports.

OPENING TIMES

Open all year.

PRICE GUIDE

Day Delegate Rate:
£30.00
24 hour Delegate Rate:
£125.00

Single Rooms:
£82.00-£85.00.
Double Rooms:
£108.00-£135.00.
Suites:
£150.00-£170.00.

All rooms have En-Suite Bathrooms

FACILITIES

- 28 Bedrooms/Suites
- Quiet location/rural setting
- Unique conference centre for up to 40
- Traditional restaurant - Country House cooking
- Award-winning gardens/200 acres parkland
- Children under 8 not accepted
- Colour TV/direct dial telephone/trouser press
- Tennis Court/Croquet Lawn
- All major credit cards accepted
- Helicopter landing facilities

CONFERENCE AND FUNCTION FACILITIES

Room	Dimensions	Capacity	Layout	Power Points	Suitable for A/V
Upper Wynn Room	9.6 x 5.4m	26	Boardroom	10	✓
		40	Classroom/Theatre		
Lower Wynn Rooms	9.4 x 5.4m	40	Formal Dinner	10	✓
		40	Buffet		
Tack Room (Syndicate Room)	4.25 x 4m	10	Small Meeting	4	✓

HARTWELL HOUSE
near Aylesbury, Buckinghamshire

HARTWELL HOUSE is a Grade I Listed Mansion built in the 17th and 18th centuries and has both Jacobean and Georgian facades. It was from 1809 to 1814 the home of Louis XVIII.

The house and gardens have been sympathetically and skilfully restored by Historic House Hotels who have created an hotel with several magnificent reception rooms, which include the rococo Morning Room with its splendid decorated ceiling, the Drawing Room and the book lined Library. The Dining Room designed in the manner of Sir John Soane, is the setting for award winning gourmet food and fine wine.

There are 47 elegant bedrooms and suites, many with fourposter beds, some in the main house and some in Hartwell Court, the restored 18th century stables. Many of the Royal rooms on the first floor of the house are exceptionally large and are named after members of the Bourbon family who occupied them.

Hartwell House is surrounded by 90 acres of parkland designed by a contemporary of 'Capability' Brown, with a lake, two tennis courts and many 18th century garden buildings.

Adjacent to the house are the Hartwell Rooms, four purpose built air-conditioned meeting rooms, and the Hartwell Spa, with a spacious swimming pool and the Hartwell Buttery serving drinks and light meals,

Hartwell House is in a rural setting in the Buckinghamshire countryside but is only an hour's drive from London. The hotel has won many awards since it first opened in 1989.

OPENING TIMES

Open all year.

PRICE GUIDE

Day Delegate Rate:
£51.00
24 Hour Delegate Rate:
£185.00

Singles Rooms:
£90.00
Double Rooms:
£135.00-£199.00
Suites:
£179.00-£299.00

All rooms have En-Suite Bathrooms

FACILITIES

- ❑ 90 acres Garden and, Parkland with Lake
- ❑ 2 Tennis Courts/ Croquet Lawn
- ❑ Leisure Spa with heated Swimming Pool, Beauty Salon
- ❑ 47 Bedrooms/Suites. All with colour TV and Direct Dial Telephones
- ❑ Award winning restaurant
- ❑ Air conditioned self contained meeting rooms
- ❑ Children over 8 welcome
- ❑ Dogs allowed in rooms in Hartwell Court
- ❑ Major credit cards accepted

CONTACT

Jonathan Thompson
Hartwell House
Oxford Road
Aylesbury
Buckinghamshire
HP17 8NL

Tel: (0296) 747444
Fax: (0296) 747450

LOCATION

From London M40, junct. 7 via A329/A418 Thame/Aylesbury Road or M40 junct 2 via A355 to Amersham and A413 to Aylesbury. Hartwell House is on the A418 Oxford Road.

Aylesbury station 2 miles. Heathrow Airport 35 miles.
There is a helicopter landing pad in the grounds.
Approach from North N.5148.43 W 00050.88

ATTRACTIONS

The Hartwell Spa contains a large heated indoor swimming pool, steam room, whirlpool spa bath, saunas, solarium and a well equipped gymnasium. Beauty salon offers a variety of treatments and a hairdresser.

Local places of interest include Blenheim Palace, home of the Dukes of Marlborough and birthplace of Winston Churchill, Woburn Abbey with its magnificent deer park and Waddesdon Manor due to re-open after extensive restoration. Guests can visit Stowe Landscape Gardens and Oxford with its colleges, museum and shops is only 20 miles away.

CONFERENCE AND FUNCTION FACILITIES

Room	Dimensions	Capacity	Layout	Power Points	Suitable for A/V
James Gibbs Room	14.7 x 6.2m	90	Various	20	✓
James Gibbs divided	12 x 12		U-Shape		
James Wyatt Room	13.7 x 6.4m	100	Various	20	✓
Eric Throssell Boardroom	7.6 x 6.2m	16	Boardroom	16	✓
Henry Keene Room	8.3 x 3.5m	12	Boardroom	12	✓

LITTLE THAKEHAM
Storrington, West Sussex

LITTLE THAKEHAM designed in 1902 by Sir Edward Lutyens is a Grade I listed Manor House set in a thousand acre estate of farms and orchards. Lutyens, the foremost architect of the last century thought of Little Thakeham as the 'best of the bunch' when referring to his works. The house and garden which have recently been restored have changed little since they were created.

Tim and Pauline Ratcliff who bought the house in 1979 have decorated and furnished the house in the Arts & Crafts period. The house is now visited by many architects, designers and connoisseurs of fine art and life style.

The gardens although not by the redoubtable Gertrude Jekyll have been planted in her style. The original owner, Edward Blackburn, was an enthusiastic gardener and plantsman and his original diaries were available to help in the restoration of the garden.

Just over an hours drive from London and in easy reach of Gatwick and Heathrow Little Thakeham is an ideal retreat from the hurly burly of city life.

The house and gardens lend themselves as a location for film or fashion shoots, private house parties and wedding receptions, in a setting of beauty and seclusion with the highest standards of comfort, food and service.

ATTRACTIONS

Sporting activities have always been a feature of life at Little Thakeham. Shooting parties, polo at Cowdray, horse riding, hunting, racing at nearby Goodwood and Fontwell and with the stables of Harwood, Dunlop and Gifford all nearby.

Cultural attractions such as Glyndebourne. The Royal Pavilion at Brighton, Arundel Castle, Parham House and the antique centre at Petworth are not far away.

CONTACT

Tim Ratcliff
Little Thakeham
Merrywood Lane
Storrington
West Sussex
RH20 3HE

Tel: (0903) 744416
Fax: (0903) 745022

LOCATION

48 miles from London on A24. 1½ miles north of Storrington on B2139.

Airport: 20 miles from Gatwick.

Rail: 5 miles from Pulborough.

OPENING TIMES

Open all year except Christmas and New Year.

PRICE GUIDE

Single Rooms:
   from £95.00
Double Rooms:
   from £150.00
Suites:
   from £200.00

All rooms have En-suite Bathrooms.

FACILITIES

- ❑ 7 Bedrooms, 2 Suites
- ❑ Credit cards accepted
- ❑ Quiet location
- ❑ Tennis, Croquet and heated Swimming Pool
- ❑ Other sporting activities arranged
- ❑ Helicopter landing
- ❑ Ideal film or fashion location
- ❑ Private parties and Wedding Receptions
- ❑ Children welcome

CONFERENCE AND FUNCTION FACILITIES

ROOM	DIMENSIONS	CAPACITY	LAYOUT	POWER POINTS	SUITABLE FOR A/V
SMALL CONFERENCES OF UP TO 30 PEOPLE BY ARRANGEMENT					

MIDDLETHORPE HALL
York

MIDDLETHORPE HALL is a gracious Queen Anne house, built in 1699 for Thomas Barlow, a wealthy Sheffield Ironmaster, and was for a time the home of Lady Mary Wortley Montagu, the well known 18th century diarist.

After many changes of ownership Middlethorpe was rescued from deterioration and decay by Historic House Hotels who carried out an immaculate restoration of the house and gardens. It has been decorated and furnished in a manner which evokes its original elegance and style. Guests can relax in the reception hall in front of a welcoming fire, the magnificent drawing room, once the ballroom of the house, or the comfortable library.

There are beautifully designed bedrooms and suites, some on two floors in the main house and some in the adjacent Classical Courtyard, and there are two further suites in a detached cottage. The panelled dining room overlooks the grounds, and the chef specialises in the best contemporary English cooking providing an imaginative menu complemented by a carefully chosen wine list.

Middlethorpe stands in 26 acres of parkland which include a sheltered walled garden, a white garden, a lake and original ha ha's. There is a magnificent cedar of Lebanon which dominates the south lawn where guests can play croquet

The Barlow Room, with its own kitchen, is detached from the main house and is ideal for meetings, receptions and private entertaining.

Middlethorpe Hall is a genuine country house in a tranquil setting yet close enough to York for guests to be able to visit its many attractions.

CONTACT

Stephen Browning
Middlethorpe Hall
Bishopthorpe Road
York
YO2 1QB

Tel: (0904) 641241
Fax: (0904) 620176

LOCATION

From the south take A64(T) off A1, follow signs to York West (A1036) them smaller signs to Bishopthorpe.

York Station (1 hour 45 minutes from London) is 1^1/2 miles.

Nearest airport Leeds/Bradford 25 miles.

Helipad in grounds
Grid ref: N5355 00`05.77

ATTRACTIONS

Middlethorpe is close to the historic city of York with its fascinating museums, Roman wall and Viking remains, medieval streets and world famous Minster.

From Middlethorpe you can visit famous stately homes like Castle Howard (setting for Brideshead Revisited) , Newby Hall, Sledmere and Beningbrough and the ruined abbeys at Fountains, Rievaulx and Jervaulx.

It is ideal for exploring the beauty of the Yorkshire dales, seaside villages and dramatic moors.

The hotel overlooks York Racecourse, known as the 'Ascot of the North' which makes it an ideal choice for the racegoer.

OPENING TIMES

Open all year.

PRICE GUIDE

Day Delegate Rate:
£30.00
24 hour Delegate Rate:
£125.00

Single Rooms:
£83.00
Double Rooms:
£115.00-£165.00
Suites:
£165.00-£189.00

All rooms have En-Suite Bathrooms.

FACILITIES

- ❏ 23 Bedrooms//7 Suites
- ❏ Colour TV with Teletext in all bedrooms
- ❏ Direct dial telephones in all bedrooms
- ❏ Peaceful setting
- ❏ 26 acres of Parkland with lake
- ❏ Croquet Lawn
- ❏ Children over 8 welcome
- ❏ Gourmet Restaurant
- ❏ Credit cards accepted

CONFERENCE AND FUNCTION FACILITIES

ROOM	DIMENSIONS	CAPACITY	LAYOUT	POWER POINTS	SUITABLE FOR A/V
Barlow Room	36'6" x 20'6"	63	Theatre	12	✓
		32	Boardroom		
		50	Dinner		
		80	Reception		
Barlow Room Divided	18'3" x 20'6"	12 x 2			✓
Boardroom		10		4	

SPECIAL EVENTS DIARY 1994

It is suggested that visitors should telephone to confirm dates and details in advance. Where a (P) is given in brackets, it indicates that the date is only provisional.

FEBRUARY

2nd   **Royal Society of Arts**
Lecture: 'The state of democracy in the United Kingdom'

4th-6th   **Leighton Hall, Lancashire**
Antiques Fair

5th   **Sulgrave Manor, Northants**
Chamber Concert - 7.30pm in Hall with light Buffet Supper

25th-27th   **Penshurst Place, Kent**
Home design and interiors exhibition

MARCH

5th   **Sulgrave Manor, Northants**
Chamber Concert - 7.30pm in Hall with light Buffet Supper

11th-13th   **Hanbury Hall, Worcs**
Home design and interiors exhibition

12th   **Oakley Hall, Shrops**
Concert, *'Baroque Opera Company'*

18th-20th   **Luton Hoo, Bedfordshire**
Antiques Fair

18th-26th   **Sulgrave Manor, Northants**
Music Weekend - *Leaflet available*

19th-20th   **Ragley Hall, Warwicks**
Craft Fair

19th-27th   **Leeds Castle, Kent**
Spring Gardens Week

25th-27th   **Luton Hoo, Bedfordshire**
Craft Fair

25th-27th   **Wilton House, Wiltshire**
Antiques Fair

26th-27th   **Ragley Hall, Warwicks**
Antiques Fair

29th-30th **Wilton House, Wiltshire**
Oct.   50th Anniversary D-Day Exhibitions

30th   **RSA, London**
Lecture: 'Whose money is it anyhow?'

APRIL

TBA   **Hanbury Hall, Worcs**
Mozart Concert - *The Impresario* Purcell Concert

1st-4th   **Athelhampton, Dorset**
Athelhampton Easter Craft Show

2nd-4th   **Leeds Castle, Kent**
Childrens Easter Egg Hunts

3rd   **Killerton House, Devon**
Horse Trials

3rd   **Wilton House, Wiltshire**
Childrens' Easter Egg Hunt

3rd-4th   **Lamport Hall, Northants**
Antiques Fair

3rd-4th   **Penshurst Place, Kent**
Classic Car Rally

10th   **Cobham Hall, Kent**
National Gardens Scheme Day

15th-17th   **Capel Manor, Middlesex**
The Spring Gardening Show

16th-17th   **Berkeley Castle, Glos**
Spring Flower Show. *2500 tulips and amaryllis on display in Great Hall.*

16th-17th   **Shugborough, Staffs**
10am-5pm: Gamekeepers' Fair. *Official B.A.S.C. Annual Country Fair. Arena demonstrations, gun dog competitions, clay shoots. Over 100 stalls, something for all the family.*

16th-17th   **Capesthorne Hall, Cheshire**
Rainbow Craft Fair

16th-24th   **Sulgrave Manor, Northants**
Living History 1664

17th   **Cobham Hall, Kent**
Spring Walk, Garden Tour, 3.00pm

23rd-24th   **Kelburn Castle & Country Centre**
Woodcraft and Forestry Fair

23rd-24th   **Wilton House, Wiltshire**
St George's Spring Festival

30th   **Hoghton Tower, Lancashire**
Antiques Fair

30th-1/5   **Hever Castle, Kent**
Traditional and Mediaeval Music and Dance in Castle grounds.

30th-1/5   **Scone Palace, Perth**
Horse Trials

30th-2/5   **Penshurst Place, Kent**
Craft Fair

MAY

TBA   **Broadlands, Hampshire**
Classic Car Roadshow

TBA   **Hanbury Hall, Worcs**
Open Air Classical Concert

30/4-1st   **Scone Palace, Perth**
Horse Trials

30/4-2nd   **Penshurst Place, Kent**
Craft Fair

1st-2nd   **Hoghton Tower, Lancashire**
Antiques Fair

1st-2nd   **Wilton House, Wiltshire**
May Day Folk

1st   **Stanford Hall, Leics**
Volkswagen Owners Club Rally (Warwicks. & Leics. Branch).

1st-2nd   **Capel Manor, Middlesex**
Country Lifestyles Show

1st-2nd   **Lamport Hall, Northants**
Craft Festival

1st-2nd   **Ragley Hall, Warwicks**
Ragley Horse Trials

2nd   **Capesthorne Hall, Cheshire**
Childrens Society Garden Party

2nd   **Killerton House, Devon**
Carriage Driving Trials

5th-8th   **Hatfield House, Herts**
Living Crafts. *The largest Craft Fair in Europe - over 400 Craftsmen selling or demonstrating their skill.*

7th-8th   **Leonardslee Gardens, Sussex**
Bonsai Weekend

8th   **Stanford Hall, Leics**
South Leicestershire MG Owners Club Rally

13th-15th   **Wilton House, Wiltshire**
Craft Fair (Wilton Park)

14th   **Oakley Hall, Shrops**
Concert 'Baroque Opera Company'

14th   **Ragley Hall, Warwicks**
Charity Concert

15th   Rover P4 Rally

14th-15th   **Chatsworth, Derbyshire**
Chatsworth Angling Fair. *The only specialised Angling Fair in the Country catering for game, coarse and sea-fishing enthusiasts with added family attractions and trade stands.*

14th-15th   **Duncombe Park, Yorkshire**
Spring Crafts Festival

15th   **Kelburn Castle & Country Centre**
Noah's Ark Carnival

15th(P)   **Stanford Hall, Leics**
Leicestershire Ford RS Owners Club Rally

15th-16th   **Leeds Castle, Kent**
Festival of English Wines

20th   **Castle Fraser, Grampian**
Classical Concert

21st (P)   **Stanford Hall, Leics**
Wartburg/IFA Owners Club (UK) Rally
Unloved Soviet and Socialist Register Rally

21st-22nd   **Sandon Hall, Staffordshire**
The Stafford County Antiques Fair

21st -5/6   **Sulgrave Manor, Northants**
Stars, Stripes and Stitches Needlework Festival

22nd (P)   **Stanford Hall, Leics**
Capri Club International Rally

27th-28th   **Luton Hoo, Bedfordshire**
Stately Homes Music Festival

28th   **Blair Castle, Perthshire**
Atholl Highlanders Parade

SPECIAL EVENTS DIARY

28th   **Hever Castle, Kent**
Mediaeval Fayre. *Mediaeval crafts on display in the grounds of the Castle.*

28th-29th   **Traquair House, Peeblesshire**
Celebration of Scottish Beer - *A beer festival held in the old walled garden including beers from every Scottish brewery.*

28th-30th   **Shugborough, Staffordshire**
10am-5pm: Shugborough Spring Craft and Country Show. *Fascinating range of traditional craft stalls, skilled craft people at work.*

28th-30th   **Stanford Hall, Leics**
National Hovercraft Racing Championships

28th-5th   **Wilton House, Wiltshire**
50th Anniversary D-Day landings - special events

29th   **Blair Castle, Perthshire**
Atholl Gathering and Highland Games

29th-30th   **Cobham Hall, Kent**
Transport Fair

29th-30th   **Belvoir Castle, Lincs**
Siege of the Castle

29th-30th   **Lamport Hall, Northants**
Lamport Country Festival

29th-30th   **Sandringham, Norfolk**
Sandringham Spectacular - Transport Through The Ages

29th-30th   **Capesthorne Hall, Cheshire**
Classic Car Show

29th-31st   **Stratfield Saye House, Berks.**
Craft Fair

31st   **Duncombe Park, Yorkshire**
Country Fair

JUNE

TBA   **Arbury Hall, Warwicks**
Craft Fair

21/5 -5th   **Sulgrave Manor, Northants**
Stars, Stripes and Stitches Needlework Festival

2nd-3rd   **Cobham Hall, Kent**
Dickens Festival (Dickens Walk at 3pm each day)

3rd-5th   **Holker Hall, Cumbria**
The Great Gardens and Countryside Festival. *A fabulous mix of Horticultural, Countryside and Environmental displays, this unique Festival also features many experts only too pleased to give advice on gardening and the countryside.*

4th-5th   **Leeds Castle, Kent**
Balloon and Vintage Car Fiesta

5th (P)   **Stanford Hall, Leics**
Lea-Francis Owners Club Rally
MG Owners Club Rally
The 39/45 Mil. Vehicle Group Rally

5th   **Arbury Hall, Warwicks**
Arbury Motor Transport Spectacular

10-12th   **Capel Manor, Middlesex**
The Summer Gardening Show

10th-12th   **Luton Hoo, Bedfordshire**
Bedfordshire Women's Institute Flower Festival

11th   **Capesthorne Hall, Cheshire**
Fireworks and Laser Symphony Concert

11th-12th   **Walcot Hall, Shropshire**
Shropshire Game Fair

11th-12th   **Burton Agnes Hall, Yorkshire**
Gardeners' Fair

12th   **Stanford Hall, Leics**
Alfa-Romeo Owners Club National Rally

12th   **Shugborough, Staffs**
11am-5pm Victorian Street Market: *Costumed street merchants set the scene as barrow boys, tinkers and piemen invite visitors to enjoy a traditional street market.*

14th   **Hoghton Tower, Lancashire**
Ballet Central

18th   **Hanbury Hall, Worcs**
Hanbury Village Fete

18th-19th   **Hatfield House, Herts**
The Festival of Gardening at Midsummer. *Set in the delightful gardens of Hatfield House. Displays of leading Nurserymen, Lectures, Question Time, Demonstrations, Trade Stands. A unique mixture of Flower Show and Garden Party.*

18th-19th   **Duncombe Park, Yorkshire**
Antiques Fair

18th-26th   **Burton Agnes Hall, Yorkshire**
1994 Exhibitions - *York & District Guild of Weavers, Spinners & Dyers.*

19th   **Lamport Hall, Northants**
East Midlands Doll Fair

19th   **Stanford Hall, Leics**
Ford AVO Owners Club Rally
Ford Executive Owners Register Rally
The Capri Collection Rally
(P)   Pre-1940 Triumph Owners Club Rally

19-17th July   **Kentwell Hall , Suffolk**
Historical Re-Creation. *Saturdays and Sundays only*

21st-25th   **Wallington, Northumberland**
Open Air Theatre: The Taming of the Shrew performed by Theatre Set-Up.

24th   **Killerton House, Devon**
Country Fair - *To celebrate the gift of Killerton to The National Trust 50 years ago.*

24th-26th   **Hever Castle, Kent**
NAFAS Flower Show - *The National Assoc of Flower Arranging Societies (Kent) Branch will hold t their annual show in the Castle grounds .*

25th   **Killerton House, Devon**
Country Show

25th   **Leeds Castle, Kent**
Annual Open Air Concert

25th   **Wilton House, Wiltshire**
Birthright Midsummer Ball

25th-26th   **Leonardslee Gardens, Sussex**
Country Craft Fair

25th-26th   **Penshurst Place Kent**
Garden of England Food and Drink Festival

25th-26th   **Ragley Hall, Warwicks**
Homes, Gardens and Crafts Fair

25th-26th   **Rockingham Castle, Leics**
Rainbow Craft Fair

25th-26th   **Sandringham, Norfolk**
Sandringham Country Weekend and Carriage Driving Trials

25th-26th   **The Gilbert White Museum, Hants**
Weekend of events including Jazz Concerts

26th   **Belvoir Castle, Lincs**
Mediaeval Jousting Tournament

26th   **Broughton Hall, Yorkshire**
Broughton Game Show

26th   **Scone Palace, Perth**
Coronation Pageant

26th   **Stanford Hall, Leics**
The Twelfth Rugby Raft Races

JULY

TBA   **Killerton House, Devon**
Jazz Night, Proms Night - *In conjunction with Exeter Festival*

TBA   **Leighton Hall, Lancs**
Midsummer Concert with Fireworks

TBA   **Rockingham Castle, Leics**
Siege Re-enactment: *Living History*

TBA   **The Queens House, Greenwich**
Greenwich Hospital - *An exhibition on the founding of the great hospital for sailors in 1694.*

TBA   **Hanbury Hall, Worcs**
Open Air Plays

19/6-17th   **Kentwell Hall, Suffolk**
Historical Re-Creation. *Saturdays and Sundays only*

2nd   **Leeds Castle, Kent**
Annual Open Air Concert

2nd-3rd   **Duncombe Park, Yorkshire**
Steam Fair

2nd-3rd   **Scone Palace, Perth**
Game/Country Fair

2nd-10th   **Sulgrave Manor, Northants**
Living History 1746

3rd   **Wilton House, Wiltshire**
Merlin Wiltshire Classic Car Tour (2pm-5pm)

3rd   **Stanford Hall, Leics**
Velocette Motorcycle Owners Club Rally

3rd   **Stanford Hall, Leics**
Club Triumph MN North London Club Rally

6th-7/8   **RSA, London**
RSA Student Design Awards

7th   **Blair Castle, Perthshire**
Charity Day in aid of Atholl Centre, Pitlochry

9th   **Wilton House, Wiltshire**
International Family Day (1pm-5pm)

10th   **Drum Castle, Grampian**
Gardens' Day

10th   **Cragside, Northumberland**
Family Funday

10th   **Glamis Castle, Angus**
The Scottish Transport Extravaganza
(Presented by Strathmore Vintage Vehicle Club).

10th (P)   **Stanford Hall, Leics**
Ford Escort 1300E Owners Club Rally

15th-16th   **Ragley Hall, Warwicks**
Stately Homes Music Festival

15th-23rd   **Wilton House, Wiltshire**
Studio Theatre - Romeo and Juliet
(Open air evening performance)

16th   **Hever Castle, Kent**
The Knights of Royal England present a Jousting Tournament

16th   **Killerton House, Devon**
Open Air Jazz Concert

16th-17th   **Luton Hoo, Bedfordshire**
Musical Event
(Classical & Light Popular)

16th-17th(P) **Stanford Hall, Leics**
BP Schools Hovercraft Competition

16th-17th   **Kelburn Castle & Country Centre**
Roots '94

17th   **Shugborough, Staffs**
11am-5pm: Goose Fair. From worm charmers to horse doctors, costume characters bring to life the raucous merriment of an 1820 Goose Fair at Shugborough Park Farm.

17th   **Broughton Hall, Yorkshire**
Performing Arts, Laser, Fireworks and Concert.

17th   **Cobham Hall Kent**
Jaguar Drivers Club Display

17th   **Hopetoun House, W. Lothian**
Hopetoun Country Fair

17th   **Killerton House Devon**
Open Air Classical Concert and Fireworks

17th   **Ragley Hall, Warwicks**
Transport Show

17th   **Stanford Hall, Leics**
Sporting Escort Owners Club Rally

22nd-24th   **Sulgrave Manor, Northants**
Tanglewood Theatre Productions

23rd   **Hever Castle, Kent**
Longbow Warfare. The Kent Bowmen demonstrate the use of the Longbow as a military weapon.

23rd/24th   **Capel Manor, Middlesex**
The Fuchsia Show

23rd-24th   **Fyvie Castle, Grampian**
Celebration of the Battle of Fyvie, 1644

24th   **Leith Hall, Grampian**
Gardens Day

24th   **Stanford Hall, Leics**
Vintage Motorcycle Club Founders Day Rally

27th   **Sandringham, Norfolk**
Sandringham Flower Show

30th   **Hever Castle, Kent**
The Knights of Royal England Present a Jousting Tournament

30th   **Ragley Hall, Warwicks**
Newfoundland Dog Trials

30th-31st   **Burton Agnes Hall, Yorkshire**
Flower Festival in support of St Catherine's Hospice.

31st   **Castle Fraser, Grampian**
Gardens' Day

31st   **Belvoir Castle, Lincs**
Mediaeval Jousting Tournament

31st   **Cobham Hall, Kent**
National Garden Scheme Day

31st (P)   **Stanford Hall, Leics**
Association of Healey Owners Rally

31st   **Traquair House, Peeblesshire**
Sheep and Wool Day. A day dedicated to sheep with sheep dog demonstrations, rare breed displays, spinning, shearing, dyeing and many stalls.

31st (P)   **Stanford Hall, Leics**
Association of Healey Owners Rally

End (P)   **Noseley Hall, Leics**
Live Crafts Fair

AUGUST

TBA   **Killerton House, Devon**
Shakespeare in the garden

TBA   **Leighton Hall, Lancs**
Shakespeare in the garden

TBA   **Broadlands, Hampshire**
Hampshire Craft Show

TBA   **Wilton House, Wiltshire**
Family Events:
Teddy Bears Picnic
Brass Rubbings
Heraldry

4th   **Castle Ashby, Northants**
Tour of garden with afternoon tea.

6th   **Hever Castle, Kent**
Longbow Warfare. The Kent Bowmen demonstrate the use of the Longbow as a military weapon.

6th   **Ragley Hall, Warwicks**
Firework and Laser Symphony Concert

6th-7th   **Cobham Hall, Kent**
Game and Countryman Fair

6th-7th   **Sulgrave Manor, Northants**
American Civil War Re-enactment

6th-7th   **Traquair House, Peeblesshire**
Traquair Fair. A wonderful weekend for all the family. Theatre, Circus, Music, Dance, Clowns, Storytelling, Crafts, Complementary Medicine and more.

7th   **Haddo House, Grampian**
Gardens' Day

7th   **Hatfield House, Herts**
Transport Spectacular. Victorian, Vintage and classic cars. Stalls, Autojumble. An ideal day for the car enthusiast.

7th   **Killerton House, Devon**
Shakespeare: 'Taming of the Shrew'

7th   **Stanford Hall, Leics**
Triumph Sports 6 Owners Club Rally

11th   **Castle Ashby, Northants**
Tour of garden with afternoon tea.

12th   **Killerton House, Devon**
Teddy Bears' Picnic

12th-14th   **Penshurst Place, Kent**
Balloon Festival

13th   **Hever Castle, Kent**
The Knights of Royal England Present a Jousting Tournament

13th-14th   **Pitmedden Garden, Grampian**
Garden Festival Weekend

13th-14th   **Kelburn Castle & Country Centre**
New Zealand Festival

14th   **Cobham Hall, Kent**
Summer Stroll - Garden Tour 3pm

14th (P)   **Stanford Hall, Leics**
Ford Fair 94

17th   **Castle Fraser, Grampian**
Scottish Concert

18th   **Castle Ashby, Northants**
Tour of garden with afternoon tea.

19th-22nd   **Fyvie Castle, Grampian**
Floral Art Weekend

20th   **Hever Castle, Kent**
Longbow Warfare. The Kent Bowmen demonstrate the use of the Longbow as a military weapon.

20th-21st   **Bicton Park Gardens, Devon**
Bicton Country Fayre at Bicton Arena

20th-21st   **Leighton Hall, Lancs**
Teddy Bears' Extravaganza

20th-21st   **Ragley Hall, Warwicks**
West Midlands Game Fair

20th-21st   **Wilton House, Wiltshire**
Wilton Horse Trials

21st   **Wallington, Northumberland**
Family Funday

25th   **Castle Ashby, Northants**
Tour of garden with afternoon tea.

25th-28th   **Blair Castle, Perthshire**
International Three Day Event and Horse Trials

SPECIAL EVENTS DIARY

26th-29th Sandringham, Norfolk
Rainbow Craft Fair

27th Hever Castle, Kent
The Knights of Royal England Present
a Jousting Tournament

27th Stratfield Saye House, Berks.
Wellington Prom - Open Air Concert.

27th-29th Athelhampton, Dorset
Athelhampton Summer Craft Show

27th-29th Stanford Hall, Leics
National Hovercraft Racing
Championships

27th-29th Sulgrave Manor, Northants
Siege of Sulgrave 1664 Re-enactment

28th Kelburn Castle & Country Centre
Viking Day

28th Holker Hall, Cumbria
M G Rally. *Post- and pre- 1955 M.G's
meet for driving trials and
concours. Entry on the day.*

28th-29th Walcot Hall, Shropshire
Bishops Castle Traction Engine Rally

28th-29th Belvoir Castle, Lincs
Mediaeval Jousting Tournament.

28th-29th Lamport Hall, Northants
Antiques Fair

SEPTEMBER

TBA Broadlands, Hampshire
Romsey Show

TBA Capel Manor, Middlesex
Autumn Show

TBA Hanbury Hall, Worcs
North Worcestershire Crafts Fair

2nd Ragley Hall, Warwicks
Last Night of the Proms and
Fireworks

3rd Hever Castle, Kent
Longbow Warfare. *The Kent
Bowmen demonstrate the use of
the Longbow as a military weapon.*

3rd-4th Arbury Hall, Warwicks
Craft Fair

3rd-4th Luton Hoo, Bedfordshire
"Lillipot Lane" Model Exhibition

3rd-4th Hatfield House, Herts
Country Fair. *2 day country Fair
spectacular for all the family,
including massed pipe and
military bands, hot-air balloons,
free fall parachuting and over 150
trade stands.*

4th Stanford Hall, Leics
Midlands Austin 7 Car Club Rally
(P) Scott Motorcycle Owners Club Rally
Salmons Tickford Enthusiasts Club
Rally

9th-11th Penshurst Place, Kent
Craft Fair

10th-11th Leighton Hall, Lancs
Rainbow Craft Fair

10th-11th Ragley Hall, Warwicks
Antique Fair

10th-11th Scone Palace Perth
Farming of Yesteryear

10th-11th Wilton House, Wiltshire
Lacemakers Weekend

16th Castle Fraser, Grampian
'An evening with Oscar Wilde'

16th Leighton Hall, Lancs
Dolls House and Miniature Fair

16th-19th Leeds Castle, Kent
Flower Festival

17th-18th Hever Castle, Kent
Patchwork and Quilting Exhibition.
*There will be a 'Miniatures"
themed section.*

17th-18th Lamport Hall, Northants
Craft Festival

23rd-27th Hatfield House, Herts
NAFAS Flower Festival.

24th-25th Capesthorne Hall, Cheshire
Rainbow Crafts Fair

24th-25th Duncombe Park, Yorkshire
Autumn Crafts Fair

24th-25th Scone Palace, Perth
Caledonian Horse Trials

24th-25th Shugborough, Staffs
11am-5pm Harvest Steam Fair. *It's
full steam ahead! at Shugborough
Park Farm, with a wide range of
steam operated vehicles from
gallopers to threshers.*

OCTOBER

TBA Hanbury Hall, Worcs
Porcelain Lectures

TBA Sandon Hall, Staffs
The Stafford County Antiques Fair

1st Sulgrave Manor, Northants
Chamber Concert - 7.30pm in Hall
with light Buffet Supper

1st-2nd Stanford Hall, Leics
Lady Fayre: Crafts at Stanford Hall

2nd Lamport Hall, Northants
East Midlands Doll Fair

3rd-4th Muncaster Castle, Cumbria
Models at Muncaster - *Models of all
kinds including steam engines and
radio-controlled cars, aircraft and
ships*

8th Sulgrave Manor, Northants
Tudor Living History

8th-9th Ragley Hall, Warwicks
Craft Fair

15th-16th Boughton Monchelsea Place
Craft Fair, Demonstrations etc.

21st-23rd Luton Hoo, Bedfordshire
Home Design Exhibition

22nd-23rd Sulgrave Manor, Northants
Apple Day Fair

29th-30th Lamport Hall, Northants
Gift and Craft Fair

29th-31st Shugborough, Staffs
6pm-9pm Hallowe'en at
Shugborough. *Victorian gothic
horror and mysteries make for a
chilling evening. Enjoy a tour of
the Georgian Mansion and
Servants' Quarters ... if you dare!*

30th Blair Castle, Perthshire
Glenfiddich World Piping
Championships

31st Glenfiddich Fiddle Championships

NOVEMBER

TBA Broadlands, Hampshire
Fireworks Display
Christmas Craft Fair

TBA Oakley Hall, Shrops
Concert 'Baroque Opera Company'

5th Leeds Castle, Kent
Grand Firework Display

5th Sulgrave Manor, Northants
Chamber Concert - 7.30pm in Hall
with light Buffet Supper

5th -6th Duncombe Park, Yorkshire
Antiques Fair

Nov Leeds Castle, Kent
Christmas Shop

DECEMBER

TBA Hanbury Hall, Worcs
Carol Concert

Dec Leeds Castle, Kent
Christmas Shop

TBA Luton Hoo, Bedfordshire
Craft Fair

3rd Sulgrave Manor, Northants
Chamber Concert - 7.30pm in Hall
with light Buffet Supper

6th-9th Shugborough, Staffs
5pm-9pm Christmas at Shugborough.
*Victorian evenings with carol
singing, candlelit Mansion House,
Christmas Market and a host of
festive entertainment.*

10th-11th Duncombe Park, Yorkshire
Christmas Crafts Festival

ACCOMMODATION INDEX

ALPHABETICAL INDEX

House names in Italics denote hotels and houses featured in the last two sections (red and green edging).

House names in Italics denote hotels and houses featured in the last two sections (red and green edging).

VOUCHER SCHEME

The following pages contain twenty vouchers, worth a total of £10.00, which may be redeemed against entry to the houses listed, with their page numbers, below. They will, however, only be accepted subject to the following conditions:-

A copy of Hudsons Historic House and Garden Directory 1994 must be produced with the vouchers.

Only one voucher per person or party accepted on any one visit.

Not redeemable for cash. No change given.

The vouchers are valid during the published opening times of the establishments concerned, and will not be valid after 31st December 1994.

The vouchers cannot be used in conjunction with any other discount vouchers.

Arbury Hall, Warwickshire	155	Hopetoun House, Scotland	197
Athelhampton, Dorset	55	Hutton-in-the-Forest, Cumbria	44
Barnsley House Gardens, Gloucestershire	66	Kelburn Castle, Scotalnd	199
Belvoir Castle, Lincolnshire	99	Kentwell Hall, Suffolk	141
Berkeley Castle, Gloucestershire	62	Killerton, Devon	49
Bickleigh Castle, Devon	51	Kingston Bagpuize House, Oxfordshire	132
Blairquhan Castle, Scotland	186	Kingstone Lisle Park, Oxfordshire	129
Blickling Hall, Norfolk	110	Lavenham Priory, Suffolk	143
Boughton Monchelsea Manor, Kent	83	Layer Marney Tower, Essex	59
Broughton Castle, Oxfordshire	128	Leighton Hall, Lancashire	94
Burton Agnes Hall, Yorkshire	172	Leonardslee Gardens, Sussex	150
Chicheley Hall, Buckinghamshire	21	Lyme Park, Cheshire	30
Cobham Hall, Kent	85	Northbourne Court Gardens, Kent	92
Dorney Court, Berkshire	18	Oakley Hall, Shropshire	134
Duncombe Park, Yorkshire	175	Owlpen Manor, Gloucestershire	67
Eastnor Castle, Herefordshire	75	Raby Castle, Co. Durham	56
Eyam Hall, Derbyshire	48	Ragley Hall, Warwickshire	157
Gilbert White Museum, Hampshire	74	Rockingham Castle, Northamptonshire	120
Great Comp Garden, Kent	91	Rotherfield Park, Hampshire	72
Haddon Hall, Derbyshire	47	Stratfield Saye House, Berkshire	19
Hanbury Hall, Worcestershire	169	Sulgrave Manor, Northamptonshire	121
Harburn House, Scotland	196	The Queens House, London	102
Harewood House, Yorkshire	177	Tredegar House, Wales	211
Hedingham Castle, Essex	61	Wilton House, Wiltshire	167
Hergest Croft Gardens, Herefordshire	76	Woburn Abbey, Bedfordshire	16
Highclere Castle, Hampshire	71		

This voucher can be redeemed for

50p

HUDSON'S
HISTORIC
HOUSE
& GARDEN
DIRECTORY
GREAT BRITAIN AND IRELAND

against admission to any one of the Houses in the 1994
Historic House Directory, listed as accepting vouchers.

Can only be redeemed in accordance with the conditions overleaf.

This voucher can be redeemed for

50p

HUDSON'S
HISTORIC
HOUSE
& GARDEN
DIRECTORY
GREAT BRITAIN AND IRELAND

against admission to any one of the Houses in the 1994
Historic House Directory, listed as accepting vouchers.

Can only be redeemed in accordance with the conditions overleaf.

This voucher can be redeemed for

50p

HUDSON'S
HISTORIC
HOUSE
& GARDEN
DIRECTORY
GREAT BRITAIN AND IRELAND

against admission to any one of the Houses in the 1994
Historic House Directory, listed as accepting vouchers.

Can only be redeemed in accordance with the conditions overleaf.

This voucher can be redeemed for

50p

HUDSON'S
HISTORIC
HOUSE
& GARDEN
DIRECTORY
GREAT BRITAIN AND IRELAND

against admission to any one of the Houses in the 1994
Historic House Directory, listed as accepting vouchers.

Can only be redeemed in accordance with the conditions overleaf.

This voucher can be redeemed for

50p

HUDSON'S
HISTORIC
HOUSE
& GARDEN
DIRECTORY
GREAT BRITAIN AND IRELAND

against admission to any one of the Houses in the 1994
Historic House Directory, listed as accepting vouchers.

Can only be redeemed in accordance with the conditions overleaf.

This voucher can be redeemed for

50p

HUDSON'S
HISTORIC
HOUSE
& GARDEN
DIRECTORY
GREAT BRITAIN AND IRELAND

against admission to any one of the Houses in the 1994
Historic House Directory, listed as accepting vouchers.

Can only be redeemed in accordance with the conditions overleaf.

This voucher can be redeemed for

50p

HUDSON'S
HISTORIC
HOUSE
& GARDEN
DIRECTORY
GREAT BRITAIN AND IRELAND

against admission to any one of the Houses in the 1994
Historic House Directory, listed as accepting vouchers.

Can only be redeemed in accordance with the conditions overleaf.

This voucher can be redeemed for

50p

HUDSON'S
HISTORIC
HOUSE
& GARDEN
DIRECTORY
GREAT BRITAIN AND IRELAND

against admission to any one of the Houses in the 1994
Historic House Directory, listed as accepting vouchers.

Can only be redeemed in accordance with the conditions overleaf.

This voucher can be redeemed for

50p

HUDSON'S
HISTORIC
HOUSE
& GARDEN
DIRECTORY
GREAT BRITAIN AND IRELAND

against admission to any one of the Houses in the 1994
Historic House Directory, listed as accepting vouchers.

Can only be redeemed in accordance with the conditions overleaf.

This voucher can be redeemed for

50p

HUDSON'S
HISTORIC
HOUSE
& GARDEN
DIRECTORY
GREAT BRITAIN AND IRELAND

against admission to any one of the Houses in the 1994
Historic House Directory, listed as accepting vouchers.

Can only be redeemed in accordance with the conditions overleaf.

CONDITIONS FOR USE

A copy of Hudsons Historic House and Garden Directory 1994 must be produced with the voucher.

Only one voucher per person or party accepted.

Not redeemable for cash. No change given.

The voucher is valid during the published opening times of the establishment concerned, and will not be valid after 31st December 1994.

The voucher cannot be used in conjunction with any other discount vouchers.

CONDITIONS FOR USE

A copy of Hudsons Historic House and Garden Directory 1994 must be produced with the voucher.

Only one voucher per person or party accepted.

Not redeemable for cash. No change given.

The voucher is valid during the published opening times of the establishment concerned, and will not be valid after 31st December 1994.

The voucher cannot be used in conjunction with any other discount vouchers.

CONDITIONS FOR USE

A copy of Hudsons Historic House and Garden Directory 1994 must be produced with the voucher.

Only one voucher per person or party accepted.

Not redeemable for cash. No change given.

The voucher is valid during the published opening times of the establishment concerned, and will not be valid after 31st December 1994.

The voucher cannot be used in conjunction with any other discount vouchers.

CONDITIONS FOR USE

A copy of Hudsons Historic House and Garden Directory 1994 must be produced with the voucher.

Only one voucher per person or party accepted.

Not redeemable for cash. No change given.

The voucher is valid during the published opening times of the establishment concerned, and will not be valid after 31st December 1994.

The voucher cannot be used in conjunction with any other discount vouchers.

CONDITIONS FOR USE

A copy of Hudsons Historic House and Garden Directory 1994 must be produced with the voucher.

Only one voucher per person or party accepted.

Not redeemable for cash. No change given.

The voucher is valid during the published opening times of the establishment concerned, and will not be valid after 31st December 1994.

The voucher cannot be used in conjunction with any other discount vouchers.

CONDITIONS FOR USE

A copy of Hudsons Historic House and Garden Directory 1994 must be produced with the voucher.

Only one voucher per person or party accepted.

Not redeemable for cash. No change given.

The voucher is valid during the published opening times of the establishment concerned, and will not be valid after 31st December 1994.

The voucher cannot be used in conjunction with any other discount vouchers.

CONDITIONS FOR USE

A copy of Hudsons Historic House and Garden Directory 1994 must be produced with the voucher.

Only one voucher per person or party accepted.

Not redeemable for cash. No change given.

The voucher is valid during the published opening times of the establishment concerned, and will not be valid after 31st December 1994.

The voucher cannot be used in conjunction with any other discount vouchers.

CONDITIONS FOR USE

A copy of Hudsons Historic House and Garden Directory 1994 must be produced with the voucher.

Only one voucher per person or party accepted.

Not redeemable for cash. No change given.

The voucher is valid during the published opening times of the establishment concerned, and will not be valid after 31st December 1994.

The voucher cannot be used in conjunction with any other discount vouchers.

CONDITIONS FOR USE

A copy of Hudsons Historic House and Garden Directory 1994 must be produced with the voucher.

Only one voucher per person or party accepted.

Not redeemable for cash. No change given.

The voucher is valid during the published opening times of the establishment concerned, and will not be valid after 31st December 1994.

The voucher cannot be used in conjunction with any other discount vouchers.

This voucher can be redeemed for

HUDSON'S
HISTORIC
HOUSE
& GARDEN
DIRECTORY
GREAT BRITAIN AND IRELAND

50p

against admission to any one of the Houses in the 1994
Historic House Directory, listed as accepting vouchers.

Can only be redeemed in accordance with the conditions overleaf.

This voucher can be redeemed for

HUDSON'S
HISTORIC
HOUSE
& GARDEN
DIRECTORY
GREAT BRITAIN AND IRELAND

50p

against admission to any one of the Houses in the 1994
Historic House Directory, listed as accepting vouchers.

Can only be redeemed in accordance with the conditions overleaf.

This voucher can be redeemed for

HUDSON'S
HISTORIC
HOUSE
& GARDEN
DIRECTORY
GREAT BRITAIN AND IRELAND

50p

against admission to any one of the Houses in the 1994
Historic House Directory, listed as accepting vouchers.

Can only be redeemed in accordance with the conditions overleaf.

This voucher can be redeemed for

HUDSON'S
HISTORIC
HOUSE
& GARDEN
DIRECTORY
GREAT BRITAIN AND IRELAND

50p

against admission to any one of the Houses in the 1994
Historic House Directory, listed as accepting vouchers.

Can only be redeemed in accordance with the conditions overleaf.

This voucher can be redeemed for

HUDSON'S
HISTORIC
HOUSE
& GARDEN
DIRECTORY
GREAT BRITAIN AND IRELAND

50p

against admission to any one of the Houses in the 1994
Historic House Directory, listed as accepting vouchers.

Can only be redeemed in accordance with the conditions overleaf.

This voucher can be redeemed for

HUDSON'S
HISTORIC
HOUSE
& GARDEN
DIRECTORY
GREAT BRITAIN AND IRELAND

50p

against admission to any one of the Houses in the 1994
Historic House Directory, listed as accepting vouchers.

Can only be redeemed in accordance with the conditions overleaf.

This voucher can be redeemed for

HUDSON'S
HISTORIC
HOUSE
& GARDEN
DIRECTORY
GREAT BRITAIN AND IRELAND

50p

against admission to any one of the Houses in the 1994
Historic House Directory, listed as accepting vouchers.

Can only be redeemed in accordance with the conditions overleaf.

This voucher can be redeemed for

HUDSON'S
HISTORIC
HOUSE
& GARDEN
DIRECTORY
GREAT BRITAIN AND IRELAND

50p

against admission to any one of the Houses in the 1994
Historic House Directory, listed as accepting vouchers.

Can only be redeemed in accordance with the conditions overleaf.

This voucher can be redeemed for

HUDSON'S
HISTORIC
HOUSE
& GARDEN
DIRECTORY
GREAT BRITAIN AND IRELAND

50p

against admission to any one of the Houses in the 1994
Historic House Directory, listed as accepting vouchers.

Can only be redeemed in accordance with the conditions overleaf.

This voucher can be redeemed for

HUDSON'S
HISTORIC
HOUSE
& GARDEN
DIRECTORY
GREAT BRITAIN AND IRELAND

50p

against admission to any one of the Houses in the 1994
Historic House Directory, listed as accepting vouchers.

Can only be redeemed in accordance with the conditions overleaf.

CONDITIONS FOR USE

A copy of Hudsons Historic House and Garden Directory 1994 must be produced with the voucher.

Only one voucher per person or party accepted.

Not redeemable for cash. No change given.

The voucher is valid during the published opening times of the establishment concerned, and will not be valid after 31st December 1994.

The voucher cannot be used in conjunction with any other discount vouchers.

CONDITIONS FOR USE

A copy of Hudsons Historic House and Garden Directory 1994 must be produced with the voucher.

Only one voucher per person or party accepted.

Not redeemable for cash. No change given.

The voucher is valid during the published opening times of the establishment concerned, and will not be valid after 31st December 1994.

The voucher cannot be used in conjunction with any other discount vouchers.

CONDITIONS FOR USE

A copy of Hudsons Historic House and Garden Directory 1994 must be produced with the voucher.

Only one voucher per person or party accepted.

Not redeemable for cash. No change given.

The voucher is valid during the published opening times of the establishment concerned, and will not be valid after 31st December 1994.

The voucher cannot be used in conjunction with any other discount vouchers.

CONDITIONS FOR USE

A copy of Hudsons Historic House and Garden Directory 1994 must be produced with the voucher.

Only one voucher per person or party accepted.

Not redeemable for cash. No change given.

The voucher is valid during the published opening times of the establishment concerned, and will not be valid after 31st December 1994.

The voucher cannot be used in conjunction with any other discount vouchers.

CONDITIONS FOR USE

A copy of Hudsons Historic House and Garden Directory 1994 must be produced with the voucher.

Only one voucher per person or party accepted.

Not redeemable for cash. No change given.

The voucher is valid during the published opening times of the establishment concerned, and will not be valid after 31st December 1994.

The voucher cannot be used in conjunction with any other discount vouchers.

CONDITIONS FOR USE

A copy of Hudsons Historic House and Garden Directory 1994 must be produced with the voucher.

Only one voucher per person or party accepted.

Not redeemable for cash. No change given.

The voucher is valid during the published opening times of the establishment concerned, and will not be valid after 31st December 1994.

The voucher cannot be used in conjunction with any other discount vouchers.

CONDITIONS FOR USE

A copy of Hudsons Historic House and Garden Directory 1994 must be produced with the voucher.

Only one voucher per person or party accepted.

Not redeemable for cash. No change given.

The voucher is valid during the published opening times of the establishment concerned, and will not be valid after 31st December 1994.

The voucher cannot be used in conjunction with any other discount vouchers.

CONDITIONS FOR USE

A copy of Hudsons Historic House and Garden Directory 1994 must be produced with the voucher.

Only one voucher per person or party accepted.

Not redeemable for cash. No change given.

The voucher is valid during the published opening times of the establishment concerned, and will not be valid after 31st December 1994.

The voucher cannot be used in conjunction with any other discount vouchers.

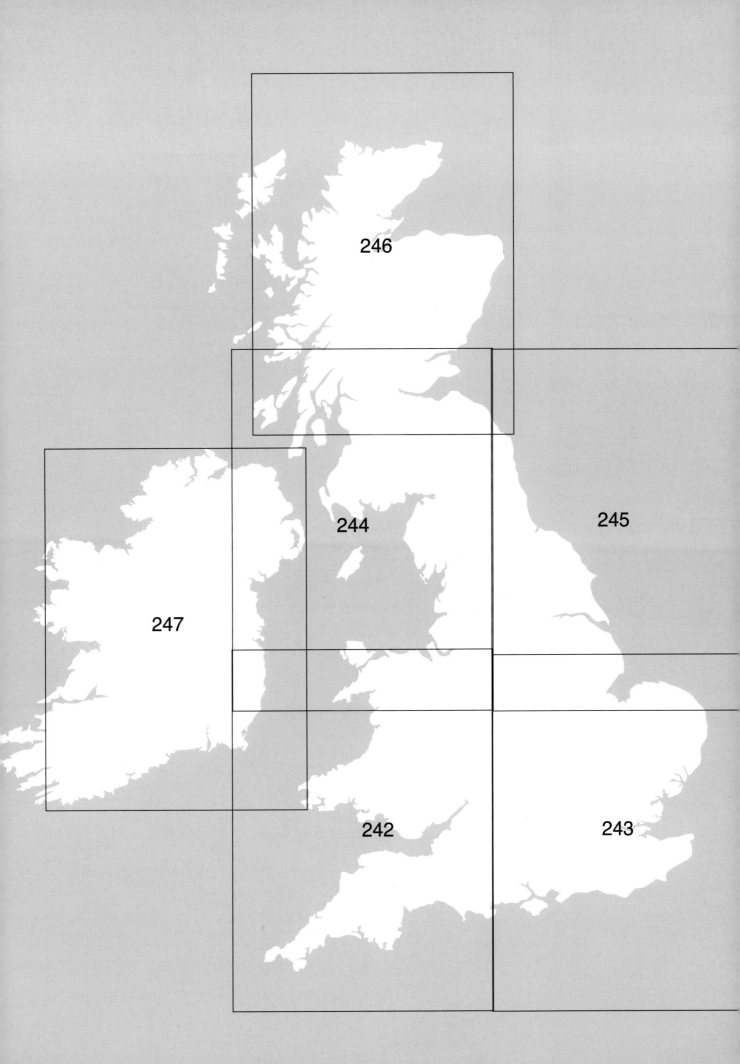

A92 Montrose

Arbroath

t Andrews

North Berwick
Dunbar
urgh
Eyemouth
Paxton House   Ayton Castle
Duns Castle   Berwick-upon
tain   -Tweed
Manderston
Melrose Floors Cast
Kelso Coldstream
                Bamburgh Castle
        A1
Chillingham Castle
                Alnwick Castle
                Alnwick
        Cragside
A68
Wallington
Northumberland   Blyth
Belsay Hall
                Newcastle
A69   -upon-Tyne
        Gibside Washington Old Hall
                Sunderland
        Durham
ia
in-the-Forest Durham   Hartlepool
                Redcar
        Middlesbrough
Raby Castle   Whitby
M6
        A66   North
Kendal Darlington Yorkshire
        A1
                Scarborough
Thorp Perrow Thirsk Duncombe Park Filey
        Newby Hall   Castle Howard
ton Hall A65
cambe Ripley Castle A19 A64
ncaster Harrogate   Bridlington
Settle Skipton Fairfax House Burton Agnes
n C S. Broughton Hall Yor   Hornsea
        Harewood House Humberside
6
ton Burnley Bradford Leeds A1
        Halifax W. Yorkshire Carlton Tower Burton Constable
Blackburn   Hull Withernsea
Rochdale Wakefield Goole
Bury   Scunthorpe Grimsby
Greater Huddersfield
Manchester Oldham Barnsley Doncaster
Manchester S. Yorkshire   Cleethorpes
m Massey M62 Stockport Rotherham Caistor
M56 Lyme Park Adlington Hall Sheffield Gainsborough Louth Mablethorpe
Tatton Park Eyam Hall   Market
Arley Hall Tabley House Renishaw Hall   Rasen
M6 Capesthorne Hall Chatsworth Worksop Lincoln Horncastle
Crewe Macclesfield Chesterfield   Doddington Place Skegness
heshire Haddon Hall Derbyshire Mansfield A1 Lincolnshire
        Leek M1 Notts. Newark
Oakley Hall Stoke-on-Trent Ashbourne   Boston
Gardens   Nottingham   Holkham Hall
Staffordshire Derby   Grantham   Sheringham
Sandon Hall   Belvoir Castle   Hunstanton Cromer
        Stafford   Melbourne Hall A15 Sandringham Blickling Hall
                        Fakenham

245

Western Isles

Stornoway

Highland

Durness
Tongue
Thurso
John o' Groats
Wick
A9
Unapool
Kinbrace
Lybster
Lochinver
Lairg
Ullapool
Dunrobin Castle
Inveran
Dornoch
Invergordon
Cromarty
Lossiemouth
Macduff
Fraserburgh
Elgin
Buckie
Banff
Nairn
Rothes
A92
Peterhea
Cawdor Castle
Huntley
Inverness
Grantown-on-Spey
Ballindalloch Castle
Fyvie Castle
Haddo House
A9
Leith Hall
Grampian
A96
Aviemore
Castle Fraser
Invergarry
Bachory
Aberdeen
Kingussie
Drum Castle
Clathes Castle
A93
Stonehaven
Fort William
Blair Castle
Pitlochry
Brechin
egan Castle
Kyle
Montrose
Mallaig
A92
Glamis Castle
Tayside
Aberfeldy
A9
Duart Castle
Dundee
Arbroath
Oban
Scone Palace
Perth
Callander
St Andrews
Inveraray Castle
Fife
Stirling
Central
Falkirk
Dunfermline
Dunoon
Dumbarton
Kirkcaldy
North Berwick
M9
Dunbar
Glasgow
Hopetoun House
Dalmeny House
A1
Greenock
M8
Eyemouth
Paisley
Harburn House
The Drum
Edinburgh
Ayton Castle
Kelburn Castle
Motherwell
Lothian
Paxton House
Berwick-upon-Tweed
A78
Hamilton
Thirlestane Castle
Duns Castle
Manderston
Mellerstain
Galashiels
Melrose
Irvine
Kilmarnock
Floors Castle
Coldstream
Traquair
Bamburgh
M74
Bowhill
Kelso
Prestwick
Strathclyde
Borders
Chillingham Castle
A1
Ayr
Campbeltown
Alnwick C
A68
Alnwi
Culzean Castle
Blairquhan Castle
Cragside
246
Girvan
Maxwelton House
Wallington
A77
New
Dumfries
Northumberland
Dumfries and
Lockerbie

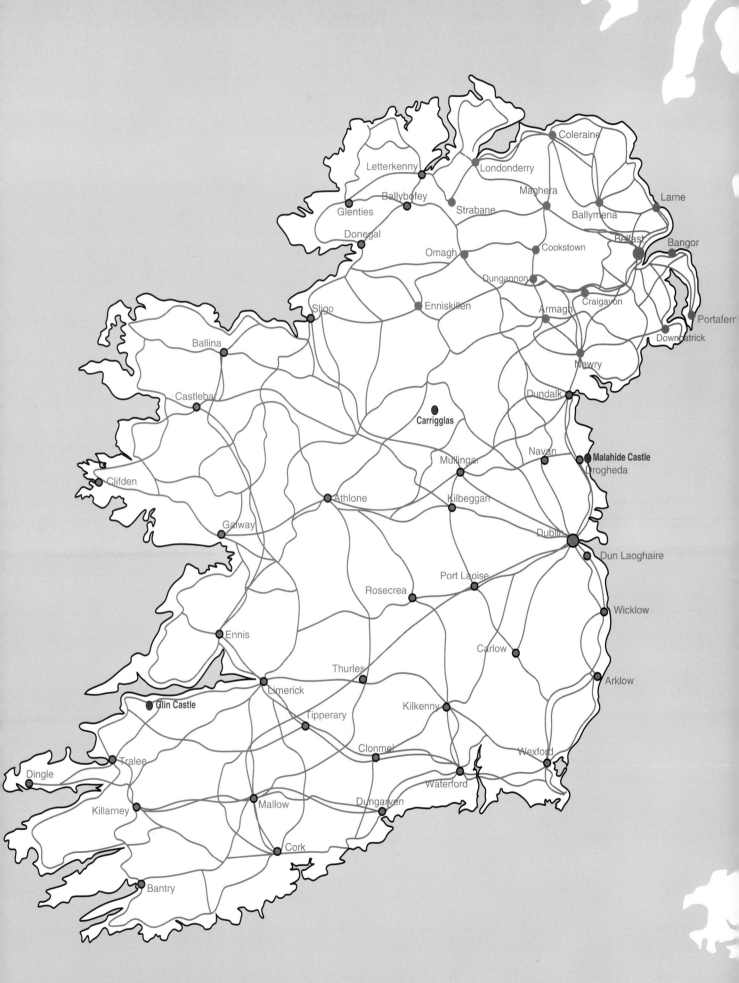

Notes

Notes

Notes